THEORY AND PRACTICE
OF EARLY READING
Volume 3

THEORY AND PRACTICE
OF EARLY READING
Volume 3

Edited by   LAUREN B. RESNICK
University of Pittsburgh

PHYLLIS A. WEAVER
Harvard University

LEA LAWRENCE ERLBAUM ASSOCIATES, PUBLISHERS
1979   Hillsdale, New Jersey

Lawrence Erlbaum Associates, Inc., Publishers
365 Broadway
Hillsdale, New Jersey 07642

Library of Congress Cataloging in Publication Data

Main entry under title:
Theory and practice of early reading.
  Based on papers presented at a series of 3
conferences, held at the Learning Research and Development Center, University of Pittsburgh, 1976.
  Bibliography: p.
  Includes indexes.
  1. Reading (Elementary)   I. Resnick, Lauren B.
II. Weaver, Phyllis A.   III. Pittsburgh.
University.   Learning Research and Development
Center.
LB1573.T46   372.4   79-23784
ISBN 0-89859-011-6 (v. 3)

Printed in the United States of America

Contents

Preface   **ix**

The Theory and Practice of Early Reading:
An Introduction
Phyllis A. Weaver and Lauren B. Resnick   **1**
The Social Press for Literacy   2
The Focus on Early Reading   5
The Issues   7

PART I: PROCESSES OF READING

1. **The Perception of Units in Beginning Reading**
   David LaBerge   **31**
   The Function of Units   32
   Selecting Unit Levels   35
   Learning New Units   40
   Difficulties and Conclusions   49

2. **How to Study Reading:**
   An Information Processing Analysis
   Lee W. Gregg and S. Farnham-Diggory   **53**
   The Perceptual Space   55
   The Semantic Space   57
   Control Programs: A Taxonomy of Reading Tasks   62
   Conclusion   69

3. **What the Study of Eye Movement Reveals About Reading**
    George W. McConkie   71
    Why There Are So Many Approaches
        to Reading Instruction   72
    What Type of Research Will Lead
        to an Understanding of Reading?   74
    The Study of Eye Movements in Reading   77
    The Future Potential for
        Eye Movement Research in Reading   85

4. **Oral Reading:**
    Does It Reflect Decoding or Comprehension?
    Joseph H. Danks and Ramona Fears   89
    Two Hypotheses About Oral Reading   89
    Research on Oral Reading   94
    The Two Hypotheses Revisited   103
    Postscript   105

    PART II: LANGUAGE DIFFERENCES AND READING

5. **Black Dialect, Reading Interference,**
    and Classroom Interaction
    Herbert D. Simons   111
    Black Language: The Deficit and Difference Viewpoints   112
    Black Dialect and Reading Interference   114

6. **Reading and the Bilingual Child**
    Diana S. Natalicio   131
    Historical Perspective   131
    The Native Language Literacy Axiom: Relevant Research   133
    Specification of the Native Language   137
    Transfer of Reading Skills   139
    Alternate Approaches to Reading Instruction   142
    Conclusions   147

    PART III: INSTRUCTION

7. **Impacts of Instructional Time in Reading**
    John T. Guthrie, Victor Martuza, and Mary Seifert   153
    Source of Evidence   157
    Statistical Analyses   162
    Results   166
    Discussion   175

8. **The ABD's of Reading: A Program for the Learning Disabled**
    Joanna Williams   **179**
    Overview   179
    The Learning Disabled Child   180
    The Program Rationale   182
    Description of the Program   185
    Evaluation in the Field   189
    Discussion   192

9. **Helping Disadvantaged Children Learn to Read**
    by Teaching Them Phoneme Identification Skills
    Michael A. Wallach and Lise Wallach   **197**
    Poor Children Frequently Lack
       Phoneme Identification Skills   199
    Phoneme Recognition is Teachable   201
    Are There Practical Means for Providing Help
       to the Children Who Need It?   204
    Concluding Observations   213

10. **Two Approaches to Initial Reading Instruction:**
    An Analysis of the *Reading Unlimited Program* and
    the *New Primary Grades Reading System*
    Helen Mitchell Popp   **217**
    Scope   218
    Teaching/Learning Strategies   222
    Testing   255
    Content   259
    Other Motivational Features   264
    Individualization   264
    Summary and Conclusions   266
    Appendix A   269
    Appendix B   275
    Appendix C   276
    Appendix D   278

PART IV: DISCUSSION

11. **Reflections on Reading about Reading**
    Tom Trabasso   **281**
    Theory   281
    Problems   286
    Programs   288
    Evaluation and Effectiveness   292

12. **Learning to Read in Classroom Interaction**
Courtney B. Cazden **295**
Time on Task 296
Focus of Attention 302
Conclusion 305

13. **Observations on Research and Practice in Beginning Reading**
Robert Glaser **307**
Using What We Know 307
Physiological Research
and Clinical Investigations 309
Curriculum Analysis 309
Testing Practices 310
Teaching Practices 311
Field and Classroom Research 312
Learning and Acquisition 313
Stages of Proficiency 314
Reading as a General Problem of Acquiring Skill 315

14. **Has the Reel Reeding Prablum Bin Lade Bear? Summary Comments on the Theory and Practice of Early Reading**
John B. Carroll and Marsha Walton **317**
The Nature of Reading 321
Programs of Beginning Reading Instruction 333
Final Comments 349

15. **Toward a Usable Psychology of Reading Instruction**
Lauren B. Resnick **355**
Two Streams of Psychological Research 356
Skilled Performance and Acquisition:
The Question of Development 358
Individual Differences in Reading 364
Invention and Discovery in Learning to Read 367
Conclusion:
Reuniting Cognitive and Learning Psychology 371

Author Index 373

Subject Index

Preface

Concern for the pedagogy of reading is almost as old as the history of the written word. Yet never before the present century has reading instruction commanded so much attention on the part of so many. A society that aspires to universal literacy must necessarily be fascinated with the question of how people read and how they learn to read. When everyone must be literate, problems that once could be solved by attrition and dropping out must now be solved by instruction. Not only those who learn easily but those who are hard to teach and even those who are reluctant to learn must be taught. Every resource, theoretical and practical, must be brought to bear on the problem of reading instruction.

These volumes explore the range and depth of our theoretical and practical knowledge about early reading instruction. Contributors—psychologists, linguists, instructional designers, reading and special education experts— were asked to address three questions: (1) What is the nature of skilled reading? (2) How is reading skill acquired? (3) What do the nature of skilled reading and the process of acquiring reading skill jointly suggest for reading instruction? In this context, issues such as the centrality of decoding in early reading, "stages" in learning to read, the role of "automatic" word recognition in reading comprehension, the role of oral language in acquiring reading skill, the effect of cultural and linguistic differences on reading acquisition and performance, and the nature of individual differences in learning to read are addressed and debated. Several major instructional programs are analyzed, and there is considerable discussion of the possible and appropriate role of theory and experimental research in guiding the course of reading instruction. Taken together, the chapters of these three volumes suggest clearly where reading research and practice stand with respect to the key questions of skilled performance, acquisition sequences, and early instruction. Accordingly, these volumes should be of interest to reading educators, psychologists, and other theorists of reading.

Many of the chapters in these volumes are based on papers that were presented and discussed at a series of three conferences held at the Learning Research and Development Center, University of Pittsburgh, in 1976. The conferences were supported by the National Institute of Education as part of the Compensatory Education Evaluation Study. Organization of the volumes is by conference, with discussion chapters appearing at the end of each volume. The thematic content of each volume and of the series as a whole is outlined in some detail in the introductory chapter.

We gratefully acknowledge those many individuals who assisted in planning and conducting the conferences and preparing these volumes. Cathlene Hardaway and Barbara Haky Viccari assisted in many details of planning and running the conferences; they and Carol Evans had responsibility for many aspects related to preparing these volumes. Shirley Tucker prepared the subject indexes to the three volumes. Charles Teggatz was technical editor for most chapters in the three volumes; his substantive suggestions and editoral assistance were invaluable. During a major part of the preparation of these volumes, one of us (Lauren Resnick) was a Fellow at the Center for Advanced Study in the Behavioral Sciences, Palo Alto, California, supported in part by a grant from the Spencer Foundation. This support is gratefully acknowledged.

LAUREN B. RESNICK

PHYLLIS A. WEAVER

THEORY AND PRACTICE
OF EARLY READING
Volume 3

The Theory and Practice of Early Reading: An Introduction

Phyllis A. Weaver
Harvard University

Lauren B. Resnick
University of Pittsburgh

> *There is a kind of idle theory which is antithetical to practice;*
> *but genuinely scientific theory falls within practice as the agency*
> *of its expansion and its direction to new possibilities.*
>
> John Dewey (1932)

Never before the present century has reading instruction commanded so much attention on the part of so many. The sources of this concern and attention lie in a combination of social and scientific developments that set the context in which these volumes and the positions on reading taken in them can best be understood and evaluated. In the social sphere, standards of literacy have been rising during the course of the past century. Virtually everyone is now expected to become literate, and the criteria for assessing literacy are more stringent today than at any previous time. The result is increased public concern for reading and increased attention to reading on the part of educators. In the scientific sphere, meanwhile, there has been a continuing press to apply scientific knowledge to practical affairs, with the result that attention has been directed most to those aspects of educational practice about which science has the most to say. Together, these social and scientific developments have shaped both the extent and the direction of current work on reading, work that is reported and debated in these volumes. In this chapter, we begin by considering how theory and practice in reading instruction have been influenced by these forces. We then outline the specific issues that are dominant in today's debates about early reading; these issues are directly addressed in the chapters of these volumes.

1

THE SOCIAL PRESS FOR LITERACY

The Expectation of Universal Literacy

A short story by Somerset Maugham helps to illustrate the ways in which social perceptions of literacy have changed. "The Verger" (Maugham, 1937) is about a man, Albert Edward Foreman, who has held the position of verger in a fashionable church (St. Peter's, Neville Square) for many years. He is illiterate, a fact that has just been discovered by the current vicar and churchwardens. The discovery leads to a request for the verger's resignation, although all involved freely admit that he performs his duties quite acceptably. Nevertheless, they find it inappropriate for a man who cannot read or write to be their verger:

> "It's the most amazing thing I ever heard," cried the [warden]. "Do you mean to say that you've been verger of this church for sixteen years and never learned to read or write?"
>
> "I went into service when I was twelve, sir. The cook in the first place tried to teach me once, but I didn't seem to 'ave the knack for it, and then what with one thing and another I never seemed to 'ave the time. I've never really found the want of it. I think a lot of these young fellows waste a rare lot of time readin' when they might be doin' something useful."

The story relates how the verger, faced with the need to earn a living in some new way, opens a tabacconist's shop, then a second, then several more. Eventually he owns a string of shops, and he is making weekly bank deposits so large that his holdings total over thirty thousand pounds. Noting this, a bank officer suggests that the funds might better be invested and offers to make out a list of securities so that all the verger-turned-businessman would need to do is to sign the necessary papers:

> "I could do that all right," said Albert uncertainly. "But 'ow should I know what I was signin'?"
>
> "I suppose you can read," said the manager a trifle sharply.
>
> Mr. Foreman gave him a disarming smile.
>
> "Well, sir, that's just it. I can't. I know it sounds funny like, but there it is, I can't read or write, only me name, an' I only learnt to do that when I went into business."
>
> The manager was so surprised that he jumped up from his chair.
>
> "That's the most extraordinary thing I ever heard."
>
> "You see, it's like this, sir, I never 'ad the opportunity until it was too late and then some'ow I wouldn't. I got obstinate like."
>
> The manager stared at him as though he were a prehistoric monster.
>
> "And do you mean to say that you've built up this important business and amassed a fortune of thirty thousand pounds without being able to read or write? Good God, man, what would you be now if you had been able to?"

"I can tell you that, sir," said Mr. Foreman, a little smile on his still aristocratic features. "I'd be verger of St. Peter's, Neville Square."

The story's ironic ending helps to illustrate the profound ways in which society's demands for literacy have changed. The story takes place in a time when an expectation of widespread literacy was just developing. The astonishment of both church and bank officials serves to highlight the expectation. Both groups seem to believe that literacy is required for satisfactory performance of the work in question; in fact, the deepest source of their astonishment is not that Albert Edward cannot read or write but that he has been performing his jobs successfully in spite of being illiterate. Albert Edward's experiences might serve to demonstrate to these people that literacy is not essential to successful performance, at least in many jobs and social functions. But that is not their interpretation. The church officials, offering the excuse of a possible accident in the church, treat literacy, even that of the verger, as a necessary status symbol for members of their organization. The bank official assumes that Albert Edward might have succeeded even more brilliantly had he been literate. Albert Edward, however, understands that his success does not depend on literacy and seems also to recognize that his inability to read is not linked to intelligence but to the accidents of birth in a period in which opportunity and expectation for learning to read were tied to social class.

Maugham wrote "The Verger" in the 1930s, an ironic commentary on an already changing scene in which formal credentials of literacy were beginning to replace functional performance and inherited status as a criterion for access to certain positions. The shifts Maugham noted fifty years ago are all the more marked now. Moreover, it is unlikely that Albert Edward today could be successful as a tabacconist. Opportunities for small business have shrunk, and even these depend heavily on obtaining credit and negotiating other formalities that require at least minimum literacy. Furthermore, it is unlikely that Albert Edward today would be so serenely accepting of his state of illiteracy, juding himself neither incompetent nor lazy for being unable to read.

The Rising Criteria for Literacy

At the same time as we have expected more people to be literate, our criteria for literacy have been rising, placing double pressures on the instructional system. Our definitions of reading competence have changed markedly over the past century, and neither our methods of teaching nor our understanding of the reading process has caught up with our social aspirations. Reviewing the history of literacy standards in Western Europe and America, Resnick and Resnick (1977) noted that until well into the present century, knowing "how to read" meant being able to recognize and respond to highly familiar texts, such as those of catechisms or other religious or civil tracts. Given this criterion, teaching reading meant teaching people to translate printed words into spoken ones—that is, to read aloud. During the 19th century, an able reader—according to the definition used in most schools—was one who could give a good public rendition of a text, declaiming it with appropriate phrasing and emphasis. Although readers undoubtedly needed to grasp at least the gist of what they were reading to achieve such a performance, there is little evidence that schools were expected to *teach* anything having to do with the comprehension of written texts. In fact, there is evidence to the contrary, suggesting that most schools explicitly understood their reading instruction mandate to end with the development of fluent oral reading skill. A description of the pedagogical aims and practices of a well-known Scottish school, drawn from an American teachers' journal of 1831, highlights this understanding (from Mathews, 1966):

> English reading, according to the prevailing notion, consists of nothing more than the power of giving utterance to certain sounds, on the perception of certain figures; and the measure of progress and excellence is the facility and continuous fluency with which those sounds succeed each other from the mouth of the learner. If the child gathers any knowledge from the book before him, beyond that of color, form, and position of the letters, it is to his own sagacity he is indebted for it, and not to his teacher [p. 55].

It is only during the present century that reading for the purpose of gaining information has become a virtually universal goal, an expectation applied in ordinary elementary schools to the entire population of students. This shift in the criteria for literacy has direct bearing on the state of our knowledge regarding reading instruction. To the extent that reading instruction is concerned with the ability to declaim print, it has a long history of pedagogical thought and effort on which to draw. Over several centuries, considerable ingenuity and thoughtfulness have been brought to bear on the problem (see Mathews, 1966, for a review), and there is a great deal of richness and depth in past discussions both of how people manage to translate print to sound and how this skill can best be taught. However, insofar as reading instruction is concerned with the process of drawing meaning from print, it has only a brief history of scientific work to draw on; and there is little richness in the range of instructional practices that have been tried. As a result, there is comparatively little in the way of empirical evidence to support competing conceptions of the nature of skilled comprehension or of how it develops. This difference in historical depth accounts in great part for the difference in how much we are able to say about decoding texts and understanding them—a difference that will become apparent to the readers of these volumes. It also suggests why professionals and scientists concerned with reading are in a position to make some meaningful prescriptive judgments about how people learn and use alphabetic codes but are able to say relatively little, with assurance, about how they develop and enhance their ability to comprehend written text.

THE FOCUS ON EARLY READING

It is in recognition of the differential state of scientific knowledge about decoding and comprehension that we chose to limit the focus of these volumes to early reading. Early reading has often been defined as learning the code, being able to recognize words, or translating print to sound. As we have just suggested, this is a definition with considerable historical tradition: Learning the code *was* learning to read for many centuries. As a result, we know more about how people use the code during both beginning and skilled stages of reading than we do about how they use the semantic or syntactic aspects of texts. If there is a part of the total process of becoming literate in which science and professional practice have an opportunity to interact fruitfully at this time, it is with respect to learning the code. A great deal of research has been conducted on recognizing printed words and translating them into oral language, and a significant amount is known about the processes involved in word recognition and how to teach this aspect of reading to young children. Research provides some knowledge of the relations between word recognition and comprehension, although this knowledge is still limited. Moreover, far less is known about the processes involved in constructing meaning from written or spoken language, and very little is known about how to facilitate the development of these processes in young learners. In fact, the study of natural language processes as part of reading is only now emerging as a major focus of scholarly research.

Code and Meaning

A decision to focus on early reading and thus on learning the code, however well justified in terms of our past history and current knowledge, immediately and inevitably raises the question of whether the equation of early reading and code learning is necessary and proper. The question is central in these volumes, for by no means all of our authors agree that the code should be central to the definition of reading or in research on reading instruction. Concern about the relationship between code and meaning is not new to reading pedagogy. In fact, our present views with respect to the roles of code and meaning in reading instruction can be understood best in light of a dialectic relation in which code and meaning emphases successively challenge, and thereby refine, one another.

Challenge to the code emphasis began in this country in the 19th century and gathered force toward the end of that century as the progressive education movement began to emphasize function and meaning over drill and stylized performance in education. But it was probably not until after World War I that reading comprehension, rather than oral reading, became a central concern of reading pedagogy. Two factors seem to have influenced the direction of this shift. One was the increasing recognition that large numbers of people who had been to school and could read certain texts aloud, although haltingly, could not gather meaning from print. This recognition was given impetus by the World War I army testing program in which about 25% of recruits were insufficiently literate to take the written form of the test (Army Alpha) used to assign men to training and jobs in the army. The other factor was the findings of early research on reading processes. Psychologists such as Cattell (1886), Huey (1908/1968), and Buswell (1920) found that people read in units at least as large as words and that meaningful phrases were the most common units of processing.

Around 1920, the combination of the emphasis on comprehension of text as the goal of reading instruction and the finding that attention to meaningful units rather than to letters and sounds characterized the reading of skilled individuals led to a radical change in reading pedagogy. Reading educators argued that if extraction of meaning is the goal of instruction and the strategy of skilled readers, then the focus from the very outset of reading instruction should be on meaning. This was to be accomplished by teaching children to recognize words as wholes, thereby allowing them—very early in their reading experience—to read sentences and stories about characters and topics of interest to them.

To make this new pedagogy work, new instructional materials were needed. If words were to be learned and read as wholes, ignoring the alphabetic principle, only a limited vocabulary could be taught. From this need grew the idea and practice of "basal readers," graded series of books in which a few words at a time are introduced and extensively reviewed in story contexts. Accompanying the readers were detailed suggestions to teachers for how to teach children to read them. The basal approach with words chosen for their relatively high frequency of occurrence rather than for their spelling-to-sound regularity, gradually replaced most of the older approaches. By the 1950s, it was the established way to teach reading. Virtually all teachers were trained in basal approaches and knew how to manage classes using such approaches. Massive publishing efforts made it possible for schools and teachers to buy varied, attractive, and complete "systems" for teaching reading, all based on the controlled vocabulary, sight recognition principle. A new "establishment" was clearly in place.[1]

---

[1]In earlier times the terms *basal* and *whole word* were used synonymously, whereas today basal reading series may stress code as well as meaning.

Inevitably, reactions to this new orthodoxy developed. Challenges to sight-word methods began to be heard in both scholarly and lay circles in the 1950s and early 1960s (see, e.g., Flesch, 1955; Fries, 1962). In 1967 Chall published a book reviewing research evidence on early reading instruction and concluded that code approaches were generally superior to whole-word and other meaning-oriented approaches in the earliest years of instruction. However, those who advocated a reemphasis on the code in the 1950s and 1960s were not suggesting a return to alphabetic drills stripped of meaning; instead, they were proposing programs of direct code instruction in the context of meaningful reading material. The proposed new code emphasis, in other words, would be systematically refined to incorporate some of the more successful and appealing aspects of basal-style instruction.

In a sense, these volumes are a reexamination of issues considered by Chall a decade ago. Somewhat modified basal reading approaches are still dominant in today's instructional practice, and they are even less favorably viewed by our contributors than they were by Chall. In both theoretical and practical chapters, there is more attention paid to aspects of teaching, learning, and using the code than to comprehending written language. Yet an interest in meaning is not absent. Indeed, a number of the contributors to these volumes express concern that in a return to code approaches to teaching reading, the heart of reading may again be lost. But most of those proposing meaning-oriented initial instruction are not suggesting that the code be abandoned in a return to a 1930s style of basal readers. Instead, emerging theories of how people understand language and how language functions in social communication are being used to refine views of what a new meaning-oriented approach to early reading instruction might become. It is in this general context of debate that a number of specific issues about the nature of reading and of early reading instruction are addressed by the contributors to these volumes. We outline next some of the major themes to be found in the chapters that follow.

THE ISSUES

In inviting contributions to these volumes, we asked each author to consider three sets of questions:

1. What is the nature of skilled reading; that is, what is the goal of reading instruction?
2. How is reading skill acquired? What are the "stages" or steps in competence in the process of going from being a nonreader to being a skilled reader, and how does one pass from one stage to the next?
3. What do the nature of skilled reading and the process of acquiring reading skill jointly suggest for reading instruction?

To answer these questions, we brought together theorists and practitioners, some who were almost exclusively concerned with documenting the nature of skilled reading and some who were largely concerned with reading acquisition and development. We defined our task as relating what is known about skilled reading performance to what is being learned about the development of that performance capability. In so doing, our hope was to shed some light on instruction. What is needed for improving reading instruction is not only a description of skilled performance but also a theory of *propaedeutics*—a theory that does not assume that processes performed early in learning will directly match those performed later but instead, suggests what kind of early preparatory instruction will help people learn subsequent more complex capabilities.

Few of the chapters in these volumes, considered individually, draw explicit connections between the three questions of skilled performance, acquisition sequences, and instruction. Yet taken together, these volumes suggest clearly where reading research and practice stand with respect to these questions. Attention to the questions emerges in the context of a number of specific issues raised by the authors, and we outline some of them here. Table 1.1 depicts these issues, the viewpoints related to them, and which contributors address the various issues. The headings in the table match those in the discussion that follows here. Therefore, the table is useful both as a summary of our discussion and as a guide to the volumes for readers with particular interests.

The Centrality of Decoding to Early Reading

Should beginning reading instruction emphasize the relationship between sounds and graphic symbols, or should it stress getting meaning from print? Although an emphasis on one aspect of reading does not necessarily exclude the other, the question of balance between them has occupied educators and researchers since at least the beginning of the 20th century. Individuals who address this issue tend to take one of several positions that vary along a continuum from: (a) learning to decode (i.e., using knowledge of phoneme-grapheme correspondences to recognize words) *is* early reading; to (b) learning to decode (through phonics instruction or some similar approach) is important because it helps develop sensitivity to orthographic regularity (i.e., recurrent spelling patterns), which is important in the transition from early to skilled reading; to (c) learning to decode is at best incidental to becoming literate and at worst, may interfere with acquiring reading skill. We examine each position briefly.

Early Reading Is Decoding.   At one end of the continuum are those who contend that reading is, to use Liberman and Shankweiler's (Vol. 2) term, *parasitic* on spoken language. That is, learning to read is viewed as learning to map graphic symbols onto speech. Once this skill is learned, the established processes of understanding spoken language "take over." This position is represented centrally in the chapters by Liberman and Shankweiler and by Perfetti and Lesgold (Vol. 1). Liberman and Shankweiler propose that children need to be taught the alphabetic principle and skills of phonemic segmentation before they are taught to read. They suggest specific strategies and sequences of instruction that include preparing children for phonemic analysis and teaching them to associate the shape of the letter with its name and sound.

Perfetti and Lesgold contend that comprehension in reading depends on highly skilled generation and manipulation of language codes. They argue that even in skilled reading, there is a form of phonological encoding, albeit an abbreviated one, that precedes comprehension; and they recommend that decoding expertise should be the basic goal of early reading instruction. They offer suggestions for developing coding skills that include games and computer-assisted instruction.

Several other chapters suggest the importance of a code emphasis in early reading instruction or discuss commercially available programs with such an emphasis. Among them are the chapters by Beck and Block and by Chall in Volume 1, by Bartlett and by Fletcher in Volume 2, and by Popp, Wallach and Wallach, and Williams in Volume 3.

Reading and Orthographic Regularity.   A less extreme position regarding the role of decoding suggests that although skilled reading may not involve phonological recoding, it involves attention to recurring letter patterns in written language. Furthermore, because direct code instruction necessarily involves attention to this orthographic detail, learning to decode helps develop the awareness of orthographic regularity that is necessary for skilled reading. This position is developed in detail by Venezky and Massaro (Vol. 1). They advocate an early phonics emphasis for both traditional reasons (e.g., it allows independence for beginning readers) and because it provides a vehicle for developing awareness of orthographic regularity. That is, phonics programs introduce almost all the orthographic patterns and do so "by procedures that give overt attention to the relevant spelling units for orthographic regularity." Thus, phonics instruction helps develop skills that are required for obtaining information from written text. A similar position is held by Juola, Schadler, Chabot, McCaughey, and Wait (Vol. 2), who discuss the development of visual search strategies and their relation to word recognition. In this context they suggest that although phonemic encoding

TABLE 1.1

Topic	VOLUME 1														
	Chall	Perfetti – Lesgold	Venezky – Massaro	Fisher	Goodman – Goodman	Frederiksen	Shuy	Sticht	Bateman	Holland	Beck – Block	Kintsch	Posner	Samuels	Gordon
	WORD RECOG				LANGUAGE				INSTR			DISCUSSION			
Centrality of Decoding — Early reading is decoding	●	●									●				
Reading and orthographic regularity			●												
Decoding not central					●	●									
Nature of Skilled Reading — Bottom-up or top-down		●	●	●	●	●	●	●						●	
Direct or mediated access		●	●		●	●									
Automaticity		●												●	
Word recognition			●												
Units of processing				●											
Lexical knowledge		●				●									
Reading and Language — Oral language transfers to written		●						●			●				
Functional language emphasis					●		●								
Richness and variety in reading materials											●				
Factors Interfering with Learning to Read — Cultural and linguistic differences								●							●
Individual differences			●						●						
Acquiring Reading Competence — Developmental theory and research	●											●			
Reading instruction and reading acquisition										●	●				
Assessing reading progress						●		●							
Teacher as an instructional variable					●			●	●		●				
Time engaged in reading										●	●				
Relations Between Theory and Practice												●	●		●

● = This topic is discussed or emphasized in the chapter

VOLUME 2															VOLUME 3														
F. Smith	Chomsky	E. Smith – Kleiman	Juola et. al.	Liberman – Shankweiler	Rosner	Clay	Calfee – Drum	Johnson	Bartlett	Fletcher	Venezky	White	Gordon	Resnick	LaBerge	Gregg – Farnham-Diggory	McConkie	Danks – Fears	Simons	Natalicio	Guthrie – Martuza – Seifert	Williams	Wallach – Wallach	Popp	Trabasso	Cazden	Glaser	Carroll – Walton	Resnick
LANGUAGE AND READING					INSTRUCTION						DISCUSSION				PROCESSES OF READING						LANG DIFF & READ	INSTRUCTION				DISCUSSION			
				•					•	•				•								•	•	•				•	•
			•																									•	
•														•			•												
•		•													•													•	
•		•		•														•										•	•
		•	•												•													•	
			•														•												
				•											•														
			•	•										•													•		
•														•							•							•	
						•	•							•			•												•
									•	•				•			•											•	•
							•		•	•				•								•	•					•	•
•		•	•												•	•							•		•			•	•
									•	•				•														•	•
								•						•			•												
					•	•								•							•	•					•	•	
									•	•				•							•		•					•	•
												•	•	•														•	•	•

11

plays a minor role in skilled reading, phonic knowledge and knowledge of English orthography are important for developing reading skill.

Decoding Is Not Central to Reading.   At the far end of the continuum is the position that decoding is secondary, even in early reading, to the task of getting meaning from print. Goodman and Goodman (Vol. 1) hold this position in its most extreme form. They suggest that written language is an alternative form of linguistic communication and like spoken language, can and should be learned in the context of its functional uses. Therefore, if appropriate experiences occur or are arranged, there is no need for explicit decoding instruction. Not only is there no need for it, Goodman and Goodman argue, but providing such instruction can actually interfere with the natural extension of general language skills to understanding the printed form. They offer suggestions for alternative learning experiences designed to promote the development of children's knowledge of language functions and to facilitate reading acquisition.

Smith (Vol. 2) also questions the value of instruction in decoding. He argues that reading is not guided by letter-by-letter or even word-by-word analysis; instead, it begins in the head with a prediction of meaning and ends with selective attention to only parts of the written text. He characterizes this as an "inside-out" process and says that children learn to read by "making sense" of written language. Therefore, he views decoding letters and combining them into words as the most difficult way to learn to read, because it does not match the processes of skilled performance. A focus on decoding, he argues, does not make sense to children and is therefore a hindrance to learning. Danks and Fears (Vol. 3) review some of the research that might provide evidence on the question of whether a hypothesis about meaning always precedes attention to the written text; they conclude that this depends on an interaction between the capability of the reader, the difficulty of the text, and the reader's purpose. The suggestion is that decoding skills are needed in at least some "skilled" reading performances.

The position held by Frederiksen (Vol. 1) reflects this sense of variability in the reading process. He contends that the primary goal in early reading instruction should be to teach children to comprehend written discourse in the same way that they comprehend oral discourse. However, because reading does involve attention to graphemic information, teaching the code is a necessary subgoal of instruction. Nevertheless, Frederiksen recommends that if achieving efficiency in the subgoal interferes with the primary goal of comprehension, then inefficiency in decoding must be tolerated.

The Nature of Skilled Reading

Many chapters in these volumes focus on the issue of how skilled readers process written discourse. Several aspects of the nature of skilled reading processes are discussed, including: (a) whether discourse processing is controlled in a "bottom-up" or "top-down" manner; (b) whether meaning is accessed directly from the graphic display or is mediated by a phonolgical recoding; and (c) what role automaticity of word recognition processes plays.

Bottom-Up or Top-Down? In a bottom-up processing view of reading, lower level processes (e.g., letter and word recognition) are thought to occur prior to and independent of higher level processes. First words are recognized, then a syntactic processing occurs, and finally a semantic interpretation is made based on the sentence syntax. Furthermore, these processes are controlled by textual input; word recognition precedes comprehension of meaning. By contrast, in a top-down conception, reading is not controlled exclusively by the textual input; instead, higher level cognitive processes (e.g., making inferences) control the system, and lower processes are called into play only as they are needed. Hypotheses regarding the meaning of the text are generated from prior knowledge of the topic, knowledge of the specific textual content, and a minimal syntactic parsing and sampling of visual cues. According to the extreme top-down view, comprehension of meaning precedes recognition of words, and complete encoding of separate words may not occur at all. (See Frederiksen, Vol. 1, for a more detailed discussion of these concepts.)

Although most researchers would not characterize skilled reading as an exclusively bottom-up or top-down process, the authors who discuss this issue tend to do so with one or the other "direction" predominating.[2] Smith and Kleiman (Vol. 2) are the main proponents of reading as predominantly a bottom-up process. Several other authors imply a bottom-up view in the context of discussions of other aspects of reading (see the chapters by Sticht, Perfetti and Lesgold, and Fisher in Vol. 1). The chapters by Frederiksen (Vol. 1) and by Smith (Vol. 2) discuss skilled reading as a top-down controlled process ("inside-out" in Smith's terms), and this position is implied in the chapters by Goodman and Goodman and by Shuy in Volume 1.

It is important to note that several authors distinguish between skilled and novice readers in this respect. They view the skilled reading process as one that is controlled from the top down but see the *development* of reading skill proceeding from the bottom up. This position is represented by Samuels,

---

[2]It is noteworthy that when these volumes went to press, views about this issue had already changed. The nature of this change is captured by Adams and Collins (1977) in their schema theoretic account of reading. They suggest and attribute to Rumelhart (in press) that "top-down and bottom-up processing should be occurring at all levels of analysis simultaneously.... Bottom-up processing insures that the reader will be sensitive to information that is novel or that does not fit his on-going hypotheses about the content of the text; top-down processes help him to resolve ambiguities or to select between alternative possible interpretations of the incoming data [p. 9]."

Shuy, Venezky and Massaro (all in Vol. 1), LaBerge (Vol. 3), and to a certain extent by Frederiksen. On the other hand, Goodman and Goodman and Smith view *both* early and skilled reading as a top-down controlled process.

Direct or Mediated Access?   Several chapters address the issue of whether there is phonological recoding during skilled reading. On one side of this issue are those who hold that even in skilled reading, graphic information is recoded into phonological information before meaning is accessed. Viewpoints on this issue are often related to those on the bottom-up versus top-down conception of skilled reading. That is, those who view reading as a bottom-up process usually hold that there is a phonolgical recoding stage, even in skilled reading (e.g., Liberman & Shankweiler; Perfetti & Lesgold); whereas those who view reading as a top-down process tend to believe that meaning is accessed directly (e.g., Frederiksen; Goodman & Goodman; Smith). Exceptions to this correlation can be found in the chapters of Venezky and Massaro and of Smith and Kleiman, both of which propose a generally bottom-up view of the skilled reading process that does not depend on phonological recoding. Danks and Fears, as we have noted, suggest that whether access is direct or mediated depends on the individual reader and the task.

The Role of Automaticity.   One argument often used to support a direct-access-to-meaning view is that skilled reading proceeds at a rate that precludes the possibility of phonological recoding. A common reply to the argument is that in high-speed skilled reading, word recognition or phonological recoding takes place in an automatic fashion. That is, words are recognized rapidly, accurately, and with minimal attentional resources. Therefore, although it appears that meaning is obtained without actually recognizing words or recoding them, it is possible that these recognition processes are present but highly automatized and abbreviated. This position is central to the discussion by Perfetti and Lesgold, and it is supported by LaBerge (Vol. 3) in his chapter on perceptual units in the reading process and by Samuels in his discussion of the chapters in Volume 1.

Other Aspects Related to Skilled Reading.   A number of other topics related to skilled reading are considered by various authors. There is now a considerable body of research literature on word (and letter-string) recognition processes in skilled reading. For reviews and discussions of this literature, see the chapters by Smith and Kleiman, Venezky and Massaro, Juola et al., and Danks and Fears. Smith and Kleiman review this literature in the context of an information-processing model of skilled reading, whereas Venezky and Massaro consider it in supporting their claims for the importance of orthographic regularity in word and letter-string recognition. Juola et al. (Vol. 2) review research on "word superiority" (faster and more accurate recognition of real words than of pseudowords that follow the rules of conventional English spelling) in their discussion of the development of visual search performance. And Danks and Fears (Vol. 3) review a selected body of literature on oral reading errors, eye–voice span, and effects of text alteration in their discussion of oral production in a decoding-comprehension model of reading.

The question of perceptual units in reading is discussed in the chapters by McConkie, Fisher, and LaBerge. McConkie (Vol. 3) reports eye-movement research related to the perceptual span in reading; Fisher (Vol. 1) discusses the effects on reading of limited peripheral-visual processing; and LaBerge (Vol. 3) discusses functions of units for perceptual processing, selection of units for specific tasks, and learning of new units.

Finally, the skilled reader makes use of an extensive body of knowledge about words and what they represent during skilled reading. The extent of this network of lexical and semantic knowledge and the effectiveness of strategies for accessing it determine in part the reader's level of proficiency. Issues related to the lexicon and lexical access are explored in the chapters by Frederiksen, Smith and Kleiman, Perfetti and Lesgold, and Gregg and Farnham-Diggory (Vol. 3).

Reading and Language

We have mentioned the question of the relation between reading and general language skills in the course of discussing other issues. As we noted, some authors argue that reading is a matter of translating print to sound and then using established language skills to derive meaning; others argue that understanding written language is a unique process, more than the sum of decoding plus understanding spoken language. Regardless of which position on the nature of the relations between oral language and reading is held, most authors seem to agree that general language competence is essential to reading skill. Differences of opinion arise, however, over when and how language skills should be taught in the context of reading.

One position is that the development of language skills should be promoted in the oral mode while initial reading (coding) skills are being taught. In this way, language skills of increasing complexity can be transferred to the written language form. Sticht (Vol. 1) develops this argument most explicitly and extensively. His "audread" model implies the need for early code teaching and assumes that training in the oral mode will transfer to reading once the learner is past the decoding stage. He defines individuals' reading potentials in terms of the discrepancy between what they can comprehend aurally and what they can comprehend in written form. A similar position on the relation of aural to written comprehension skills is espoused by Beck and Block (Vol. 1), Perfetti and Lesgold, Liberman and Shankweiler, and by Rosner (Vol. 2).

A contrasting position holds that written language is an alternative functional form of language and that skill in using it does not transfer directly from oral competence as a result of learning the code. Instead, children should be taught reading in the context of the various functional modes that are relevant to them. In this way, written language can become a form of communication that is as useful as oral language. The functional language approach to reading is discussed extensively by Goodman and Goodman and by Shuy in Volume 1, and it is implicit in the chapters by Smith (Vol. 2), by Cazden (Vol. 3), and by Simons (Vol. 3). It is worth noting that whereas a functional language emphasis is usually accompanied by an anticode stance in instruction, this negative relation between functional language and code orientations is not a necessary one. Shuy, for example, recognizes a need for direct code teaching while emphasizing functional aspects of language in reading instruction.

A concern for richness of content and form of language within code-oriented instruction characterizes Bartlett's chapter (Vol. 2) comparing the *Distar* and *Open Court* beginning reading programs. Bartlett speculates that literary forms, or genres, can function as cognitive structures, serving to organize verbal information and to aid comprehension and memory. Both reading programs, Bartlett notes, are organized to facilitate code learning, but they provide a different range of literary experience. Bartlett suggests that the relative literary limitation of one of the programs may foster an impoverished kind of literacy. The need for phonics teaching in a semantically rich context is also acknowledged in the other chapters in which instructional programs are analyzed (Beck & Block in Vol. 1, Fletcher in Vol. 2, and Popp in Vol. 3). Similar concerns are expressed by Clay (Vol. 2), who suggests that reading programs that focus only on word attack and have tightly controlled vocabularies may actually be counterproductive to developing independent reading skills. She advocates programs rich in many aspects of language that may support, to use Clay's term, a *self-improving system* of language development.

Factors That Interfere With Learning to Read

The motivation for extended research in reading, and especially for the present attempt to explore the implications of theory and research for instructional practice, derives from the fact that large numbers of people in our society are not achieving expected standards of literacy. The efforts of many researchers and educators are directed at improving or preventing this situation. Children who fail to learn to read or who do so slowly and with extreme difficulty are therefore a major concern of many of the contributors to these volumes. In discussing those who have difficulty learniing to read, it is possible to distinguish between students who encounter difficulty because the expectations and habits of their social-cultural group do not match those of the schools and students who have difficulty because of individual differences in ability. These groups have overlapping memberships, even in the most elegant and theoretical classifications, and they are often very difficult to distinguish in practice. Despite this, it is important, for purposes of analysis, to consider separately these different sources of reading difficulty.

Cultural and Linguistic Differences.   The chapters that focus explicitly on social-cultural origins of reading difficulty are those by Shuy, Simons, Natalicio (Vol. 3), Wallach and Wallach (Vol. 3), and Gordon (Vols. 1 & 2). Shuy discusses the mismatch between the language that children bring to school and the language used by teachers and in texts. He suggests that for children who are culturally and linguistically different from the majority, the language mismatch is not so much a phonological or grammatical one as it is a mismatch of functional language competence—the ways in which language is used for various communication purposes. Shuy suggests that research in the area of language functions may be the most promising of all for determining causes of reading difficulty and failure.

Simons reviews the literature on phonological and grammatical in- terference in reading among speakers of a black dialect. Like Shuy, Simons concludes that there is little evidence to suggest that speaking a dialect interferes with comprehending written texts once basic skills have been mastered. However, according to Simons, the evidence on the role of dialect speech in *acquiring* reading skill is inconclusive, and speaking a dialect may indeed interfere. Simons proposes to study the question by examining reading instruction as it actually occurs in the classroom; he describes several studies that examine reading interference and classroom interaction by analyzing videotaped instructional sequences.

Natalicio reviews the existing literature on reading and the bilingual child. Although there is currently considerable pressure among Hispanics and others to teach reading in the child's native language, Natalicio suggests that there is little empirical evidence for such an approach. She calls for more research on bilingualism and second-language learning to resolve what have become largely political arguments regarding the best way to teach reading to bilingual children. Trabasso (Vol. 3), in discussing Natalicio's paper, suggests that parallel teaching of reading in both English and the home language should also be considered, in the spirit of what has been called by Riegel and Freedle (1976) "independent bilingualism." It is not surprising that we know less about the problems of bilingual children than about those of bidialectic children. As Natalicio points out, the recognition of reading problems among bilinguals is relatively new in the United States, and they have only recently gained the attention of researchers.

Gordon (Vol. 2) addresses issues of social-cultural differences and reading from a broader perspective. He discusses compensatory education, characteristics of the groups served by compensatory education, and the effects of various compensatory educational programs. His comments on the teaching and learning of reading are set in this broader context.

Individual Differences. The chapters by Fisher and by Bateman in Volume 1, by Johnson and by Rosner in Volume 2, and by Wallach and Wallach and by Williams in Volume 3 are concerned primarily with individuals—rather than members of social or ethnic groups—who have difficulty learning to read. Fisher and Johnson focus on individuals who are from a clinical population, those with severe learning or reading disabilities; the other authors focus on individuals whose reading difficulties are less severe and for whom instruction can take place in a regular classroom setting.

Fisher discusses the visual-neurological origins of severe reading disability and describes experiments that show sharply reduced peripheral-visual processing among the severely reading disabled. He discusses the importance of the visual periphery in obtaining information and guiding eye movements, and he suggests that instruction for the severely disabled should compensate for these difficulties. Johnson discusses a variety of factors as possible sources of learning or reading disabilities, and she proposes a systems analysis approach to diagnosis and remediation. By this, she means identifying the various psychosensory systems and processes that are involved in reading and determining which are intact and which are impaired. She stresses that the population of children with learning disabilities is heterogeneous and that children with learning disabilities require individual remedial instruction. Examples of these individual remedial strategies are described in her chapter.

The chapters by Bateman, Rosner, Wallach and Wallach, and Williams are concerned with classroom instructional procedures for the hard to teach, whether they are labeled disabled, retarded, or culturally different. Although there are differences in the approaches recommended, a common thread in these chapters is an assumption that those who have difficulty learning to read require a structured curriculum that attends to the phonemic nature of the language and to the relationship of the phonemic to the graphemic code. Bateman recommends using principles of applied behavioral analysis and task analytic programming. Operationally, according to Bateman, this means direct practice with many trials to ensure acquisition and development of the decoding aspect of reading. She suggests that *Distar* is an exemplary program for teaching beginning reading (but cf. Bartlett, Vol. 2). Wallach and Wallach and Williams report on programs they designed and implemented to teach certain beginning reading skills to children who are at high risk for reading failure. The Wallachs report an apparently successful attempt at teaching phoneme identification and segmentation skills to inner-city children in Chicago. Williams designed and is testing a program with learning disabled children from inner-city neighborhoods in New York City. Like Bateman, she recommends that the cognitive and perceptual skills necessary for reading be taught in the context of reading rather than apart from it. Her program follows a sequence in which segmentation and blending of syllables are taught before segmentation and blending of phonemes. Both the Wallachs' program and Williams', then, teach the kinds of skills Liberman and Shankweiler stress as necessary for learning the code. Rosner, discussing the general problem of teaching poor-prognosis children, outlines the components of an instructional system in which he believes it is possible to match student traits with instruction so as to optimize learning. His suggestions are slated for children he views as hard to teach, but his outline appears to be for an instructional system that would benefit all students.

Acquiring Reading Competence

As we have noted earlier, it is important in discussing reading and reading instruction to distinguish between descriptions of the skilled reading process and accounts of how reading skill is acquired. In reading as in other skills, it is probable that the novice performs differently from the expert. Novice readers probably are not only slower, but they probably also attend to different features of text, perceive text in different-sized units, and bring knowledge that is both less extensive and less well structured to the reading activity. Therefore, for example, the skilled reader may read in phrase or clause units, whereas the novice may attend to every word or even to every letter. Despite growing knowledge of the processes involved in skilled reading, much less is known about the ways in which the reading process changes in the course of its development (see Gibson & Levin, 1975, for a discussion of developmental research related to reading), and there is virtually nothing that can reliably be said about how transitions from one stage of competence to another occur. Several authors in these volumes call for additional developmental research on reading; others have begun such investigations. Still others have analyzed existing early reading programs and offer comments on the sort of literacy skill that may result from different instructional procedures.   ·

Developmental Theory and Research. In several chapters, preliminary models or schemes of reading and its development are offered. Chall (Vol. 1) offers a theory of the stages of reading development that can serve to organize much of the subsequent discussion in these volumes. The first three of Chall's stages include a prereading stage; a decoding stage, during which the learner acquires the elements of the code; and a confirmation and fluency stage, during which the code is mastered through the reading of largely familiar material. Following these are stages in which the reader focuses primarily on meaning: first reading for learning from one viewpoint, then reading from multiple viewpoints, and finally reading with what Chall terms a "world view." A stage theory of this kind is of potentially great significance for organizing and focusing the debate over the proper role of the code in reading acquisition. It poses the question of *when* rather than *whether* the code should be emphasized, and it also stresses the role of practice on meaningful and familiar texts. Chall clearly places the code emphasis at the beginning of the acquisition process, but her scheme also emphasizes high levels of comprehension as central to the full cycle of reading development. Other authors would order the emphases differently. What is important is that a stage-oriented theory provides a framework for empirical studies that are both developmental in nature and attentive to the instructional environment in which acquisition proceeds (cf. Kintsch, Vol. 1).

Gregg and Farnham-Diggory (Vol. 3) view reading as a special case of information processing and see the processing system as having three major parts: the perceptual system, the semantic system, and the operations and programs for performing reading tasks. Each of these systems develops greater capability with age and experience. They also offer a taxonomy of reading tasks that is arranged along two dimensions: size of unit and number of operations. The authors suggest that as the processing systems mature, tasks involving larger units and more operations can be performed. Trabasso (Vol. 3), in his discussion chapter, calls for more work on such a taxonomy (and suggests some possible modifications), because it contains an implicit developmental model of reading from prereading to skilled levels with a potential focus on task demands. This, he feels, would force researchers to concentrate on the mechanisms by which skills required for reading are *acquired.* That such schemes have begun to be formulated is promising for our eventual understanding of reading acquisition and development.

The chapters by Chall and by Gregg and Farnham-Diggory offer a relatively macroscopic view of the development of reading skill. By contrast, the chapters by LaBerge (Vol. 3), Juola et al., Liberman and Shankweiler, and Chomsky (Vol. 2) examine aspects of reading acquisition more microscopically. A focus of LaBerge's chapter is on how readers acquire the cognitive structures necessary for recognizing a word, with an emphasis on units of processing. Juola et al.'s chapter examines the appearance and changes over time of visual search strategies in reading and the development of a word superiority effect. Liberman and Shankweiler examine the relation between spoken and written language and describe the phonemic segmentation skills learners need to acquire (on their own or through direct instruction) to be able to map written onto spoken language. Theirs is a developmental theory with explicit implications for instruction. Chomsky offers evidence to support the view that the ability to construct written language (i.e., to write and spell) developmentally precedes the ability to read, at least in some children. She suggests that children can be introduced to reading through a form of creative writing where they are not formally taught spelling but use a spelling system that they themselves invent.

Reading Instruction and Reading Acquisition. Instructional implications have been considered throughout our discussion of issues in reading. However, a few instructional topics did not lend themselves to discussions in other contexts, and we mention them briefly here. Attention should perhaps first be directed to several chapters that address matters related to reading acquisition in the course of describing and assessing instructional programs. The chapters by Beck and Block and by Holland in Volume 1, by Fletcher and by Bartlett in Volume 2, and by Popp in Volume 3 analyze a number of early reading programs. Each is interspersed with comments on the processes of reading acquisition. These chapters are major sources for information on the current state of the art in American reading instruction and the kinds of questions that skilled analysts are raising about this practice.

Assessing Reading Progress. Several chapters stress the importance of assessment as an integral component of the reading instructional process. In order to "deliver" instruction at the proper pace and level of difficulty, the teacher must be able to measure every child's progress in an ongoing way and incorporate the results in daily instruction. This is the major focus of the chapter by Calfee and Drum (Vol. 2), who discuss the goals, methods, and criteria for assessment in the context of instruction. Their emphasis is on measurement of specific skills for short-term instructional decisions rather than on long-term placement decisions. The other chapters that include discussion of assessment are those by Frederiksen, Sticht, and Danks and Fears. Frederiksen suggests that a taxonomy of inference types could be used to construct achievement-test items to measure aspects of discourse processing and that the methods he uses for analyzing children's recall of stories could be adapted for classroom instructional decisions. Sticht describes a procedure for assessing the reading potential of adults. The Literacy Assessment Battery measures the "gap" between auding and reading abilities and reveals the degree to which reading problems are indicative of problems with the printed language specifically or of low levels of general language ability. Danks and Fears offer an experimental task that may be applicable to classroom assessment procedures. They propose a hierarchy of processing levels in reading and describe a series of experiments with texts that have been systematically altered or disrupted. By building the disruptions into the text according to the level in the processing hierarchy that one wishes to study, they argue, it is possible to analyze oral reading behavior to determine if the text is processed at least to the level of the disruption.

The Teacher as an Instructional Variable.   The importance of the teacher both as the deliverer of instruction and as a creator of the learning environment is stressed in several chapters. All authors explicitly or implicitly recognize that the quality of instruction depends in great part on the teacher. Those authors whose chapters emphasize the importance of the teacher are Bateman (Vol. 1), Clay and Rosner (Vol. 2), and Simons, Cazden, and Glaser (Vol. 3). Many other chapters discuss the role of the teacher in the context of other topics (e.g., Beck & Block, Goodman & Goodman, Natalicio, and Shuy). A point that can be drawn from all these discussions is that we know more about the reading process and reading instruction than is currently being used. The teacher is of course pivotal in this matter. Bateman, for example, claims that we already know how to teach the decoding aspect of reading. What we need to do is help teachers to apply the proper methods.

Both Simons and Cazden implicate the teacher and the social interactions in the classroom as possible sources of reading difficulty for some children. They describe observational reasearch suggesting that the quality of instruction may vary for different children even within the same classroom. Rosner describes the traits that teachers must have to be able to teach reading effectively to children who are hard to teach. They must be familiar with basic concepts of reading (many are not), able to be precise and repetitive, able to perform in a structured, relatively nondynamic environment, and able to sustain efforts even when progress is slow and results are small.

Clay describes a program of instructional change in New Zealand. She, like Rosner, emphasizes the importance of teachers' knowledge of reading and reading instruction. She refers also to the importance of teachers as sensitive observers of reading progress, suggesting that observation is itself an assessment technique. She includes an interesting account of in-service training designed to make teachers better informed regarding reading theory and research and more able to apply this knowledge to their teaching.

Time Engaged in Reading.   The importance of time spent in direct instruction in reading is touched on in many of the chapters that analyze and compare different reading instructional approaches. These discussions are found in the chapters by Beck and Block; Bartlett; Fletcher; Guthrie, Martuza, and Seifert (Vol. 3); and Popp. The most direct consideration of this issue is found in the chapter by Guthrie et al., who reanalyzed data collected by the Educational Testing Service on compensatory reading programs. Using that data, they examined the impacts of instructional time in reading on reading achievement among middle- and low-socioeconomic-status (SES) groups. They concluded that amount of time spent in formal reading instruction influenced achievement more than the specific approach used to teach reading. Their findings suggest that a large amount of instructional time benefited sixth graders from low-SES groups but not those from middle- and high-SES groups. Findings at the second-grade level suggest that the amount of instructional time in reading affected achievement but that different SES groups were not affected differently. The authors stress that it is not time itself that affects achievement but the specific events that occur during that time, and they conclude with a recommendation that we improve the measures of instructional intensity by quantifying the events that occur among students and teachers.

Holland focuses explicitly on issues related to the quality rather than the quantity of time spent on reading. Proceeding from a behavioral engineering point of view, he suggests the importance of arranging sequences of contingent interrelations among materials and of clear consequences contingent upon students' responses to details of the materials. Resnick's review chapter (Vol. 2) summarizes and evaluates research on engaged time and instructional programs and suggests that for several reasons, decoding approaches to instruction have probably been correlated with high amounts of time engaged in reading and with more tightly engineered instructional programs. She argues that at least until meaning-oriented instruction can be organized to promote heavy engagement in the actual tasks of reading, code approaches to instruction will best serve the needs of hard-to-teach populations.

On the Relations Between
Theory and Practice

We noted earlier that certain chapters—primarily the discussion chapters at the end of each volume—focus on the actual and potential relationships between theory and research on one hand and practice of reading instruction on the other. Other authors also discuss issues of theory and practice relationships in the context of their specific substantive concerns. Belief in the power of scientific pedagogy is far from universal, as a reading of these volumes will amply demonstrate. Practitioners succeed in teaching reading to many children without being informed of or directly influenced by the results of research. And psychologists themselves are not always convinced that current theory and research can improve educational practice. Depending partly on how individuals became interested in the study of reading and partly on their experiences in applying scientific theory and knowledge to social needs and practices, expectations for the relation between theory and practice differ. All agree, however, that drawing instructional implications directly from current laboratory-based experimental findings is extremely difficult.

Of the several discussants, Venezky (Vol. 2) and Kintsch (Vol. 1) are the least optimistic about the possibility of a direct link between laboratory research and classroom practice. Venezky claims that applying theory to practice is not only difficult but at times has actually led to poor instruction. He argues, not for the direct application of laboratory research, but instead for a "separate but equal" discipline of applied research that is grounded in classroom experimentation. Kintsch, on the other hand, sees a need for more, rather than less, interaction between laboratory and classroom. He holds that although work on reading instruction and basic research in reading are both flourishing, the interaction between them is insufficient. Furthermore, he argues that the lack of a serious theory of reading is a main source of the problem: Instruction is based more on intuition than on research, and research often circumvents important instructional issues.

Kintsch directs attention toward increased efforts in the theoretical realm as an eventual basis for scientifically grounded practice. He perhaps would be joined in this judgment by Posner (Vol. 1), who in addition, points out the ways in which theory can limit as well as expand our work in reading instruction. Posner characterizes theory as both a lens and a set of blinders for practitioners and curriculum developers. He suggests that theory tends to magnify those aspects of a problem on which scientists have worked (the lens), making them more understandable. At the same time, the existence of well-elaborated theory tends to reduce attention to other important aspects of a problem on which there has been little work (the blinders). Posner's chapter elaborates this lens–blinders metaphor with reference to specific issues discussed in the papers on which he comments.

Two discussants, Glaser (Vol. 3) and White (Vol. 2), offer more positive views of actual and potential theory–practice relations. Glaser contends that we know enough now from theory and research to produce positive changes in the outcomes of reading instruction. He suggests that although psychological knowledge is imperfect, it can and should be applied, in an artful and heuristic fashion. White goes a step further. Not only does he think that theory and research can and should change practice; he also suggests a scheme for effecting a more successful change. He argues that the traditional approach of researchers conducting experiments in laboratories and then shipping the results to the classroom has not worked. Instead, he proposes that researchers leave the laboratory to conduct their research in classroom settings and allow their hypotheses to be formulated from actual instructional problems. He argues convincingly that his new scheme may be as important for theory as for education.

It is noteworthy that although Glaser, White, and others seem to be generally satisfied with the state of theory with respect to reading instruction, they all point to a need for more elaborated theories of reading acquisition. The discrepancy between theories of skilled reading and those of reading acquisition and development is discussed by Gordon (Vol. 1), Venezky (Vol. 2), and Trabasso (Vol. 3). Regardless of disagreements on other issues, all contributors whose discussion focuses on this topic unite in calling for more research on reading acquisition. The need for this shift in theoretical and research direction is clarified by Trabasso. He notes that current work in cognitive psychology is preoccupied with the description of processes used for engaging in tasks rather than with how the processes required for engaging in them are learned. To remedy this, Trabasso calls for renewed attention to some of the questions of classical learning theory but within the new context of an enriched cognitive psychology. Resnick (Vol. 3) echoes the need in her summary discussion and develops a proposal for the kinds of questions a psychology of reading instruction would need to address and the methods it may require.

General Issues

The final chapters of each of these volumes are discussion chapters. In most of these, commentary is limited to issues raised in the chapters of the volume itself. However, four of the discussion chapters—those by Gordon and Resnick in Volume 2 and those by Carroll and Walton and by Resnick in Volume 3—present a more general set of reflections. These chapters, written after all the other chapters were submitted and discussed, are intended as integrative reviews highlighting particular issues in early reading instruction that were considered in the volumes as a whole. They do not attempt to respond chapter by chapter or point by point to the other contributions; instead, they use the issues raised in all three volumes as points of departure in considering broad concerns of research and practice in reading instruction.

Gordon's integrative chapter (Vol. 2) is concerned with the problem of reading instruction in the context of compensatory education programs. The chapter begins with a discussion of the concept of compensatory education itself—how the concept developed, the assumptions about the poor that surround it, and common conceptions of the children who receive compensatory education. Gordon suggests that these children have too often been grouped together under the label *disadvantaged* and characterized by their differences from the white, middle-class "norm," rather than being seen as individuals, with individual strengths and weaknesses. He proposes that it is these individual characteristics, and not group labels, that should be taken into account in the design of instruction for all populations. Against this background, Gordon discusses various chapters in the volumes with respect to their implications for compensatory reading programs.

Resnick's integrative chapter in Volume 2 represents an effort to distill from the many specific points of view presented in these volumes the major competing positions on the nature of reading and appropriate reading instruction. She identifies two major views of the nature of reading—reading as translation of print to sound and reading as an autonomous language process. These two positions, Resnick points out, lead to different prescriptions for reading instruction: Adherents of the reading-as-translation view prescribe early and systematic instruction on the alphabetic code; supporters of the reading-as-autonomous-process view prescribe early attention to functional and meaningful use of written language. After reviewing empirical research on instructional program effects, Resnick picks code-oriented instruction for the early years of reading, but cautions that this will not "solve" the reading problem. She goes on to suggest the kinds of research and development that are needed for more successful instruction in comprehension and the functional aspects of reading.

Carroll and Walton's chapter in Volume 3 reviews previous attempts at organizing knowledge about early reading, and discusses these volumes as part of this series of efforts to solve the reading problem. The chapter contains an extensive discussion of the positions and points of view expressed in the chapters of these volumes. This discussion is organized into two major sections: (1) conceptions of the nature of reading, and (2) how well early reading instruction as it is currently conducted reflects theory and knowledge about learning to read. The section on the nature of reading includes detailed analyses of particular points of view expressed in the various chapters of these volumes. It is thus an excellent guide to the often confusing and tangled arguments on topics such as the centrality of decoding, top-down versus bottom-up processing, direct versus mediated word access, and the role of language skills in becoming a good reader. The section on instruction includes a detailed discussion of beginning reading programs, which both comments on and extends the discussion of curriculum and pedagogy presented in various chapters. Throughout their integrative chapter, Carroll and Walton take definite positions on controversial instructional questions.

Finally, Resnick's chapter in Volume 3 addresses the questions of whether and how theory and basic research can contribute to practical pedagogy in reading. Resnick first considers some of the reasons that most basic research in reading has not been as helpful to practice as might be wished. She then proposes a variety of research questions and research methods that she believes would make future reading research both more useful in instructional design and better science in its own right. The result of such research, she suggests, would be a psychology of reading focused directly on instruction, a psychology centrally concerned with processes of acquisition and with the role of intervention (i.e., instruction) in these processes.

REFERENCES

Adams, M. J., & Collins, A. *A schema-theoretic view of reading* (Tech. Rep. No. 32). Urbana, Ill.: Center for the Study of Reading, 1977.
Buswell, G. T. An experimental study of eye–voice span in reading. *Supplementary Educational Monographs,* No. 17. Chicago: University of Chicago, 1920.

Cattell, J. M. The time it takes to see and name objects. *Mind,* 1886, *11,* 63–65.

Chall, J. S. *Learning to read: The great debate.* New York: McGraw-Hill, 1967.

Flesch, R. *Why Johnny can't read, and what you can do about it.* New York: Harper, 1955.

Fries, C. C. *Linguistics and reading.* New York: Holt, Rinehart & Winston, 1962.

Gibson, E. J., & Levin, H. *The psychology of reading.* Cambridge, Mass.: MIT Press, 1975.

Huey, E. B. *The psychology and pedagogy of reading.* New York: Macmillan, 1908. Republished by the MIT Press, Cambridge, Mass., 1968.

Mathews, M. *Teaching to read: Historically considered.* Chicago: University of Chicago Press, 1966.

Maugham, W. S. The verger. In *Cosmopolitans.* New York: Doubleday, Doran, 1937.

Resnick, D. P., & Resnick, L. B. The nature of literacy: An historical exploration. *Harvard Educational Review,* 1977, *47*(3), 370–385.

Riegel, K., & Freedle, R. Bilingualism. In D. Harrison & T. Trabasso (Eds.), *Black English: A seminar.* Hillsdale, N.J.: Lawrence Erlbaum Associates, 1976.

Rumelhart, D. E. Toward an interactive model of reading. In S. Dornic (Ed.), *Attention & performance VI.* Hillsdale, N.J.: Lawrence Erlbaum Associates, 1977.

PROCESSES OF READING

1 The Perception of Units in Beginning Reading

David LaBerge
University of Minnesota

The main concern of this chapter is the particular way that perceptual units are involved in the reading process. My remarks are not aimed at describing a complete theory of reading nor even a theory of beginning reading. Instead, I would like to treat a restricted aspect of reading that asks questions about units, their functions, their sizes, and their development in the experiences of the person. My remarks may provide more questions than answers, but I would be content if in the course of this chapter, one or two basic issues in this area were clarified so that a set of productive hypotheses could be generated for further research.

Most of the examples treated here are related less to comprehension than to the perceptual aspects of reading—for example, word recognition and decoding, which are important issues in beginning reading. However, it would be a bonus if some of the principles discussed at the perceptual end of the reading process would generalize to comprehension processes deeper in the cognitive system.

The chapter has three parts. First I discuss what I consider to be the main function of units for perceptual processing in general and for reading in particular. This involves a description of a class of models that interrelate these units. The second part of the chapter is concerned with the question of how we manage to select the particular set of units appropriate to the task at hand. Finally, I discuss in a general way some important factors that may influence the learning of new units.

THE FUNCTION OF UNITS

It is rare that we hear anyone talk about reading without mentioning units. Certainly our conventions of measurement require that we agree on the definition of a unit. In measuring reading speed, we usually count words. In measuring immediate memory span, we may count letters; And when we measure a line of poetry, we may count syllables. However, many psychologists consider words, syllables, and letters to be more than simply objective units of measurement. They also regard them as conceptual representations of perceptual events or structures (Melton & Martin, 1972). They assume that readers have a network or code representation for each of the many familiar patterns they have experienced, ranging from simple line features to more complex patterns such as letters, words, and faces. These codes may be considered as part of long-term memory or, to be more precise, as part of long-term perceptual memory; It is these structures that are first encountered when information comes off the sensory surfaces of the eye and ear. For example, when we are shown a new word, the name of a new flower that I will call a *sidularium,* not everything we see when we look at it is new. The letters and probably the letter clusters are familiar enough so that we can spell the word and pronounce it. We may even try to relate that word to other things or rehearse it so that we can recall it later. However before we do any of these things, the word stimulus falling on our retina has already made contact with the memory of certain letters and letter clusters, and it seems as if the recognition of these familiar patterns simply happens to us. Therefore, this point of view introduces perceptual units very early in the processing system, and the outputs from these perceptual units are used in higher-order operations such as naming, rehearsal, and comprehension.

A schematic representation of perceptual units related to reading based on the assumptions set forth in the LaBerge and Samuels model (1974) is shown in Fig. 1.1. There are three major systems that contain an array of codes or units: the visual perceptual system, the phonological system, and the semantic–syntactic system. (I use the terms *unit* and *code* interchangeably in this chapter.) Graphemic information from the printed page enters from the top and makes contact with (i.e., activates) the codes of the visual system, represented by dots. Solid dots refer to codes that are well formed in long-term memory through many experiences with a particular stimulus pattern, such as a common letter or word. Open dots refer to codes that are unfamiliar and therefore have been only temporarily formed—for example, a Greek letter or a new flower name.

Although the visual codes are spatially arranged in a hierarchy in Fig. 1.1, there is no specific indication of how they are interrelated here, hence the omission of any lines connecting codes with one another. There are several alternative models (LaBerge, 1976) by which the codes may be linked

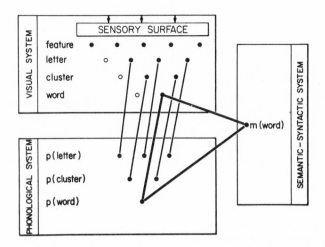

FIG. 1.1. Representation of units in the visual, phonological, and semantic–syntactic systems. Solid dots represent familiar memory codes that can be activated automatically from the sensory surface. Open dots represent unfamiliar codes that require additional activation by attention. Lines connecting codes represent intersystem associations.

together. These models are discussed in detail later in connection with learning new codes. However, regardless of which of these models is assumed, outputs from many of these visual codes become associated with units in other systems. For example, we learn to name letters and words, and we may give meanings to words not only from their phonological units but also directly from their visual units.

The name and sound units are represented by codes in the phonological system, and a hierarchical arrangement of these codes may be assumed, as shown in Fig. 1.1. For example, when children sound out a new word, *clam.* they may visually code *cl* and *am* and by association produce the sounds /kl/ and /aem/, which they then blend into a higher order sound /klaem/. With practice, they may learn to associate the whole word *clam* directly with the sound /klaem.

Other associative links in Fig. 1.1 are assumed to connect phonological codes to meaning codes (which children typically have learned before they begin to read) and to connect visual codes directly to meaning codes. These associations are assumed to be activated by outputs from unitary codes. And herein lies one of the advantages of perceptual unitizing. If no unitization occurred before intersystemic associations were attempted, then a good deal of confusion would accompany an association. For example, assume that *cl* and *am* were separately associated directly to the word sound /klaem/. Then the child would say / klaem/ to any word that began with *cl* or ended with *am*. Obviously, to avoid confusions such as this one, the child must either unitize the visual clusters into a visual word before learning the association or else always rely on associating spelling patterns with the appropriate syllables; The latter approach will run into the same problem, however, when patterns such as *th* and *ough* are encountered. These letters must be unitized into spelling patterns before the appropriate sounds can be associated with them without confusion.

A parallel line of reasoning is assumed for the case in which sounds are associated with meanings and visual units are associated with meanings. It is difficult to imagine how intersystemic associations can effectively occur unless there are unitizations of the perceptual codes, that is, the child must unitize the pattern to sound it or get its meaning. Therefore, units can be regarded as transformers of information; they take information from the sensory surface, directly or indirectly through other subordinated units, and put it into a unitary form to transmit to other major cognitive systems for further processing. This transformation is not merely a matter of convenience; it is somewhat of a necessity. Evidently some associative transformation must take place between the information falling on the sensory surface and the phonological and meaning systems, because the acoustical codes and the meaning codes assigned to this information are almost always arbitrarily related to the form of the physical object. A unit seems to be an appropriate form assumed by perceptual information in order that arbitrary associative relationships can be made in an efficient and relatively unambigous manner.

Units also act as filters of incoming sensory information (Estes, 1974). If perceptual units were omitted from the design of the human reader, then the myriad details of information at the sensory surfaces would have to be processed at the deeper cognitive levels. This would reduce the efficiency of processing, especially in view of the limited capacity characteristics of processing.

The size of the unit may vary depending on the task demands. For ordinary reading purposes, the larger the perceptual unit, the better (Gibson & Levin, 1975). Some stages of processing have limits on the number of units of information that can be processed simultaneously. One of these systems is immediate memory, which is said to have an upper limit of 7 plus or minus 2 units (Miller, 1956) or 5 plus or minus 1 unit (Mandler, 1967). Presumably, we use this kind of memory to keep in mind the first part of a sentence while perceiving the last part of a sentence, so that we can put the whole sentence together for comprehension. Another system with a sharply limited capacity is attention, which may be limited to operating on only 1 unit at any given moment (Broadbent, 1958; Moray, 1969; Treisman, 1964), although with rapid shifting, attention may appear to maintain several units at a state of heightened activity. Given that immediate memory and attention capacities are so small, skilled readers evidently process information in text as fast as they do because they pack more information into each unit.

The information-carrying capacity of perceptual units (and meaning as well) can be very large, but a considerable amount of learning is required to be able to compress information into a unit quickly and reliably. Perceptual learning is considered to proceed at a relatively slow rate as compared to the rate of associative learning, which may often occur in all-or-none fashion (Estes, 1970). Nevertheless, learning to perceive information in terms of large units is critical for fluent reading and for higher cognitive functions such as creative thinking. Therefore, it is not surprising that it takes years for reading skill to become fluent.

One of the benefits of unitizing perceptual patterns is that the processing usually becomes more automatic with each exposure. This means that less attention is needed to process a given unit, so that attention can be devoted to others aspects of the task at hand such as comprehension and coding for recall (LaBerge & Samuels, 1974). For example, recognizing a new word at first takes attentional effort, but later, as the word becomes more familiar, it seems to be recognized with no effort; in fact, we cannot easily stop ourselves from recognizing it. The relationship between familiarity and automaticity has been studied in experiments by Shiffrin and Gardner (1972) and by LaBerge (1973). Currently, I am exploring other ways to measure automaticity and relate it to measures of unitizing during perceptual learning.

At this time, I feel relatively secure in assuming that the familiar units represented in Fig. 1.1 are processed automatically. Therefore, when a familiar word is shown to a person, not only the word code but also the letter codes and feature codes are activated. This result is assumed to hold independently of the particular word-recognition model chosen (see Fig. 1.4). But this immediately presents a new problem: If all the familiar codes at all levels are activated, how do we select a particular code for association with codes of another cognitive system? How do we insure, when we are reading, that the highest level of perceived units is the one processed for meaning? When the first-grade teacher holds up a card with a word on it, how can one know whether a child is attending to the letter units, or the spelling units, or the whole word?

SELECTING UNIT LEVELS

The issue of selecting a level of processing has been a major concern in our laboratory over the past several years. We have tested the processing of letters and familiar bigram units with a task that simply requires the person to match these patterns. For example, the subject is shown two letters positioned side by side, with several spaces between them, and is asked to press a button if the two letters match but to withhold the response if they do not. Sometimes we have the subject press another button when the two patterns do not match, but the data of interest are the latencies of correct matching operations. Sometimes we use novel letters as well as familiar letters and sometimes novel letter strings as well as familiar spelling patterns and words. The basic assumption of this method is that we can measure the visual perception of a pattern relatively directly, as opposed to the more indirect method of measuring the time to name a pattern or categorize it. These latter tasks have other components that take up processing time, namely, the association between the visual code and the code in the other system and the processing of the code in the other system (see Fig. 1.1).

Consider a stimulus display containing two bigrams, *cl, cl,* that the subject is instructed to observe. If the two patterns match, the subject is to press a button. According to Fig. 1.1, the familiar letters *c* and *l* will be automatically activated. Notice that the subject could perform the task by matching each letter one at a time—(two matching operations)—or by matching the clusters as units—(one matching operation). Which way is used? Even if the subject were sounding the letters and bigrams, something would have to determine which way is chosen. We have run several control conditions that indicate that the subjects' reaction times seem to be based on visual matching, even though they often report that they are aware of naming or pronouncing the patterns (see also Baron & Thurston, 1973; Pollatsek, Well, & Schindler, 1975).

Rohn Petersen and I (Petersen & LaBerge, 1975) set out to determine whether we could control the level of processing of bigram clusters. To do this, we used two kinds of lists of items. One list contained predominantly familiar bigrams or clusters such as *sl, ph, sh,* and *br.* The other list contained predominantly unfamiliar clusters such as *ls, hp, hs,* and *rb.* Our hypothesis was that for the first list, subjects would process the bigrams as units and make one matching operation, whereas for the second list, they would process the bigrams letter by letter and make two matches. With this method we hoped we could exert control over the unit level at which the stimulus display would be processed for a match.

What we needed was an indicator of the processing level used in each list. We inserted into these two kinds of lists, two kinds of test items—a familiar bigram pair such as *cl, cl,* and an unfamiliar bigram pair such as *lc, lc.* We reasoned that in the list of unfamiliar bigrams, these two test items should be processed similarly, that is, letter by letter. Therefore, their latencies should not differ. However, in the list of familiar bigrams, there should be a difference in the time required to process these test items. The unfamiliar test item should take longer than the familiar test item, because the subject is expecting to match the cluster as a whole but cannot do it quickly because the

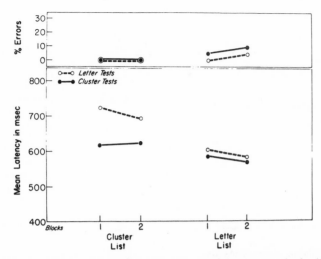

FIG. 1.2.   Mean latency and percent errors of matching responses for familiar digram (clusters) and unfamiliar digram (letters) test items for two types of list contexts.

cluster is unfamiliar. Even if the subject tries to match it letter by letter, it should probably take more time to switch attention to the letter level to make the match.

The results of this experiment are shown in Fig. 1.2. The mean latency to test patterns is plotted over two blocks of trials for each type of list. Familiar bigrams are labeled *clusters,* and unfamiliar bigrams are labeled *letters.* When cluster and letter bigrams are embedded in lists of letters, there are no significant differences in the time to match them. But when the same cluster and letter bigrams are embedded in lists of clusters, there is a significant and substantial difference between them. Clearly, the type of list context has an effect on the way a given stimulus pattern is processed. Thus, we can take as our indicator of level of processing of the list items the difference in latency between unfamiliar and familiar test items. When there is no difference in latency between the types of test items, then we infer that the subject is processing the list of items at the letter level; when the unfamiliar items show a longer latency than the familiar items, then we infer that the subject is processing the list of items at a higher level.

The fact that the latency of matching an unfamiliar bigram changes with the type of list context indicates that list context must exert some kind of influence on the processing of the units. Along with Estes (1974), I represent the influence of contextual conditions on perceptual processing by special contextual nodes, as shown in Fig. 1.3. The arrows indicate that a contextual node can activate the entire set of pattern codes at one level of processing. For example, when the letter contextual node is activated, it activates all the letter

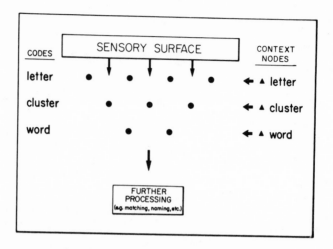

FIG. 1.3. Representation of units in the visual system for three levels of processing. Contextual nodes activate all units at the indicated processing level.

codes. This internal activation combines multiplicatively (Estes, 1974) with incoming sensory information, so that individual letters appearing on the sensory surface are given emphasis compared to units representing groups of letters. This results in a higher activity of readout from the letter codes to the matching operation, so that the first match completed is made on the basis of letter units. It is possible that readout from unit codes representing clusters would also reach the matching operation; but it they did, they would reach it some time after the letter code readouts arrived. In this way, a context node selects the level of processing by which a given task operation is carried out. Typically, selection can move upward or downward in the hierarchy of processing, although sometimes special training is needed to induce a child to read out from lower levels, as in segmenting words or syllables into phonemes. Again, it is important to note that Fig. 1.3 represents a modification of the original LaBerge and Samuels (1974) model, because as it stood before, there was no mechanism by which a particular unit level could be selected. The change that is suggested here is the addition of context nodes that combine with stimulus inputs to determine which level of units has highest priority for further cognitive processing.

If a mechanism like the context nodes is tentatively accepted, another problem arises: How is a particular context node activated? Something makes us look at letters when we proofread a manuscript for spelling errors and controls our processing of words and phrases when we proofread a manuscript for sense, for example, to determine whether a sentence as been left out. Similarly, something controls the child's choice of units when the teacher holds up a card with the word *pen* and instructs the child to tell what the word means—in which case he or she processes it at the word level—or instructs the child to tell how many letters it contains—in which case he or she selects a letter unit. In all these examples, instructions determine the unit level selected. In the experiment just described, which called for matching units at different levels, the unit level was presumably determined by the list context. Exactly how experience with the first several items of a list produced an activation of a particular context node is not spelled out here.

We believe the questions concerned with the selection of context for a given task requre research involving converging operations in order to provide clear and firm answers. As a step in this direction, we have carried out a series of experiments (LaBerge, Petersen, & Norden, 1977) to determine whether subjects can be instructed or cued to select visual units by directing their attention to a specific level of processing. Using the bigram materials in the experiment just described, we mixed the familiar and unfamiliar bigrams within the same block of trials but always presented familiar bigrams in the lower part of the screen and unfamiliar bigrams in the upper part of the screen. Before each trial, a circle was shown in the upper or lower position to tell the subject the location and therefore the type of bigram to expect. We hoped that this very obvious spatial cue would induce the subject to process the items in the upper position letter by letter and the items in the lower position bigram by bigram. Using the same probe tests as before, we found no significant differences in mean latencies between the two presentation positions. This result apparently tells us that subjects could not easily switch levels of visual processing from trial to trial. It also suggests that it may take several trials to establish a stable context level. Although much more research is needed to clarify this issue, it does appear that even college subjects have difficulty in directly shifting attention effectively and quickly between levels of processing of visual units. It appears that we cannot easily focus attention on a context in the way that we can focus on a given pattern or even on an operation such as adding or subtracting. It seems more likely that we can more directly select phonological levels because we can respond by pronouncing a letter or a syllable. Selection of a level in the phonological system might then feed back to the visual system and select the corresponding level of units.

Thus, although there remains work to be done to solidify and extend these results, there are two conclusions from this discussion that seem to me to be of considerable import in the understanding of the role of units in perceptual processing. First, since subjects have an option as to what unit they will process when they are shown a word, some source of information other than the immediate stimulus display must determine the unit selected. Second, at least for the visual system, the selection of unit level by direct deployment of attention to that level is not easily done by the average person.

LEARNING NEW UNITS

The foregoing discussion of the function of context nodes in the selection of perceptual units suggests strongly that the context node may also have a crucial role in the acquisition of new units. If the activation of a response from the perceptual system is presumed to require the joint action of the information from the stimulus display and the activation of a context node, then we cannot expect to teach children to respond on the basis of a new unit unless they already have its context node available and functioning. For example, it they are sounding a word on the basis of letter units, how can we expect them to shift to higher orthographic units unless there is control by the contextual node at this higher level? Thus, it seems quite likely that the formation of context node precedes, or is contemporaneous with, the formation of a unit at that level of processing.

It would appear, then, that two main questions concerning the learning or development of perceptual units must be addressed: First, how is a unit formed when the appropriate contextual node is in active existence? Second, how is a unit formed when the appropriate contextual node is not available and must be developed at the same time? On the one hand, we learn new units most frequently at a level of processing at which we have already acquired some units, but on the other hand, it follows that we must occasionally learn a unit that is the first one acquired at a new level of processing. In the latter case, the child must acquire or develop the appropriate context node before or at the same time as the first unit as that level is formed.

A very important issue in the perceptual learning of a word involves the regularities or rules of combinations of spelling patterns (Spoehr & Smith, 1973). For example, consonant cluster units seldom follow each other; instead, a vowel or vowel cluster usually intervenes. The present discussion does not elaborate the relationships of visual units and otherographic rules; instead it concentrates on the implications of contextual nodes for the processing of simplified displays of various units. If this approach is successful in these situations, then hopefully a subsequent paper will give more discussion to orthographic rules.

Learning a Unit at a Familiar Level

How are letter units formed by children who have already learned a few letters of the alphabet? Or consider the unitizing of a new word by a child who already has several words in his or her visual vocabulary. For these children, it is assumed that there exist context nodes for letter units and word units. Thus, all that the child needs to do is to form a new unit of a somewhat familiar kind. This is the type of situation in which I have studied the perceptual learning of novel letters (LaBerge, 1973), and others have studied the perceptual learning of new letter strings (e.g., Barron & Pittenger, 1974). This kind of perceptual learning has been conceived of as having three stages (LaBerge, 1976)— namely, feature discovery, unit formation, and the automatic unitization. For example, in the perceptual learning of artificial letters, the subject must first discover the distinctive features—in a way similar to Gibson's (1969) notions that distinctive-feature pickup takes place in perceptual learning. However, since typical subjects have already encountered many letters, they will find the selection of a single feature will not suffice to distinguish the new letter from the others they have learned. For example, suppose the new letter contains two lines that cross. Taken alone, this feature will lead to a confusion of the lower case letters t and f if the crossing lines are horizontal and vertical. Seldom does one feature distinguish one letter from all the rest of the letters that the person is called on to distinguish.

This fact forces the learner to observe more than one feature in order to discriminate patterns from each other. When patterns are presented side by side in a same–different task, subjects can scan each contrasting feature independently, especially when the two patterns are positioned close enough to each other to facilitate scanning back and forth. But if the subjects are presented one pattern at a time for identification, then they must learn the combination information of the two features. When we learn to identify letters by name, we have to note the particular combinations of features by which each letter is uniquely identifiable. This stage of perceptual learning, therefore, requires that information in the distinctive features be combined. I consider this to be a second stage of perceptual learning in which a letter unit is formed.

The perceptual learning of a word may be considered in a parallel manner. For the four words *at, it, an,* and *in,* the task of merely discriminating pairs of these words can be carried out by scanning the first and second letter positions. For example, if subjects are given the pair *at, an* to distinguish, they look at the first letter position and find a match, then scan the second letter position and find a mismatch, and then respond, indicating that the two patterns are different. But if the subjects are required to identify (e.g., by four different responses) each of these words in isolation, they may scan each letter position, but they must remember the first letter when noticing the second letter. It is the combination of the two letters that determines the correct response. The perception of this combination information is assumed to be the second stage of perceptual learning.

Exactly how the combination information is processed is currently a very active controversy in the study of perception. Perhaps the most well known form of the question asks what information in a string of letters produce word recognition. The vast array of experiments on the word-advantage effect centers on this issue, since it asks how a letter is more easily detected when it is embedded in a word than in a nonword (e.g., Estes, 1975: Reicher, 1969). For a word, the particular combination (including order) of letters has been learned, but for a nonword, the combination information has not been learned, especially if it is a nonpronounceable nonword. Thus, this problem falls under the second stage of perceptual learning. It is clearly not a first-stage problem, since subjects have no difficulty discriminating a novel string of letters from other strings of letters.

The relationship of a word unit to its constituent letters perhaps can be clarified in terms of the network models shown in Fig. 1.4. It is hoped that this kind of classification of coding models will help to set priorities in research to determine what it is in graphemic stimuli that activates a word unit.

The pure hierarchy model assumes that letter code outputs converge to activate a word code; that is, a word is recognized by outputs from its constituent letter units. Of course, a word code may be activated by spelling patterns as well as by individual letters. However, for convenience in expositions of the six models, the cluster level of units that are included in Fig. 1.1 is omitted. In the quasi-hierarchy model of word recognition, there are inputs to the word code from word features such as word length, contour, and internal relations. This model assumes, then, that a word is recognized on the basis of component letters together with features unique to the word pattern.

The two-level models assume that a word code is activated from the feature level only, so that the processing of a letter unit is not a necessary prior

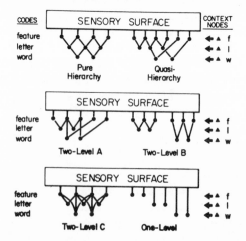

FIG. 1.4. Six coding models for word recognition. Solid dots represent familiar memory codes at three levels of processing (spelling pattern codes are ommited here for convenience of illustration). Context nodes activate all units at the indicated level of processing.

condition to the recognition of a word. The two-level models differ with respect to characteristics of the inputs. In the two-level model A, some of the imputs to a word code come from features that also activate letters. In two-level model B, the word code is activated only by distinctive features of words such as length, contour, and internal relations. In two-level model C, the inputs to a word code come only from features that also activate letter codes.

The five models just described assume that a word unit is activated by outputs from either letter codes or feature codes and that usually at least two of these inputs are required to activate the word code. The one-level model, on the other hand, assumes that each unit extracts its information directly from the sensory surface without intermediating codes. In this way there is no fusion of two or more inputs, but there is instead a direct relation between the stimulus information and the unit.

It should be noted that one- and two-level models do not have the hierarchical property whereby the codes of one level feed into the codes of the next level. The arrangement of units in these models is stratified in Fig. 1.4 only to reflect the conventional way we order features, letters and words in our descriptions. I would like to point out again that the inclusion of the spelling-pattern level, which is critical for the functioning of orthographic relationships [Eds. note: see also Venesky & Massaro, Volume 1, this series], is not expected to alter the main contrasts being drawn among these six models. If the spelling-pattern units were added to Fig. 1.4, the additional crossings of lines would produce a rather noisy array that would tend to obscure the main differences among the models.

Perhaps we can summarize the main principles of these models by borrowing on variations of an old Gestalt principle. For the pure hierarchy model, the word is the sum of its letter parts. For the quasi-hierarchy model, the word is more than the sum of its letter parts. For the one- and two-level models, the word is different from the sum of its letter parts. Thus, there appear to be at least six different ways that a word code might be activated once the stimulus information falls on the sensory surface. I am not suggesting that only one model is true for all cases. It may be that we shift from one way of processing to another under different reading demands; and it may be that in the course of learning to read, a child shifts from one way to another as the predominant way of processing a word.

If we assume a pure hierarchy or quasi-hierarchy model, then one interpretation of unitizing is that a word is fused from component letter units or some feature units that are unique to the word. But if we assume the two-level B model, then it might be said that the word unit is fused from its own unique set of features. In this case, second-stage perceptual learning is not based on previously formed units but instead on a reselection of features such as particular internal relations in a word. This process may be considered quite close to the process of first stage perceptual learning, since it involves discovery of the appropriate features. However, it differs in at least three respects from the search for distinctive features. First, the purpose here is not usually that of discriminating two patterns from each other, since this can already be easily done on the basis of the known letter units. Second, the word features are likely to be relational features that are not "point-to-able" in the sense that letters can be singled out. This implies the third difference, namely, that the reselection is not likely to involve a search by reorientation of the eyes to other locations within the word pattern but must be guided in some way to a new relational feature based on the raw information already existing in the print of the letters. After all, if the ink marks were removed, the word could not be perceived. Therefore there is something about the marks on the page that gives rise to word perception as well as to letter perception.

Regardless of whether second stage unit learning is regarded as a fusion of letters or features as a direct extraction process or as some other process, it would seem that there must be a shift in the context node from activating units at the letter level to activating units at the word level.

Once the subject perceives the word as a unit, further exposures are needed to consolidate the unit so that eventually the unit can be activated without attention to fusion and/or to reselection of features. In this way, perception becomes automatic. If the second stage unit learning for words proceeds by fusion of letter code outputs, then in the third stage the fusion occurs without the attentional scanning of the letter. If the second stage occurs by an extraction of relational features, then during the third stage the deployment of attention to this process becomes less and less.

Learning a Unit at a New Level[1]

The situation of learning a new type of unit is much like that confronting a child who has no trouble identifying or naming letters of the alphabet but who now must perceive a cluster of letters—for example, the bigram *ch* or *sh*—and notice the regularities of their combinations (which is involved in what some mean by learning orthographic "rules"). These letter clusters must be perceived as units to associate effectively a unitary phonological response with them. Similarly, after phonics training with parts of words, the child must learn to blend the parts into a word. This may involve shifting context levels in the phonological system. Listening to children trying to blend a word for the first time can be very instructive. For example, in blending the two patterns *ch* and *at* into /caet/, the pause between /c/ and /aet/ indicates quite

---

[1] I hope the reader will keep in mind that my comments in this section of the chapter are speculative. However, it is in view of the practical importance of initial unit learning that I stray so far from supporting data. I hope the ensuing remarks will stimulate some productive tests of these notions.

directly that they are processing these as separate units. Later, after "something clicks in their heads," they pronounce the word *chat* in a quick, uninterrupted manner, which seems to the observer to indicate that they have processed the word at the phonological level holistically. One can be even more convinced of this unitization if they recognize the meaning of the word at the time that they successfully blend it. The point is that once children have learned to blend successfully one or twice, the blending of new cases seems to proceed faster. Similarly, when children learn to identify one or two bigrams as units, they seem to pick up new bigrams, trigrams, and so on quite quickly. The problem appears to be located at the point of getting children to identify a bigram as a unit or to blend parts of a word for the first time. We often say that they have to "learn the skill" of blending or unitizing; this is perhaps not unlike the learning-to-learn phenomenon described by Harlow (1949). In terms of the present model, when they can activate the appropriate context node to perform the appropriate unitizing, they have learned an acquisition skill. By means of this skill, they go on to acquire new units at that level.

It might be remarked that the appropriate context nodes of letter groups and whole-words sounds are available and actively used by children at the time they first learn to blend and unitize letter strings. In their daily conversation they use spoken words, and they can almost always recognize their written names and usually a few common written words. Doesn't this mean that they already have an active node for these particular perceptual units, and therefore, for all other units at these levels? I would venture to guess that they do not necessarily have the appropriate context nodes for other units, because the context is not the same. Consider how a child recognizes his written name among other names presented to him. Suppose *John E.* is written above a coat hanger in the kindergarden classroom. John's task is to discriminate the visual pattern of the written name from other names he sees. In a typical group of 20 or 30 children in his class, there is not likely to be another written name very similar to his. If there is a John F. or a Joan E., he might show some confusion, and a teacher often foresees this problem and places the labels at different spatial locations so that spatial cues can be used to help discriminate the names. If pressed, I would suggest that the context node involved here is at the feature level. Thus, young children generally can identify their written names on the basis of a few features that are quite different from the information they must learn to pick up when they identify the vast range of words in their visual vocabularies years later.

The parallel argument for phonological units is more difficult and admittedly somewhat tentative at this time. But I would ask the reader to consider that before children learn to read, they do not segment spoken words very often. [Eds. note: see also Liberman & Shankweiler, Volume 2, this series]. A sentence is heard as a continuous stream of sounds, and boundaries are often not at all distinctive to children until after they have learned to read.

Therefore, the way they hear and utter words in normal speech probably involves contextual controls altogether different from those appropriate for the sounding of words in isolation. Although one has seen and heard one's name many times before beginning to read, one may eventually come to hear and see the name differently after learning to read. By *hear and see differently,* I mean that a different context node is involved, and this implies that one must be able to pick up stimulus information from the same words differently.

Let us return to the case in which children have learned to identify individual letters and now are called on by task requirements to process strings of letters as units, for example, bigrams or short words. Their training with letters has sensitized them to the locations within a word that carry the information that distinguishes one word from another. For example, there are many words in our language that differ by only one letter. Children who have focused attention on letter units must now free themselves from this narrow range of information and take in new information whose source is no longer individual letters but is in the combination information in the string of letters. As has been pointed out before, there are several viewpoints as to how the information in a string of letters gives rise to a new unit representing a spelling pattern or a word. Regardless of the view adopted, the word unit is assumed to be controlled by an appropriate contextual node. And this node must either be present genetically through maturational readiness or somehow acquired by appropriate experiences. If it is available, then the child learns the new unit and moves rapidly ahead. If it is not available, we either wait until it matures, or we try to induce the context by instructional means.

Instruction and Unitizing Skills

Although scientists prefer to control the events in their domains as opposed to waiting for them to happen, and although our practical educational objectives also press us to control beneficially the learning of a student, it may turn out that the development of a contextual mechanism is not subject to direct control and therefore may be resistant to efforts to "teach" it. Recall the experiments just described in which we tried to cue the level at which a subject would match pairs of bigrams. The results indicated that subjects apparently do not directly activate levels of processing, implying that the context nodes may be so remote from attentional control that efforts to teach a subject to use them when they have never before used them may be entirely fruitless. It seems to me that the notion of readiness captures the flavor of this problem. If we have to wait for a child to become ready to learn a skill, then this implies that the basic processing mechanisms are not receptive to our attempts to control them. This does not mean that some skills already in the child's repertoire could not substitute for the one in question. A child who does not perceive the bigram *sl* as a visual unit may stay at the visual letter level and combine letters phonologically by sounding them one after another. On a more general level, a reader may compensate for an inability to perceive many whole word units by sounding out syllables.

If control of visual unit levels is not easily accomplished directly, then perhaps other routes to the activation and selection of visual units are employed. In the experimental example described, in which the familiarity of a list of bigrams apparently determined the level of processing, there must have been some pathway by which the visual nodes were selectively activated. Our best guess is that the operation of matching the patterns produced a feedback to that level of units that yielded the faster matching. The ultimate control of level of units in this case was the environment, since it was the type of display that determined the context. Similarly, we often find that a child can "get into the swing" of performing a new skill under the strong control of classroom stimulation but when faced with the same task alone, cannot perform the new skill. What seems desirable is to provide the child with a means of controlling his or her level of perception rather than leaving it to the preceding sequence of stimulation.

One promising direction for providing internal control of visual processing levels looks to the phonological system, in which control is typically exerted by speech. Adults find it relatively easy to listen to whole words, the last rhyming syllable, or the sound of the first phoneme. This may be done quickly, because they can sound these units to themselves. In this way they select a level of processing. If they have learned sound-to-sight associations— that is, can categorize sounds as words, clusters, or letters—then they can control the level of visual processing by attentional activation of appropriate sound units, which then activate corresponding visual control of visual processing levels. Children who have not learned to segment phonemes within a word and have not learned the relations between sound levels and sight levels should have considerable difficulty in selecting the appropriate visual units in processing graphemic displays. Thus, the acquisition of new visual units, especially at a new level, is regarded here not as a simple selection and/or fusion of sensory inputs from the bottom up. Because of the important interactive role of the contextual nodes with incoming stimulation, perception and acquisition of new units require that appropriate activation of contextual nodes be controlled. The major direction of this control is assumed to come from higher cognitive systems.

It may be the case that fast learners differ from slow learners because of a difference in the availability of contextual mechanisms. There is evidence that slow and fast learners apparently do not differ with respect to speed of forming associations (Estes, 1970; Zeaman & House, 1963) but do differ with respect to perceptual learning. Specifically, lower mental-age subjects require more time to discover the appropriate perceptual features or dimensions of the perceptual patterns in a task. Similarly, one might expect to find differences in learning rates at other stages of perceptual learning, such as in coding new units. Perhaps one of the most dramatic differences between individuals may be in terms of the speed at which they acquire new unit levels. Some children move from letters to higher orthographic units to whole phrases so rapidly that it is difficult sometimes to believe that for these children there are separable subskills at all. But for others, the contextual levels may become available relatively slowly, and for a time the child cannot move from one level to the next.

I have been talking about the learning of units in the same way that some researchers refer to the learning of skills. In view of the similarity of the conceptualizations of skill learning and unit learning, it should not be surprising to find that they share common questions. For example, it is reasonable to assume that a global skill such as reading can be appropriately segmented into subskills for the purpose of effective instruction. If so, does the most effective way to teach these skills proceed from the bottom up, that is, beginning with smaller units and proceeding to the larger units? Furthermore, when we find ourselves spending a great amount of time on some particular subskill, how do we motivate the child appropriately? For example, if the motivation for reading is to comprehend written language, how do we most effectively motivate subskill learning at the level of orthographic units?

To what extent are unitizing skills teachable? I believe that instruction, whether by a teacher or by a book, exercises control over the student's perception most effectively by presenting material that is "point-to-able." The teacher can make sure that the student picks up the critical information by saying "consider *this*" or "look at *that*," whether it is a feature of an airplane, a note of music, a sentence, or a mathematical expression. When a point-to-able item is the critical feature, then learning apparently proceeds quickly, because the "pointing" function of the teacher controls the attentional focusing of the student. But when the feature is not so easily pointed out, then attentional focusing of the student is not directly controlled by the teacher, and there will be uncertainty about the material the teacher intends the student to perceive. Many relational features are this type. For example, when two pitches are presented simultaneously, it is not clear whether the student percieves the musical interval or just the two individual notes. Similarly, when the teacher points to the word *man,* it is not clear that the student perceives the visual relations within the word. Compare the words *man* and *mat*. It is tempting to say that the difference is perceived in terms of the different terminal letter units, because the terminal letters *n* and *t* can be pointed to. But it is more likely that the reader perceives the whole word, and the first two letters—*ma*—and the last letter are interrelated. How does a teacher effectively point to such a relation? Indeed, it is far more convenient to point to a letter than to a relation. And this may mean that it is very difficult to "point the way" to new levels of perceiving, especially when they involve relational features.

However, once a level has been brought under the control of a contextual mechanism, then the teacher may have several means of promoting the acquisition of units. Two of the methods have already been described. The first way uses units that are at the new level to induce activation of the context mechanism by presenting them as a series of examples before presenting the new unit. For example, if the bigram *dr* is to be learned as a unit, it can be presented folowing *sl, fl,* and *gr,* which by assumption are familiar units at that level. The second way of promoting unitizing uses sound-to-sight relations to induce the appropriate visual level. For example, sounding the series of visually presented words, *mink, sink, pink,* and then *drink,* may promote perceiving *dr* as one visual unit if the child already can segment the initial phoneme and the initial letter in the first three words. If, however, the child has neither visually unitized a bigram prior to *dr* nor learned to visually segment the first letter or letters of a word and associate sounds to these visual units, then teaching the child to unitize *dr* visually will be more difficult. If the teacher points to *dr,* the child is likely to perceive two letters. If the teacher pronounces it "druh," the child may not isolate the initial phonemes from the neutral syllable "uh" and more important, he or she may hear the two phonemes /a/ and /r/ separately. If the child hears two sounds, then he or she may look for two symbols, and although this may be desirable in some tasks, it is not desirable for promoting visual unitization.

Although the foregoing examples are quite rough attempts to illustrate ways that unitizing might be taught, it hoped that they do provide a contrast between teaching a new unit when the appropriate contextual control of a level is available and when it is not available.

DIFFICULTIES AND CONCLUSIONS

It is obvious that considerable research is needed to fill in the gaps in the contextual control modifications of the LaBerge–Samuels model (1974). It is difficult to formulate optimal algorithms for acquiring units when there is considerable uncertainty as to how a word code is activated. Figure 1.4 shows six different models, and there are undoubtedly others. Quite probably, the acquisition of word codes proceeds by stages that may be arranged hierarchically. Initially, the child may recognize a word in terms of letters and spelling patterns and only later as a single unit. But if the learning sequence proceeds hierarchically, this does not necessarily imply that when the word is finally recognized as a unit, it is processed hierarchically—that is, from outputs from letter and spelling pattern codes. Fluent readers, in fact, probably learn new words directly as single units without going through letter and spelling pattern stages, due to the use of contextual nodes of a high order. Before these questions can be probed, reliable indicators are needed of the level at which a word is processed in any given instance. Figure 1.2 illustrates one way this might be done, but the test has drawbacks in terms of ease of administration.

Another difficulty standing in the way of prescribing ideal conditions for acquiring units is the lack of detailed knowledge of the way contextual information interacts with sensory input. Furthermore, as was mentioned before, it is not clear how visual contextual nodes are activated by the phonological system and perhaps the syntactic–semantic system

If the importance of learning a unit at a new level were compared with learning a unit at a familiar level, there would be no question that the accomplishment of the first is the more momentous educational event. A contextual jump presents a new class of units within the grasp of the child, and these moments are often referred to as times when the child has "made a leap" or is "over a hump." When the child has learned to use a new contextual node, he or she has in effect learned an "acquisition skill" by which a host of new units at that level can be acquired. It may be that contextual jumps are events that cannot be directly pointed out to the child but instead must happen to him or her, and all teachers can do is provide the best conditions under which these happenings can occur. Defining what those conditions are may be a fruitful direction of research in efforts to understand the role of perception in the very complex skill called reading.

ACKNOWLEDGMENTS

This research was supported in part by United States Public Health Service Grant HD-06730 and in part by the Center for Research in Human Learning through National Science Foundation Grant BMS-75-03816. The author acknowledges the helpful discussions with S. Jay Samuels, Rohn J. Petersen, and Lee Brownston.

REFERENCES

Baron, J., & Thurston, I. An analysis of the word-superiority effect. *Cognitive Psychology,* 1973, *4,* 204–229.

Barron, R. W., & Pittenger, J. B. The effect of orthographic structure and lexical meaning on "same-different" judgments. *Quarterly Journal of Experimental Psychology,* 1974, *26,* 566–581.

Broadbent, D. E. *Perception and communication.* London: Pergamon Press, 1958.

Estes, W. K. *Learning theory and mental development.* New York: Academic Press, 1970.

Estes, W. K. Memory, perception, and decision in letter identification. In R. L. Solso (Ed.), *Information processing and cognition: The Loyola symposium.* New York: Wiley, 1974.

Estes, W. K. The locus of inferential and perceptual processes in letter identification. *Journal of Experimental Psychology: General,* 1975, 104, 122–145.

Gibson, E. J. *Principles of perceptual learning and development.* New York: Appleton-Century-Crofts, 1969.

Gibson, E. J., & Levin, H. *The psychology of reading.* Cambridge, Mass.: M.I.T. Press, 1975.

Harlow, H. F. The formation of learning sets. *Psychological Review,* 1949, 56, 51–65.

LaBerge, D. Attention and the measurement of perceptual learning. *Memory & Cognition,* 1973, 1, 268–276.

LaBerge, D. Perceptual learning and attention: In W. K. Estes (Ed.), *Handbook of learning and cognitive processes,* (Vol. 4.). Hillsdale , N.J.: Lawrence Erlbaum Associates, 1976.

LaBerge, D., Petersen, R. J., & Norden, M. Exploring the limits of cueing. In S. Dornic (Ed.),*Attention and performance VI.* Hillsdale, N.J.: Lawrence Erlbaum Associates,1977.

LaBerge, D., & Samuels, S. J., Toward a theory of automatic information processing in reading. *Cognitive Psychology,* 1974, 6 293–323.

Mandler, G. Organization and memory. In K. W. Spence & J. T. Spence (Eds.), *Psychology of learning & motivation I.* New York: Academic Press, 1967.

Melton, A. W., & Martin, E. (Eds.). *Coding processes in human memory.* New York, Wiley, 1972.

Miller, G. A. The magical number seven, plus or minus two: Some limits on our capacity for processing information. *Psychological Review,* 1956, 63 81–97.

Moray, N. *Attention: Selective processes in vision and learning.* London: Hutchinson, 1969.

Petersen, R. J., & LaBerge, D. *Contextual control of letter perception* (Tech. Rep. No. 15 of the Minnesota Reading Research Project). Minneapolis, Minn.: University of Minnesota, 1975.

Pollatsek, A., Well, A. D., & Schindler, R. M. Familiarity affects visual processing of words. *Journal of Experimental Psychology: Human Perception and Performance,* 1975, 1, 328–338.

Reicher, G. M. Perceptual recognition as a function of the meaningfulness of the material. *Journal of Experimental Psychology,* 1969, 81, 275–280.

Shiffrin, R. M., & Gardner, G. T. Visual processing capacity and attentional control. *Journal of Experimental Psychology,* 1972, 93, 72–82.

Spoehr, K. T., & Smith, E. E. The role of syllables in perceptual processing. *Cognitive Psychology,* 1973, 5, 71–89.

Treisman, A. Selective attention in man. *British Medical Bulletin,* 1964, 20, 12–16.

Zeaman, D., & House, B. J. The role of attention in retardate discrimination learning. In N. Ellis (Ed.), *Handbook of mental deficiency: Psychological theory and research.* New York: McGraw-Hill, 1963.

2 How to Study Reading: An Information Processing Analysis

Lee W. Gregg
Carnegie-Mellon University

S. Farnham-Diggory
University of Delaware

We have read in several places lately that the time is not yet ripe for a comprehensive reading model. For example, Gibson and Levin (1975) wrote: "It is indeed a question whether looking for a model is a worthwhile enterprise. A model implies a paradigm, or a pattern to be closely followed. That any one model will suffice to typify the reading process is doubtful [p.481]." And Smith, in a 1975 National Institute of Education (NIE) report, said: "The absence here of any discussion of the complete model for the reading process published in the last 10 years is intentional. After intensive analysis of such models [e.g., those found in the Davis, 1971, collation] we believe that we know too little about the component processes to justify attention to complete models [p.2]." Why, then, in the face of this collective wisdom, are we about to discuss a comprehensive reading model?There are two major reasons. First of all, it is not true that we lack comprehensive models of reading. We have dozens of them, hundreds. Everyone has a model or theory of reading. But in whole or in part, they are implicit theories, and most of them are not formulated in a testable way. If it was possible, as the quotation from Smith suggests, to identify components of the reading process (e.g., decoding and comprehension) and to study them experimentally, then a model that defined the component boundaries must have existed. That is, an implicit comprehensive theory of reading must have led the NIE study group on models to propose that word recognition is necessary to reading. The problem is not to invent a model; the problem is to make public and testable the consequences of the models we already have.

A second major reason for discussing an overall theory of reading is to provide a framework to account for experimental data. Reading involves only a few types of processes and information structures. They are not really a mystery. What is uncertain is how these components go together at high speed. We need ways of characterizing the conditions under which certain processes are evoked. We need the decision rules that fire one cognitive function rather than another. We need to specify characteristics that determine which process gets activated initially and which produces the final output. Without an explicit model of these control factors, we have no way to integrate the piecemeal data that our reading laboratories have generated. In this chapter, then, we offer a framework for a comprehensive theory of reading.

Figure 2.1 is a schematization of the human information-processing system. There are three major parts to it. First, we discuss the perceptual system, the discrimination nets or P-space. We talk about the outcome of perceptual processing—the act of recognition. Those acts are signified here by terminal nodes labeled *I*. Second, we talk about the semantic system, or S-space. Note that we have not referred to a decoding system or a comprehension system. The P-space is not a decoding space, nor is the S-space equivalent to comprehension. *Decoding* and *comprehension* refer to ways in which both these spaces are used. (One reason there is much confusion about the terms *decoding* and *comprehension* is that we have not been sufficiently careful to specify task demands and stage of practice.) The third part of the human information-processing system, then, is the collection of basic operations and learned programs for performing reading tasks. A great deal of confusion arises from not taking into account differences among reading tasks. To demonstrate how perceptual processes and semantic processes—as diagramed here—operate during reading, it is necessary to be very specific about the type of reading task referred to. For that reason, we have developed a taxonomy of reading tasks. We return to an analysis of these tasks after presenting an overview of the structure common to all of them.

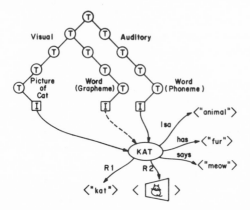

FIG. 2.1.   Perceptual and semantic elements of the human-information processing system.

THE PERCEPTUAL SPACE

Earlier in the history of psychology, as well as in the history of reading instruction, perception was considered to be a holistic process, something that happened all of a piece. Over the past two decades, however, we have learned that this is not the case. The discoveries have been partly a matter of experimental design and partly a matter of apparatus development. It is now an accepted fact that perception is a process of noticing a series of features sequentially. We do not perceive the letter E all at once. We perceive a set of horizontal and vertical lines, one at a time. Or possibly, we perceive a single higher order feature—a pattern of horizontal and vertical lines. We refer to this noticing process as feature testing. That means, in effect, that such questions are asked as: Does the letter have a vertical line in it? Is the letter closed at the top? The tests are made at high speed, in a few hundredths of a second. With regard to perceiving the English alphabet, we have a first approximation to what kinds of tests can be expected in an adequate model of feature detection: tests for verticals, horizontals, symmetries, and so forth (Gibson, 1969). The perceiving mind, even the mind of a young child, after some experience with the alphabet, "grows" a testing program to discriminate among the letters. We think of this program as a tree of tests.

The first theory that attempted to make this growth process and the subsequent testing process explicit was in the form of a computer program called the Elementary Perceiver and Memorizer (EPAM) developed in the late 1950s by Feigenbaum (1959). This program simulated the process of growing a new test structure, as well as the process of using it. Interestingly, one of the first applications of the EPAM program was to reading. Feigenbaum and Simon (1963) showed that a system capable of performing paired-associate memory tasks is capable of reading names of objects. The important requirement for this is that a minimum of three distinct encodings or representations of the stimuli in reading are necessary. The net must discriminate among phonemes—the sounds of words, letters; another set of tests must distinguish among visually presented letters and syllables; and a third must recognize objects in terms of their visual characteristics—shape, color, and the like.

The importance of the simulation was that it forced the simulators, the theorists, to confront problems that are all too often swept under a theoretical rug. For example, there is the problem of understanding the natural, unschooled development of feature-testing abilities. When children look at Daddy's or Mommy's copy of the New York Times—especially when they look at it upside down—what tests are they growing? In psychological laboratories and in schools, we manage to avoid that question. But if we tried to simulate the growth process, we would not be able to avoid it. We would be forced to make our speculations explicit and to design ways of testing them. Perhaps the most crucial issue to emerge in constructing an explicit model of an association memory is the number of levels of indirection necessary for such a structure to operate. At least two levels of indirection, via pointers to tokens of an object, are necessary in a node-linked recognition memory. Otherwise, removing the object from sight would remove it from memory (Gregg, 1971).

Although there is little research on humans, there is a growing body of animal research on the neurophysiological nature of feature detectors. Specific brain cells respond to specific kinds of visual information—horizontal lines, vertical lines, diagonal lines, and so forth. Groups of these cells, when activated, fire higher order cells—pattern detectors. Thus, a single higher order cell assembly may be responsible for the detection of a pattern. The animal evidence also indicates the existence of critical periods in the development of feature detecting abilities. Clearly some kind of learning, exposure to patterns, imprinting—whatever we want to call it—must go on at a very early age.

Someday we will have detailed models of the development of human feature detectors—models that will describe neurophysiological changes in the growing brain and specify the extremely high speed operations that we refer to as P-space tests. An important component of these models will be specification of how the P-space increases in complexity. With age and experience, the P-space grows rich and intricate. Tests develop the ability to test syllables, spelling patterns, word roots, prefixes, and so forth. These perceptual abilities become, in some sense, built in neurophysiologically.

Or at least they should. There is probably a class of disorders included in that catch all term *dyslexia* that result from growth problems at this level. The P-space in some children does not become elaborated in normally organized ways. This may be a type of perceptual confusion analogous to astigmatism or other types of visual disorders. The point is that for practical puposes, it is a neurophysiological disorder, a brain dysfunction. Someday, when we have proper models of normal P-space functioning, we may be able to fix these disorders just as we can fix astigmatism by fitting glasses. Many other so-called dyslexic disorders, however, are probably not P-space disorders but are difficulties involving the outcome of P-space operations. When we say that a child is "learning to perceive letters," we are implicitly referring not only to the child's ability to detect features at a high speed but also to the ability to associate test outcomes to some other learned information—like the name of the letter or its sound. Those two kinds of processing—perceiving and associating—are governed by different principles. We turn now to some of the principles of association.

Recognizing Familiar Objects

In Figure 2.1 a terminal node, a square box, is distinguished from test nodes that appear earlier in the perceptual sequence. If graphemic stimuli can be sorted to a terminal node, an act of recognition has occurred. At the termination of feature testing, there is an internal name, a symbol pointing to whatever information has been associated with that graphemic stimulus. When we say a word has been recognized, we are really saying that it now has symbolic form that will permit it to be associated with other symbols.

It is important to distinguish between the visual recognition of graphemes and the recognition of previously learned speech sounds. Children may be able to perceive a word perfectly well visually but not recognize it because there is nothing in their memory that the percept is pointing to. On the other hand, children may recognize a word when they hear it—that is, when they test acoustic features—but may not be able to process the graphemes visually

There has been a major controversy in reading over whether recognition must always involve auditory recoding. In our terms, the question is, "Must the pointer always be to the sound of the word?" The relationship labeled *R1* in Fig. 2.1 is the articulatory code for saying "cat." A word sound may be the only thing a beginning reader recognizes. We come back to this issue later. For now, the point is that recognition is the termination of a perceptual testing process, a termination that exists in the form of a pointer to other previously learned information. What happens after that is a semantic issue.

THE SEMANTIC SPACE

The semantic space is symbolized in the lower right portion of Fig. 2.1. There are several fundamental parts to the space, and there are a number of different ways of representing them, depending on the notational system one chooses. In our system, a closed area represents what we ordinarily call a concept, an addressable location in the memory. It is a node, a symbolic entity, an internal name, that serves to index the properties and relations that define it. In Fig. 2.1 the index is called *KAT,* so we are able to refer to it.

The node has associated with it a set of properties—such things as color, shape, size, texture—plus additional information: functions, contextual information (where the concept is likely to be found, for example), linguistic properties, and everything else that one knows about the particular concept in question. The links between the properties and the conceptual node are relations. There can be superordinate relations—a cat "is a[n]" animal—and properties—a cat has fur. There are also related actions—a cat scratches.

As the diagram suggests, it is possible to get from any part of a semantic network to any other part. The idea of bouncing can lead to the idea of ball which in turn can lead to the idea of red. If all those entities are activated by a syntactically correct program, one has the idea of a bouncing red ball.

Because it is theoretically possible to get from one part of the semantic network to any other part, what keeps the entire net from "lighting up" at once? Presumably, the limitation is in our short-term memory capacities. We are able to use only a very small portion of our knowledge at any one time. This severe constraint affects the way in which knowledge is gathered and stored, as well as the way in which it is later accessed. Because of this constraint, semantic memory is organized.

What is the nature of this organization? A good deal of research suggests that the organization is categorical and that the categories are arranged in hierarchies. Much research has also been directed toward the notion that we have schemata or frames or scripts that make it possible for us to use semantic information efficiently and selectively (Abelson, 1976; Bobrow & Norman, 1975; Rumelhart, 1975; Winograd, 1977). For example, when we read or hear the word *hit,* we expect that some kind of object—a ball—is involved. We have a schema for verb–object relations of this type, a schema that is independent of any particular verb in the class. We have schemata for picking up many kinds of semantic information that direct us to look for other information. Thus, initial information is verified or disconfirmed by subsequent information. Verification of schemata is an important aspect of reading comprehension. Most of the developmental research in the area is concerned with schemata for single words like *buy, sell,* or *give.* We have recently completed the only study we know of on the development of semantic schemata of a more complex, sentential sort.

We were concerned with the young child's ability to activate schemata involving an agent, an action, and an object. For example, think of a baseball player at bat and then of a baseball. Does the ball "go with" the first scene? Does a hot dog go with it? Does a letter go with the scene of a postman walking down the street? Does a tricycle go with the postman scene? We used 10 different agent–action slides and 4 different types of objects that were more or less related to each of the 10 stimulus slides. After each pair of slides, the subject was asked, "Does this go with the picture you just saw?" The subject's decision time to answer, yes or no was recorded, and the subject was then asked for an explanation.

The explanations were scored in terms of the simple process model shown in Fig. 2.2. The levels represent three types of schemata that could be employed in making a decision. A Level 1 schema includes a belief that the object—the baseball, say—is an inevitable part of the agent–action scenario. For example, as one child said. "When someone's hitting a ball, they need a ball." There is a very high frequency of association. We can think of the

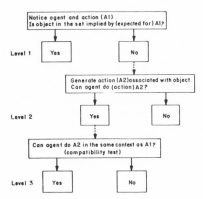

FIG. 2.2. Process model for belongingness decisions.

schema as a frame with a blank for the agent, a blank for the action, and a blank for the object. When the first two blanks are filled, a candidate for the third one is quickly detected.

But suppose that instead of seeing a baseball, the subject saw a hot dog. Does a hot dog "go with" the baseball player at bat? The subject might decide yes, but in order to do so, he or she would have had to generate some actions associated with hot dogs and perhaps some other actions associated with the baseball player—the fact that he or she eats, for example. That is more complex type of schema, which we call a Level 2 schema. If it has been activated, the subject will say something like, "Yes, the baseball player and the hot dog go together, because baseball players can eat hot dogs."

A yes followed by that type of explanation should have a longer latency, because the subject probably generated and tested the Level 1 schema first and then generated some more ideas after rejecting the Level 1 possibility. Under the guidance of the schema, the subject noticed additional properties associated with particular nodes and explored a more remote area of the semantic network.

Of course, the Level 2 possibility might also be rejected. We would consider that to have happened if the subject said something like, "Yes, the baseball player and the hot dog could go together, because the player would be hungry after his game and would then go and eat a hot dog." That kind of answer contains what we call a compatibility test: Even though the action of hitting a baseball and the action of eating a hot dog could be connected through the node of the player, those two actions are not simultaneously compatible. The player could not do both of them at the same time or, perhaps, in the same place. The compatibility test in a verbal explanation is a higher order functional rule than the tests at Level 1 or Level 2, because two different agent–action schemata must be generated and tested. That type of "yes" decision should have the longest latency of all.

So far, we have discussed only "yes" decisions. "No" decisions should take somewhat longer than "yes" decisions at each level. The assumption is that a "no" decision includes some kind of tranformation from positive to negative, and these take a small but measurable amount of additional time (Clark & Chase, 1972; Just & Carpenter, 1976).

The experiment was carried out using eight adults and eight 5-year-olds. Each subject saw, in a random order, all 10 stimulus agent–action pictures paired with each of 4 object pictures. That amounted to 40 slide pairs. Decision times were recorded automatically by means of a voice key. Verbal explanations were recorded on audiotape. Table 2.1 provides a summary of the results.

To begin with, children are generally slower than the adults, by about half a second on the average. Second, when the "yes" and "no" judgments are conbined, the adults and children show about the same relative increase in response time from Level 1 to Level 2 to Level 3 decisions. The interval from Level 1 to Level 2 is shorter than the interval from Level 2 to Level3 for both children and adults. The general pattern is consistent with our model, and it suggests that the 5-year-olds went through roughly the same semantic decision processes as the adults did, when the children went through any decision processes at all. To understand that last clause, the "yes" and "no" means should be examined. For the adults, the "no" judgments—with all levels combined—take about 200 msec longer to make than "yes" judgments, as is consistent with a large amount of "yes"–"no" literature. Among the 5-year-olds, however (and this is actually a replication of a previous experiment using different groups of children and adults), there is a very different

TABLE 2.1
Response Times for Belongingness Decisions

Type of Response[a]	Children Response Time[b]			Adults Response Time			C–A Difference
Level 1	1904	(56)		1344	(44)		560
Difference (2–1)			218			140	
Level 2	2122	(23)		1484	(37)		638
Difference (3–2)			468			547	
Level 3	2590	(21)		2031	(19)		559
"No"	1891	(64)		1716	(44)		175
Difference (No–Yes)			–628			193	
"Yes"	2519	(36)		1523	(56)		996
Mean	2205	(100)		1619	(100)		586

[a]Level refers to the model shown in Fig. 2.2, and "No" and "Yes" refer to the outcomes of the decisions.

[b]Response times and differences in milliseconds are classified for children and adults by type of response. Percent of total responses is shown in parenthesis for each type of decision.

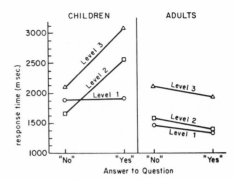

FIG. 2.3. Response times for belongingness decisions.

situation. The children take much longer to decide yes than to decide no. The effect is especially striking when we separate the levels, as shown in Fig. 2.3.

For adults, a "no" decision always takes a longer time than a "yes" decision; the effect replicates from level to level. Among the children, only the Level 1 decisions begin to look like the adult functions. Level 2 and Level 3 decisions are much slower when they are affirmative than when they are negative. Why should this be?

We think that the "no" times do not contain the decision functions. The child said no first and figured out why afterwards. The "yes" times do contain the decision functions. The child thought about a particular decision before making it. In terms of our model, we can think of it this way: The children either decide no on the basis of a Level 1 schema, or they decide that they are going to say yes. Having decided to say yes, they then choose a Level 1, Level 2, or Level 3 schema for formulating their judgments. This suggests that even though 5-year-olds are capable of activating higher order schemata, they do not use that capability in making any particular decision. If they have used it—that is, if they have explored the semantic net and have constructed some relatively remote hypotheses—then they are likely to view the outcomes of their labors positively. This may be something like a dissonant situation: Because I am going to so much trouble, any connection that I finally turn up must be a valid one. Whatever the reason, it is apparently easier and faster for 5-year-olds to acknowledge semantic disconnections than it is for them to activate schemata that permit higher order connections. That is the first point. The second point is that having invented a higher order connection, the child respects it.

The pedagogical implications of such research are straightforward. We should base beginning reading materials on schemata that children find natural and easily activated. Because we do not yet have detailed models of what these natural schemata are, our best recourse is to use the child's own language. This may give rise to schemata that strike adults as unusual. Figure 2.4 is a language-experience chart that seems somewhat ungrammatical in terms of how adults think of sentence rules. But the schemata represented are

Funny Colored Pictures

Blue pictures, red pictures, zebra pictures.

There were small pictures and big pictures.

The pictures were not real.

Just colors.

Many colored pictures.

FIG. 2.4. Language-experience chart as an example of natural schemata.

the ones that were natural to this particular group of children following a particular kind of experience—they had just visited a museum. It is the research scientist's job to discover and specify the nature of such schemata. We should design reading materials that are based on the natural integrative structures of children. If we do not, we may be forcing beginning readers to spend precious attentional capacity on schemata that are not natural to them but that are based on ones that are natural for adults. We take up the complex matter of attention in the next section.

CONTROL PROGRAMS: A TAXONOMY OF READING TASKS

We have sketched some of the basic structures and functions that are involved in any reading task. For any type of reading, some kind of stimulus material— letters, words, or whatever—must first be discriminated, sorted through P-space structures. The outcome of the sort shifts the processing into the semantic space, where different kinds of processing occur. To construct a theory of any reading task, we must be able to specify a unique program of attentional control. Attention is directed by the program from one type of cognitive activity to another. Since skilled readers can perform a variety of reading tasks, it must be the case that a control program for one type of task bears some kind of systematic relationship to control programs for other tasks. This is also implied by the fact that the programs are operating on the same P-space and the same S-space structures, which are highly stable for normal individuals.

Table 2.2 is a taxonomy of reading tasks. The tasks are arranged along two dimensions that we believe to be key parameters: size of unit and number of operations. Units can increase from letters, or pieces of letters, to whole passages of words. The number of operations in any given act of reading may be few, or it may be many. Within this general framework, it is intuitively helpful to list some familiar categories. We are used to thinking in developmental terms of prereading, beginning reading, reading, and skilled reading levels, so those categories are marked. We are also used to thinking in terms of such tasks as reading-to-learn, or constructive reading, as compared to confirmatory types of reading. These categories are marked along the top of the table, and we explain them in more detail as we go along.

TABLE 2.2
Taxonomy of Reading Tasks

Sight-sound Correspondences	Verification Tasks		Construction Tasks	
	Perceptual	Conceptual	Understanding	Remembering
Saying letters (Prereader)	Letter recognition	—	—	—
Iteration ↓	*Integrating concrete operations* →	*Cognitive synthesis* →	*Invoking schemata* →	*Generating strategies* →
Saying words (Beginning reader) ↓	Word recognition →	Word meaning	Clarifying ambiguous words	Reading for specific facts
Reading sentences aloud (Reader)	Object relations	Narrative	Following directions	Reorganizing semantic memory
Reading passages with feeling (Skilled reader)	Map reading	Logical propositions	Making logical inferences	

Cognitive Hurdles

63

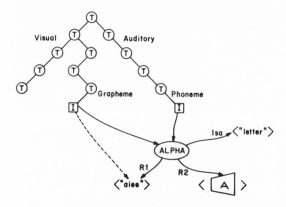

FIG. 2.5. Sight–sound corres-pondences for saying the name of the letter *a*.

Let us think first of what is often considered the simplest, most fundamental reading task of all: saying the name of a letter. That is our first level of sight–sound correspondence learning. Figure 2.5 shows what kind of P-space and S-space operations are to be expected. The child sees the letter *A* and sorts the features to a terminal node that indexes a semantic node. We have designated the semantic node as *alpha*. Alpha is recognized, its internal address is accessed. It indexes the image of *A*, assuming that such an image is stored in the long-term memory of the reader. It indexes information like "first letter of the alphabet," in some memories at least. It also indexes the sound (articulatory code) *aiee*. Note that through the sound, the speech–motor program for pronouncing the sound is obtained. By saying the letter aloud, the sound is recognized.

As the reader becomes more skilled, the control program operates on larger units. The situation becomes more complicated when the unit size goes beyond the span of immediate apprehension. Then the reader cannot take in all the necessary text elements at once. Some information must be held in a short term store while additional information is gathered. We can chart the control program as shown in Fig. 2.6.

The program is described in very general terms to show how broadly it may be applied. First, some goal (*R1* in the figure) must be specified—for example, finding the name of a concept. Attention then scans a portion of the material and holds it. The program then tests for completion of the terminal recognition unit: Is there anything more to be perceived—the rest of the word, say? If the unit is not complete, the program must cycle back and pick up the rest of the information before it can move into the S-space and get the name it is after. When it finds the name, the speech-motor code can then be executed.

This cycling operation, the ability to scan and hold pieces of a recognition unit, is a developmental milestone. Constructing an iterative control program may be just the hurdle that every child must get over in order to get beyond primary reading. The capacity of short term memory—the holding capacity—is critical. It should not surprise us to learn, as we reported earlier,

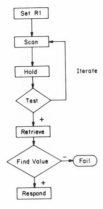

FIG. 2.6.   Flow chart of the control program for sight–sound correspondence tasks.

that disabled readers have short term memory problems (Farnham-Diggory & Gregg, 1975).

As we developed the taxonomy, we found hurdles of other types. For every class of reading task, defined by our columns, there appears to be a type of new subroutine that the reader must be able to devise in order to become reasonably skilled.

The rather elaborate taxonomy of reading tasks tries to capture two dimensions that are important to an understanding of reading processes. Both imply increasing sophistication in terms of the demands placed on the reader. The left-hand column is labeled *sight–sound correspondences*. Going down that column, we find larger and larger units of text—from single letters that a prereader can decode to entire prose or poetic passages whose interpretation by a skilled reader calls for much knowledge and practice. To the right of the sight–sound column are four additional columns of increasing complexity, organized into two broad categories: verification tasks and construction tasks.

Verification Tasks

By *verification* we mean that the text confirms something that the reader already knows or sees. The written material is intended to verify a previously observed relation. Thus, in the early stages of reading, a child may be requested to "find the letter *A* " or when shown a picture of a dog, to "find the word that goes with the picture." Verification can refer to perceptual events or conceptual ideas. At the level of reading sentences, the relation between objects can be verified: "Is the star above the cross?" Or, "Jack and Jill went up the hill to fetch a pail of water." The child who has the story committed to memory verifies that narrative event at the proper time. Most verification occurs during the acquisition of reading skill. Subsequently, verification becomes a subprocess of comprehension.

As the size of the unit increases, we find such tasks as reading descriptions of objects or places. Here, the control program must get over a new type of hurdle. It must invent subroutines for handling multidimensional information. To read about a bright red beach ball, a child must have the ability to notice several dimensions simultaneously—brightness, redness, roundness. According to Piaget (1965), this kind of control is a hallmark of the concrete operational stage. Hence, moving from a beginning to a skilled reading level on tasks of this type requires more than the simple iterative capacities required for a similar developmental step on sight–sound tasks. However, this higher order program may include iterative subroutines.

Verification tasks do not always have a concrete representational component. That means simply that nonphysical properties of a semantic unit may be accessed. There are many other properties: ideas of lower-and uppercase letters, grammatical properties of words like *and* and *the,* as well as words like *run.* And to get from word meanings to sentence meanings, one has to be able to integrate ideas. That poses another hurdle.

Since the verification programs are quite similar, the single flow diagram of Fig. 2.7 is used to outline the processing sequences. Notice that the subroutine called "get value" essentially embodies the sight–sound correspondence program shown in Fig. 2.6, except that now a new property of the semantic unit is called for. In the case of perceptual verification, *R2* is the physical, sensory description of the object. Conceptual verification tests ideas established by the teacher or by the demands of the task. Verification tasks require search of the text for confirmation through words, sentences, and the like.

In our view, the most important new component is the ability to compare a previously set referent with information extracted from the text. The comparison operation can fail for two reasons: First, the multidimensional

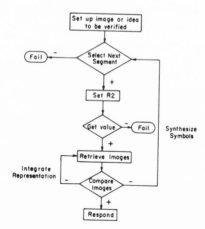

FIG. 2.7.   Flow chart for reading verification tasks.

test of object properties may be beyond the developmental capabilities of the reader. Two (or more) dimensions must be tested on Property 1 and then on Property 2 for both the stored image and the image derived from the reading process. Or, second, the comparison may fail because the reader is not able to synthesize ideas extracted from the separate segments of the text.

We have labeled this hurdle *cognitive synthesis* (see Table 2.2) a term that refers to some earlier experiments (Farnham-Diggory, 1967). In these experiments, children learned whole word symbols, or logographs, for familiar words. The aim was to test the integrative capacities of children who were too young to have learned the alphabetic writing system. After learning the logographs, the children were shown sets of them in simple sentences, like "jump over block." They could read the logographs perfectly. They were then asked to "do what you said." Young children, instead of jumping over the block (a block just happened to be on the floor), jumped up in the air, made a sign for over and pointed to the block. They acted out each symbol one at a time, instead of putting all the symbols together mentally and then acting out their combined meaning.

That research was without a satisfactory theoretical context until recently. Now we think of synthesis as a type of simple linear schema. To get conceptual meaning out of a sentence, the reader must apply a basic schema of collecting a set of words before computing meaning. This is a version of the scan-and-hold program discussed earlier.

Purely conceptual programs of this type are apparently more difficult than similar programs that contain representational cues. Rebus languages are said to be pedagogically simpler than alphabetic languages (Farnham-Diggory, 1972). However, the trick here is to select pictorial cues that are exactly what you want semantically, so that the comparison operation is direct. We experimented with a rebus task of the following type: A child was shown, for example, the numeral 1, a swatch of red yarn, and a wooden square. In response to instructions, he read aloud, "one red square." He was then shown a card containing such things as blue circles, green triangles, and red squares and was asked to "find what you said." Young children pointed to any old square. They did not integrate the number, color, and form properties unless they were specifically instructed to listen to what they themselves were saying. If they listened, then they integrated all the information.

The experiment suggests that semantic integrative schemata are associated with spoken language before they are associated with written language, which is no surprise. But the experiment carries a warning for rebus pedagogy. Do the schemata elicited by pictures match those of natural language? Does a picture of tin can elicit the same schema as the word *can?* Unless we can be sure of that match, or at least sure that the child is attending to his or her spoken schema rather than to the pictured schema, we should be wary of rebuses.

Constructive Reading

In a constructive reading task the criteria are not given—readers must generate them as they go along. Of course this type of reading involves verification, which is to say that programs for tasks in the rightmost columns of Table 2.2 include subroutines from columns to their left—verification subroutines and sight–sound subroutines.

We were not able to think of a type of constructive reading task that could be carried out by the prereader except, perhaps, making up meanings to go along with graphemes.

Beginning readers demonstrate constructive skills when they recognize, for example, the difference between the meaning of the word *run* in the sentence *I can run* and its meaning in the sentence *He hit a home run.* To understand either sentence, the reader must construct a meaning test and then verify it.

To get beyond that level of simple disambiguation, beginninng readers must become able to use semantic schemata we described earlier. One important characteristic of the language-experience method of teaching reading is that it puts children into a constructive mode from the outset of reading instruction. The development of language-experience reading programs always involves connections with semantic information the reader already has.

In the taxonomy, comprehension is viewed as a constructive reading process. The hypotheses are supplied from the running context provided by the task and from prior knowledge of the reader. For example, scripts and plans may represent episodes in long term memory that the reader invokes to understand the meaning of a particular text. A cake-baking script, where ingredients are measure, mixed, combined, and placed in an oven, prescribes a series of anticipated events that makes understanding of a recipe possible.

Constructive reading tasks are shown at the right of the table. There are two major divisions: understanding tasks and remembering tasks. Roughly, the distinction is whether information is only retrieved from long term memory or whether it is retrieved and then stored. The latter class of tasks is more complex and requires that the reader generate strategies for selecting which elements of the text to store and which already learned elements of memory serve to index the new information

In the final column, headed *Remembering,* are tasks that involve reading with the intent to learn. According to Flavell (1970), we should not expect that sort of reading in a beginner. Indeed, we do not find it in many adults. However, reading-to-learn involves the construction of strategies for altering the S-space. At the beginning level of reading, the learner may alter only a few semantic elements. At the skilled level, however, the reader takes in information that may serve as the basis for reorganizing large portions of semantic memory. For example, reading Chall's book (1967) caused many people to reorganize extensively interconnected ideas they had about learning to read.

CONCLUSION

Reading comprehension consists of verifying perceptual and conceptual elements of schemata invoked for the purpose of understanding new information or generated for the purpose of remembering information for later use. We have described what we believe to be a plausible mechanism for the perception of the visual and auditory elements essential to the reading process. We subscribe to a current view that semantic memory is organized along certain linguistic and episodic lines. We have emphasized the importance of studying reading in the context of specific reading tasks, presented in our taxonomy, for which detailed information-processing models can be constructed. The flow charts presented in this chapter are less than a first approximation to the level of detail that is required to make specific predictions about the proficiency of reading performance in reading tasks.

One additional feature of Table 2.2 should be mentioned. Through the central row are labels for the *Cognitive Hurdles* that we believe characterize the growth of cognitive skills in reading. Each of the hurdles has created a body of research and knowledge. There are five of them. *Iteration* denotes the ability of the reader to scan and hold on to individual letters, syllables, words, or phrases while the process of recognition memory operates. This rather simple procedure of keeping track of one's place while reading aloud comes about because of the limitations of the attentional span of the visual system and the limitations of short-term memory. *Integrating concrete operations* is a phrase expressing the task requirements imposed when the reader must keep track of a set of physically present objects while visually scanning the written materials. *Cognitive synthesis* requries holding two conceptually defined streams of thought. *Invoking schemata* occurs when the appropriate episodic plan must be followed while simultaneously decoding text. And finally, *generating strategies* implies a very high level problem-solving process that must go on while the basic reading functions are being performed.

This concludes our highly oversimplified walk through a taxonomy of reading tasks. You are no doubt seething with alternative suggestions—and that is the point: By looking at reading tasks within the framework of a single set of theoretical principles, we can see contradictions, discrepancies, and inconsistencies. But we can also see commonalities, developmental trends, instructional hypotheses, and regions for transfer of training. We can see how basic perceptual and semantic research may relate to reading. With a broad theoretical map before us, we can all work more confidently toward a program of experimental priorities.

ACKNOWLEDGMENT

This research was supported by Public Health Service Grant No. MH-07722 from the National Institute of Mental Health.

REFERENCES

Abelson, R. P. Script processing in attitude formation and decision-making. In J. S. Carroll & J. W. Payne (Eds.), *Cognition and social behavior*. Hillsdale, N.J.: Lawrence Erlbaum Associates, 1976.

Bobrow, D. G., & Norman, D. A. Some principles of memory schemata. In D. G. Bobrow & A. Collins (Eds.), *Representation and understanding*. New York: Academic Press, 1975.

Chall, J. S. *Learning to read: The great debate*. New York: McGraw-Hill, 1967.

Clark, H. H., & Chase, W. G. On the process of comparing sentences. *Cognitive Psychology*, 1972, *3*, 472–517.

Davis, F. B. (Ed.). *The literature of research in reading with emphasis on models. Project No. 2: The literature search*. New Brunswick, N.J.: Rutgers—The State University, Graduate School of Education, 1971.

Farnham-Diggory, S. Symbol and synthesis in experimental "reading." *Child Development*, 1967, *38*, 221–231.

Farnham-Diggory, S. The development of equivalence systems. In S. Farnham-Diggory (Ed.), *Information processing in children*. New York: Academic Press, 1972.

Farnham-Diggory, S., & Gregg, L. W. Short-term memory function in young readers. *Journal of Experimental Child Psychology*, 1975, *19*, 279–298.

Feigenbaum, E. A. An information processing theory of verbal learning (Paper P-1817). Santa Monica, Calif.: RAND Corporation, 1959.

Feigenbaum, E. A., & Simon, H. A. Performance of a reading task by an elementary perceiving and recognizing program. *Behavioral Science*, 1963, *8*, 72–76.

Flavell, J. H. Developmental studies of mediated memory. In H. W. Reese & L. P. Lipsitt (Eds.), *Advances in child development and behavior* (Vol. 5). New York: Academic Press, 1970.

Gibson, E. J. *Principles of perceptual learning and development*. Englewood Cliffs, N.J.: Prentice-Hall, 1969.

Gibson, E. J., & Levin, H. *The psychology of reading*. Cambridge, Mass.: MIT Press, 1975.

Gregg, L. W. Similarities in the cognitive processes of monkeys and man. In L. E. Jarrard (Ed.), *Cognitive processes of nonhuman primates*. New York: Academic Press, 1971.

Just, M. A., & Carpenter, P. A. The relation between comprehending and remembering some complex sentences. *Memory & Cognition*, 1976, *4*, 318–322.

Piaget, J. *The child's conception of number*. New York: Norton, 1965.

Rumelhart, D. E. Notes on a schema for stories. In D. G. Bobrow & A. Collins (Eds.), *Representation and understanding*. New York: Academic Press, 1975.

Smith, M. S. (Ed.). *Modeling the reading process* (NIE conference on studies in reading, Panel 4). Washington, D.C.: National Institute of Education, 1975.

Winograd, T. A framework for understanding AI approaches to discourse. In P. A. Carpenter & M. A. Just (Eds.), *Cognitive processes in comprehension*. Hillsdale, N.J.: Lawrence Erlbaum Associates, 1977.

3 What the Study of Eye Movement Reveals About Reading

George W. McConkie
Cornell University

At the present time, there is a great variety of approaches being advocated for teaching people to read and for helping people who read poorly to improve. One approach may emphasize the formation of accurate hypotheses, another may emphasize widening the perceptual span and speeding up the perceptual processes, another may place its emphasis on building a sight vocabulary, and still another may attempt to teach a series of specific skills that are thought to be critical for successful reading. Each approach has its advocates and its critics. It is easy for someone who is first encountering the field of reading to be baffled by this seeming chaos and to raise the obvious question, "Why doesn't someone do some research and find out what is the best way to teach people to read?" Our answer—that research of this type has been going on for decades and that we are still seldom able to determine that one method is better than another—will probably cause our novice to wonder why so much research (so many millions of dollars and hundreds of thousands of man hours) should leave us in such a state of ignorance. The excuses given in response to that question will probably not sound convincing.

In this chapter I first address the question of why so many approaches to reading can exist at the same time and what it would take to change our present state of ignorance. My answer is an argument for more basic research in reading, and I then describe an example of such research and show the kinds of implications it can have for reading instruction.

WHY THERE ARE SO MANY APPROACHES
TO READING INSTRUCTION

A person who develops a curriculum for the teaching of reading is in reality working from two sets of assumptions. First, there is a set of assumptions about the nature of the final product sought, which I will refer to as *skilled reading*. Second, there is a set of assumptions about the sorts of exercises that will move a person from where he or she is to some point closer to being a skilled reader.

As I peruse various materials designed to teach reading, it appears that the authors often make very different assumptions about what it is they are actually trying to teach. In fact, in the reading field generally, there is great disagreement about the nature of skilled reading. What is even more disconcerting is that often where there is some agreement, there is little evidence to justify the position being agreed on. To a great extent, we must admit that we do not know what a successful reader does while reading; we do not know the nature of either the perceptual processes or the cognitive processes involved in converting visual language patterns into meaning. If we were to make a list of the assertions about the nature of skilled reading that we know to be true or of which we have sufficient evidence to feel highly confident, the list would be depressingly short.

One of the things we can do with facts is to show that certain theories are incorrect. If we know Fact A, and Theory B is not consistent with Fact A, then we have some reason to reject Theory B as an acceptable account of the phenomenon we are interested in or at least to require that it be modified. However, when few facts are known, there is little empirical basis for selecting one theory over another, that is, for keeping some theories and rejecting others. In such a situation, it is possible for many creative people to devise alternative views of the phenomenon, few of which can be rejected on an empirical basis. This seems to be the present condition in the field of reading. Each person is free to adopt or develop a view of the nature of skilled reading and then to create a set of exercises that he or she believes will guide people to be able to read in that way. There is little basis, in terms of facts known about skilled reading, on which to select views that are most accurate. In this situation, people tend to make choices among the alternatives more on the basis of emotional factors (which approach is most compatible with the way I think about reading, which approach was favored by my favorite professor, etc.) and less on the basis of consistency with known facts. Hence, discussions and criticisms often seem to produce more heat than light.

If this analysis is correct, then one of the great needs of the reading field is for well-established facts about the nature of skilled reading. The bulk of past research in reading has not been aimed at this goal. Only by adding to the list of things we are confident are true about the nature of skilled reading can we begin rejecting certain views of reading, together with curriculum programs based on these views. Of course, gaining an increasingly accurate view of the nature of skilled reading does not itself answer the question of how to help people become skilled readers. But it should lead to greater agreement on the nature of the goal of reading instruction. Our work would be greatly enhanced if we had enough knowledge to be able to agree on our goal, and then we could focus our arguments on the most effective ways of achieving it.

There are many things we need to learn about the skilled reader, including the size of the perceptual span, the aspects of the text attended to in reading, how the piecemeal input from a series of fixations is integrated into a coherent meaning representation, what aspects of the passage are retained, the nature and amount of flexibility exhibited in reading different materials and for different purposes, and what characteristics of the task and the text influence the retention of various aspects of the passage read. However, the main point I wish to make is that the experimental investigation of skilled reading, if it can succeed in revealing facts about the nature of the reading skill, is of vital concern to our attempts to improve reading instruction. It is a most needed, and perhaps the least developed, aspect of reading research today. The entire enterprise of curriculum development in the area of reading is to some degree held back because of the lack of a clear understanding of skilled reading. If people do not know the nature of their goal, it is not likely that they will be able to develop an optimally effective means of achieving it. In fact, if a curriculum developer were to have an incorrect view of the nature of skilled reading and were successful in producing a curriculum that was highly effective in teaching children to read in the way he or she believed they should, the results could be very undesirable.

Also blocked to a great extent by the lack of clear knowledge of skilled reading are the processes of identifying and remedying reading disorders. A reading disorder is basically a deviation from skilled reading. Diagnosis and remediation are the processes of identifying precisely the nature of the deviation and moving the person in the direction of skilled reading. However, without a clear understanding of skilled reading, it is very difficult to identify precisely the nature of the deviation. Without precise identification, it is less likely that an optimally appropriate approach will be selected for helping the person change in the manner desired. The enterprise of assessment of reading development is also held back by the lack of a clear understanding of the nature of skilled reading, because that lack make its difficult to know just what aspects of the reading process, or of the product resulting from reading, are the important ones to measure.

Although knowledge about the nature of skilled reading does not by itself answer the practical problems associated with teaching people to read, it does have a strong influence on the way we think about how to achieve the practical goals. It determines how we conceptualize the goal, which places restrictions on the types of activities we perceive as having some potential for usefulness in reading instruction. Thus, although it does not provide direct solutions to practical problems, it has the potential for fundamentally affecting curriculum development and instruction.

WHAT TYPE OF RESEARCH WILL LEAD TO AN UNDERSTANDING OF READING?

A few factors should be kept in mind if one intends to employ empirical research to add to the list of assertions about reading in which we have confidence. Because the eventual goal is improving reading, it is common for studies in the reading area to be aimed directly at the goal. A common design is to treat two or more groups of subjects in somewhat different ways, one of which is often said to be "standard" instruction, and then to test with a unidimensional measure of reading performance to see if the different treatments improved reading performance differentially. This approach to research arises from a desire to find immediately more efficient means of improving reading. However, it is important to realize that this research design has little potential for increasing our understanding of the nature of the reading processes. Although it may show that certain treatments are more effective than others (and even this has seldom been shown conclusively in such research), it provides little or no information about why this is so. It reveals little about the nature of the mental operations involved and thus little about the basis for why one treatment should be superior to another.

If we are truly interested in gaining a better understanding of the mental processes involved in reading, we must first recognize the complexity of those processes. A unidimensional measure of the "goodness" of a person's reading behavior captures little of this complexity. A more useful approach would be one that avoids the "goodness" question and focuses on understanding what effects certain variables have. Rather than asking whether a variable X improves reading, we could study what effects X has on the person's reading behavior, irrespective of whether those effects are seen as improvements. Such study would require as detailed an assessment as possible of the effects of X on various aspects of the person's mental activities during reading. This sort of detailed descriptive approach to the study of reading has a greater likelihood of adding to our knowledge of the reading processes. A second useful approach is to study a specific aspect of reading (the formation of inferences, the likelihood of retaining certain aspects of information from the passage, the likelihood of making regressive eye movements, etc.) and determine what effect certain manipulations of interest have on this aspect of reading. Again, the result is likely to be added knowledge about the reading processes.

The knowledge generated by these approaches to research is useful for theory building, and it may also be useful for practical applications. For instance, such data may show which variables do seem to improve reading. However, improvement can be specified only with respect to some particular goals. Investigators are forced to specify the nature of the goal they have in mind (in what specific ways they wish to change reading behavior); then, having done this, they can turn to knowledge obtained from research to find out what sorts of manipulations are most likely to produce these changes. Of course, two people may have different goals and thus may select quite different means for producing improved reading. However, the sort of knowledge acquired from the research approaches I have described would provide a knowledge base useful to each.

It appears to me that the type of research I have suggested is particularly important in the study of beginning reading. It is often difficult to determine what constitutes success in improving reading. If we manage to teach children to decode, but as a result of the instructional methods the children refuse to look at books at home, it is doubtful that we have succeeded. Or if one program gives them a large sight vocabulary so that they do very well on a standardized reading test when finished, but we find that they fall behind for some unknown reason at the third and fourth grades, we have not been successful. In a way, teaching reading is like raising children. It is extremely encouraging to see progress in a 3-year-old, but we have to remind ourselves that we do not really know whether we are succeeding until we see the person at age 20 or 25 or 30. What may look like a success at age 3 may be putting the child on a line of development the end product of which we would not view as a success at all.

A type of research we seem to need, then, is research that investigates the effects of variables rather than research that simply asks whether certain manipulations improve reading. And wherever possible, the assessment should include a wide range of effects, including the child's attitudes toward reading, what the child does with the knowledge or skill outside of formal reading instruction, and how the child responds to later forms of instruction. Detailed observation of a relatively few children may give much more knowledge about the effects of reading instruction variables than does a national study involving thousands where the only measure is some single index of amount of improvement.

A second factor that must be borne in mind in doing research in reading comes from the complexity of reading and the difficulty of studying it. Rapid silent reading involves vision, psycholinguistic processing, production of a memory representation, eye-movement coordination, formation of inferences, and many other complex processes—most of which occur extremely rapidly and so subconsciously that readers have little notion of what they are doing as they read. There is little for the researcher to observe during the course of reading. Readers move their eyes rapidly, may make some facial gestures, and then are able to answer questions they could not answer before reading.

A common strategy in psychological research is to turn one's attention to the study of some task that is simpler than the task one eventually wishes to understand but that seems to have elements in common with it. However, recent research has convinced us that people are very flexible in their cognitive functioning, being able to adopt different approaches and strategies to tasks that make them more efficient at those tasks but that may not generalize to other, apparently similar, tasks. There have been many studies in which subjects identify tachistoscopically presented word or letter strings, scan text to find targets, fill in missing words in text, and so on. Assertions are then made about the nature of reading on the basis of the results of these studies. In view of the difficulty of investigating the reading processes directly, studies such as these are certainly necessary. However, it is important to recognize that subjects in these tasks may not be behaving in the same manner, in the aspects being studied, as they do when they read. Thus, results from such studies must always be viewed with some degree of suspicion until similar results have been obtained from studies of people actually engaged in the act of reading a passage to understand its meaning.

If we wish to understand the mental activities occurring during reading and to study the act of reading itself rather than some other task, there are two approaches we can take. First, we can monitor the act of reading as it is in progress by some means that provides information about the nature of the processes involved. Second, we can obtain information about the product of reading by testing after the act of reading is finished, and on the basis of this information, we can attempt to say something about the nature of the processes that must have taken place. Both these approaches are fraught with difficulties. The second approach requires one to infer processes from products. Certainly the nature of the knowledge a person has acquired from a passage places constraints on inferences about the nature of the processes involved during reading; the processes must be capable of yielding this product. However, in most cases the information we have about the product falls far short of specifying precisely the nature of the processes that led to it. The first approach to the study of reading is clearly the most desirable if our goal is to understand the nature of the cognitive processes involved in reading. However, there is very little that can be observed during the reading act. The most obvious type of behavior that can be recorded is eye movement behavior. In the next section I turn to the question of whether eye movement research can reveal useful information about the nature of skilled reading.

THE STUDY OF EYE MOVEMENTS
IN READING

It appears that many (probably most) people in the field of reading today are convinced that the study of eye movements can reveal little about the nature of skilled reading. This conclusion is the natural result of several decades of painstaking research on eye movements in reading that has made little contribution to our understanding of the nature of reading. In addition, a number of writers in the field have developed models of eye movement control of a type that I refer to as *visual buffer models* (e.g., Bouma & deVoogd, 1974; Shebilske, 1975), which assume little relation between eye movements and cognitive processes in reading. They postulate a buffer memory for visual input, a place for information obtained during fixations to be stored until it is needed for mental processing. Thus, on each fixation, visual information is added to the buffer, and when the mind needs more visual information to continue its identification and interpretation of the text, it simply draws some from the buffer. According to this model, eye movements are only controlled within broad limits. The eye must move along fast enough so that the buffer always has information available when the mind needs it, but it must not go so fast that too much information is put into the buffer, causing some to be lost before the mind is ready to use it. According to this model, then, it matters little where the eye happens to be directed, so long as there are regular fixations across the line of print. The good reader is assumed to make rhythmic eye movements across the page, with fixation durations of .20 to .25 of a second and saccade lengths of about 8 or 9 letter positions. One would expect variability in fixation durations and saccade lengths on two bases: One would be physiological error, and the other would be the result of differences in reading rate for easy and difficult parts of the text, with the eye slowing down (i.e., longer fixation durations and shorter saccades) in areas where the mind requires more time to process the text and speeding up where the text is easier to process. This model also assumes that the information obtained during a fixation is processed only after the fixation; during the fixation, it is simply placed in the buffer, ready to be withdrawn at some later time when needed. How much later (that is, how big the buffer is) is not known.

If this model were accurate, there would be little reason to examine eye movement data in an attempt to understand the reading process. The regular movements of good readers would tell little about their mental processes and perhaps only indicate where the more and less difficult parts of the text occur. Even here, they give a delayed indication, because it would be a fixation or two after visually encountering a difficult area before the information would be processed and the eye slowed down.

However, in our research at Cornell, we have become convinced that this model is not an accurate description of eye movement behavior in reading, that the eye is being quite precisely controlled on the basis of momentary processes taking place in reading, and that there is much we can learn from eye movement studies about both the perceptual and psycholinguistic processes involved in reading. From the earliest literature on reading, it has been asserted that good readers show a "rhythmic pattern" of eye movements, that saccade lengths and fixation durations show little variability for good readers. When we began our studies, therefore, I was amazed to find that even good readers show a large amount of variability in their eye movement behavior. Their fixations range from .10 of a second to as much as a full second in duration, and the lengths of saccades vary from 1 or 2 letter positions to 14 or 15 as they read a single passage. It is true that they average around .20 of a second and 9 letter positions, but to ignore the variability present is akin to asserting that all human adults are of essentially the same height because they average around 5.75 feet.

The visual buffer models do admit a certain amount of variability. The eye is expected to speed up and slow down during reading. As Rayner and I (1976) have explained, such models give rise to the hypothesis that the durations of fixations and the lengths of the saccades immediately preceding or following them will be correlated. However, we found a correlation of $-.006$ between these measures. Thus, these two components of eye movement behavior are independent of one another in reading. They cannot be controlled by a single unitary mechanism like visual buffer mechanisms but must be controlled separately. Also, there is little correlation between the durations of successive fixations ($r = .11$) or the lengths of successive saccades ($r = .13$). If these individual eye movements and fixations are controlled, they are controlled almost completely independently of one another. Again, these results question the type of control proposed by visual buffer models.

Two types of theories of eye movement control would be compatible with the correlations just reported. Either these aspects of eye movements are essentially random (perhaps with the variability arising from physiological error as the eye attempts to achieve a regular pattern but where little precise control is exerted), or the durations of individual fixations and the lengths of individual saccades are being specifically controlled by information available at the moment (momentary mental states). The latter possibility is particularly interesting, because if it were so, then eye movement measures may be closely linked to aspects of mental processing during reading. As a general strategy, it would seem best to try to look for nonrandom patterns in the eye movement data in an attempt to reject the first alternative. Only if this were to fail should the random movement position be accepted.

What Determines Where the Eye Will be Sent?

In a study designed to investigate the size of the perceptual span, McConkie and Rayner (1975) were able to determine whether subjects obtained visual information about word length patterns from text in their peripheral vision as they were reading. The subjects read from text displayed on a computer-controlled cathode-ray tube (CRT) as the computer monitored where they were looking. When subjects made each fixation, the computer was able to quickly change the display so that normal text appeared in their central vision, but in their peripheral vision the spaces between words were replaced by letters. We found that when subjects did not obtain word length information from their peripheral visual area, they tended to make shorter saccades. Control of eye movement behavior was thus shown to be somewhat related to word length patterns.

With this in mind, we calculated the probability of fixating each letter in the passage[1] as a function of the length of the word the letter was in. We found that for letters in 2-letter words, there was a 10% chance of a direct fixation. This rose to 13% for 6-letter words, a 30% increase, and then dropped back to 11% for 10- and 11-letter words. Again, something about the word length pattern was influencing where the eye was being sent.

O'Regan (1975) reported a study in which he found that at a particular point in his text, the length of the next saccade depended on the length of the next word. Longer words resulted in longer saccades.

Finally, Rayner and McConkie (1976) found that there were substantially fewer fixations than normal in the area between sentences. There was only a 7% chance of fixating a space between sentences as compared to about 12% for the rest of the text.

It seems safe to conclude, then, that the eye does not simply move rhythmically across the page but that the distance it is sent for each saccade is determined to some degree by characteristics of the text at that point. In particular, word length patterns are involved in where the eye is sent. However, since word length patterns are related to both perceptual factors and to syntactic structure of the text, we do not know at this time the precise nature of the control exhibited.

What Controls the Durations of Fixations?

The next question that arises is whether the durations of fixations are also controlled on a momentary basis. Again, there is evidence that specific

---

[1]When speaking of eye position, I refer to the eye as "fixating" at a certain location. This simply indicates that the position of the eye is approximately what would occur if the subject were asked to look directly at that location. It is not meant to suggest that the reader is specifically giving attention to that particular letter or word.

control is present. First, it is a commonly reported observation that abnormally long fixations frequently occur on names, dates, other numbers, and sometimes on unusual words. If it is true that names, dates, and numbers are likely to occur in a comprehension test of the passage, there may be good reason for the reader to spend extra time ensuring that these pieces of information are well stored. Conversely, Rayner (1975a) found that when fixations fell in the regions between sentences, which contain no substantive information, they averaged about 20 to 40 milliseconds shorter than fixations elsewhere in the text.

We have wondered whether different subjects tend to spend about the same relative amount of time fixating at different locations in the text. This is somewhat difficult to determine, since two subjects do not fixate at the same locations, and so the information they have access to on their fixations is slightly different. As a first step around this problem, David Zola, a graduate student at Cornell, prepared text in which the words were spaced farther apart than normal. He simply inserted 8 spaces after each word, thus placing them far enough apart so that when subjects fixated one word, the amount of visual information they received about other words was substantially reduced. We recorded the eye movement of a few subjects as they read this passage after having read a practice passage. We then ran correlations between the fixation durations of pairs of subjects on each of the words in the passage. Prior to computing the correlation, we deleted all data for regressions, for words fixated more than once, and for first and last words on the line, since the readers showed idiosyncratic eye movement patterns at the beginnings and ends of lines. The correlations that we have obtained so far averaged about .35. Although the study is crude, the correlation indicates that to some degree at least, different subjects spend somewhat similar relative amounts of time fixating the same areas of the text. Thus, the durations of fixations appear to be controlled to some degree by the text and the cognitive activities involved in processing it.

Finally, Rayner (1975b) provided additional evidence that the durations of fixations are affected by the cognitive processes being carried out, along with evidence on the question of processing lag—that is, on the length of time between obtaining visual information and using it in reading. (I indicated earlier that the visual buffer models suggest that there should be such a lag.) The subjects in this study read a number of short paragraphs displayed by computer on a CRT. The computer also monitored their eye movements as they read. As they read a particular line, a change was made in the text during a specific saccade. On one fixation, a particular word was present at a point a specific distance to the right of the fixation point; as the eye made its saccadic movement, this word was replaced by another word at that location, so on the next fixation the display was not the same as before. Both words fit syntactically and semantically into the passage, began and ended with the same letter, and had the same external word shape (ascending and descending letters in the same locations). He examined the duration of the fixation immediately following the display change and found that if the previous fixation had been sufficiently close to the word that was changed, the fixation after the change was longer than normal. In some way, the subjects detected the change in the text pattern from one fixation to the next, and the change influenced the duration of the fixation on which the change was first detected. Thus, visual information acquired on a fixation influenced the duration of that fixation—not several fixations later as the visual buffer models might have predicted. How long it takes to complete syntactic and semantic processing is another question we are presently exploring via eye movement studies.

It seems safe to say, then, that characteristics of the text or of the processing of the text influence both where the eye is sent and how long it lingers for the fixation. Models of reading that suggest that the eye is under little specific control, such as the visual buffer models, appear to be incorrect. The eye movement pattern is neither a completely rhythmical pattern nor a random pattern; instead, it shows regularities associated with characteristics of the text. Furthermore, it is likely that there is not a substantial lag between the input of visual information and the processing of that information; eye movement behavior can be influenced by information acquired on the present fixation. All of this suggests that the eye's behavior may be closely associated with the perceptual and cognitive processing occurring at the moment. This opens the door to the possibility of investigating the nature of those processes through eye movement data. Variability in eye movement data likely reflects events in the perceptual and cognitive processing taking place in reading.

How Large Is the Perceptual Span?

To me, one of the most fundamental questions in reading concerns the size of the perceptual span during a fixation. From how wide an area does the reader acquire useful visual information during a fixation in reading? The answer to this question will have important implications for the theory of reading. For instance, if the span were quite narrow, just a word or two on the line being fixated, the information-handling characteristics of the mind would be quite different from what they would be if the span were very large, encompassing most or all of a line and perhaps more than one line on a fixation. It is also important to point out that the size of the perceptual span during reading may be similar to or different from that during other tasks, such as viewing pictures or attempting to recognize word or letter strings presented tachistoscopically. Determining the size of the perceptual span during actual reading requires finding some means of obtaining data from people as they read rather than as they perform some other task. I now describe one approach we have used to study this question, both as an example of how such questions can be answered through eye movement research and as an attempt to summarize what we know about the perceptual span at this point.

Actually, there is probably not a single perceptual span. It is likely that the reader acquires different aspects of the visual information at different distances into the visual periphery. Perhaps at some distance into the visual periphery, only word length patterns and other very distinct visual differences are detected. Somewhat closer to the center of vision, external word shape (location of ascending and descending letters) and beginning and ending letters (those bounded by space and thus not subject to interference from adjacent letters) may be detected. Finally, full featural detail concerning internal letters in the words may be available only for words within a fairly restricted area around the fovea. It is also likely that there is a region within which words can be identified sufficiently well that their meanings may be assessed, whereas farther into the periphery, visual information is obtainable but not sufficient for identification. It is also possible that these areas vary at different places in the text due to visual or psycholinguistic factors.

One method we used to investigate the size of these perceptual spans was reported by Rayner (1975b) and was previously mentioned. The subjects were asked to read a series of short paragraphs, each displayed on the computer-controlled CRT, while their eye movements were monitored. Each paragraph contained one word location, called the *critical word location,* where a display change might occur during reading. When a paragraph was first displayed, the critical word location contained either the original word, called the *base word,* or one of four other alternatives: a word having the same first and last letters and word shape as the base word and that fit syntactically and semantically into the paragraph; or one of three nonword letter strings—one having the same first and last letters and word shape as the base word, one having the same first and last letters but different word shape, or one having the same word shape but different first and last letters. Thus, each alternative stimulus differed from the base word in certain specified ways: whether or not it was a word; whether or not it maintained the same word shape; and whether or not it maintained the same first and last letters.

As the subject read the passage, during a specific saccadic eye movement on the line containing the critical word location, the word in that location was removed and replaced by the base word. Thus, if one of the other alternatives appeared initially, then there was some fixation on which the content of that location was different from what it had been up to that point. If the subject had obtained visual information from the critical word location on the prior fixation, then that information might be incompatible in some manner with the information obtained following the change. If so, we anticipated that the duration of the fixation immediately following the change would be lengthened somewhat as the reader carried out the added processing required by the discrepancy. As data, Rayner considered the duration of the fixation immediately following the display change and then only if that fixation were centered directly on the critical word location. Thus, he considered how long the subjects looked at the base word in the critical word location immediately after the display change had occurred, as a function of two variables: First, what sort of stimulus alternative resided in that location prior to the change; and second, how far to the left of that location had the previous fixation been? We assumed that if the previous fixation had been quite far to the left of the critical word location, little visual information would have been acquired from it, and the change would not be detected.

The results showed that when the prior fixation was more than 12 letter positions (3° of visual angle) to the left of the critical word location, little or no specific information about the word was acquired from it (another study showed word length to be an exception). That is, when the prior fixation was that far to the left of the word, the durations of fixations on that word following a display change were no different from the durations when no change had occurred. When the prior fixation was less than 12 letter positions to the left of the word, a display change in that word location caused a substantial increase in the duration of the next fixation. Thus, it appeared that information about both word shape and about initial and final letters was obtained from words that began less than 12 letters to the right of the fixation point. Finally, if the prior fixation was more than 6 letter positions from the critical word location, it made no difference whether that word location initially contained a word or a nonword letter string. Apparently, the subjects obtained visual information from words beginning 7 to 12 letter positions to the right of their fixation point but did not make semantic interpretations of words in this region. When the eye was less than 6 letter positions from the critical word location, the occurrence of a nonword in that location both inflated the duration of the fixation prior to the display change and substantially increased the duration of the fixation following the change. In summary, the results indicated that the subjects acquired certain visual information from words beginning up to 11 or 12 letter positions to the right of their fixation point, but they seemed to make semantic interpretations of words lying no more than 6 letter positions to the right.

Other studies we have conducted have indicated that good readers obtain word length information from words lying more than 12 letter positions to the right of the fixation point (McConkie & Rayner, 1975) and that they acquire little if any useful visual information more than 4 letter positions to the left of the fixation point, if that far (McConkie & Rayner, 1977). The word length information, as previously mentioned, seems to be used in guiding the eye. The visual information about letters beyond the region of semantic identification may also be facilitating reading. Rayner and I are presently conducting a study in which subjects fixate a point on the screen, a letter string is then displayed some distance to the left or right of their fixation point, and they look over the word and speak it aloud. We measure the time until vocalization begins. In most conditions, the stimulus initially displayed on the screen is replaced by another word as the subject's eye moves over to look at it. The main independent variable is the relation between the initially displayed string and the word with which it is replaced and that the subject must identify. Generally, the more similar the initial stimulus is to the final word, the faster the subjects are able to say the word when they fixate it. Thus, they must obtain some useful visual information from the original letter string on one fixation that then facilitates identification of the word on the next fixation. This study does not involve normal reading, so its results can only be suggestive about the reading process itself. However, it gives some support to the possibility that information about visual characteristics of words lying more than 6 letter positions to the right of the fixation point on one fixation is useful in facilitating the identification of those words on the next fixation.

Thus, by tying specific display changes to the subjects' own eye movement behavior and then carefully analyzing their eye movement records in reading, we have obtained evidence that the region from which the subjects acquire useful visual information during a fixation is much narrower than we had previously supposed. The region from which these relatively skilled readers identified words during a fixation was less than the size of most phrases in text, even if their fixations happened to be centered optimally within the phrase for its perception. This region was also smaller than the region from which subjects are able to identify words when they are presented tachistoscopically (Bouma, 1973). Thus, the assembling of information concerning phrases and larger linguistic structures must occur across fixations rather than being directly perceived on each fixation.

Clearly, much additional work needs to be done on this question in order to investigate individual differences, differences at different points in the text, and differences between skilled and less skilled readers, but the techniques seem quite capable of providing answers to these questions. And for now, we at least have a "ball-park" answer to the question of the size of the perceptual span of skilled readers that begins to have educational implications.

Educational Implications

Being able to identify the size of the perceptual span in reading is but one small part of a total understanding of the nature of skilled reading. However, if further studies support the work that we have done so far, the facts that will be established will place specific constraints on the types of models of skilled reading that can be viewed as acceptable. Any theory that supposes that the reader obtains visual information from and semantically interprets a large area of text (a phrase, sentence, or line at a time) during a single fixation is probably out of harmony with reality. Any view of reading instruction that assumes that the distinguishing characteristic of poor readers is their small perceptual span and that this small span causes them to be unable to assemble the meaning from the text is also likely to be rejected. We have not studied the size of the perceptual span of poor readers, but we have artificially reduced the span of good readers to see what effect this would have on their reading. We are able to do this through computer techniques for controlling the text display so that at the point of the subject's fixation, only 9 letters of the text were seen, and the letters to the left and right of this small area were replaced by x's. Thus, only 9 letters of useful visual information were available on each fixation. This essentially turned the subjects into "word-by-word" readers. The question was, did this cause their comprehension to drop substantially—something that has been suggested to occur with word-by-word reading? The results indicated that the subjects' reading rate was substantially slowed, with shorter saccades, longer fixations, and more regressive eye movements. However, there was only a slight, nonsignificant drop in their scores on the retention test. To the extent that retention reflects comprehension, it is clear that there was no great drop in comprehension as might have been expected. We have not yet carried out the studies necessary to establish whether poor readers do have narrower perceptual spans than good readers do, but the results just presented provide no support for the notion that a narrow perceptual span necessarily causes poor comprehension. This being the case, it becomes doubtful that performing exercises that try to broaden the size of the perceptual span are likely to directly improve comprehension in reading. It should also be noted that we do not have evidence at the present time that exercises commonly believed to broaden the perceptual span actually increase the size of the perceptual span in reading. With the technology described earlier, we are now in a position to test this claim. It should also be noted that even if these exercises do not broaden the perceptual span, they may still have a facilitating effect on reading for some other reason. That possibility also needs further exploration.

THE FUTURE POTENTIAL FOR
EYE MOVEMENT RESEARCH IN READING

As I have tried to show, recent research seems to have established that skilled readers do not simply move their eyes in a rhythmical pattern but that where the eye is sent and how long it remains in that location is controlled on a momentary basis and reflects certain aspects of the processing occurring at the time. It is this characteristic that opens the door to using eye movement research to study aspects of reading other than the eye movements themselves. The studies described that investigated the size of the perceptual span, using eye movements both to control the display and to provide a detailed record of the reading behavior, are an example of how this can be done. I believe that we now have the potential for seeking answers to a number of other questions about the nature of skilled reading through eye movement research. The fact that eye movements are rather sensitive indicators of disruption in reading makes it possible to detect whether and when certain irregularities in the text are detected during reading. It appears likely that fixation durations reflect the amount of processing, at some level, that must occur involving the visual information being perceived on that fixation. Detailed theories of visual, psycholinguistic, and memory processing will undoubtedly predict differences in the amount of cognitive work required at different points in the text, and fixation duration patterns are likely to become a primary data source for testing such theories. Finally, the capability of making display changes contingent on eye position so the display is modified from one fixation to another, provides a powerful method of exploring aspects of the perceptual processing in reading.

The study of eye movements in reading is obviously only one approach to the study of reading. At Cornell, we are also engaged in an attempt to identify what information is retained from a text and how the characteristics of the text and of the task demands influence this. These questions and many others will require quite different research approaches. However, the important thing about a number of approaches to reading research that are presently being developed is that they have the potential for yielding specific knowledge about the perceptual and cognitive processes involved in reading. Careful studies using these approaches will add to the list of assertions that we can make about reading, things about which we have substantial supportive evidence. This body of facts should allow us to gradually weed out views of skilled reading that are not in harmony with reality and will exert pressure on us to produce new theories that are in harmony with the available facts. As our understanding of skilled reading develops, the activity of curriculum building and reading instruction will have a firmer foundation on which to build. I believe that progress in the study of skilled reading will be reflected in all aspects of the field of reading.

REFERENCES

Bouma, H. Visual interference in the parafoveal recognition of initial and final letters of words. *Vision Research,* 1973, *13,* 767–782.

Bouma, H., & deVoogd, A. H. On the control of eye saccades in reading. *Vision Research,* 1974, *14,* 273–284.

McConkie, G. W., & Rayner, K. The span of the effective stimulus during a fixation in reading. *Perception & Psychophysics,* 1975, *17,* 578–586.

McConkie, G. W., & Rayner, K. Asymmetry of the perceptual span in reading. *Bulletin of the Psychonomic Society,* 1977, *8,* 365–368.

O'Regan, J. K. *Structural and contextual constraints on eye movements in reading.* Unpublished doctoral dissertation, University of Cambridge, 1975.

Rayner, K. Parafoveal identification during a fixation in reading. *Acta Psychologica,* 1975, *39,* 271–282. (a)

Rayner, K. The perceptual span and peripheral cues in reading. *Cognitive Psychology,* 1975, *7,* 65–81. (b)

Rayner, K., & McConkie, G. W. What guides a reader's eye movements? *Vision Research,* 1976, *16,* 829–837.

Shebilske, W. Reading eye movements from an information-processing point of view. In D. W. Massaro (Ed.), *Understanding language: An information processing analysis of speech perception, reading and psycholinguistics.* New York: Academic Press, 1975.

4 Oral Reading: Does It Reflect Decoding or Comprehension?

Joseph H. Danks
Ramona Fears
Kent State University

How do most elementary school teachers determine whether a child can read? It is likely that the teacher hands the child a book at the child's estimated reading level and asks the child to read. That the reading is to be aloud is usually not stated but understood implicitly by both teacher and child. What reading activity is commonly found in most traditional lower-elementary-grade classrooms?—children reading aloud individually or in unison. Oral reading provides the teacher with a quick evaluation of each child's progress and provides the child with practice on at least some aspects of reading. Although oral reading is a widely used procedure, we lack well-developed theories concerning what specific components of the reading process are assessed and what reading skills are developed by oral reading.

TWO HYPOTHESES ABOUT ORAL READING

A general model of reading that is commonly assumed proposes that print input is first decoded into a phonological code that has most of the characteristics of an oral verbal input. This code is then comprehended by the usual routines of language comprehension that the child has developed for speech. These two stages of reading are usually seen as discrete stages that can be taught independently. This assumption has led to a division of reading instruction into teaching decoding and comprehension. Decoding depends only minimally on comprehension, although some investigators posit "downstream" effects on the basis of top-down models of comprehension. For example, a major aspect of Goodman's (1967) informed-guessing model is that previously comprehended material facilitates the decoding of print. However, these downstream influences of comprehension on decoding are usually not thought to be essential for successful decoding but only helpful when the contextual information is available. On the other hand, comprehension is necessarily dependent on decoding for the representation on which to operate. Except for providing the input for comprehension, however, the decoding process does not directly affect the comprehension process [Eds. note: See also Frederiksen, and Goodman and Goodman, Volume 1, this series].

Given this rough two-stage model of reading, where does oral production fit? The motor production aspect of oral reading must be "tacked on" to the model of the reading process, because there is no production component explicit in the model. There are two general hypotheses as to when oral production is initiated in the reading process. These hypotheses are illustrated in Fig. 4.1.

The decoding hypothesis is that oral production is initiated immediately following decoding (point A in Fig. 4.1). Oral production is initiated on the basis of the phonological code that is the output of decoding. (Oral reading then serves as practice during the initial decoding stage.) In this case, there might be no comprehension of the text at all; or oral production and comprehension might progress in parallel; or comprehension might occur much later than the oral production, perhaps as the reader hears him- or herself talk. Children sometimes imitate speech without comprehending it, so it would not seem unreasonable that beginning readers might initiate oral production on the basis of the phonological code without comprehending the message first.

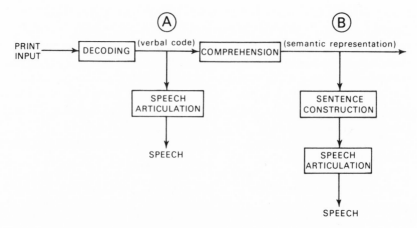

FIG. 4.1.   Two hypotheses about oral reading performance.

The comprehension hypothesis is that oral production is initiated only after comprehension processes have constructed a semantic representation of the message (point B in Fig. 4.1). Oral production is initiated from the semantic representation and not from the phonological code that existed at an earlier point in the process. In fact the verbal code may no longer exist at the time at which oral production is initiated. The oral production process beginning with the semantic representation resembles sentence production in its essential components. A speaker has an idea to express, and he or she translates that idea into lingusitic form and then expresses it in speech. In oral reading, the semantic representation of the printed message constitutes the idea that serves as the input to the production process.

These two hypotheses represent classes of hypotheses, with variations depending on the specific conceptions of decoding, comprehension, and speech production. For example, comprehension is described as if it were a single process with a fixed beginning and ending. However, comprehension may be a loose collection of processing strategies rather than a single routine. The possible variations in these two classes of hypotheses will become evident. For the moment, they serve as convenient touchstones for conceptualizing the question of how oral production meshes with the reading process. The two hypotheses can be differentiated further by comparing two types of readers that appear to embody each hypothesis.

Word Callers

The decoding hypothesis appears to be supported by reading disabled children labeled *word callers* (Smith, Goodman, & Meredith, 1976). These are children who can read aloud but who do not understand what they have read. One would assume on the basis of their oral reading performance that they understand. However, when they are tested for comprehension of the message, they have at best a minimal understanding of what they have just read. Word callers' understanding is not improved when they are permitted to read silently. Although it is not clear what they are doing when they are silent reading other than staring at the page, their understanding is not increased. So the problem is not that their normal comprehension process is disrupted by the additional task of having to read aloud. In terms of our general model, then, word callers support the decoding hypothesis in that their oral production must be initiated immediately following decoding but before comprehension occurs.

At one time or another, many adults have had the experience of reading aloud without comprehending. When learning a foreign language, many people pass through a phase when they can read aloud in the second language but not understand what they read. Or when reading some particularly difficult text like a philosophic treatise, one might read it aloud to allow more time to think about what is being said but still might not understand what is written. It seems possible, then, that at an early point in reading acquisition, some beginning readers might be able to read aloud on the basis of their decoding skills but not comprehend the message.

There is considerable dispute, however, over whether word callers really exist and over what the criteria should be for so labeling a child. Goodman (1973) claimed that "remedial reading classes are filled with youngsters in late elementary and secondary schools who can sound out words but get little meaning from their reading [p. 491]," although he adduced no statistics to support that claim. Other reading specialists claim that the number of true word callers is exceedingly small, because children who are labeled "word callers" by classroom teachers actually have poor decoding skills or poor language comprehension skills.

What criteria should be considered in classifying a child as a word caller? According to the traditional definition, the child must be able to read aloud reasonably well and not understand what was read. What is meant by *reasonably well?* At minimum, the child must read at close to the typical rate of comprehending readers with about the same number of errors and with normal intonation. There is some question of whether word callers can meet these criteria. For example, poor readers tend to read with a list intonation (Clay & Imlach, 1971). Reading with a list intonation is a clear clue to a lack of comprehension, because decoding punctuation and combining that information with the meaning of the passage leads to intonation patterns more typical of speech. What is meant by *not understand?* The key test is whether the child can understand the passage if it is presented aurally. If adults had the foreign language text or the philosophy essay read aloud, they would not understand it any better than when they read it themselves. If the child does not comprehend when listening, the problem may be attributable to a general language or conceptual deficit rather than to a deficiency in reading-specific comprehension skills or in the coordination of decoding and comprehension processes.

Word callers may be related to a class of children labeled "hyperlexics," who are superficially similar to word callers in their reading behavior (Mehegan & Dreifuss, 1972; Silverberg & Silverberg, 1967, 1968– 1969). The common distinguishing feature is that "they manifested an unusual and premature talent in reading [aloud] against a background of generalized failure of development, or marked impairment, of other language functions" (Mehegan & Dreifuss, 1972, p. 1106). Their reading is a voracious compulsion that frequently develops in the preschool years. In addition, they are frequently retarded, autistic, or hyperkinetic. Perhaps these children represent an extreme instance of word calling mixed with an intellectual or emotional disturbance, or they may be a qualitatively different type of reader. Given the disagreements about both word callers and hyperlexics, careful investigations and descriptions of both are needed.

Dialect Speakers

Readers whose oral reading appears to support the comprehension hypothesis are those whose oral language dialect is different from the dialect of the primers. The most salient example in the United States are children who speak a Black dialect and learn to read from primers printed in standard English. When asked to read aloud, they produce numerous "errors" in oral production; that is, their speech does not match the speech that one would expect, based on the print. However, their deviations are not arbitrary with respect to the meaning of the text. Many of these "errors" do not change the meaning of the text but are a translation of the message into the reader's dialect. [Eds. note: See Shuy, Volume 1, this series, and Simons, this volume.]

Dialectal variation occurs at all linguistic levels, although phonemic miscues are the most frequent in oral reading (Burke, 1973). Although Black children may "mispronounce" a printed word (e.g., /ro/ for *road*), they comprehend the meaning of the printed word (Melmed, 1973). Many other Black English responses in oral reading are morphological variations, such as dropping regular past-tense and third-person singular endings on verbs and plural and possessive markers on nouns (Rosen & Ames, 1972a, 1972b; Weber, 1973). Lexical substitutions also occur; for example, *bucket* for *pail* and *gym shoes* for *sneakers* (Burke, 1973). However, we have found no studies that have reported cases where dialectal variations changed meaning more than oral reading errors of standard English speakers changed meaning.

To translate the text into their oral dialect without a change in meaning necessitates that Black children first comprehend the printed text. A fortiori, they must decode the standard English text correctly before comprehending it. It is incorrect to claim that these children have deficient decoding skills. In fact, it is inappropriate to label these children as having a reading problem. They know how to read. The variation in oral reading results from a variation in speech that is different from standard English.

At the very least, oral reading is an inappropriate assessment tool when applied to these children unless the "errors" are interpreted in terms of the child's own dialect. Hunt (1974–1975) scored Black children's responses on the Gray Oral Reading Test both according to the manual and correcting for dialectal responses. She found an increase of only 0.1 grade level between the two scoring systems, although that difference was statistically significant. However, the better readers (as defined by the standard scoring of the test but who were still below grade level) were helped more by the dialectal scoring. They gained one-half grade level on the average with some children gaining more than a whole grade level.

Using oral reading as an instructional device in the classroom must be tempered by a teacher who understands that a child who translates into his or her own dialect is reading correctly (Goodman, 1965a; Goodman & Buck, 1973; Labov, 1967). Otherwise, the teacher may underestimate the child's level of reaching achievement and may put undue pressure on the child by constantly "correcting" his or her oral productions. The child also may be confused by not understanding why the teacher is correcting what he or she is reading correctly (Fasold, 1969).

These children who read orally by translating the standard English of the primers into their own dialect provide convincing evidence for the comprehension hypothesis. Accurate comprehension (and therefore accurate decoding) must have occurred before the child initiated oral production.

RESEARCH ON ORAL READING

Given the identification of these two types of readers, one of whom apparently supports each hypothesis, what empirical evidence is available? Three sources of evidence are reviewed. One source is the analysis of oral reading errors. The errors or miscues are evaluated with respect to the reading processes that underlie the performance. A second source of evidence is studies of eye–voice span. If the eye–voice span varies with the semantic, syntactic, or conceptual difficulty of the text, then the reader may be comprehending the meaning before initiating the oral production. The third source of evidence is a task in which the text material is altered—for example, a misspelled word, a wrong part of speech, a semantically anomalous word, or a logical inconsistency. Whether the oral reader is disrupted by a particular type of alteration in the text indicates whether he or she is using that type of information to process the text.

Oral Reading Errors

A major problem with the literature on oral reading errors has been the lack of agreement on a classification system to analyze the errors (Weber, 1968). The classification schemes reflect the investigators' underlying assumptions about the nature of the reading process. Those who view oral reading primarily as a performance skill score as errors hesitations, poor enunciation, and inappropriate intonation and phrasing (Weber, 1968). Those who view oral reading as a reflection of underlying processes have focused on the graphic–phonetic similarity and syntactic–semantic acceptability as two major determinants of oral reading errors.

Using specially constructed word lists, Shankweiler and Liberman (1972) found that optical confusability, as exemplified by reversals of letter sequence and orientation, was a much less significant factor in producing oral reading errors than were orthographic factors, such as position of the sound segments and phoneme–grapheme correspondences. Initial segments were better read than medial or final ones, and consonants were read better than vowels. Errors on vowels were predicted by the number of possible orthographic representations.

Using word lists as opposed to prose precludes any evaluation of syntactic and semantic determinants. Shankweiler and Liberman (1972) justified their use of word lists by the fact that there were significant correlations (averaging .70) between error scores on oral reading of lists of words and error scores on the Gray Oral Reading Test in each of four groups of children. They concluded that "the problems of the beginning reader appear to have more to do with the synthesis of syllables than with scanning of larger chunks of connected text [p. 298]." However, since the word list data accounted for only about 50% of the variance on the Gray Oral Reading Test, considerable variance remains to be explained by syntactic and semantic components of connected text. Goodman (1965b) reported that many words that were missed when they appeared on a list of isolated words were read correctly when they appeared in a story context. In fact, first graders read 64%, second graders read 75%, and third graders read 82% of the missed words correctly, given the syntactic and semantic constraints of the story.

The term *semantic constraints* is usually used to refer to the meaning of the sentence constraining what lexical items might meaningfully complete the sentence. *Semantic constraints* also can be used to refer to access to the meaning of a word in the lexicon, or "mental dictionary." Two experiments with isolated words are particularly relevant. Perfetti and Hogaboam (1975) reported that more skilled comprehenders were more rapid at word recognition (and pronunciation) than were less skilled comprehenders, even when all words were known to both groups. The difference between the groups was larger for infrequent than for frequent words. Golinkoff and Rosinski (1976) used a somewhat different task in which automatic semantic access would interfere with the subject's performance on picture naming. They found that although less skilled comprehenders were weak on decoding, their semantic access skills were not imparied. The results of these two studies are inconsistent with respect to whether more and less skilled comprehenders differ in semantic access. However, the fact that variation in semantic access affected naming responses indicates that semantic access occurred before the naming response was initiated.

Other investigators have compared the effects of graphic and syntactic–semantic constraints on errors in connected text. They have uniformly reported that oral reading errors are represented more accurately as alternatives that are syntactically and semantically plausible than as alternatives that match graphic constraints. Out of 7,674 substitution errors committed by first graders, Clay (1968) reported that 72% were syntactically appropriate but that only 41% could be attributed to grapheme–phoneme correspondences. Biemiller (1970) found that first graders' graphically similar substitution errors were less frequent than were contextually appropriate substitutions. A similar finding has been reported by Weber (1970a, 1970b); however, good first-grade readers were more influenced by graphic similarity than were poor readers. Visual graphic form appears to constrain the choice of a response from a set of possible words previously limited by syntactic and semantic constraints. The graphic form of a word does not appear to be a primary factor per se.

That the large majority of substitution errors in oral reading tend to be syntactically and semantically appropriate is well documented. In one case, oral reading errors of college students were not just syntactically appropriate but were predicted by a formal grammar, an augmented transition network (Stevens & Rumelhart, 1975). Studies by Biemiller (1970), Clay (1968), Cohen (1974–1975), Goodman (1965b), and Weber (1970a, 1970b) reported that first graders' oral reading errors tend to be grammatical and meaningful for the context up to the point of the error. Frequently, the error is grammatically and semantically consistent with the remainder of the sentence as well. If not, self-correction usually occurs (Clay, 1969; Goodman, 1965b; Weber, 1970a). Weber (1970a) reported that ungrammatical errors were more graphically similar to the printed word than were grammatical errors, illustrating a trade-off between these two determinants. Biemiller (1970) studied first graders longitudinally through the first grade. He found an initial phase in which the errors were semantically appropriate to the prior context but were minimally related to the graphic form of the stimulus word. During a second phase called the nonresponse phase, the number of errors dropped, and there was an increase in graphically similar substitutions whereas the percentage of contextual (semantically appropriate) substitutions remained constant. Finally, in the third phase, the percentage of contextual substitutions increased whereas the percentage of graphic substitutions remained stable. A comparable sequence has been reported by Clay (1969) for self-corrections by first-grade children (5 years old in New Zealand). Initially, errors were self-corrected only if they did not make sense in the context; then visually dissimilar errors were corrected; and finally, both factors were relevant, so that only a substitution that made sense and was graphically similar was left uncorrected.

There is some evidence that certain types of oral reading errors may be a partial function of the instructional program. The children observed by Biemiller, by Weber, and by Clay were receiving reading instruction in meaning-emphasis programs. Cohen (1974–1975) analyzed the oral reading errors of first graders being taught with a code-emphasis approach. Her results were a bit different from Biemiller's in that she found only a few readers who went through an initial phase of giving contextual responses. Instead, most started out in a brief nonresponse phase. In the next phase, these children produced a significant number of nonsense words. Evidently, the emphasis on sounding out words and attempting to pronounce them induced children to make up words based on the graphic stimulus. Following the phase in which nonsense errors predominated, the children began producing meaningful word substitutions as the context gained in importance.

It appears that the primary conclusion to be derived from studies of oral reading errors is that readers proceed through the comprehension stage before initiating oral production. How else could syntactic and semantic constraints have such a powerful effect on oral reading errors unless such were the case? Not only is this conclusion true for skilled adult readers, but it also holds for beginning readers and for good readers as well as poor readers. Thus, the comprehension hypothesis is substantially correct, and word callers exhibit a clear reading disability that is qualitatively different from typical reading.

Although this logic is appealing, we argue that it is incorrect. From the fact that a child makes a grammatically and semantically appropriate error, one cannot conclude with certainty that he or she has comprehended the intended meaning of the text before initiating oral production. The child may have constructed an interpretation or meaning for the prior text and filled in unknown, missing, or unsampled words on the basis of the constructed meaning. On some occasions, the constructed meaning may be the same as the textual meaning, but this correspondence does not necessarily indicate that the child obtained that meaning by processing the text word through to its semantic representation and then substituting a synonym at production. If a child accurately comprehended the text prior to making an error (the comprehension hypothesis), then not only would the error be acceptable in the sentence up to that point; it would be a close paraphrase as well. A syntactically and semantically acceptable error is not necessarily a close paraphrase. For example, substituting *car* for *cat* in "The girl saw the cat run across the road" does not yield a close paraphrase of the sentence even though *car* is syntactically and semantically acceptable. There would be no need to correct an error that is a close paraphrase, because there would be no inconsistency with the remainder of the sentence. However, substitution errors are frequently self-corrected because they are ungrammatical or inconsistent with the remainder of the sentence (Clay, 1969; Goodman, 1965b; Weber, 1970a). Thus, the self-correction phenomenon suggests that although the substitution errors are syntactically and semantically acceptable, they are not close paraphrases. The child predicts a meaning, produces an oral response that is appropriate for that meaning, realizes that the substitution is inconsistent with the later text, and then repeats to correct the error.

Our argument is that there are at least two possible mechanisms by which syntactically and semantically appropriate errors are produced in oral reading. One is what we originally suggested as the comprehension hypothesis; that is, the error is an output error in which the message was correctly comprehended but then was translated into the reader's idiolect. This mechanism results in close paraphrases and describes what happens with dialect readers. The second possible mechanism is that the substitution is generated on the basis of the preceding context. In this case, the text word is not actually read, but a response is produced based on the semantic representation of the preceding text. This might occur primarily under speed pressure or when the word is unknown but a response is required. This latter mechanism corresponds in many respects to Biemiller's (1970) first phase, in which the first graders respond with a contextually appropriate response that may not have a close correspondence to what is actually printed. "The actual graphic display takes second place to grammatical acceptability. Reasonable as this might be as a tactic for the young reader, he [or she] must sooner or later read what is actually written rather than what he invents" (Gibson & Levin, 1975, p. 281).

The difference between the two mechanisms may be reflected by comparing the reading errors with the child's own idiolect. If the oral production is an accurate translation of the message of the printed text into the child's idiolect, then one would be justified in concluding that the "error" is an oral production change. If a Black child deleted markers for past tense, third-person singular, plurality, or possession (Rosen & Ames, 1972a, 1972b), then one reasonably could conclude that the "errors" were oral production changes. Taking an example from Weber (1970a), however, if a reader substituted *dimes* for *money,* it is more likely that he or she ignored the graphic stimulus and generated the error from the prior context.

Perhaps the two mechanisms can be differentiated by the level of the error. Pronunciation and morphological errors would be the result of oral production differences, but more complex syntactic and semantic substitutions would be contextually based responses. This interpretation probably is not adequate. Consider another example from Weber (1970a). She called "I will see what *is it*" an ungrammatical response to the printed sentence, "I will see what *it is.*" It is possible that the erroneous response was "grammatical" in the child's idiolect. The failure to invert the subject and predict in embedded relative clauses is characteristic of one stage in children's acquisition of embedded clauses (Menyuk, 1969). Although the failure of inversion more typically is found in nursery-school children than in first graders, any one of several factors—for example, slight oral language delay in this particular child—could explain its presence. Although no information was reported about this child's idiolect, the example does illustrate that we cannot identify any particular level of oral reading error as either an output error or a contextual error without a comparison with the child's oral language.

From the fact that a child produces syntactically and semantically appropriate errors in oral reading, the teacher should not infer automatically that the child is comprehending and therefore reading adequately. The source of the errors must also be determined. Only after a comparison with the child's idiolect, rather than a comparison with an adult's responses to the same graphic stimulus, can one determine whether the error is a translation based on a veridical semantic representation or a guess based on the preceding text.

Eye-Voice Span

When moderately skilled readers read aloud, the eye is fixated on the line of print somewhat in advance of the word being vocalized. This difference (typically measured in words) is called the eye–voice span. The eye–voice span is influenced by a number of factors—age and skill level of the reader (Levin & Turner, 1968), difficulty of perceptual processing (Resnick, 1970), syntactic structure (Levin & Kaplan, 1968, 1970; Rode, 1974–1975; Schlesinger, 1968), difficulty of the material (Buswell, 1920; Fairbanks, 1937), and task demands for the reading (Levin & Cohn, 1968). For the current discussion, the most important conclusions drawn from among the studies are that the eye–voice span is responsive to syntactic structure and tends to terminate at phrase and clause boundaries. The usual interpretation has been that readers read in phrase or clause units. The reader may actively construct a hypothesis about what is being read and then test that hypothesis against the printed text. Thus, if reading is an active sampling, constructing, and testing process, then one would expect hypothesis generation to be defined by syntactic and semantic units. If so, the reader comprehends the material before initiating oral production; in fact, it is the semantic representation that permits correct continuations after the visual stimulus has been removed from view.

This interpretation of eye–voice span is subject to the same objection that we raised to the usual interpretation of oral reading errors. Even if the eye–voice span is influenced by the preceding context and comprehension of the preceding meaning, one does not have certain evidence that the reader comprehended the printed material before vocalizing it. One may object that our argument rests on the premise that the reader has comprehended the preceding material. Although such may indeed be the case, the reader may have comprehended the preceding material only after he or she had vocalized it, perhaps by having comprehension and oral production run in parallel or perhaps by comprehending the oral output itself. In any case, comprehension prior to initiation of oral production is not required by our premise.

If readers in eye–voice span experiments base their responses in part on informed constructions of preceding material, then errors should be made in the eye–voice span. Rode (1974–1975) reported such errors for third, fourth, and fifth graders. On 15% of the trials, an erroneous word was substituted for a printed word between two (or more) correct words. She found that 62% of these errors were syntactically and semantically appropriate, and even fewer violated the syntax of the sentence. In a recognition test following eye–voice span measurements, Levin and Kaplan (1968) found extremely few false-positive responses (0.1%), indicating that readers were not purely guessing. In both studies, subjects responded at least partially on the basis of the preceding text.

Text Alterations

Although the analysis of spontaneously occurring oral reading errors provides a wealth of information, not infrequently the type of error needed to answer a specific question is not committed. We then are faced with the uncertainty of not knowing whether the reader was not influenced by that particular aspect of reading or whether the text we chose for reading did not give the reader the opportunity to commit such an error. The uncertainty can be alleviated by inserting inconsistencies of the type we wish to study the text. Various types of structure in the text (e.g., graphic, syntactic, semantic) are used by one or more components of the reading process. Altering a specific type of structure will disturb any component that uses that information. Moreover, the types of structure and the corresponding processing components can be ordered from perceptual processing, using graphic information, to more abstract levels, such as components that use syntactic, semantic, and prose structure. If we are interested in whether semantic access occurs, a very infrequent word, one unlikely to be known by the reader, or a pronounceable nonsense word can be inserted in the text. Or if we are interested in whether the reader is integrating sentence meaning, we can insert a word that produces an inconsistency in meaning. If oral reading is disrupted in either instance, then we can reasonably conclude that the text was processed at least by the components using the changed structure.

Siler (1973–1974) attempted to differentiate between syntactic and semantic determinants of oral reading errors. He introduced semantic disruptions (a word that was the correct part of speech but that was anomalous in the context) and syntactic disruptions (an inversion of one pair of words). Syntactic disruption produced a larger effect on both oral reading time and oral reading errors than did the semantic one. Both types of disruption had an effect on oral reading, but it is difficult to draw a comparative conclusion because there is no common scale on which to compare the relative magnitudes of the syntactic and semantic manipulations (Danks, 1969; Dooling & Danks, 1975).

Lazerson (1974–1975) had college students read Caxton's preface to the *Eneydos* (1490), which was printed in Late Middle English with variable spellings and an archaic syntactic–semantic system. In some conditions, Lazerson corrected only the syntax–semantics to conform with Modern English; in some conditions, both the spelling and the syntax–semantics were corrected. Archaic syntax–semantics increased oral reading time, and the addition of variable spelling increased it even more, but there were no differences in comprehension. The variable spelling and the archaic syntax–semantics probably affected the performance system but not reading comprehension per se.

In both Siler's and Lazerson's experiments, the disruptions in oral reading were measured in terms of total time and total errors in reading a passage. These overall measures demonstrate that processing involved syntactic and semantic components, but they are too gross to determine whether processing occurred before or after oral production had been initiated. If oral reading "disfluencies" (i.e., disruptions) are measured relative to a specific alteration in the text, then the point of initiation of oral production can be specified more precisely. Where the oral reading disfluency occurs relative to the change in the text provides a means of deciding between the decoding and comprehension hypotheses. If the disfluency occurs before the reader has uttered the altered part of the text, then the text must have been processed to that level prior to initiating production. However, if the disfluency occurs after the altered section has been uttered, then the processing at that level occurred much later, perhaps even in response to the oral output itself.

Three experiments have used a more precise procedure of introducing specific alterations and measuring oral reading disfluencies in the immediately surrounding text. These three experiments introduced alterations corresponding to three levels of processing—lexical access, syntactic and semantic integration, and intersentence integration.

To determine the effects of disrupting lexical access, Miller (1975) introduced four types of modifications into paragraphs—infrequent words, pronounceable nonsense words with and without syntactic markers, and phonologically impossible sequences. He measured substitution errors in the original text surrounding the inserted word; hesitations, incorrect intonation, and other performance variables were not measured. In second graders' oral reading, there were increased errors on the two words immediately preceding and following the inserted word, but there was no effect due to the type of text alteration. Since none of the inserted words were available in the "mental dictionary" of the child (including the infrequent words), the reader was unable to locate the word before pronouncing it. Thus, attempts at semantic access occurred prior to oral output. The type of alteration did not make a difference, because the same process, lexical access, was disrupted by all alterations.

Miller and Isakson (1976) assessed intrasentence integration by substituting verbs in sentences. Semantic integration was disrupted by replacing a transitive verb with another transitive verb that was semantically unacceptable. For example, *paid* replaced the verb *planted* in the sentence: "The old farmer planted the bean seeds in the rich, brown soil." Both syntactic and semantic integration were disrupted by substituting a semantically anomalous intransitive verb—for example, *went*—in the foregoing sentence. Subjects were groups of fourth graders who had been divided into good and poor comprehenders (more than or less than one-half year above or below grade-level placement on the reading comprehension subtest of the Iowa Test of Basic Skills, respectively; all readers were within one-half year of grade placement on the vocabulary subtest). The only effect of the verb substitutions was increased oral reading errors at the verb position by good comprehenders. Only the readers who performed at a relatively high level of comprehension skill processed the semantic and syntactic information. The results suggest that integration occurred prior to the initiation of the oral response, because the production of the altered word itself was disrupted. Perhaps with even more skilled readers, the disruption would occur one or more words prior to uttering the altered word.

In a recently completed study, we[1] assessed the disruptive effect of a conceptual inconsistency or contradiction. Within a paragraph, a sentence was altered such that it was inconsistent with a single critical word in the next sentence but not inconsistent with the rest of the paragraph either preceding or following. For example, the first sentence was replaced in the following pair of sentences (taken from Patton's memoirs of World War II); "I then told him that, in spite of my most diligent efforts, there would be some raping. I should like to have the details as early as possible so that we can hang these men. He said that this was . . . ." The replacement was: "I told him there would unquestionably be some helping by the soldiers," which produced an inconsistency with the critical word *hang* in the second sentence. Note that the second sentence containing the critical word was not altered in any way. There were 10 experimental paragraphs, and the location of the text

[1]This experiment was designed in collaboration with Karen Fischer. We thank Mark Germano for his assistance in conducting the experiment.

alteration varied in the paragraphs. Two groups of 10 college students read these passages aloud, and the readings were tape-recorded. Half the passages for each group were altered to produce the inconsistency, and half were left unchanged. Complementary sets of changed and unchanged passages were presented to the two groups of readers. The intervals between saying each of the 5 words preceding and following the critical word in the second sentence, as well as the length of time to say the critical word, were measured by playing back the tape at one-fourth the recording speed. Because the time distributions were skewed, the data were transformed logarithmically.

Subtracting the control group means from the experimental group means, the curve depicting differences in interword time intervals across position in the sentence showed a significant disruption 2 and 3 words following the critical word. The time to say the critical word itself was longer for the experimental group than for the control group, a difference that was significant across both readers and passages.

The results suggest that the reader had comprehended the material prior to initiating oral production of the critical word itself. Detection of the inconsistency required detailed and integrated comprehension. It depended not just on access to the lexical item in semantic memory and not just on comprehension of the sentence currently being uttered but on integration with the semantic representation of the preceding sentence as well. This integration with prior context requires additional time to accomplish (Dooling, 1972). Even if one assumes a constructive or top-down comprehension process, the match between the expected meaning of the second sentence and the actual meaning must have occurred at an abstract level of representation, because the inconsistency could not have been detected on a perceptual level or by comparing individual words or phrases. Thus, comprehension must have occurred well ahead of oral production.

THE TWO HYPOTHESES REVISITED

Our conclusion is that neither the decoding nor the comprehension hypothesis holds all the time but that the particular processes involved in oral reading are reader and task specific. A given reader with specific materials and a definite purpose for reading processes the text to the extent that he or she is capable and to an extent consistent with the implicit or explicit purposes. The reader then initiates the oral production process at that point. Word callers are unable to progress beyond the decoding stage before initiating their oral production, but dialectal speakers are able to comprehend the text before initiating production. Reader limitations, textual variation, and purpose affect processing in somewhat different fashions. The reading level of the reader, whether limited by level of acquisition or by skill, is a limitation of the system. It sets an upper limit on the level of processing that the reader is able to attain. The other two factors, difficulty of the text and the purpose of reading, result in variation in the level of processing.

Reading Level. The level of reading skill sets an upper bound on the processing that a reader can accomplish prior to the initiation of oral production. A limitation resulting from level of acquisition is most often indexed by the age or the grade level of the child. Good and poor readers typically are defined by whether or not they exceed or fall below the grade level corresponding to their chronological age.

The level of processing is not independent of rate of processing and memory limitations. There is evidence that children do not differ from adults in the absolute size of their memory capacity but that children use their memory stores less efficiently (Chi, 1976). This impoverished ability to select and store relevant information is particularly critical in reading where integration of information must occur over a span of input. The reader must develop strategies for the effcient intake and storage of printed information. The rate must be fast enough that the requisite information exists simultaneously in memory so that it can be integrated. However, if the initial stages of the reading process are not sufficiently fluent or are not sufficiently automatic to proceed with minimal or no attention, then the rate of input will not be sufficiently rapid to overcome memory limitations. The beginning phases of reading acquisition are occupied with the practice of decoding skills. When they become sufficiently automatic, attention can be directed to the later comprehension stages (LaBerge & Samuels, 1974). [Eds. note: See Perfetti and Lesgold, Volume 1, this series.]

With increasing age, readers become better able to control the strategies necessary for processing efficiently so that they can be directed toward the particular task set for them. Just as they can better control the strategies involved in the efficient storage and retrieval of material, they can control the reading process to particular ends.

Purpose or Task. The reading task influences the level of processing accomplished. Keeping in mind that the level of reading acquisition sets an upper limit and that the general developmental level of the reader may determine his or her ability to control the reading strategies, a reader can focus on decoding, on comprehension, or on oral production. If the reader expects to be tested on his or her knowledge of the content of the passage, then the reader will attempt to comprehend the passage more thoroughly. However, if the reader expects to be evaluated solely on oral production, then he or she may focus attention on decoding and pronunciation, thereby ignoring comprehension.

The schoolchild who must read for the teacher with the class listening probably pays particularly attention to decoding and oral production so as not to make a mistake. Typically, the teacher and the other children follow the text, so they know immediately if a mistake is made. Pehrsson (1974) tested fifth graders under such conditions. When the teacher focused attention on correct decoding and oral production, reading rate and comprehension decreased, as one might expect. But unexpectedly, oral reading errors increased. Conversely, Pehrsson found that if the children were permitted to read aloud without interruption and had to retell what they had read, then comprehension increased.

Text Difficulty. The text can vary in difficulty at several different levels. The type font may make it difficult to discriminate the letters, the vocabulary may be difficult, the syntactic structure may be complex, and the ideas and conceptual organization may be abstract or obscure. These levels of difficulty interact with the level of reading of which the reader is capable. If the reader is concentrating attention on decoding, either because of ability limitations or task orientation, then the complexity of the syntax and the difficulty of the conceptual structure will not have an effect on oral production. If there is an inconsistency at a higher level than the reader is capable of processing, then there will be no disfluency in oral production.

Comprehension processes in oral reading cannot be evaluated by using a list of words. Lexical access can be assessed, but accessing meaning of isolated words is but a small part of the processes involved in the comprehension of paragraphs. In prose comprehension, words must be amalgamated for sentence meaning, and sentences must be integrated for textual meaning.

In summary, the decoding hypothesis of oral reading holds in certain contexts with particular materials and for certain types of readers, and the comprehension hypothesis holds in others. All three factors interact to determine the specific level of processing of the text. Whether oral production is initiated prior to or after comprehension is determined by these factors.

POSTSCRIPT

In his comments on our chapter, Trabasso discusses the lack of clear definitions of decoding and comprehension. Decoding typically refers to the translation of print input into an appropriate phonological code. Comprehension refers to the process of extracting meaning from the phonological code. Neither of these definitions is precise enough to know what operations to use to investigate each. Trabasso correctly asserts that procedural definitions of decoding and comprehension are needed.

The basic reationale for our discussion of the research in oral reading is that oral reading reflects processing at a variety of levels. Oral reading errors were classified as being related to the graphic properties of the stimulus or as related to syntax or semantics. Several levels of processing in reading were identified in terms of alterations in text, the effects of which were measured by disfluencies in oral reading. This processing hierarchy effectively has eliminated the need for a distinction between decoding and comprehension. Which processing levels are involved in decoding, and which are involved in comprehension? The distinction is no longer formally necessary, because the levels of processing in reading have been defined by the particular operations used to disrupt each processing level.

The original question as to whether oral production is initiated after decoding or after comprehension has been divided. One question is whether or not a particular level of processing (as defined by a manipulation of the text) is involved in oral reading. Any disruption in oral reading provides evidence of processing at that level. The second question is whether oral production is initiated before or after processing at a particular level has occurred. This question is answered by the point of disfluency in oral reading relative to the point of alteration in the text. Disfluencies prior to when the altered text is uttered indicate that processing at that level has been completed; disfluencies after the altered text has been uttered indicate that oral production was initiated prior to processing at that level. Using this rationale, one's model of reading is implicit in the selection of what processing levels are interesting to manipulate.

ACKNOWLEDGMENT

The research was supported in part by Grant No. MH 21230-02 from the National Institute of Mental Health.

REFERENCES

Biemiller, A. The development of the use of graphic and contextual information as children learn to read. *Reading Research Quarterly,* 1970, *6,* 75–96.

Burke, C. Dialect and the reading process. In J. L. Laffey & R. Shuy (Eds.), *Language differences: do they interfere?* Newark, Del.: International Reading Association, 1973.

Buswell, G. T. An experimental study of the eye–voice span in reading. *Supplementary Educational Monographs,* 1920, (Whole No. 17).

Chi, M. T. H. Short-term memory limitations in children: Capacity or processing deficits? *Memory & Cognition,* 1976, *4,* 559–572.

Clay, M. M. A syntactic analysis of reading errors. *Journal of Verbal Learning and Verbal Behavior,* 1968, *7,* 434–438.

Clay, M. M. Reading errors and self-correction behaviour. *British Journal of Educational Psychology,* 1969, *39,* 47–56.

Clay, M. M., & Imlach, R. H. Juncture, pitch, and stress as reading behavior variables. *Journal of Verbal Learning and Verbal Behavior,* 1971, *10,* 133–139.

Cohen, A. S. Oral reading errors of first grade children taught by a code emphasis approach. *Reading Research Quarterly,* 1974–1975, *10,* 616–650.

Danks, J. H. Grammaticalness and meaningfulness in the comprehension of sentences. *Journal of Verbal Learning and Verbal Behavior,* 1969, *8,* 687–696.

Dooling, D. J. Some context effects in the speeded comprehension of sentences. *Journal of Experimental Psychology,* 1972, *93,* 56–62.

Dooling, D. J., & Danks, J. H. Going beyond tests of significance: Is psychology ready? *Bulletin of the Psychonomic Society,* 1975, *5,* 15–17.

Fairbanks, G. The relation between eye-movements and voice in the oral reading of good and poor silent readers. *Psychological Monographs,* 1937, *48*(3, Whole No. 215), 78–107.

Fasold, R. W. Orthography in reading materials for Black English speaking children. In J. C. Baratz & R. W. Shuy (Eds.), *Teaching Black children to read.* Washington, D.C.: Center for Applied Linguistics, 1969.

Gibson, E. J., & Levin, H. *The psychology of reading.* Cambridge, Mass: MIT Press, 1975.

Golinkoff, R. M., & Rosinski, R. R. Decoding, semantic processing, and reading comprehension skill. *Child Development,* 1976, *47,* 252–258.

Goodman, K. S. Dialect barriers to reading comprehension. *Elementary English,* 1965, *42,* 853–860. (a)

Goodman, K. S. A linguistic study of cues and miscues in reading. *Elementary English,* 1965, *42,* 639–643. (b)

Goodman, K. S. Reading: A psycholinguistic guessing game. *Journal of the Reading Specialist,* 1967, *6,* 126–135.

Goodman, K. S. The 13th easy way to make learning to read difficult: A reaction to Gleitman and Rozin. *Reading Research Quarterly,* 1973, *8,* 484–493.

Goodman, K. S., & Buck, C. Dialect barriers to reading comprehension revisted. *Reading Teacher,* 1973, *27,* 6–12.

Hunt, B. C. Black dialect and third and fourth graders' performance on the Gray Oral Reading Test. *Reading Research Quarterly,* 1974–1975, *10,* 103–123.

LaBerge, D., & Samuels, S. J. Toward a theory of automatic information processing in reading. *Cognitive Psychology,* 1974, *6,* 293–323.

Labov, W. Some sources of reading problems for Negro speakers of nonstandard English. In A. Frazier (Ed.), *New directions in elementary English.* Urbana, Ill.: National Council of Teachers of English, 1967.

Lazerson, B. H. The influence of highly variable spelling upon the reading performance of skilled readers of Modern English. *Reading Research Quarterly,* 1974–1975, *10,* 583–615.

Levin, H., & Cohn, J. A. Studies of oral reading: XII. Effects of instructions on the eye–voice span. In H. Levin, E. J. Gibson, & J. J. Gibson (Eds.), *The analysis of reading skill.* Washington, D.C.: U.S. Government Printing Office, 1968.

Levin, H., & Kaplan, E. L. Eye–voice span (EVS) within active and passive sentences. *Language and Speech,* 1968, *11,* 251–258.

Levin, H., & Kaplan, E. L. Grammatical structure and reading. In H. Levin & J. P. Williams (Eds.), *Basic studies on reading.* New York: Basic Books, 1970.

Levin, H., & Turner, A. Sentence structure and the eye–voice span. In H. Levin, E. J. Gibson, & J. J. Gibson (Eds.), *The analysis of reading skill.* Washington, D.C.: U.S. Government Printing Office, 1968.

Mehegan, C. C., & Dreifuss, F. E. Hyperlexia: Exceptional reading ability in brain-damaged children. *Neurology,* 1972, *22,* 1105–1111.

Melmed, P. J. Black English phonology: The question of reading interference. In J. L. Laffey & R. W. Shuy (Eds.), *Language differences: Do they interfere?* Newark, Del.: International Reading Association, 1973.

Menyuk, P. *Sentences children use.* Cambridge, Mass.: MIT Press, 1969.

Miller, J. W. Disruptive effect: A phenomenon in oral reading. *Reading Horizons,* 1975, *15,* 198–207.

Miller, J. W., & Isakson, R. L. *The effect of syntactic and semantic violation on high and low reading comprehenders.* San Francisco: American Educational Research Association, 1976.

Pehrsson, R. S. V. The effects of teacher interference during the process of reading or how much of a helper is Mr. Gelper? *Journal of Reading,* 1974, *17,* 617–621.

Perfetti, C. A., & Hogaboam, T. Relationship between single word decoding and reading comprehension skill. *Journal of Educational Psychology,* 1975, *67,* 461–469.

Resnick, L. B. Relations between perceptual and syntactic control in oral reading. *Journal of Educational Psychology,* 1970, *61,* 382–385.

Rode, S. S. Development of phrase and clause boundary reading in children. *Reading Research Quarterly,* 1974–1975, *10,* 124–142.

Rosen, C. L., & Ames, W. S. An exploration of the influence of dialect on the oral reading of sentences by Black children, grades three through six. *Reading World,* 1972, *11,* 201–209. (a)

Rosen, C. L., & Ames, W. S. An investigation of the influence of nonstandard dialect on the oral reading behavior of fourth grade Black children under two stimuli conditions. In J. A. Figural (Ed.), *Better reading in urban schools.* Newark, Del.: International Reading Association, 1972. (b)

Schlesinger, I. M. *Sentence structure and the reading process.* The Hague, Netherlands: Mouton, 1968.

Shankweiler, D., & Liberman, I. Misreading: A search for causes. In J. F. Kavanagh & I. G. Mattingly (Eds.), *Language by ear and by eye.* Cambridge, Mass.: MIT Press, 1972.

Siler, E. R. The effects of syntactic and semantic constraints on the oral reading performance of second and fourth graders. *Reading Research Quarterly,* 1973–1974, *9,* 583–602.

Silverberg, N. E., & Silverberg, M. C. Hyperlexia—specific word recognition skills in young children. *Exceptional Children,* 1967, *34,* 41–42.

Silverberg, N. E., & Silverberg, M. C. Case histories in hyperlexia. *Journal of School Psychology,* 1968–1969, *7,* 3–7.

Smith, E. B., Goodman, K. S., & Meredith, R. *Language and thinking in school* (2nd ed). New York: Holt, Rinehart & Winston, 1976.

Stevens, A. L., & Rumelhart, D. E. Errors in reading: An analysis using an augmented transition network model of grammar. In D. A. Norman & D. E. Rumelhart (Eds.), *Explorations in cognition.* San Francisco: Freeman, 1975.

Weber, R. M. The study of oral reading errors: A survey of the literature. *Reading Research Quarterly,* 1968, *4,* 96–119.

Weber, R. M. First-graders' use of grammatical context in reading. In H. Levin & J. P. Williams (Eds.), *Basic studies on reading.* New York: Basic Books, 1970. (a)

Weber, R. M. A linguistic analysis of first-grade reading errors. *Reading Research Quarterly,* 1970, *5,* 427–451. (b)

Weber, R. M. Dialect differences in oral reading: An analysis of errors. In J. L. Laffey & R. Shuy (Eds.), *language differences: Do they interfere?* Newark, Del.: International Reading Association, 1973.

II LANGUAGE DIFFERENCES AND READING

5 Black Dialect, Reading Interference, and Classroom Interaction

Herbert D. Simons
University of California at Berkeley

A major problem that continues to plague American education is the fact that large numbers of Black students are not learning to read well enough to function in a society that requires its citizenry to attain a high degree of literacy. Black students' lack of reading skills remains a problem, despite the great deal of attention that it has received and the enormous amount of federal, state, and local money that has been and continues to be spent in attempts to solve it. Our past performance on this problem leads one sadly to predict that the current emphasis on skill hierarchies, behavioral objectives, management systems, and the like will produce the same meager results that programmed instruction, computer-assisted instruction, performance contracting, talking typewriters, and so on have produced. There are at least three reasons for this dismal state of affairs. First, there is a lack of basic understanding of the reading acquisition process. We do not have any comprehensive developmental theories of reading acquisition. Despite the voluminous research literature, reading instruction is mostly art and very little science. Second—as a result of this lack of basic knowledge—most innovations such as the ones mentioned end up organizing or arranging instruction in different ways, but their content—that is, the set of skills that they are designed to teach—remains the same. The same old content is presented in a new way, and it is not surprising that students do not read any better under the new program than under the old ones. Finally, research and instruction in reading has tended to focus on materials and methods rather than on the instructional interchange between teachers and students as it takes place in the classroom. This focus on methods and materials is, in my opinion, misguided and unlikely to prove fruitful in the future. This focus has had a major influence on the research on Black dialect and reading.

BLACK LANGUAGE:
THE DEFICIT AND DIFFERENCE VIEWPOINTS

Over the past decade, one explanation that has been advanced for Black students' poor reading performance is their language. Two essentially different views of Black children's language have been proposed to explain their reading failure. They are the deficit and difference views. The deficit view holds that the language of Black children is an inferior form of standard English that is unacceptable in school and society and is an inadequate vehicle for thinking and learning to read. Thus, Black children are handicapped by the inadequacy of their language in learning to read. Although Labov (1969) and others have shown that Black language is not inferior to standard English, the deficit viewpoint still appears to be the predominant view in the schools and in society in general. My impression is that some progress has been made among faculty members at schools of education and among writers of reading textbooks who no longer favor the deficit view, or at least no longer publicly espouse it. Unfortunately, in the places where most reading instruction takes place—the schools—the deficit view is still predominant.

The difference view holds that Black children speak a dialect of English that is referred to in this chapter as Black dialect. Black dialect, as an expression of Black culture, is a viable system of communication, and as such, it is different from standard English but in no way inferior to it as a vehicle for thinking and learning to read. According to the difference viewpoint, the problems that Black children have in learning to read are due to the fact that the schools operate with and recognize only standard English and are unwilling and unable to accommodate Black children and their language. The difference viewpoint is held by most linguists and anthropologists and by some psychologists and educators. The difference view is the prevailing notion among academics who study language, and there is now very little debate about the relative merits of the deficit and difference views. The issue is settled, and the difference view prevails. Unfortunately, the majority of teachers of Black children, I would guess, ascribe to the deficit view; and those who ascribe to the difference view have only a dim understanding of it and even less understanding of what it means in terms of reading instruction.

Both the deficit and difference points of view hold that there is a close relationship between language and reading and that the mismatch between Black children's language and the language used in schools and in reading texts interferes with Black children's reading. Proponents of each view differ profoundly in assigning blame for the problem and consequently in proposing remedies for it. The deficit viewpoint assumes that the Black child's language is defective and focuses on changing it. Its advocates propose either eliminating Black dialect entirely and replacing it with standard English or adding standard English as a second dialect. The instructional means for accomplishing this is usually borrowed from second-language teaching techniques. All this changing of the Black child's language is to take place either before reading instruction begins or concurrently with it. The objective is to remove the source of the problem.

The difference viewpoint assigns the blame to the schools and proposes that the schools accommodate Black dialect. Its proponents would do this by changing the methods and materials used to teach reading. Their proposals fall into two categories. The first would change the books that children learn to read with by writing them in Black dialect.[1] The second, proposed by Goodman (1965), would retain the standard English materials but allow children to produce a Black dialect rendition of them. Thus, in the first proposal the materials are changed, whereas in the second the materials remain the same and the teachers must adopt a strategy of accommodating dialect.

The proponents of the two viewpoints have simply assumed that the mismatch between Black children's language and the language of the school causes reading interference. They (myself included) have adopted this assumption without proposing any detailed explanation of the interference. Thus, little if any of the research in reading has been directed at describing the mechanisms of the interference. And since the proposals for remedying the problem concern methods and materials, the research has focused on materials and has attempted to demonstrate the existence of reading interference by examining the effect of prototypical instructional materials. For example, one major way of studying reading interference has been to compare Black children's reading of Black dialect and standard English texts. If the Black dialect texts are read better, then both reading interference and the usefulness of dialect reading texts is presumably demonstrated. These texts can then serve as prototypes for dialect readers.

A notable exception to the emphasis on materials is the Goodman (1965) proposal, which would retain the existing materials and focus on the teacher's response to the Black child's dialect rendition of the text. Labov (1967) and a few others have focused on the teacher rather than on the materials. However, beyond the general call for teachers to know about dialect and its features and not to reject the child's language, and the more specific suggestion that dialect-based miscues not be corrected, there has been no real discussion of

---

[1]A related version of this proposal is to write materials that avoid features that correspond to Black dialect features. Wolfram (1970) has pointed out some of the problems with this approach. It has not been researched to my knowledge, and not much interest has been shown in it.

either the mechanisms of interference or detailed strategies for teachers to follow in dealing with it. And since materials are easier to study than teachers, there has been almost no research on the Goodman proposal. The Piestrup (1973) study is the only one that I am familiar with that focused on teachers. Her study and an analysis of some of her data are discussed in the last part of this chapter.

I next examine the empirical evidence on the question of reading interference and the efficacy of the proposed remedies. This evidence is much more equivocal than one would expect, given the forceful rhetoric that surrounds the issues.

BLACK DIALECT
AND READING INTERFERENCE

Black dialect and standard English differ in phonological and grammatical features and in lexical items. Most of the research has been directed at questions of phonological and grammatical interference and has tended to study one or the other, and only in some cases have both been studied.[2]

Phonological Interference

The pronunciation of certain written English words by Black dialect speakers is different from that by standard English speakers. The results of these differences are words that have a pronunciation unique to Black dialect, for example, "ness" for *nest*, "ress" for *rest*, and "han" for *hand*. In addition, there are words whose Black dialect pronunciation results in a different word, for example, "tess" for *test*, "men" for *mend*, "walk" for *walked*, "coal" for *cold*, and so on. The latter result in an extra set of homophones for Black dialect speakers. These differences in pronunciation presumably could interfere with word recognition, even though the precise way they interfere has never been spelled out. Several of the studies discussed later have looked at comprehension and word recognition without explaining how Black dialect phonology interferes with comprehension.

---

[2]The distinction between grammatical and phonological features of Black dialect is not clear-cut. First, there are features that are wholly phonological such as consonant cluster simplification in monomorphemic words—for example, *test-tess, desk-dess*. Second there are features that are phonological in origin but intersect with consonant cluster simplification in words with past-tense morphemes—for example, *liked-like, passed-pass,* and so on. Third, there are features that are clearly grammatical such as the invariant *be*. In this discussion, phonological and grammatical interference are discussed separately in the full recognition that there are many features in the second category.

Melmed (1971) conducted one of the first empirical studies of phonological interference. He compared third-grade Black children with third-grade White children on their ability to discriminate auditorily, to produce, and to comprehend in oral and silent reading certain major phonological features of Black dialect. He found that the Blacks differed from the Whites in auditory discrimination and production of the selected features, demonstrating that they were dialect speakers. If phonological interference exists, then the speakers who exhibited the most dialect features—in this study the Black children—should do less well on the reading comprehension measures than the Whites, who in this study exhibited fewer dialect features. If there is no phonological interference, then there should be no difference on the reading comprehension measures. The latter was found to be the case in Melmed's study. Although Black subjects differed from Whites on auditory discrimination and production of Black dialect phonological features, they did not differ on their ability to comprehend them in oral and silent reading. Thus the Melmed study does not support the hypothesis of phonological interference. There are, however, some questions about the representativeness of his subjects' reading ability and degree of dialect speaking that tend to weaken his findings.

Another study of phonological interference was conducted by Simons (1974), in which second-, third-, and fourth-grade Black children read real and nonsense Black dialect homophone pairs—for example, *bus-bust, hus-hust*. It was hypothesized that the first member of each pair would be easier to read than the second member, because its spelling is closer to Black dialect phonology. In all three grades, there either were no differences between the word types or the difference favored the second member. Thus, the phonological interference hypothesis is again not supported.

A third study of phonological interference was conducted by Rystrom (1970), who compared the effect of training in the production of standard English phonology on the reading achievement of first-grade Black dialect speakers. The experimental group received training in producing standard English phonology; the control group received language arts training without particular emphasis on standard English. If phonological interference exists, then the experimental group should exhibit less dialect as a result of the training and should read better than the control group, which should exhibit more dialect because they received no standard English training. He found training in standard English phonology did not produce significant differences in reading achievement on three measures of reading achievement. One significant difference was found, but it favored the control group. Thus, it appears that the Rystrom study also fails to support the hypothesis of phonological interference.

Rentel and Kennedy (1972) conducted another study relevant to the question of phonological interference. They studied the effects of pattern drill (similar to that used in second-language teaching techniques) in standard English on first-grade Appalachian dialect speakers and its influence on reading achievement. Since Appalachian dialect was studied and not Black dialect, the study is not an exact test of the question for Black dialect. However, Black dialect and Appalachian dialect have some features in common, and they are both dialects of English; so the results may have some bearing on the question for Black dialect speakers. Rentel and Kennedy employed the same research strategy as Rystrom in that they attempted to manipulate the amount of dialect to see if it affected reading achievement. If dialect interferes, the group that receives training in standard English should experience less interferences and do better in reading than a comparable group who have no training and thus presumably experience more dialect interference. Rentel and Kennedy found no difference in reading achievement between the experimental and control groups. Thus, this study also fails to support, phonological interference. However, in both the Rental and Kennedy and the Rystrom studies, the standard English training failed to work, so that one could argue that the phonological interference hypothesis was not adequately tested.

Further but indirect evidence on the question of phonological interference is provided by Osterberg (1961), who studied reading acquisition in a dialect area of Sweden. He conducted an experiment in which a group of first-grade children were taught for the first 10 weeks of the school year with books especially written to conform to the phonological features of the dialect they spoke. A control group received instruction using standard texts that conform to standard Swedish speech. If phonological interference with learning to read Swedish exists, then teaching students to read with texts that conform to their phonological system should reduce this interference and thus increase reading achievement. Osterberg found that the experimental group was superior to the control group after 10 weeks as well as at the end of 1 year on various measures of reading achievement. This study offers some support for the hypothesis of phonological interference.

With the exception of the Osterburg study, the evidence on phonological interference tends to be negative. However, there are methodological problems with the studies concerning both internal and external validity that tend to weaken the findings (Simons, 1971), and the question of phonological interference is still not closed.

Grammatical Interference

The evidence on grammatical reading interference is even more conclusively negative. Grammatical reading interference is presumably caused by the mismatch between the Black child's syntax and the standard English syntax of texts (Baratz, 1969; Stewart, 1969). The sources of this proposed interference are not very clear. Proposed hypotheses involve cases where standard English sentences are interpreted as nonequivalent Black dialect sentences. For example, *He will be busy* might be interpreted as a habitual action because of the *be* (Stewart, 1969). They also involve such things as failure to interpret *ed* as a past-tense marker because it is not pronounced. And finally, there is the extra-step or translation hypothesis, which proposes that Black children go through an extra step in reading because they have to translate from the standard English text to their own Black dialect grammatical system. None of these proposals are very convincing.

The empirical research on grammatical interference has with few exceptions been concerned with attempting to show that Black children read texts written in Black dialect grammar better than texts written in standard English. Two studies, Ruddell (1963) and Tatham (1970), provide indirect evidence on the question. They both found that standard-English-speaking White elementary-school children comprehended material written in grammatical sentence patterns more frequently used in their oral language better than material written in sentence patterns less frequently used in their oral language. The findings of these studies support the notion that children comprehend written language better if its structure is closer to that of their oral language and that less familiar structure interferes with reading. If these findings can be demonstrated with Black-dialect-speaking children, then the reading interference hypothesis would receive strong support.

Unfortunately for the proponents of dialect readers, the same results have not been found in studies of dialect speakers. Walker (1975), in a study of third-grade children who speak a Newfoundland dialect, found that the standard English texts produced faster reading speeds and fewer errors than the dialect texts. Studies of Black-dialect-speaking children in grades two through four have been conducted by Schaaf (1971), Sims (1972), Simons and Johnson (1974), Nolen (1972), Mathewson (1973), and Marwit and Newman (1974). Taken altogether, they used a variety of reading materials, including stories written especially for the studies, folktales, and standardized passages from reading tests, each written in a Black dialect and standard English version. The criterion measures included multiple-choice comprehension questions, free-recall tests, and oral reading tests. The results were either no differences between the versions or better reading of the standard English version. In no instance was the Black dialect version read better. Thus, all these studies of dialect speakers, including the Rentel and Kennedy (1972) study mentioned earlier—which also studied grammatical interference—offer no support for the grammatical reading interference hypothesis. The only support for it is the very indirect evidence provided by the Ruddell (1963) and Tatham (1970) studies.

Overall, the empirical evidence in support of grammatical or phonological interference is very thin indeed. There is almost no positive evidence to support either. On the basis of the empirical evidence discussed in this chapter, Black dialect as an explanation for Black children's poor reading performance seems almost a dead issue. However, the issue is not as moribund as it appears to be.

An Alternative Explanation for Negative Evidence on the Reading Interference Hypothesis

The negative evidence on reading interference may be due more to the way it has been conceived and studied than to its nonexistence. As mentioned earlier, grammatical interference has been almost exclusively studied by comparing Black children's reading of texts written in standard English and Black dialect. These studies have been criticized because of the size and nature of their sample of subjects and the appropriateness of the materials—that is, whether and to what degree the Black dialect versions matched the Black children's speech (Baratz, 1971; Simons, 1974). These criticisms tend to weaken the negative findings on interference. And although these criticisms may have some validity, I believe that the findings are essentially valid; that is, Black children will not read a text written in Black dialect with any better comprehension than they will a text written in standard English. In fact they will probably read it with less comprehension than the standard English text due to the novelty of encountering their dialect in print, even though they may prefer to listen to spoken Black dialect and comprehend it better. This latter point is supported by Mathewson (1973). He found that Black children had a more positive attitude toward and better comprehension of folktales when they were told to them in Black dialect than when they were told to them in standard English; the reverse was true when the folktales were presented in written form.

The reason, in my opinion, for the finding of no advantage for the Black dialect texts is that the places in the standard English texts that present conflict points with Black children's dialect do not cause any serious loss of comprehension. For example, even though *ed* is not read as past tense, there are other redundant syntactic and semantic cues that provide the same information. Thus, there is no loss of information. In the studies under discussion, when the Black dialect text was presented with conflict points removed, there was no increase in comprehension over the standard English text, because the conflict points did not cause any real problems in the first place. Some evidence for this conclusion is provided by Labov (1970), who studied interference caused by the past-tense morpheme *ed*. More specifically, he investigated whether or not Black adolescents understood that the *ed* signaled past action. He had subjects read aloud isolated sentences like the following: "When I passed by, I read the posters," and "I looked for trouble when I read the news." Their pronunciation of the homograph *read* indicated whether or not they had understood the *ed* to be a past-tense marker. Labov found that his subjects were able to comprehend the past-tense marker only 35% to 55% of the time. This fact suggests that failure to pronounce the *ed* interfered with comprehension of the sentences a substantial part of the time. He also found that performance on this task did not correlate with overall reading skills as measured by a standardized reading comprehension test. This lack of a correlation between comprehension of the past-tense marker and overall reading skill suggests that even though specific features of dialect may not be comprehended, they do not interfere with overall comprehension of connected discourse.

Comprehension of connected text is aided by the fact that any ambiguities that may arise in individual sentences concerning tense, plurality, possessive, and so on are compensated for by syntactic and semantic information in the rest of the text or by other semantic information within the same sentence. Thus, one would expect no comprehension problem with a sentence like, "Yesterday when I passed by, I read the posters," because a redundant cue— yesterday—to the past-tense interpretation has been added. One would also expect that even the original Labov sentence would be understood when embedded in a passage that provided other redundant cues for the past tense.

Thus, there appears to be no interference from dialect during actual reading of texts because of the availability of redundant cues to meaning. I would like to argue, however, that reading interferences may exist but that the studies reviewed here have conceived of it and attempted to demonstrate it in an inadequate way. A number of the studies reviewed have (with the exception of Osterberg, 1961) asked whether there would be differences in comprehension in reading texts with and without dialect conflict points, that is, in standard English and Black dialect. The real question, in my opinion, is not whether Black children's dialect interferes with their actual reading of texts but whether their dialect interferes with their acquisition of the skills necessary to read these texts. The problem is that Black-dialect-speaking children have not acquired reading skills sufficient to read texts written for their grade level, whether they are written in standard English or Black dialect. I would like to propose that Black-dialect-reading interference should be conceived of as interference with the process by which children acquire reading skills rather than as interference with their actual reading of texts. Reading acquisition is a developmental process, and it should be studied as such. One-shot experiments in which children read standard English and Black dialect texts do not tell us much about reading interference or the reading acquisition process.

One approach to demonstrating interference that is more valid than the one-shot approaches has been suggested by Baratz (1969), Stewart (1969), and others. This approach is to teach Black children to read using dialect readers and to compare their reading achievement to that of other Black children using conventional readers. If Black children were to learn to read better with the dialect readers than with traditional readers, then not only would reading interference be demonstrated but the solution to the problem would be verified—that is, use dialect readers.

This approach to the issue, in my opinion, offers little hope for either demonstrating interference or solving Black children's reading problem. There are a number of reasons for my pessimism. First, there is the problem of constructing the reading texts. Black children differ in the frequency of the dialect features they produce, so there is the general problem of which children's speech is to be matched. Second, there is the problem of conducting large-scale, long-term, comparative curriculum experiments in the schools. There are a multitude of methodological problems, the most severe of which is lack of control over teacher variables that are, in my opinion, insurmountable. For example, the inconclusiveness of the decoding versus meaning reading methods experiments is in part due to their failure to overcome the methodological problems that are inherent in large-scale intact classroom experiments. Third, there is the vehement opposition of some Black teachers, administrators, and parents. They object to dialect readers, because they see them as perpetuating the use of dialect they consider an impediment to achieving full participation in society. Because of this opposition, as far as I know, no large-scale dialect reader experiment has ever been attempted. I am not optimistic about overcoming this opposition, at least in the short run.

Fourth, in reading methods studies where one set of materials is compared to another, differences—when they are found—usually have a magnitude of a few months on a standardized reading test. These differences could just as easily be attributed to teacher difference as to method. On the other hand, the discrepancy between the scores of Black and White children can range from 5 months to 5 years, depending on the grade level tested. It seems unlikely that differences in reading materials alone could explain the gap between Whites and Blacks. It seems highly improbable that dialect readers alone would make enough difference, even if they did prove to be superior to standard English readers.

Fifth, there is also the problem that large-scale methods comparison studies concentrate on comparing end products—that is, standardized achievement test scores. There is rarely any examination of the process by which those scores are achieved. Thus, whatever the findings of these studies, one is hard presed to extract any usable information that can be applied in the schools.

Finally, the most serious problem with a methods comparison study, which often boils down to a materials comparison study, is that the variables being manipulated—the materials—may not be important in the first place. In my opinion, materials alone are not that significant a factor in children's reading achievement.

The most fruitful way to study reading interference is to study directly the reading acquisition process and the role that Black children's dialect plays in it by examining reading instruction as it actually takes place in schools.

Learning to read in school involves two types of activities. In the first, the student works alone and interacts with written materials. The research reviewed in this chapter is relevant for examining the degree of reading interference that takes place during this type of activity. The negative research evidence and the discussion of it already presented suggest that reading interference during this type of activity is not a major problem. However, since the research has not provided a detailed analysis over time of this type of activity, this source of interference cannot be ruled out completely.

The second type of activity that children engage in when learning to read provides a more promising site for reading interference. This activity involves what is usually thought of as direct instruction. It consists of a teacher instructing or guiding a child or group of children in some reading-related activity. The medium for this activity is spoken language, and the activity involves a language interchange between teacher and child or children. I would like to suggest that what takes place during this activity is a major determinant of the degree of reading skill that Black children develop. The study of the language interchange during this activity should provide important information about the reasons Black children have so much difficulty learning to read and about the role that their dialect plays in this difficulty.

A Linguistic and Sociolinguistic Framework for Studying Classroom Interaction

The recent research in linguists and sociolinguistics provides a useful framework for analyzing the interaction that takes place during classroom reading instruction. The theory of speech acts focuses on the effects that utterances produce. In this theory a distinction is made between the propositional content of an utterance (its literal meaning) and its elocutionary force (its intended effect on others). These two aspects often differ. For example, a statement by a teacher to children like, "We don't sit on the tables," has a literal meaning related to the fact that certain people don't sit on tables. its elocutionary force is that of a request or order not to sit on the tables. The interpretation of speech acts is dependent on shared background information, shared principles of cooperative conversation (Grice, 1975), and the ability of the learner to make inferences (Searle, 1975).

Gumperz (1976, in press) and Gumperz and Herasimchuk (1973) have built upon the theory of speech acts by proposing the notion of situated meaning. The situated meaning of an utterance is the speaker's intent in a particular context. Context includes the speaker's perception of the social situation and social relations, the type of speech activity, and the relation of the utterance to the utterances surrounding it and to the discourse as a whole. The comprehension of the situated meaning of an utterance is dependent on the interpretation of its literal content and the use of metacommunicative cues— that is, contextualization cues that signal the meaning in a particular social situation. Some contextualization cues that have been identified include intonation, code switching, stress, choice of lexical items and syntactic structure, rhythm, loudness and softness, and utterance-sequencing strategies. Thus, effective communication involves interpretation of the situated meaning of messages, which is in turn dependent on the proper interpretation of the literal meaning and the contextualization cues. The type of communicative strategies employed and the meaning of contextualization cues are largely matters of social convention. Thus, as Gumperz (1976) explained it, shared communicative background experiences are a major determinant of communicative strategy that includes the use and interpretation of contextualization cues: "Since the conventions governing the interpretation of contextualization cues are not overtly verbalized, they must be learned indirectly through regular and direct associations with their uses. Understanding of contextualization cues is therefore in large part a matter of shared background, of similarity of past communicative experience and values [p. 284]." Since there are cultural differences in communicative background, there will be cultural differences in communicative strategies and in the interpretation of the situated meaning of passages. This could lead to miscommunication between members of different cultural groups. In this way, cultural differences can cause miscommunication.

The problems that Black children encounter when learning to read in school may be, in part at least, the result of miscommunications of situated meanings between teacher and student that result from not sharing a communicative background.

Reading Interference and Classroom Interaction

One obvious way to study the problem of miscommunication is to examine classroom interaction during reading instruction. Piestrup (1973) conducted one of the only studies that looked at the language interchange during reading instruction of Black children. She observed and tape-recorded the reading instruction in 14 Black inner-city first-grade classrooms. She focused on episodes where dialect usage occurred during reading instruction, as well as episodes where other language instruction took place. She found teacher-style differences in handling of Black children's language, and these differences were reflected in some differences in reading scores among classrooms. These findings must be treated cautiously, because the children in the classrooms were not equated in ability; so that differences in end-of-year reading scores among classrooms may be due to differences in initial ability rather than to influences of teacher style. The episodes Piestrup described are the most important aspect of the study. The episodes involving dialect usage provide the data from which some clues to the mechanisms of interference may be inferred. The remainder of this chapter is devoted to an analysis of one of these episodes.

Reading Interference Episode.   In this episode, children are seated around a large table, reading sentences printed on long manila strips. Each child has a printed sentence that is large enough for the group to read (Piestrup, 1973):

1. Teacher (T) This one, (C₁). This way, (C₁). Come on you're right here. Hurry up.
2. C₁ /dey/
3. T Get your finger out of your mouth.
4. C₁ call (child continues without hesitation)
5. T Start again.
6. C₁ /dey/ call, What is it? What is it?
7. T What's this word? (pointing out the word "They")
8. C₂ /dey/
9. C₁ /dæt/
10. T *What* is it? (contrastive stress on "What")
11. C₃ /dæt/
12. C₂ /dey/
13. C₁ /dey/
14. T Look at my tongue. *They.* (stress on "th")
15. C₁ They
16. T They. Look at my tongue. (between her teeth)
17. C₁ /they/ (between /ᵹ ey/ and /dey/ but closer to /dey/)
18. T That's right. Say it again.
19. C₁ /they/ (between /ᵹ ey/ and /dey/ but closer to /dey/)
20. T They. O.K. Pretty good. O.K. ... C₁ [p. 54–55].

The discussion that follows is speculative in nature and is meant to be suggestive and provocative of further research rather than definitive. The discussion and conclusions are limited by the unavailability of the nonverbal information communicated in the episodes, and the inability to question the participants about the cues used and their intentions inevitably leads to ambiguity. Gumperz (1976) has proposed a questioning strategy to be employed with participants in a conversation that will help reduce these ambiguities. There is also the problem that the theory of situated meaning is still evolving and has not been worked out in detail. Thus, its application in any verbal interchange leaves room for different interpretations. Furthermore, the generality of the conclusions is limited by the sample of teachers that Piestrup studied, since there is no information about their representativeness.

The crux of the communicative problem in this episode appears to be the fact that the participants do not share background knowledge about standard English and Black dialect pronunciation, and the teacher employs unsuccessful verbal strategies for eliciting the response that she wants. The episode begins with C_1 in Line 2 pronouncing the word *they* in a manner consistent with his own dialect, indicating successful recognition of the word. The child's definition of the reading task at this point in the episode is to correctly recognize and pronounce the words in his own dialect. by his definition of the task, he is successfully accomplishing it in a way that is consistent with his communicative background. The teacher's definition of the task is similar to that of the child's, but it is different in one crucial way. For her, the task is also to recognize and pronounce the word, but the pronunciation must be in standard English. In the first part of the episode, it is not clear whether she believes that correct recognition of words in reading is only indicated by standard English pronunciation or whether she is consciously attempting to teach standard English pronunciation as a part of the reading task. The rest of this episode can be seen as an unsuccessful attempt by the teacher, through the use of communicative strategies, to get the child to adopt her definition of the task.

The child's first word in Line 2 does not fully conform to the teacher's definition of the task. To get him to adopt her definition of the task, she says in Line 3, "Get your finger out of your mouth." On one hand, this is a command to the child to take his finger away from his mouth. On the other hand, it may also indicate that the child has made a mistake in pronouncing the word due to his finger being in his mouth. It is also probably a command to go back and "correct" the word to standard English pronunciation. C_1 in Line 4 fails to interpret the situated meaning of the teacher's utterance and continues reading. In Line 5 the teacher interrupts the child's reading again with the statement, "Start again." The utterance is a command to start reading the sentence again. The situated meaning is a command to correct his "mistake." The child fails again to respond to the situated meaning but responds only to the literal meaning, and in Line 6 he attempts to read the full sentence without correcting the "mistake."

In both the teacher's utterances, the contextualization cues are lexical, and the child fails to respond appropriately to them and fails to get the situated meaning of the utterances. This failure to interpret the situated meaning of these utterances may be due to his failure to correctly interpret the contextualization cue that in the school situation—"Start again" and "Get your finger out of your mouth"—means you have made a mistake and you must correct it. But even if he has interpreted the contextualization cues correctly and understands that he made a mistake, his background knowledge does not enable him to correct it. Furthermore, the teacher, in her ignorance of his dialect, expects him to be able to hear and produce the distinction between /$\eth$/ and /d/ in initial position in words; whereas the fact that he is a Black dialect speaker makes this difficult if not impossible. The fact that later on in the episode his presumably standard pronunciation in the teacher's eyes is closer to dialect than to standard supports the contention that the distinction is not in his repertoire. He also may not see its salience to reading. The fact that he makes no attempt to change his response, as he does later on in the episode in response to different contextualization cues, suggests that there is a problem interpreting these contextualization cues. In Line 7, the teacher changes her contextualization cue to a question—"What's this word?"—accompanied by a nonverbal cue—pointing. The situated meaning of the utterance is the same—that is, correct the mistake. However, here she is more specific in showing which word is to be corrected and in providing a redundant cue. C_1 correctly interprets the cue, as is shown by his changing his pronunciation of the word on which the teacher has focused. But he produces a different word, /dæt/, which indicates again his inability to produce the standard English pronunciation that the teacher expects. C_1's response, /dæt/, in Line 9 departs considerably from the actual printed text, and C_1 ignores the notion that words should fit into the context of a sentence. The teacher responds with the question in Line 10—"*What* is it?"—with contrastive stress on *what*. Here the contextualization cue is stress and intonation, indicating again that the response is wrong and should be corrected. C_1 correctly interprets the cue and changes his answer. Unfortunately, he does not produce the right answer because of his dialect. C_3 and C_2 also produce wrong answers because of their dialect. At this point in the episode, the children's definition of the task has shifted from one of reading to one of trying to guess what the teacher wants them to say. They have given up the reading task and switched to a guessing game. The rest of the episode turns into an unsuccessful lesson in standard English pronunciation in which the teacher eventually accepts as correct a pronunciation of *they* that is closer to Black dialect than standard English. It is not clear that the children have learned anything about reading or about standard English from this episode.

Another aspect of this episode that is of interest is the teacher's questioning strategy and, in particular, the utterances she uses to signal to C_1 that his response is incorrect and that he should correct it. She uses utterances such as; "Get your finger out of your mouth," "Start again," "What's this word?" and "What is it?" Other teachers on the Piestrup tapes us "Pardon me," "I can't hear you," and repetition of children's responses with questioning intonation. All these utterances that teachers use to correct children are characterized by their indirectness. They only indirectly tell the children what is wrong. This indirectness, which characterizes the episode under discussion and other episodes in the Piestrup data, often results in children not producing the "right" answer-that is, the answer the teacher wants. The indirectness may cause communication problems in the following ways. Indirectness is an effective strategy when there is a great deal of shared backround knowledge. In the case of Black children, there is probably less shared background knowledge than teachers assume, because in addition to adult–child differences, there are cultural differences in communicative background experiences.[3] When shared background knowledge is missing or low, then the child must rely more heavily on contextualization cues to draw inferences about the situated meaning. There also may be cultural and adult–child differences in the selection and use of contextualization cues (Gumperz, 1976). In addition, it has been pointed out that indirectness is not very useful when new information is being conveyed, and instruction in school often presumably involves new information (Cook–Gumperz, 1976). In everyday conversation, where there is a great deal of indirectness, when listeners do not understand the meaning of an indirect speech act, they can ask the speaker to explain in a more direct may. In the tapes under study, this does not happen very often. It may be that it is not encouraged or accepted in school discourse. If this is the case, then the children are put at a further disadvantage in interpreting indirectness than they would be in everyday conversation, because they cannot use their normal "repair" strategies when they do not understand something. Finally, indirectness often leads to a series of questions when the first question is not answered correctly. The simple length of the interchange may increase the probability that the children will be distracted from the original task.

The issue of the use of indirectness by teachers is particularly important because teachers are taught to use strategies that require students to draw inferences and work things out for themselves. Indirectness is a widely used way of accomplishing this. If further research bears out some of the foregoing speculation, then important implications for teacher training could be drawn.

This episode suggests some of the ways in which Black children's dialect may interfere with learning to read. The lack of shared knowledge between teacher and child about dialect, the children's problems with interpreting contextualization cues, and the teachers' indirect teaching strategies all combine to distract the child from the reading task. In other episodes, the children are not distracted from the reading task as completely as in the

---

[3]The miscommunication problems described here are not limited to White teachers and Black students. Black teachers can have the same types of communication problems with Black students, because they often have the same standard English expectations that White teachers have and because they may be ignorant of the particular features of Black dialect.

episode discussed. Reading simply gets defined as the production of pronunciations that no one uses. In one episode, for example, children are made to pronounce the word *pond* as pond $+/\wedge/$ by a teacher attempting to get them to produce the final consonant. Thus, reading becomes a strange activity that differs substantially from everyday language use.

Whether the sources of reading interference discussed in the preceding section are prevalent enough or important enough to account for the magnitude of the reading failure of Black children must remain and open question until more research has been conducted. My guess is that dialect is only part of the problem. There are other differences between various aspects of Black children's culture and the school culture that could lead to interference with learning to read. There are peer-group influences (Lewis, 1970), audience participation expectations (Abrahams & Gay, 1972; Kochman, 1971), turn-taking rules, and nonverbal communication strategies (Johnson, 1971) in Black culture that may conflict with the instructional situation in schools. There is also teachers' failure to build on modes of communication that are specific to Black culture such as verbal play and the emphasis on form rather than content (Kochman,1969). All these factors, including dialect, when added to a more adequate knowledge of the psychological processes involved in learning to read than we presently possess, could go a long way toward explaining and remedying the reading problem of Black children. The research must have its main focus on the classroom and on the description and analysis of how these factors influence Black children's learning

As far as reading instruction is concerned, there should be a shift of emphasis away from instructional materials and to attempts to change teachers' strategies for teaching Black children that take into account their language and cultural differences. Unfortunately, it is not clear at the present time what teachers should be taught, since we do not have a very clear idea of the sources of interference. Nor do we have a very detailed idea of what teachers are presently doing. Research that provides detailed descriptions of classroom instruction will provide some of this information. Working with teachers in describing and analyzing classroom episodes such as those contained in the Piestrup study may provide a good starting point for our efforts to change teachers' strategies for teaching for teaching Black children.

ACKNOWLEDGMENTS

The author is grateful to John Gumperz and Jenny Cook–Gumperz for the generous amount of time they spent with him explaining the sociolinguistic concepts employed in this chapter. He takes full responsibility, however, for any misinterpretations of these concepts contained in this chapter.

REFERENCES

Abrahams, R., & Gay G. Black culture in the classroom. In R. D. Abrahams & R. C. Troika (Eds.), *Language and cultural diversity in American education*. Englewood Cliffs, N.J.: Prentice-Hall, 1972.

Baratz,J. Teaching reading in an urban Negro school system. In J. Baratz & R. Shuy (Eds.), *Teaching Black children to read.* Washington, D.C.: Center for Applied Linguistics ,1969.

Baratz,J. *A review of research on the relationship of Black English to reading.* Paper presented at the meeting of the International Reading Association, Atlantic City, New Jersey, May 1971.

Cook–Gumperz, J. Personal communication, April 1976.

Goodman, K. S. Dialect barriers to reading comprehension. *Elementary English,* 1965, *42* 639–643.

Grice, H. P. Logic and coversation. In P. Cole & J. Morgan (Eds.), *Syntax and semantics.* New York: Academic Press, 1975.

Gumperz, J. J. Language, communication, and public negotiation. In P. Sandoz (ED.), *Antropology and the public interest: Fieldwork and theory.* New York: Academic Press, 1976.

Gumperz, J. J. The sociolinguistics of interpersonal comunication. New York: Academic Press, in press.

Gumperz, J., & Herasimchuk, E. Conversational analysis of social meaning: A study of classroom interaction. *Report of the Twenty-Third Roundtable Meeting on Linguistics and Language.* Washington, D.C. Georgetown University Press, 1973.

Johnson, K. Black kinesics-Some nonverbal communication patterns in the Black culture. *Florida FL Reporter,* 1971,*9,* 17–20; 57.

Kochman, T. Reading, culture and personality. *Florida FL Reporter,* 1969,*7,* 24–26; 49.

Kochman, T. Cross-cultural communication: Contrasting perspectives, conflicting sensibilities. *Florida FL Reporter,* 1971,*9,* 3–16; 53–55.

Labov, W. A. Some sources of reading problems for Negro speakers of non-standard English. In A. Frazier (Ed.), *New directions in elementary English.* Champaign, Ill.: National Council of Teachers of English, 1967.

Labov, W. A. The logic of nonstandard English. *Florida FL Reporter,* 1969, *7,* 60–74.

Labov, W. A. The reading of the -ed suffix. In H. Levin & J. P. Williams (Eds.), *Basic studies on reading.* New York: Basic Books, 1970.

Lewis, L. Culture and social interaction in the classrom: An ethnographic report (Working paper No. 8). Berkeley: University of California, Language-Behavior Research Laboratory, 1970.

Marwit, W., & Newman, G. Black and White children's comprehension of standard and nonstandard English passages. *Journal of Educational Psychology,* 1974, *66,* 329–332.

Mathewson, G. *The effects of attitudes upon comprehension of dialect folktales.* Unpublished doctoral dissertation, University of California, Berkeley, 1973.

Melmed, P. J. Black English phonology: The question of reading interference. *Monographs of the Language Behavior Research Laboratory,* University of California, Berkeley, 1971 (No. 1.).

Nolen, P. Reading nonstandard dialect materials: A study of grades two and four. *Child Development,* 1972, *43,* 1092–1097.

Osterberg, T. *Bilingualism and the first school language.* Umea, Sweden: Vastenbottens Togckeri AB, 1961.

Piestrup, A. M. Black dialect interference and accommodation of reading in struction in first grade. *Monographs of the Language Bahavior Research Laboratory,* University of California, Berkeley, 1973 (No. 4).

Rentel, V., & Kennedy, J. Effects of pattern drill on the phonology, syntax, and reading achievement of rural Appalachian children. *American Educational Research Journal, 1972, 9* 87-100.

Ruddell, R. B. *An investigation of the effect of the similarity of oral and written patterns of language structure on reading comprehension.* Unpublished doctoral dissertation, University of Indiana, 1963.

Rystrom, R. Dialect training and reading: A further look. *Reading Research Quarterly, 1970, 5* 581-603.

Schaaf, E. *A study of Black English syntax and reading comprehension.* Unpublished master's thesis, Univesity of California, Berkeley, 1971.

Searle, J. Indirect speech acts. In P. Cole & J. Morgan (Eds.), *Syntax and semantics.* New York: Academic Press, 1975.

Simons, H. *Black dialect and reading interference: A review and critique of the research evidence.* Unpublished manuscript, 1971.

Simons, H. Black dialect phonology and work recognition. *Journal of Educactional Research,* 1974, *68* 67-70.

Simons, H,. & Johnson, K. Black English syntax and reading interference. *Research in the Teaching of English,* 1974, *8,* 339-358.

Sims, R. *A psycholinguistic description of miscues created by selected young readers during oral reading of text in Black dialect and standard English.* Unpublished doctoral dissertation, Wayne State University, 1972.

Stewart, W.A. On the use of Negro dialect in the teaching of reading. In J. Baratz & R. Shuy (eds.), *Teaching Black children to read.* Washington, D.C.: Center for Applied Linguistics, 1969.

Tatham, S. M. Reading comprehension of materials written with select oral language patterns: A study at grades two and four. *Reading Research Quarterly,* Spring 1970, *5* 402-426.

Walker, L. Newfoundland dialect interference in oral reading. *Journal of Reading Behavior,* 1975, *7* 61-78.

Wolfram, W. A. Sociolinguistic alternatives in teaching reading to nonstandard speakers. *Reading Research Quarterly,* 1970, *6* 9-33.

6 Reading and the Bilingual Child

Diana S. Natalicio
University of Texas at El Paso

HISTORICAL PERSPECTIVE

Until relatively recently, no special provisions were made in public schools for children from non-English-speaking backgrounds. Such children were totally immersed in an English language curriculum along with their native-English-speaking counterparts, and little or no recognition was given to their native language. In some cases, in fact, the use of the native language was actively discouraged by the imposition of disciplinary measures. This educational practice reflected the accepted social premise of the time—that all ethnic groups would blend into the great U.S. melting pot. The school experience was thought to be a crucial factor in integrating non-English-speaking children into the dominant culture, and an exclusively English-language-learning environment—yesterday's version of today's "total immersion" program—was thought to be the most efficient means of accomplishing this goal. Although thousands upon thousands of immigrant children were educated in such English language programs, success in reducing minority groups to a single "all-American" linguistic and cultural group appears to have been somewhat limited. Andersson and Boyer (1970) wrote:

> Immigrants to America did not cease being what they were and did not, except in rather superficial ways, become something different when they were naturalized as American citizens. Changes that occurred were far less extensive and less structural than they were believed to be. In most cases a bicultural style developed which enabled American and ethnic identities to coexist and influence each other over time [p. 3].

131

Despite the monolingual, monocultural orientation of most American schools, linguistic and cultural pluralism prevailed, sustained by early and more recent immigrant groups.

Bilingual education in the United States received its major impetus during the decade of the 1960s. A specific event helped to highlight the need: A large number of Cubans, many of them professionals, entered Florida, and suddenly thousands of Cuban children were enrolled in Florida schools. Special programs were seen as required, Cuban professionals were recruited to assist in the development of the programs, and the feasibility of bilingual education in the United States was demonstrated. The response was no doubt also due to the general sociopolitical climate in the 1960s. Arguments that non-English-speaking children were not faring well in our educational system, that they were dropping out at higher rates and earlier ages than their native-English-speaking counterparts, and that the school system's insensitivity to their native language and culture was primarily responsible found a receptive audience. In 1967 the Bilingual Education Act, designed to meet the needs of children from non-English-speaking backgrounds, was passed.

Since then, additional federal and state legislation has been passed, and judicial decisions have been rendered concerning linguistically different pupil populations. Most recently, the Office of Civil Rights of the Department of Health, Education and Welfare (HEW) issued a set of guidelines for schools to comply with the 1974 Supreme Court decision in the case of Lau v. Nichols, which requires school districts to provide equal educational opportunity for students from non-English-speaking backgrounds.[1] The guidelines require that school districts having 20 or more students from a single language background develop bilingual education programs.[2] HEW has estimated that between 1.8 and 2.5 million children in the United States should receive their initial schooling in bilingual programs. Bilingual education, once the lofty ideal of a few visionaries, is now an every day challenge to school districts throughout the country.

The educational system is suddenly under pressure to comply with new regulations, to prepare teachers, to identify appropriate pupil populations, to prepare teaching materials and methodologies, and to develop a philosophy of bilingual education upon which all of the aforementioned are to be based.

---

[1]The full text of the opinion of the Supreme Court, written by Justice William O. Douglas, appears in *The Linguistic Reporter,* 1974, *16(3),* 6–7.

[2]The guidelines are reproduced in their entirety in *The Linguistic Reporter,* 1975, *18(2),* 5–7. It should be noted that a recent (April 1976) memorandum distributed by the Office of Civil Rights of HEW attempts to clarify these guidelines. The result appears to be a relaxation of the requirements governing the implementation of bilingual education programs.

Without a tradition of bilingual schooling in the United States and lacking lead time to prepare for this educational revolution, it is no surprise that school districts were and are ill prepared and that little research has been conducted in the United States that bears directly on the major issues of educating children bilingually. (The limited research that is cited typically reports on experiences in other countries.) The result is that many of the basic principles guiding the development of bilingual education in the United States have been stated as axioms.

One such axiom, involving reading instruction, states that literacy should be achieved first in the child's native language. This is subsequently referred to as the *native language approach.* (This approach may be contrasted with the direct method where a second language is at least initially the primary language of instruction; children are introduced to reading through the second language and only after oral fluency is demonstrated.) Two standard works on bilingual education, *Bilingual Schooling in the United States* (Andersson & Boyer, 1970) and *A Handbook of Bilingual Education* (Saville & Troike, 1971), unequivocally support the native language approach. Referring to a 1953 UNESCO report, Andersson and Boyer stated, "Educators are agreed . . . that reading and writing in the first language should precede literacy in a second [p. 45]." Saville and Troike agreed, stating that "the child should begin reading in his dominant language [p. 50]." Such statements are extensively quoted and expanded on in bilingual education literature. So widely is this notion accepted, in fact, that to suggest that it may be open to question is to run the risk of being labeled confused, insensitive, ultraconservative, or even racist.

Cognizant of this risk, I attempt to examine critically some of the issues involved in teaching reading to bilingual children. I briefly examine research that appears to bear directly on the question of the priority of native language literacy, and I explore various issues that, although not explicitly articulated, appear to be closely tied to current policies and practices in bilingual education. Finally, I raise some practical questions concerning the implementation of native language literacy programs.

THE NATIVE LANGUAGE LITERACY AXIOM: RELEVANT RESEARCH

The native language literacy axiom appears to have been originally based on a widely accepted notion that reading should not be taught until oral fluency in a language is demonstrated. This notion has served as a basis for the sequencing of the four skills in foreign language instruction (i.e., understanding, speaking, reading, and writing). In the area of reading, it underlies arguments favoring instructional materials that relate closely to children's prior linguistic backgrounds, including the use of child-generated language experience materials. It is also fundamental to recommendations that dialect readers be prepared for those children whose dialects differ significantly from the standard written language.

Although there is considerable agreement that initial instruction in reading should occur only after a degree of oral language competence has been attained, accounts of Dick-and-Jane readers being thrust into the hands of native-Spanish-speaking first-grade pupils, who were not provided even minimal oral language instruction in English, are all too recent and too familiar. Proponents of bilingual education frequently cite such abuses in attempting to justify the native language literacy approach. Viewed from this perspective, the basis for many of the arguments in favor of native language literacy appears to be simply a rejection of admittedly improper pedagogical practices. It is unlikely that anyone would quarrel with this criticism. It is also clear, however, that advocates of the native language literacy approach cannot expect to base their arguments solely on negative evidence from poorly implemented direct method programs, because such claims are easily contested. Specialists in the area of English as a second language (ESL), for example, have challenged the categorical denunciation of direct method ESL programs contained in the Office of Civil Rights Guidelines for bilingual education (i.e., "since an ESL program does not consider the affective nor cognitive development of students...[it] is not appropriate," [OCR Sets Guidelines, 1975, p.6]). These ESL specialists point out that there have been many successful direct method ESL programs that they believe have considered both affective and cognitive development and that have carefully developed oral language skills prior to introducing reading (see Galvan, 1975).[3]

Stronger and more positive claims about the efficacy of the native language approach must be made. Saville and Troike (1971) attempted to strengthen their argument by stating that "the basic skills of reading transfer readily from one language to another [p. 50]." Gutierrez (1975) added, "children learn to read best through their native language. The decoding skills learned in Spanish will establish a firm base for the Spanish-speaking child and will transfer to the development of reading and writing skills in English without loss of time and energy [p. 5]." Unfortunately, these stronger claims are

---

[3]One must ask at this point what is meant by the suggestion that literacy approaches explicitly consider psychological variables such as the affective and cognitive development of students. To raise this question is not to deny the psychological impact on children of their educational experience but rather to make explicit the requirement that empirical evidence support any claim that one approach leads to greater psychological benefit than another. Without such evidence, arguments such as this one become meaningless exercises.

supported by little convincing research evidence. Even the most frequently cited study, Modiano's (1968) research in Chiapas, Mexico,[4] is, by the author's own admission, not a convincing demonstration of the superiority of the native language approach.

Briefly, Modiano compared Indian pupil achievement in two educational settings, a direct Spanish language approach in federal and state schools and a native language approach in Indian schools. Her results indicated that children taught Spanish reading after receiving native language reading instruction in the Indian schools scored higher on Spanish reading tests than did children taught exclusively in Spanish in the federal and state schools. But among with other problems the study (see Engle, 1975, pp. 297–298), Modiano's results were contaminated by the fact that the direct Spanish language instructional approach used in the federal and state schools was poorly implemented. Children in these schools were far from fluent in Spanish before reading instruction was begun, and Spanish language instruction was not systematic. As Engle (1975) concluded, "it is not surprising that [Modiano's] results suggest that the native language approach ... schools were superior. The study does not present a comparison of the good use of the direct method with the native language approach [p. 297]."

Other studies that purport to contrast the native language literacy approach with the direct method reveal highly contradictory results. The data do not provide a sound empirical basis for assertions about native language reading instruction in bilingual education programs in the United States. Engle (1975), in her excellent critical review of 24 studies related to the topic of medium of instruction in early school years for minority group children, concluded that the studies "varied in every conceivable way, and most provided no substantial evidence as to which approach is better [p. 320]." Among problems identified in these studies are the lack of information concerning the cognitive and psycholinguistic mechanism of transfer involved in learning to read a second language, the inadequacy of data concerning the political and cultural relationships between language groups that influence language acceptance, and the uneven quality of the educational programs studied.

A position favoring the native language approach is further complicated by the results of experimental bilingual programs in Canada, which appear to demonstrate the value of the direct method approach. The St. Lambert Project, begun in Montreal in 1965, exposed native-English-speaking children to a total-immersion, French language and literacy program during

---

[4]The fact that a study published in 1968 continues to be the most widely cited in support of the native language literacy approach, in spite of the tremendous growth in the number of bilingual education programs in the United States since then, attests to the paucity of relevant research in this area.

the first years of school. Test results indicated that Anglophones achieved a high degree of fluency in French and that their English language skills compared favorably with those of English-speaking children in regular English programs (Lambert & Tucker, 1972). Because the original subjects in the experimental program were middle-and upper middle-class children volunteered for participation by their parents, there existed the possibility that English language literacy instruction was provided at home (although program personnel discouraged it), and another study was conducted with lower middle-and upper lower-class children (Tucker, Lambert, & d'Anglejan, 1973). Results obtained with this subject population were highly similar to those reported earlier, but it is important to note that the subjects continued to be volunteers. Subsequent studies in Ottawa (Barik & Swain, 1975) have revealed similar results.

Cautiously interpreted, these results appear to indicate that a carefully implemented direct method approach enables children to successfully learn a second language and to transfer reading skills acquired in the second language to the native language. The argument that children learn best through their native language would appear to be weakened by the results of the Canadian experiments.

Endorsement for English immersion programs in the United States based on the Canadian model (e.g., Campbell, 1970) has not been forthcoming for several reasons. In the first place, the bilingual education context in the United States differs significantly from that in Canada. Canada is officially a bilingual nation; the United States is not. Subjects in the Canadian experiments have been members of the dominant group; bilingual education in the United States has typically been viewed as a compensatory program for minority-group children. Finally, participants in the Canadian experiments have been volunteers whose parents encouraged their participation; bilingual program participants in the United States have been selected on the basis of surname or, more recently, performance on language diagnostic measures. It is not at all clear whether the success attained in the Canadian context would be realized here given these significant differences.

On the one hand, then, research studies supporting claims about the superiority of the native language approach are limited in both number and quality. On the other, the carefully documented research demonstrating the success of the direct method approach in Canada may not be directly relevant to bilingual education contexts in the United States, except perhaps for majority-group volunteers. It may be concluded that most previous research on how best to teach reading to children in bilingual settings provides few answers, primarily because this research was conducted in settings that differ markedly from those in the Uninted States and because much of this research was beset with serious methodological weaknesses (e.g., lack of proper controls on variables such as teacher competencies and program quality and design problems resulting in a Hawthorne effect in the experimental samples). Clearly, there is a need for carefully designed and conducted research into those issues that are basic to the teaching of reading to bilingual children in the U.S. context. Two such issues underlying native language literacy programs—namely, the specification of the native language and the transfer of reading skills—are considered in the following sections.

SPECIFICATION OF THE NATIVE LANGUAGE

One of the first issues with which the proponents of native language literacy must deal is the specification of the native, first, or dominant language of the child who is to be taught to read. Remarks here are limited to Spanish-speaking populations and specifically to Mexican–American children, but there are undoubtedly parallels among all minority-group populations, including speakers of Black English (cf. Melmed, 1973).

Much of the prior research in native language literacy has been conducted among subject populations who appear to be more linguistically homogeneous than are most minority groups in the United States. The geographical or social isolation that characterized some of these research populations (e.g., Indians in Modiano's Chiapas study) is not typically present in the United States. Even recent immigrants are immediately exposed to the cultural and linguistic features of the English-speaking environment that have permeated not only the speech of most residents but also all forms of media. Fifteen minutes of Spanish language radio broadcasting in the El Paso/Juarez area revealed, among many others, the following examples of English integration: "La funeraria X le ofrece servicio personal basado en interés; "La instalación es obtenible a bajo precio"; "X abre sus puertas a las cinco con happy hour hasta las diez"; and "Son veinte minutos después de las dos P.M."[5] Nash's descriptions of "Spanglish" (1970) and "Englañol" (1971) in Puerto Rico reveal similar phenomena.

Terms such as *native Spanish-speaking* and *bilingual* are often used loosely to refer to a group of children whose linguistic backgrounds and language competencies may vary considerably.[6] (It is interesting to note the shifts in terminology, from "Spanish-surnamed" to "Spanish-speaking" or "bilingual" to the more recent "Spanish-heritage," that have characterized efforts to identify the population in question. Not one of these labels is entirely

---

[5]For the benefit of those not familiar with Spanish, these examples involve the use of both English lexicon (e.g., "happy hour" and "p.m.") and English syntactical patterns.

[6]The title of this chapter provides an excellent example of the problem. *Bilingual* is used to refer to a broad range of linguistic competencies, from monolingualism in a language other than English to fluent bilingualism in both English and another language.

satisfactory, largely because of the heterogeneity of the group, i.e., some Spanish-surnamed are not Spanish-speaking, some Spanish-speaking are not bilingual, and so on.) In the first place, there are three principal dialect origins of Spanish spoken in the United States: Mexican, Cuban, and Puerto Rican. Discrepancies between these dialects and standard written Spanish-on the phonological, grammatical, and lexical levels—are similar to those observed between regional American dialects of English and the standard written form of the language. Monolingual children in Spanish-speaking countries have successfully dealt with these dialect variations, as have their English-speaking counterparts in the United States. Spanish dialect variations in the United States are, however, much more complex than their mere geographical origins suggest. Differences among and within these three dialect groups have been heightened by their existence in an English language context. Mexican–Americans in Los Angeles speak a dialect considerably different from that spoken in New Mexico and from that spoken in South Texas. Although all these dialects have their origins in Mexican Spanish, they, differ in pronunciation, grammar, and lexicon. The extent to which English is integrated into these dialects and the specific lexical and grammatical features of English that are integrated vary from place to place as a result of multiple variables in each language contact setting. For example, Mexican–American girls in El Paso may celebrate their fifteenth birthday with *una fiesta de quinceañera* whereas their counterparts in south-central Texas may have *una fiesta de* "sweet fifteen." *Grocería* is commonly used for "grocery store" in one location and is ridiculed in another. Archaic Spanish forms such as *asina (así)* are used regulary in one area and not in another. Social variations also occur; for example, some Chicano activists use the term *carnal* for "brother" whereas more traditional Mexican–Americans do not (cf. Elias–Olivares, 1976).

Language attitudes also significantly affect the language each native-Spanish-speaking child brings to school. In the same neighborhood, some families continue (consciously or unconsciously) to speak a dialect of Mexican Spanish. Others speak some Spanish and some English, depending on the topic and the presence of certain family members (e.g., grandparents) and outsiders. Others freely mix English and Spanish within the same conversation and even the same sentence; for example, "Her leg, *estaba asi,* sticking out." Still other families make a very concerted effort to use only English, which in their view will better prepare their children for school and later life. A recent conversation with two speech therapists in the El Paso area is illustrative of this wide variation. In attempting to devise a diagnostic language test for "Spanish-speaking" preschool children, these therapists' frustration had become intense, because although approximately the same age and from the same area, they were unable to agree on labels for some very common objects that were to be used as test stimuli. They represent, in my experience, the rule rather than the exception. It is not at all uncommon to enter a first-grade classroom where there are wide discrepancies in the prior language experience of the pupils in the class.

In the absence of investigations related to teaching Spanish-dialect-speaking childen to read in standard Spanish, it is perhaps appropriate to review the extensive literature concerning the question of Black dialect interference in learning to read standard English (see Shuy, 1973; Somervill, 1975). Some researchers (e.g., Baratz, 1973) argue that the significance of Black dialect differences on both phonological and grammatical levels requires the development of specialized dialect reading materials. Others, however, have concluded that dialect variation on the phonological level has little disruptive effect on the reading process and that dialect involvement on the morphemic and structural levels is extremely limited (Burke, 1973). Regardless of the outcome of these arguments, important questions are being raised concerning possible Black dialect interference in learning to read standard English. The same questions should be investigated when dialects of Spanish are the issue; lexical variation alone strongly suggests that dialect interference in learning to read standard Spanish may occur.

Those who argue for teaching reading first in Spanish—citing the psychological, social, linguistic, and pedagogical advantages to initial reading in the native language—often seem to ignore the wide divergence between the Spanish in written materials and that spoken by the children for whom the native language approach is recommended. The issue is not simply one of a native language approach versus a direct English Approach; the dialect factor, widely discussed in terms of Black English speakers, may be of greater relevance within the context of teaching reading to Spanish-speaking children.

TRANSFER OF READING SKILLS

A second issue that must be dealt with by proponents of native language literacy in bilingual education programs involves the transfer of reading skills from one language to another. Although the successful acquisition of reading skills in two languages revealed in the Canadian immersion and some other bilingual programs appears to provide some support for the claim that these skills transfer quite readily (Gutierrez, 1975; Saville & Troike, 1971), it is not at all clear how such transfer takes place or what factors are relevant to its occurrence.

It seems reasonable to assume that the nature of the two languages involved in the transfer and the specific characteristics of the writing systems of the two languages play some role in the ease with which transfer takes place. Languages that present to the reader markedly different cues on the morphological and syntactical levels might be expected to present greater obstacles to transfer than those languages that are more closely related. If such differences are also accompanied by significant differences in the writing systems (e.g., ideographic vs. alphabetic, or even Cyrillic vs. Roman alphabetic), difficulties might be expected to be even greater. The difficulties I encountered as an adult attempting to learn to read Swahili and Russian after successful experiences with English and several Romance languages attest to the importance of both linguistic and writing system differences in transferring reading skills from one language to another. It appears that if claims about the transfer of reading skills are to be made, some consideration must be given to the similarities and differences between the languages in question and their writing systems. Such claims probably can most safely be made about languages that are closely related, but even here, caution must be exercised. Considering the close relationship between Black and standard English, for example, the recommendation that transitional readers be used to facilitate the transfer from dialect readers to standard English written material (see Ching. 1976, p. 8) suggests that transfer is far from automatic.

Related to the claim about the transfer to reading skills is the notion that some languages provide for easier reading acquisition than others. It is argued that this advantage should be exploited in teaching children to read. Thus, Saville and Troike (1971) stated:

> The child who learns to read first in Spanish or Navajo may have, in fact, a definite advantage over the child who must learn first in English. The writing system of English is not regular, and children must learn that a single sound may be spelled in many different ways. The writing system of Spanish and that which has been developed for Navajo are very regular, with close correspondence between sounds and letters. The child's ability to recognize the relationship between sound and symbol is a major factor in his [or her] success in initial reading instruction [p. 50].

Thus, it is argued that since transfer occurs almost automatically, reading instruction is facilitated by learning in a language that is more regular in its sound–symbol correspondences. To put this argument in perspective, it is interesting to examine more closely specific features of the Spanish writing system (a "regular" system).

A truly regular writing system would involve a consistent one-to-one correspondence between sounds and symbols. Nuclear vowels in Spanish do bear such a correspondence. Diphthongs, on the other hand, do not; for example, *hay* (there is) versus *aire* (air). Consonants vary considerably. The Spanish writing system includes both a *b* and a *v* that correspond to the same sound; that is, the initial sounds in *beso* (kiss) and *vez* (time) are pronounced the same. The *h* in words such as *hombre* (man) and *hora* (hour) represents no sound. In Spanish, /s/ may be represented by *s* (*sábado*/Saturday), *c* (*cielo*/sky), or *z* (*zapato*/shoe); /k/ by *c* (*casa*/house) or *qu* (*quince*/fifteen); /y/ by *i* (*hielo*/ice), *y* (*yo*/I), or *ll* (*calle*/street); /h/ by *x* (*México*), *j* (*hijo*/son), or *g* (*gente*/people); and so on. Learning to read in Spanish involves learning the rules for mapping these spellings to the sounds they represent.

Transferring reading skills from Spanish to English involves the readjustment of the sound–symbol correspondences characteristic of Spanish to those of English. Thus, for example, the letter *h*, which in Spanish is always mute, is sometimes mute in English, as in *hour*, but may also represent an /h/ in words such as *hat* and *her*. The *ll*, which in Spanish corresponds to /y/, typically represents /l/ in English as in *bullet* or *pulling*. The letters *b* and *v* which correspond to a single sound in Spanish, represent two distinct sounds in English. Finally and perhaps most important for the learner, the regular correspondences between vowel symbols and sounds in Spanish must be adjusted to a variety of vowel sound–symbol correspondences in English. Thus, in addition to acquiring a new phonological system in oral English (new vowel and consonant sounds in new positions and combinations), the native-Spanish-speaking child who learns to read initially in Spanish will also have to learn new sound–symbol correspondences as he or she moves from reading in Spanish to literacy in English. Considerable research is required before a claim can be made that a language with relatively more regular sound–symbol correspondences facilitates the acquisition of reading skills and the subsequent transfer of these skills to reading in another (less regular) language. Such research would have to involve a rank ordering of languages on a scale of orthographic "regularity" as well as a matrix of orthographic correspondences (both regularities and irregularities) among languages.

Furthermore, learning grapheme–sound correspondences is only one aspect of learning to read. Reviewing approaches to beginning reading instruction, Weber (1970) pointed out that "grammatical structure as an aspect of context has hardly been considered in regard to reading despite its central position in the language as the vehicle for semantic as well as extralinguistic content and despite the well-known restrictions on the occurrence of words in sentences that grammar entails [p. 147]." Levin and Kaplan's (1970) studies of experienced readers demonstrate the effects of grammatical constraints on reading—namely, that such constraints enable the reader to formulate correct hypotheses about what will follow. "When the prediction is confirmed, the material covered by that prediction can be more easily processed and understood [p. 132]." The transfer of reading skills from one language to another must necessarily involve such higher-level constraints in both languages. Claims about the ease with which the transfer of reading skills occurs—especially those that appear to rest primarily (or even exclusively) on the regularity of given orthographic systems—are clearly overstated. The studies reviewed in Engle (1975) reveal that almost no consideration has been given to the identification of those specific aspects of reading that should transfer from learning to read in one language to learning to read in another.

The transfer process has been of considerable interest to researchers in the area of second language acquisition. Recent research suggests an underlying linguistic system in second language speech, an "interlanguage," that is at least partially distinct from both native and target languages (Selinker, 1972). Interlanguage involves strategies or cognitive activities relating to the processing of second language data in the attempt to express meaning. Although the emphasis of this work has been on language production, it seems reasonable to consider the possibility that a similar underlying interlingual system may be involved in learning to derive meaning from written materials in a second language. Related here is Kolers' (1970) research into the coding of isolated words and the reading of bilingual connected discourse by skilled French–English bilingual readers, where it is suggested that "words are perceived and remembered preferentially in terms of their meanings and not in terms of their appearance or sounds [p. 111]." Becoming a bilingual reader requires more than the mere acquisition of new grapheme–sound correspondences, just as becoming a bilingual speaker involves more than learning new sounds and a new vocabulary.

The present state of our knowledge about second language acquisition and the acquisition of reading skills in a first language is such that we can only speculate about how reading skills transfer from one language to another. Brown (1970) suggested that a child "operates on speech with a large number of effective heuristics. The majority of these, with accommodations for the visual medium, are probably applicable also in reading [p. 186]." Since we are only now beginning to have an idea of the nature of these heuristics, claims about how they transfer from one language to another are probably premature.

ALTERNATE APPROACHES TO READING INSTRUCTION

In the light of the historical background of reading in bilingual education and the paucity of research directly relevant to the basic issues just discussed, it is interesting to consider some practical implications of three possible alternatives to reading instruction in bi- or multilingual settings. (It is noted that no mention is made of the "common core" or "neutral" approach suggested for speakers of Black English, where an attempt is made to minimize dialect and cultural differences in reading materials. In addition to the problem of the awkward and unnatural product that is likely to result from such an effort in one language, there is obviously no way that the differences between two languages can be "minimized"; that is, there is no common core, except perhaps for a few cognate words.)

Reading in the Standard Native Language

Reading instruction in bilingual settings may be introduced in the standard native language, for example, standard Spanish. As was indicated earlier, instruction in standard Spanish as a second dialect is probably a necessary prerequisite for most Spanish-dialect speaking children if standard Spanish reading instruction is to be seriously considered (see Barker, 1971, pp. iii–iv). Although the dialects of some children reveal a rather well-developed phonological, grammatical, and lexical control of the standard dialect, others show considerable deviation from the standard; and still others, a high level of English integration on both grammatical and lexical levels.

Teaching a second dialect, once highly recommended as the solution to preparing speakers of Black English to read in standard English, has proved to be a much more difficult task than was initially anticipated. Although some researchers (e.g., Venezky & Chapman, 1973) continue to recommend standard-English-as-a-second-dialect training for nonstandard-dialect-speaking children, others (e.g., Kochman, 1969; Wolfram, 1970) question whether such training should or even can be accomplished. Factors that appear to be relevant to the difficulties encountered in second-dialect training include peer-group pressure on the language of children in the initial school years, broad sociocultural pressures against standard language teaching in some minority-group settings, and—as verbal learning research suggests— the difficulty of learning highly similar material.

Teaching Standard Spanish as a second dialect will inevitably involve many of the same problems encountered in attempting to teach standard English as a second dialect. Despite the considerable time and expertise that have been applied to such efforts in English, results indicate that we have been "grossly inefficient in teaching standard English at any level" (Shuy, 1973, p. 13). Although there is very little direct experience on which to base predictions of success in teaching standard Spanish as a second dialect, the English example does not make such efforts appear promising.

The teacher variable seems particularly significant in the case of Spanish. Most teachers who have been abruptly drafted into teaching in bilingual education programs on the elementary school level have little or no experience in teaching standard Spanish. (A few may have limited experience in the area of teaching Spanish to speakers of English.) Many teachers who have become involved in bilingual education programs are themselves native speakers of various dialects of Spanish, but few have had formal training in the standard language. Some read standard Spanish only with great difficulty. Teachers who are aware of their limited competence in the standard language are naturally insecure when expected to teach it, and classroom experiences often contribute to this insecurity. (For example, I once observed in a bilingual classroom a bulletin board containing pictures of common objects and their Spanish names. Next to a picture of a toy appeared the label *hugete*. Shortly thereafter, an alert first grader remarked to the teacher that in his book the word for "toy" looked different. The teacher then realized that the correct spelling of this word was *juguete*.) The situation is even more complicated in bilingual classrooms where a monolingual English-speaking teacher is assisted by a Spanish-speaking aide whose formal education may be quite limited. Teaching standard Spanish under conditions such as these is not likely to be successful.

In-service training of teachers in standard Spanish might appear to be the answer, and such training is being conducted in some bilingual endorsement and certification programs. The difficulties encountered in attempting to teach standard English should be borne in mind, however, when contemplating the preparation of teachers to teach standard Spanish as a second dialect. If teaching a second dialect is indeed as difficult as it appears to be, training in standard Spanish may create teacher expectations that will never be realized. (On the other hand, an indirect benefit of such instruction may be a greater sensitivity on the part of teachers to the problems encountered by the nonstandard dialect speakers in their classrooms. Such increased teacher sensitivity is strongly recommended by most specialists in the area of education for the linguistically different, regardless of the divergence in their opinions about how such education should be carried out.)

If oral language training in Spanish must precede the introduction of reading, there will of course be some delay in introducing reading. Minority-group parents, many of whom are eager to see their children aspire to higher educational goals than those they themselves were able to attain, would probably be as intolerant of delayed reading instruction as middle-class parents have proven to be (Baratz, 1973). Furthermore, it is not at all clear that parents support an early school emphasis on Spanish. Anecdotal evidence from interactions with school administrators and teachers in the Southwest suggests that at least some Mexican–American parents feel that the school's responsibility is to teach their children to speak and read "good" English; Spanish, irrespective of variety, is not considered to be a crucial component of their children's education. (It should be noted that schools tend to reinforce such attitudes by phasing out the use of Spanish language materials after the initial school years. Thus, although it is claimed that learning to read in Spanish in the first grade offers long-range educational benefits, curricula from the middle-school years onward contain no application of Spanish literacy skills.)

Finally, teaching children a second dialect of Spanish, if indeed possible, must inevitably be accompanied or followed by instruction in English. Thus, during the initial years of classroom instruction, Spanish-dialect-speaking children must learn both a second dialect and a second language. We know very little about how second language and second dialect acquisition occur (Ervin–Tripp, 1970), but there is some recent evidence to suggest that the optimum age for second language learning is not between 4 and 10 years of age. Ervin–Tripp (1974) found that older children learned number,gender, and syntax more rapidly than did younger children. Initial pronunciation and retention of vocabulary were found to increase with age by Politzer and Weiss (1969). Research conducted by Fathman (1975) revealed that preteen children appeared to be more successful at learning phonology, but children betweeen 11 and 15 years of age were more successful in learning grammar. Engle (1975), citing research conducted by Stern in Sweden and Lavallee in Switzerland, suggested that the initial school years (6 to 8 years of age) may in fact be the least appropriate for teaching a second language; children younger than 6 and older than 10 years of age appear to show greater motivation and achievement. The advisability of attempting to teach a second dialect and a second language (and literacy in both) during the early school years must thus be seriously questioned.[7]

Spanish Dialect Readers

A second possible approach to the introduction of reading to native-Spanish-speaking children involves the use of Spanish dialect readers. Experience with Black dialect readers should be indicative of the problems that might result from attempting to pursue this approach to beginning reading instruction (see Baratz, 1973; Leaverton, 1973). The wide variations in Spanish dialects rule out the publication of a single U.S. Spanish dialect reader (cf. Fishbein, 1973). Questions concerning the use of English borrowings—such as *tichar* (from *teach*) and *huachar* (from *watch*)—would have to be dealt with as would nonstandard Spanish dialect forms such as *semos* (*somos*), *haiga* (*haya*), *suidad* (*ciudad*), and *aigre* (*aire*). If a dialect reader could be agreed on for one location, its acceptability in other areas would be unlikely. Teachers could of course construct ad hoc dialect readers using the language experience approach, but time constraints would undoubtedly prohibit widespread use of such teacher-made dialect materials. Some teachers might also be expected to react negatively to materials containing what they consider to be

---

[7]Examples of young children who successfuly learn two or more languages, often without apparent effort, probably do not provide strong counterevidence to this statement, just as preschool chilren who learn to read without formal instruction do not negate the need for attempts to improve the teaching of reading in our schools.

nonstandard or even incorrect Spanish. Parents, whose expectations of schools are high, might even be shocked to find "bad" Spanish in their children's school materials, and problems in community relations might result (cf. Baratz, 1973, p. 109). Finally, the apparently complex series of learning requirements involved in the transitions from Spanish dialect readers to standard Spanish readers and subsequently to standard English readers would seem to represent an extremely ambitious set of objectives for the initial years of schooling.

Teaching Reading in English

A third alternative to teaching reading to Spanish-dialect-speaking children is the direct method, where initial contact with reading is made in the second language, English. As was discussed earlier, French language programs in Canada that use this approach have proved to be highly successful. In such programs children are first introduced to oral language skills in the second language and fluency in the oral language is required before reading is introduced. Children are permitted to use their native language with each other and with their teacher during the first year of school; the teacher interacts with the children only in the second language, translating their questions and comments and responding to them exclusively in the target language. (It should be noted that this approach differs somewhat from earlier English immersion programs in the United States, where use of the native language was usually discouraged.)

The question of the appropriateness of teaching a second language to children in the initial years of schooling, mentioned earlier in connection with teaching standard Spanish as a second dialect, is relevant here. Although the results of the Canadian studies appear to indicate that the total immersion approach is highly successful in second language teaching at this age level, further research into the optimal age for second language acquisition, especially among minority-group children, is necessary before final conclusions can be drawn.

Also relevant here is the problem of delaying reading instruction until the direct method approach has successfully developed oral language competence in the children who are to be taught to read in a second language. Teacher and parental attitudes that evaluate the success of a school by how quickly children begin to read would require reshaping. Also relevant is the requirement in most school districts that standardized achievement testing be conducted in areas such as reading. Teachers, even those who recognize the inappropriateness of given tests to the context in which they work, often feel pressured to prepare their pupils for annual testing, and requisite steps in the learning process may be bypassed. The direct English language approach seems particularly vulnerable to such pressures, and the result may be the introduction of reading in English prior to the establishment of a solid oral language foundation.

Finally, regardless of research results concerning the efficacy of one pedagogical approach over another, the importance of the sociopolitical context within which bilingual education takes place should not be underestimated. The climate for English language immersion programs in the United States is decidedly unfavorable (Cohen & Swain, 1976). Evidence of poorly conceived and implemented direct method, English language programs and a growing interest in the definition of ethnic languages and cultures are strong factors in support of the native language approach. Furthermore, research in language planning (see Drake, 1975) suggests that if bilingualism is a desired goal, the social prestige of minority languages must figure in the design of language instruction in the early school years, since lower-prestige languages are more likely to be abandoned. Lambert and Tucker (1972), for example, stated that "priority for early school should be given to the language or languages least likely to be developed otherwise, that is, the languages most likely to be neglected [p. 216]." Thus, the probability of preserving bilingual/biculturalism in a given location is apparently greater when the lower-prestige language is the initial language of instruction in the early school years, either as a native language for minority-group children, or—as in Canada—as a second language for majority-group children.

CONCLUSIONS

There is obviously no ready answer to the question of how best to teach reading to children from non-English-speaking backgrounds. Everyone seems to agree that schools must give proper recognition to such children and to what they know upon entering school, but there is little or no agreement about how best to proceed from what they know to what they ought to learn nor even about what ought to be learned. Most current discussions focus on social, political, and even emotional factors, not only because such factors are real and must be acknowledged but also because data concerning the linguistic, psychological, and pedagogical bases and implications of one or another approach are extremely limited and often contradictory. We still know relatively little about the dialects of non-English-speaking groups in the United States, about how a second dialect or second language is acquired, about optimal ages for such acquisition, or about how reading skills transfer from one language to another.

A large number of bilingual programs are currently being implemented throughout the United States, and almost all such programs contain a research component. Unfortunately, however, the single research interest that such components most often serve is that relating to program justification. Such evaluation research is unlikely to provide insights into the basic issues of teaching reading to the bilingual child. Basic research in connection with bilingual programs is a clear necessity. In the absence of data from such basic research, arguments about which approach to reading is best will go on without significant progress toward resolution.

REFERENCES

Andersson, T., & Boyer, M. *Bilingual schooling in the United States* (Vol. 1). Austin, Tex.: Southwest Educational Development Laboratory, 1970.

Baratz, J. C. Relationship of black English to reading: A review of research. In J. L. Laffey & R. Shuy (Eds.), *Language differences: Do they interfere?* Newark, Del.: International Reading Association, 1973.

Barik, H. C., & Swain, M. Three-year evaluation of a large scale early grade French immersion program: The Ottawa study. *Language Learning, 1975, 25,* 1–30.

Barker, M.E. *Español para el bilingüe.* Skokie, Ill.: National Textbook Company, 1971.

Brown, R. Psychology and reading: Commentary on chapters 5 to 10. In H. Levin & J. P. Williams (Eds.), *Basic studies on reading.* New York: Basic Books, 1970.

Burke, C. Dialect and the reading process. In J. L. Laffey & R. Shuy (Eds.), *Language differences: Do they interfere?* Newark, Del.: International Reading Association, 1973.

Campbell, R. N. English curricula for non-English speakers. In J. L. Alatis (Ed.), *Twenty-first annual roundtable: Bilingualism and language contact.* Washington, D.C.: Georgetown University Press, 1970.

Ching, D. C. *Reading and the bilingual child.* Newark, Del.: International Reading Association, 1976.

Cohen, A. D., & Swain, M. Bilingual education: The "immersion" model in the North American context. *TESOL Quarterly, 1976, 10,* 45–53.

Drake, G. F. Integrity, promise and language planning. *Language Learning, 1975, 25,* 267–279.

Elias–Olivares, L. Chicano language varieties and uses in East Austin. In M. R. Mazon (Ed.), *SWALLOW IV: Linguistics and education.* San Diego, Calif.: San Diego State University, Institute for Cultural Pluralism, 1976.

Engle, P. L. Language medium in early school years for minority language groups. *Review of Educational Research, 1975, 45,* 283–325.

Ervin–Tripp, S. M. Structure and process in language acquisition. In J. L. Alatis (Ed.), *Twenty-first annual roundtable: Bilingualism and language contact.* Washington, D.C.: Georgetown University Press, 1970.

Ervin–Tripp, S. M. Is second language learning like the first? *TESOL Quarterly, 1974, 8,* 111–127.

Fathman, A. The relationship between age and second language productive ability. *Language Learning, 1975, 25,* 245–253.

Fishbein, J. M. A nonstandard publisher's problems. In J. L. Laffey & R. Shuy (Eds.), *Language differences: Do they interfere?* Newark, Del.: International Reading Association, 1973.

Galvan, M. ESL *is* appropriate.. *TESOL Newsletter, 1975, 9,2* 2–3; 19–20.

Gutierrez, A. L. Bilingual education: Reading through two languages. In D. E. Critchlow (Ed.), *Reading and the Spanish speaking child.* Waco, Tex.: Texas State Council of the International Reading Association, 1975.

Kochman, T. Social factors in the consideration of teaching standard English. In A. C. Aarons, B. Y. Gordon, & W. A. Stewart (Eds.), Linguistic-cultural differences and American education. *Special Anthology Issure of Florida Foreign Language Reporter, 1969, 7.*

Kolers, P. A. Three stages of reading. In H. Levin & J. P. Williams (Eds.), *Basic studies on reading.* New York: Basic Books, 1970.

Lambert, W. E., & Tucker, G. R. *Bilingual education of children.* Rowley, Mass.: Newbury House, 1972.

Leaverton, L. Dialectal readers: Rationale, use and value. in J. L. Laffey & R. Shuy (Eds.), *Language differences: Do they interfere?* Newark, Del.: International Reading Association, 1973.

Levin, H., & Kaplan, E. L. Grammatical structure and reading. In H. Levin & J. P. Williams (Eds.), *Basic studies on reading.* New York: Basic Books, 1970.

Melmed, P. J. Black English phonology: the question of reading interference. In J. L. Laffey and R. Shuy (Eds.), *Language differences: Do they interfere?* Newark, Del.: International Reading Association, 1973.

Modiano,N. Bilingual education for children of linguistic minorities. *America Indigena,* 1968, *28,* 405–414.

Nash, R. Spanglish: Language contact in Puerto Rico. *American Speech,* 1970, *46,* 106–122.

Nash, R. Englãnol: More language contact in Puerto Rico. *American Speech,* 1971, *46,* 106–122.

OCR sets guidelines for fulfilling Lau decision. *The Linguistic Reporter,* 1975, *18,* 4–7.

Politzer, R., & Weiss, L. Developmental aspects of auditory discrimination, echo response and recall. *The Modern Language Journal,* 1969, *53,* 75–85.

Saville, M. R., & Troike, R. C. *A handbook of bilingual education.* Washington, D.C.: Teachers of English to Speakers of Other Languages, 1971.

Selinker, L. Interlanguage. *International Review of Applied Linguistics,* 1972, *10,* 209–231.

Shuy, R. Nonstandard dialect problems: An overview. In J. L. Laffey & R. Shuy (Eds.), *Language differences: Do they interfere?* Newark, Del.: International Reading Association, 1973.

Somervill, M. A. Dialect and reading: A review of alternative solutions. *Review of Educational Research,* 1975, *45,* 247–262.

Tucker, G. R., Lambert, W. E., & d'Anglejan, A. Cognitive and attitudinal consequences of bilingual schooling: The St.Lambert project through grade five. *Journal of Educational Psychology,* 1973, *65,* 141–159.

Venezky, R. L., & Chapman, R. S. Is learning to read dialect bound? In J. L. Laffey & R. Shuy (Eds.), *Language differences: Do they interfere?* Newark, Del.: International Reading Association, 1973.

Weber, R. First-graders' use of grammatical context in reading. In H. Levin & J. P. Williams (Eds.), *Basic studies on reading.* New York: Basic Books, 1970.

Wolfram, W. Sociolinguistic alternative in teaching reading to nonstandard speakers. *Reading Research Quarterly,* 1970, *6,* 9–33.

III INSTRUCTION

7 Impacts of Instructional Time in Reading

John T. Guthrie
International Reading Association

Victor Martuza
University of Delaware

Mary Seifert
International Reading Association

In elementary schools in the United States, reading instruction is almost a universal phenomenon. In nearly every school, teachers attempt to help children acquire fundamental reading processes and proficient reading practices. To a greater or lesser degree, teachers engage children in certain activities, the sole purpose of which is to teach them how to read (Chall, 1967). Yet we also know that at least some children can acquire reading proficiency without formal instruction. As Durkin (1966) has documented, a few children learn how to read before entering school. In addition, as we later point out, some schools commit such a small amount of time and resources to formal reading instruction that children who learn how to read must do so incidentally rather than as a result of instruction.

During the past decade many people have held a skeptical view about schools, due partly to the reports by Coleman, Campbell, Hobson McPortland, Mood, Weinfeld, and York (1966) and by Jencks, Smith, Acland, Bane, Cohen, Gintis, Heyns, and Michelson (1972). After reanalyzing the data from the equality of educational opportunity study conducted by Coleman, the Jencks report stated in reference to elementary schools that "school effects probably account for only two or three percent of the total variance...in verbal scores [p. 124]." It also said that "no measurable school resource or policy shows a consistent relationship to schools' effectiveness in boosting student achievement.... The relationship between student achievement and such things as school size, class size, ability grouping and curriculum point to the same conclusion. Some show benefits, some show losses, and some no effect either way [p. 96]." The authors' view about the importance of high schools is even more conservative; they claimed that the average effect of a high school on its students' scores in reading comprehension and mathematics, controlling for socioeconomic status (SES) and educational aspirations, accounts for about .0001% of the variance. Appearing in many kinds of publications, statements such as these have led too many people to conclude that the educational enterprise, including reading programs, has little effect on student achievement.

One criticism of the Coleman and Jencks reports is that they did not analyze educational programs appropriately. In their approach, school effects were determined by examining achievement across a variety of schools using the school as the unit of analysis. However, a school is merely a place. The aggregation of teachers, students, and materials in that place is primarily an administrative convenience. Educational events that occur within such places are extremely variable and are likely to be critical to achievement. Consequently, the benefits of schools should not be determined on the basis of how schools differ from one another but rather on how educational events within them influence the achievement of children who are involved in those events.

The fact that differences between schools account for a relatively small amount of variability in achievement does not imply that what goes on in schools is not important. In the Coleman report, schools were described in terms of such factors as: whether the school had a speech therapist, a librarian, a principal with an MA degree or higher, free textbooks, a large library, highly experienced teachers, and so forth. However, none of these factors has any direct bearing on what skills and capabilities children are taught, how children are taught, and what is learned. Instructional events and learning events that are most closely related to educational achievement are not necessarily influenced by these factors.

In the present study, reading programs within schools were examined. Gains in achievement scores over the course of 1 year, as revealed by tests administered before and after the occurrence of a program, were studied. This contrasts with Coleman and Jencks, who analyzed the variables that related to achievement as reflected by one test score administered at one point in time. In addition, Coleman and Jencks referred to achievement at 6th, 9th, and 12th grades, whereas we examined achievement at 2nd and 6th grades. It is likely that the strongest schooling effects appear early in children's school history and are associated with the teaching program in which they are placed.

Professionals in the field of reading, including both teachers and researchers, have not questioned whether reading instruction is beneficial in learning to read. Convinced that some form of reading instruction must be valuable, they often debate what type of teaching is most effective and seldom (or never) question whether instruction in reading is needed at all. For example, Chall (1967) did not make a systematic comparison of reading instruction versus no instruction. In a review of 147 references on innovations in teaching beginning reading, Wittick (1968) assumed that direct instruction increases achievement in reading, but she provided no evidence or documentation. She searched strenuously, however, for the superior strategies. A similar viewpoint is held by Huus (1968) regarding the teaching of reading at intermediate and junior high school levels. She noted a plethora of techniques for reading improvement and the paucity of evidence that any of them is superior to any others in producing reading achievement, but she did not raise questions about whether formal instruction in reading might be ineffective for this age group in some environmental conditions.

Evaluating the importance of reading instruction presents many dilemmas. Not the least of them is that the absence of reading instruction is notably absent. However, the amount of instruction in reading varies widely. The issue of whether instruction increases achievement may be addressed in terms of whether larger and smaller amounts of instruction are differentially effective.

The value of amount of instruction has been highlighted by Wiley and Harnischfeger (1974). In a reanalysis of Coleman's equality of educational opportunity survey, Wiley and Harnischfeger found that, controlling for socioeconomic status, instruction measured in terms of hours of schooling per year is highly related to achievement. They reported that "in schools where students received 24% more schooling, they will increase their average gain in reading comprehension by two-thirds [p. 9]." Not withstanding the facts that this account seems to exaggerate the impact of exposure to instruction and that Karweit (1976) failed to replicate this analysis, the findings seem reasonable. Wiley and Harnischfeger presented a model suggesting that achievement is determined by the difference between total time needed for a student to learn a task and the total time the pupil spends learning the task. Support for this model was reported by Harris and Serwer (1966) in a study of reading instruction. In 12 schools containing primarily disadvantaged children in New York City, Harris and Serwer found that the amount of time devoted to reading activities correlated at .56 with achievement in word recognition and at .55 with achievement in comprehension for first-grade children. Reading activities included work in basal readers, experience charts, sight word drill, and phonics activities. Supportive activities, such as writing, art, discussion, and dramatization, did not correlate significantly with achievement. Apparently, instruction must be targeted to reading-related activities if it is to influence reading achievement.

Amount of exposure to instructionlike activities has been related to achievement by Ball and Bogatz (1973) in an evaluation of "Sesame Street." They reported that disadvantaged children who viewed "Sesame Street" frequently (more than five times a week) showed more gain in achievement during 1 year than middle-class children who viewed "Sesame Street" less often (two to three times a week). Although frequency of viewing "Sesame Street" increased achievement for both middle-class and disadvantaged children, quantity of instruction was more influential than socioeconomic background in facilitating cognitive growth that is relevant to education. In view of these effects, we selected amount of time as a variable that could be used to study the impact of reading instruction.

Since it is possible that a reading program in which a large amount of time is invested may differ qualitatively from one in which a small amount of time is invested, we included a variable that represents differences in reading methods. To identify this variable, we examined the largest single investigation of reading instruction, the first-grade studies reported by Bond and Dykstra (1967). Although the report is difficult to interpret, we drew some tentative conclusions on the basis of the following decision rules. First, we examined the word reading and paragraph meaning subtests of the Stanford Achievement Test (SAT) as the dependent variables. Second, we ignored analyses of variance and examined only the analyses of covariance. We decided that if a given contrast—for example, between a basal and phonics/linguistic method—was significant on both analyses of covariance, it was reliable. Third, we looked for contrasts that did not vary across the different sites in the study or that varied in the same direction across sites (we accepted ordinal interactions).

Using these guidelines, we concluded that children learned word recognition (SAT word reading) more readily by skills methods such as linguistics or phonics/linguistics than by basal methods. Word recognition was also taught more efficiently by a combination of phonics and basal methods than by traditional basal approaches alone. Reading comprehension (SAT paragraph meaning) was not reliably facilitated by any one procedure; however, adding a small skills component such as phonics or phonics/linguistics to a basal program in which considerable language stimulation is provided in basal stories seemed to have an edge in effectiveness. Because an emphasis on decoding seemed beneficial, at least for word recognition, we elected to examine whether amount of emphasis on skills influenced achievement in reading.

We decided to investigate the relationship of reading instruction and reading achievement, since it has been underrated in sociological surveys and neglected in educational studies. We viewed amount of instructional time in reading, a contrast of negligible and substantial amounts of time, as a realistic approximation of the presence and absence of formal reading instruction. To examine the association of instructional time in reading and reading achievement, we attempted to control for the effects of several pupil characteristics, including chronological age, previous reading achievement, sex, and socioeconomic status. We attempted to avoid confounding instructional time with one prominent characteristic of instruction, emphasis on skills, by making the latter a separate independent variable.

SOURCE OF EVIDENCE

The Data Base. This study consists of a reanalysis of data collected by the Educational Testing Service (ETS) under a contract titled, "A Descriptive and Analytic Study of Compensatory Reading Programs." In Phase 1 of the ETS study, a national sample of schools was constructed that was representative of the population of schools in the United States in terms of average income, percentage minority, geographic region, degree of urbanization, and school size. Thus, the findings from the present study are considered to be projectable on a national basis. A subsample of 264 schools and 57,694 children was drawn from the original population of 731 schools. The latter sample was given performance tests in reading achievement and attitudes. Questionnaires were filled out by the principals and teachers of regular and compensatory programs. The present analysis is based on that subsample.

Many analyses of the effects of education are conducted at the school level. However, instructional variables are likely to differ from teacher to teacher and from program to program within a given school. Consequently, the analysis of instructional conditions, unlike the analysis of organizational or administrative characteristics, should be made at the program rather than at the school level. One might choose the individual child as the sampling unit; however, reading programs are seldom planned and implemented for the individual child. Instruction is provided in groups, although a substantial amount of individualization may sometimes occur. Therefore, we decided that a group of children designated by the school principal and teacher as the recipients of a distinct program should be the unit of analysis. Our sampling unit was an instructional group in reading.

The data received from ETS on Phase 2 of their study were culled for quality. Information that was inconsistent or incomplete was eliminated from the data base. Attendance records on each instructional group were used. Children were included only if they attended the instructional group to which they were assigned on 75% or more of the required meetings of the group. Chidren were eliminated from the sample if they did not have both fall and spring test scores on all the tests and subtests that were administered to their age and reading level groups. Instructional groups were omitted from the data base in a few cases in which information on teacher characteristics could not be associated with the reading groups they taught. An instructional unit was omitted if the information on socioeconomic level, instructional time, or instructional emphasis on skills was omitted from the questionnaire that was filled out by the teacher.

The original ETS sample had four subgroups of children: (a) compensatory only—consisted exclusively of children who were assigned to a reading group "because they were reading below their grade level"; (b) compensatory mixed—a group of children who were behind in reading and who attended the same reading program as did normally achieving children; (c) regular only—normally achieving children who received a reading program; (d) regular mixed—normally achieving children who attended a reading program that contained some compensatory readers. Groups (a), (c), and (d) were used for the present analysis. The initial ETS sample included samples of second-, fourth-, and sixth-grade children. For purposes of economy, the second- and sixth-grade levels were selected for analysis in this survey. Instructional units that received a moderate amount of instructional time (defined in a later section) were excluded in favor of units receiving maximum or minimum instructional time. After these exclusions, there remained 931 sampling units that constituted our data base. The numbers of children included: compensatory second, 1,086; regular second, 2,833; compensatory sixth, 884; regular sixth, 3,282; total, 8,085. To determine whether the sample after exclusions was similar to the original group, we compared scores on all measures that were used in the analyses of covariance. The raw score means differed by less than one point except for three instances: 1.38, 1.45, 1.35. These negligible differences lead us to believe that the exclusions did not produce any bias in the sample.

Achievement Tests. In the ETS study, reading tests were administered to the sample of 264 schools in the fall of 1972 and the spring of 1973. The tests given in grade 2 were the Cooperative Primary Tests, 12A and 12B, and the Metropolitan Achievement Tests, Primary I, F, and G (Word Knowledge and Reading). In grade 6 the tests included Sequential Tests of Educational Progress, Series II, 4A and 4B, and Metropolitan Achievement Tests, Elementary, F and G (Word Knowledge and Reading). The tests were administered by classroom teachers with the supervision of ETS staff. The materials provided to students were specially prepared booklets and answer sheets at the second-grade level, whereas the normal forms and materials were used for sixth graders. ETS scored, coded, and transposed the scores.

Questionnaires. The questionnaires consisted of four units. A school principal questionnaire contained 49 items and elicited information about the school populations, organization and implementation of programs, and other school-level information. A teacher characteristics questionnaire was filled out by each teacher in the study. It contained 16 items, including demographic characteristics of training and beliefs. A modest inventory of 17 items was included that questioned teachers' beliefs about compensatory reading children and programs. A regular class and program characteristics questionnaire was filled out by teachers who had a regular reading program, groups (c) and (d). It contained 45 items, including the specification of teaching goals, pupil characteristics, and classroom activities. A compensatory class and program characteristics questionaire was filled out by each teacher who had a compensatory instructional group, group (a). This questionnaire included 49 items very similar to the items on the regular class and program characteristics questionnaire.

Socioeconomic Status.   From these questionnaires, we selected items for analysis in the investigation. From the regular and compensatory program questionnaires, we selected an item that reflects the socioeconomic status of the instructional groups based on family occupations. The distribution of socioeconomic status in reading groups was examined for the total population of the ETS study. Children from the initial ETS sample, including second, fourth, and sixth graders in the four instructional group categories, were included. Results of this analysis are displayed in Table 7.1. The first 27.2% of the distribution was designated as high SES; the next 47.7% of the population as middle SES; and the last 25.1% as low SES.

To determine whether the socioeconomic distribution within grade level and reading level categories was sufficient to permit analysis, the distribution was partitioned as shown in Table 7.2. It is apparent that within second-grade compensatory programs, the percentages of sampling units in the SES categories were as follows: high SES, 15%; middle SES, 45.8%; low SES, 39.2%. In other words, there was a sufficient number of high-SES sampling units to allow inclusion of this category in the statistical analyses for second-grade compensatory programs. Similar conclusions can be drawn about the sixth-grade compensatory programs and regular programs at both grade levels.

Instructional Time.   The variable of instructional time was based on an item from the class and program characteristics questionnaires. Teachers described their programs in terms of minutes per period and periods per week. We multiplied these to obtain an estimate of minutes per week. Range in time was from 8 to 600 (or more) minutes per week of formal instructional time. The allocation of instructional time to reading groups contains more variation than one might have supposed. The bottom 22.6% (approximately one-quarter) contained 80 minutes per week or less of formal reading instruction. About two-thirds of this bottom group received 31 to 40 minutes per week of instruction, an average of about 6 to 8 minutes a day. We have not analyzed the scheduling of this time over the course of a week. That is, 40 minutes may appear in two 20-minute periods or four 10-minute periods.

TABLE 7.1

Distribution of Socioeconomic Status among Regular and Compensatory
Second, Fourth, and Sixth-Grade Instructional Groups

| | Socioeconomic Status | | | | | | | | | |
| | High | | | Middle | | | | Low | | |
Regular and Compensatory	1–9	10–19	20–29	30–39	40–49	50–59	60–69	70–79	80–89	90–100
Absolute frequency (%)	253	239	269	380	266	344	347	189	183	330
Relative frequency (%)	9.0	8.5	9.6	13.6	9.5	12.3	12.4	6.8	6.5	11.8
Cumulative frequency (%)	9.0	17.6	27.2	40.7	50.2	62.5	74.9	81.7	88.2	100.0

Note. High SES is generally associated with occupational categories of white collar workers, business owners or managers, and professionals.
Middle SES is generally associated with occupational categories of white collar and skilled workers.
Low SES is generally associated with occupational categories of unskilled or service workers or unemployed.

TABLE 7.2
Frequency of Instructional Groups According to SES and Reading Level at Second and Sixth Grades

SES		Second Grade		Sixth Grade		Total Group
		Compensatory	Regular	Compensatory	Regular	
High	Frequency	16	103	10	115	244
	Column percent	15.0	24.3	11.6	29.2	24.1
Middle	Frequency	49	231	46	213	539
	Column percent	45.8	54.5	53.5	54.1	53.3
Low	Frequency	42	90	30	66	228
	Column percent	39.2	21.2	34.9	16.7	22.6

Note. Column percentages are percentages of the cell over the total for its column. The frequency of 16 is 15% of 107, which is the sum of 16, 49, and 42.

Further analysis is necessary to make these distinctions. The upper quarter of the distribution (25.3% of the instructional group) consists of 221 to 600 minutes per week. About half these units received 221 to 230 minutes per week, which is 45 minutes per day of reading instruction.

These descriptions were based on the entire distribution of regular and compensatory second, fourth, and sixth graders. The distribution of time in compensatory programs is remarkably similar to regular programs. That is, 22.4% of the instructional groups received 80 minutes per week or less, and 26.1% of the instructional groups received 221 minutes per week or more of formal reading instruction. In other words, the amount of reading instruction for children varies markedly in this sample, which is presumably representative of variation in public schools.

Instructional Emphasis. The independent variable of instructional emphasis on skills was determined from a combination of four items from the class and program characteristics questionnaires that were identical for compensatory and regular programs. These items included: (a) whether instruction was organized around skill deficiencies: (b) amount of emphasis on phonics and/or structural analysis; (c) the importance of word recognition as a goal; and (d) a self-evaluation of success in teaching skills. Each program was rated from a low of 0 to a high of 4 on this variable. The distributions of skill emphasis on compensatory and regular programs are presented in Table 7.3. Emphasis on skills decreased markedly from second to sixth grade. Orientation to skills in teaching is about the same for compensatory and regular programs at both second grade and sixth grade. There is slightly, but not dramatically, more skill-oriented instruction in compensatory than in regular reading programs.

STATISTICAL ANALYSES

Design. The design included an array of pupil characteristics and instructional characteristics. A number of analyses of covariance were conducted (Finn, 1974). For example, one analysis of covariance was conducted for compensatory readers in second grade. In this analysis, the factors were 2(Sex) × 3(SES) × 2(Instructional time) × 2(Skill emphasis). For each instructional group the dependent variable was the spring score on the word knowledge subtest of the Metropolitan Achievement Tests (MAT), and the covariate was the fall score on that subtest. A separate analysis was made for the MAT reading subtest scores. Analogous analyses of covariance were conducted for compensatory readers at sixth grade, regular readers at second grade, and regular readers at sixth grade. With this design, it is apparent that the influence of instructional variables of time and skill

TABLE 7.3
Distribution of Skill Emphasis in Compensatory and Regular
Reading Programs at Grades 2 and 6

	Grade		Skill Emphasis					Total
			Low 0	1	2	3	High 4	
Compensatory Program	2	f	4	20	44	42	12	122
		%	3.3	16.4	36.1	34.4	9.8	100
	6	f	11	38	28	15	2	94
		%	11.7	40.4	29.8	16.0	2.1	100
Regular Program	2	f	24	91	180	122	36	453
		%	5.3	20.1	39.7	26.9	7.9	100
	6	f	100	150	109	58	9	426
		%	23.5	35.2	25.6	13.6	2.1	100

emphasis are examined when pupil characteristics including previous achievement, reading level (compensatory vs. regular), grade level, socioeconomic status, and sex are controlled. The number of sampling units included in these sets of analyses were: compensatory second, 118; compensatory sixth, 96; regular second, 365; and regular sixth, 352.

Rationale. In recent years there has been considerable controversy concerning the proper method(s) for analyzing change data, and there still is no consensus. Kenny (1975) and others (e.g., Campbell & Erlebacher, 1971) have stressed the importance of considering the various alternative approaches to analyzing "quasiexperimental" change data to minimize the effects of factors like regression and treatment by maturation interaction, especially in the evaluations of compensatory programs that seem to be susceptible to these effects. In particular, Kenny suggested that the decision to use: (a) analysis of variance (ANOVA) with raw change scores, (b) ANOVA with standardized gain scores, (c) analysis of covariance (ANCOVA), or (d) ANCOVA with reliability correction ought to take into account the manner in which the assignment of subjects to various treatment groups takes place. The concerns of Kenny and others seem to have been motivated primarily by the controversy emanating from past compensatory program evaluations that, for the most part, indicated that the compensatory treatments, when compared to a nonequivalent control, tend to be ineffective or perhaps detrimental in their effects (e.g., see Campbell & Erlebacher, 1971). Since the analyses in the present study do not involve the types of comparison on which their concerns are based (i.e., compensatory treatment vs. noncompensatory control), and because the sampling units are teacher/class means (computed separately for each level of student sex) rather than individual student scores, the effects of factors such as those mentioned previously appear to be minimal. As a result of these considerations, two reasonable approaches to data analysis in the present study were (a) ANOVA using raw change scores and (b) ANCOVA using pretest data. Primarily because of statistical power considerations, we chose the latter. In summary, a separate ANCOVA was run on each dependent variable of interest (cell n's were too small to permit multivariate analyses). Pretest data from the same instruments served as the covariate within each cell of the design.

Preconditions. We used several statistical and psychometric preconditions for interpreting the analyses of covariance. First if ceiling effects were observed in a certain data set, analyses of covariance were not conducted on that set. This occurred for regular second-grade MAT word knowledge and reading subtests and for the regular sixth-grade MAT word knowledge subtest. Next we checked for: (a) comparability of pretreatment populations; (b) homogeneity of regression; and (c) adequate cell n. These properties of the data had to be satisfactory before a significant effect in an analysis of covariance could be interpreted confidently.

The precondition of comparable pretreatment populations refers to the degree of correlation between the covariate and stratification or instructional variables. If equal populations are observed, we may rule out a treatment by maturation interaction as a threat to the validity of the inferences. Suppose, for example, that we wish to evaluate the impact of instructional time, minimum vs. maximum time conditions, for second-grade compensatory programs on word knowledge. We wish to be certain that prior to the treatment, the children who are allocated maximum time do not differ in word knowledge achievement scores from children who are allocated minimum instructional time. If that were not the case, previous achievement would be confounded with instructional time as a variable that might account for differential gains in the two instructional time conditions. The precondition of comparable populations was met by the large majority of the analyses of covariance. One violation of the equal populations precondition occurred for regular sixth-grade programs. Low-SES children who were in maximum instructional time conditions had lower pretest scores on the MAT reading subtest than did other groups such as low-SES children in minimum time conditions or middle-SES children in maximum instruction. Consequently, these low-SES, maximum-time groups may be expected to make smaller gains than other groups; and as a result, their relatively small achievement over the course of the year cannot be easily interpreted.

The precondition for homogeneity of regression refers to the requirement that the regression slopes for the dependent variable and the covariate be not significantly different across the cells of the analysis of covariance design. Since some of the cells in a number of analyses were empty or had a very small number of sampling units, tests of the parallelism assumptions in each case were based only on cells in which the number of sampling units was three or more. This precondition was met in all cases, with the exception of the MAT reading subtest for sixth-grade regular programs. Our conclusions regarding this group, program, and test are attenuated accordingly.

The precondition of adequate cell n refers to the need for stability in all the cells of the analysis of covariance. In this study, several analyses of compensatory programs contained cell n's that were too low (less than 5) to permit interpretation of higher order interactions with confidence. The cell n's were adequate for main effects and lower order interpretations.

Procedures. The main purpose of these statistical analyses was to examine the effect of instructional variables on reading achievement. We wished to examine these effects while controlling for pupil characteristics of socioeconomic status and sex. The analyses of covariance included four factors: socioeconomic status, sex, instructional time, and skill emphasis. In analyzing balanced data, the order in which these variables are entered does not influence the significance of the outcomes. However, in unbalanced designs such as those in this study, the sum of squares associated with the variable will be larger if it is entered first than it will be if it is entered last. We used a priori rules to establish that the blocking variables of sex and SES should be entered first and the instructional variables of time and emphasis should be entered last to provide conservative estimates of the effects of the variables of primary concern. The order used for all analyses was sex, SES, instructional time, and instructional emphasis. We conducted exploratory reordering of these main effects and found that the differences were negligible. Consequently, we assumed that the a priori rules were justifiable. One benefit of this analysis is that it provides a partitioning of the sum of squares that allows the calculation of percentage of variance accounted for by the different effects.

The principal means for reporting the outcomes of the analyses of covariance are the percentages of variance accounted for. The importance of different factors such as instructional time or socioeconomic status are discussed in terms of the percentage of variance attributable to these factors. A description of their impact is given in percentile points. Other results could have been reported, including gains in raw score units or gains in grade-equivalent units. The use of raw scores was excluded, because different tests were used in second and sixth grades with different numbers of items and different scales for the tests. The use of grade-equivalent units is limited in value for this study, primarily because two of the tests—the Cooperative Primary Test and the Sequential Test of Educational Progress—did not convert to grade-equivalent units. Another reason is that reports of gains in grade-equivalent units must include both means and standard deviations for the different groups that are being described, and often comparisons of the magnitude of effects are difficult. We expected that the combination of percentage of variance accounted for and changes in percentile scores would be appropriate.

Several limits to these statistics should be noted. First, the strength of association that is reflected by the percentage of variance attributable, for example, to instructional time in a given study may be interpreted only within the limits of the amounts of time used in that study. As Glass and Hakstian (1969) noted, a percentage of variance attributable to instructional time or quantity of schooling can never be stretched to refer to a universal relationship between these variables. The relationship is particular to the specific levels and ranges of the dependent and independent variables in the study. Second, the index used in the present study is one of many indices. We used epsilon squared, which is very similar to omega squared (Glass & Hakstian, 1969). However, slightly different approximations of strength of association are given by these two formulas. Third, the unequal n analyses that we conducted yield estimates of the percentage of variance accounted for that are partially a function of the ordering of factors. Due to these limitations, the percentage of variance accounted for reported in this study should be regarded as an approximation of a relationship between two variables; the figures should not be interpreted in an absolute sense.

RESULTS

Instructional Impacts in Compensatory Programs

We first outline the outcomes for children in compensatory reading programs. In second-grade compensatory reading programs, amount of instructional time had a significant effect on the word knowledge subtest of the MAT ($p < .01$). The difference between minimal instructional time, about 5 minutes a day, and maximum instructional time, about 45 minutes or more a day, accounted for about 4% of the variance. Children who received maximum time in compensatory reading programs made larger gains than did children who received minimum instructional time (see Table 7.4).

A second effect of instructional variables on children in second-grade compensatory reading programs was an interaction between instructional

TABLE 7.4
Percentages of Variance in Reading Achievement Attributable to Instructional and Pupil Characteristics in Compensatory Reading Programs

	Grades					
	2			6		
Source	*MWK*	*MREAD*	*COOP*	*MWK*	*MREAD*	*STEP*
Pupil						
SES						
Sex						
Instruction						
Time	4***					3*
Emphasis						
IT × Emphasis			3*			
Interaction						
IT × SES				9****		8***
Emphasis × SES		5**				

*p < .03
**p < .02
***p < .01
****p < .005

time and instructional emphasis. This effect occurred on the Cooperative Primary Reading Test. This interaction was significant at $p < .03$ and accounted for about 3% of the variance. About one-third of the items on this test might be primarily measures of word knowledge; however, most items require sentence and paragraph comprehension, and the measure may be viewed as mainly a test of reading comprehension.

We interpret the significant interaction to mean that for compensatory programs in which there was a high skill emphasis, amount of instructional time did not influence gains in reading comprehension during the second-grade year. However, in programs in which there was a low skill emphasis, amount of instructional time had a distinct impact. Maximum time produced larger gains than did minimum time.

For sixth-grade compensatory reading programs, instructional time was found to have a significant effect on reading comprehension as measured by the Sequential Test of Educational Progress. This effect was significant at $p < .03$ and accounted for about 3% of the variance. However, the interpretation of this effect is not clear, because instructional time interacted with socioeconomic status. In other words, the effects of time do not occur similarly across different socioeconomic levels. As Table 7.4 reveals, the interaction of instructional time and socioeconomic status accounted for 8% of the variance on the test ($p < .01$). In brief, this effect suggests that more instructional time had a beneficial effect on children of low socioeconomic status, but it did not benefit children in middle and high socioeconomic levels.

This interacton also may be viewed in light of changes in percentile scores (see Table 7.5). For low-SES children who received minimum instructional time in compensatory programs, there was no change in their raw score from fall to spring, and this represents a loss of 6 percentile points. For low-SES children who received maximum instructional time, a considerable gain in raw score points was observed, but it was not sufficient to increase their percentile score; they lost 2 percentile points. Thus, whereas low-SES children in compensatory programs tend to lose ground to their peers,

TABLE 7.5
Percentile Scores on the Sequential Test of Educational Progress for Sixth-Grade Compensatory Groups of Different Instructional Time and SES Categories

| | Instructional Time | | | | | |
| | Minimum | | | Maximum | | |
	Fall	Spring	Change	Fall	Spring	Change
SES						
High	64	67	+3	36	31	−5
Medium	20	24	+4	29	24	−5
Low	16	10	−6	10	8	−2

maximum instructional time tends to reduce the loss and is consequently beneficial, at least relative to minimum instructional time. On the contrary, middle- and high-SES children who received minimum instructional time in compensatory programs gained a considerable number of raw score points and a few percentile points—3 for high-SES and 4 for middle-SES children. On maximum instructional time, both groups made smaller raw score gains and lost 5 percentile points. This suggests that smaller gains in reading comprehension were made under conditions of maximum time than under conditions of minimum time for middle- and high-SES children. If this effect is replicable, it warrants further research. Several plausible hypotheses could account for this result and should be examined in future investigations.

A significant interaction between instructional time and socioeconomic level was also observed for the word knowledge subtest of the MAT. This effect was significant at $p < .005$ and accounted for 9% of the variance. The interaction is very similar to the one just described. Parallel to their performance in reading comprehension, low-SES children benefited from more instructional time in their acquisition of word recognition skills. Under conditions of minimum instructional time, low-SES children made negligible progress; but under conditions of maximum instructional time, low-SES children made substantial gains on the word knowledge subtest. For middle-SES children, on the other hand, maximum instructional time produced slightly smaller gains than minimum instructional time.

One puzzling outcome of this analysis is that high-SES children performed more like low-SES than like middle-SES children, showing higher gains in maximum instructional time than in minimum instructional time. Why this effect occurred is not immediately apparent. What is both reasonably clear from the statistical analyses and fairly important for education is that instructional time benefited low-SES children at the sixth-grade level in both word recognition and comprehension. In contrast, increasing amounts of time did not benefit middle-SES groups and had an inconsistent effect on high-SES children.

The relative benefits of compensatory programs for second graders compared to those for sixth graders may be judged by examining the changes in percentile scores (Table 7.6). The children in second-grade compensatory

TABLE 7.6
Percentile Scores on COOP and STEP in Regular and Compensatory Programs for Grades Two and Six

	Regular			Compensatory		
	Fall	Spring	Change	Fall	Spring	Change
Grade 2	63	48	−15	16	27	+11
Grade 6	50	53	+ 3	22	21	− 1

TABLE 7.7

Percentages of Variance in Reading Achievement Attributable to Instructional and Pupil Characteristics in Regular Reading Programs

	Grade					
	2			6		
Source	MWK	MREAD	COOP	MWK	MREAD	STEP
Pupil						
SES	#	#		#		
Sex	#	#		#	1*	
Sex × SES	#	#		#		1*
Instruction						
Time	#	#		#		
Emphasis	#	#		#		
IT × Emphasis	#	#		#		1*
Interaction						
IT × SES	#	#		#	1**	3***
Emphasis × SES	#	#		#	2**	

*$p < .05$
**$p < .01$
***$p < .001$
#Not tested due to ceiling effects.

programs gained 11 percentile points, from 16 in the fall to 27 in the spring; children in sixth grade lost 1 percentile point, from 22 in the fall to 21 in the spring. Apparently, compensatory reading programs had more impact on reading achievement in second than in sixth grade.

Instructional Impacts in Regular Programs

Results of the statistical analyses of data from regular reading programs are presented in a form parallel to that used for compensatory reading programs (see Table 7.7). At second grade, the MAT word knowledge and reading subtests exhibited ceiling effects, and consequently, analyses of covariance were not conducted on them. On the Cooperative Primary Reading Test, there were no significant effects for second graders.

In the sixth-grade regular programs, there were a number of significant effects that accounted for relatively small percentages of variance. The effect for sex on the MAT reading subtest, accounting for 1% of the variance, was that girls had higher gains than boys. However, sex interacted with SES on the Sequential Test of Educational Progress ($p < .03$), accounting for 1% of the variance. The smallest gains were made by low-SES girls and high-SES boys; high-SES girls and low-SES boys made relatively larger gains. The instructional time by instructional emphasis interaction for the Sequential Test of Educational Progress revealed that amount of time made little difference for low skill emphasis. The largest gains were under the conditions of minimum time–high skill emphasis; the smallest gains occurred for maximum time–high skill emphasis.

The most pronounced effect in the regular programs at sixth grade was an interaction between instructional time and socioeconomic status that accounted for about 3% of the variance ($p < .001$). This effect is attributable to the fact that instructional time influenced low-SES but not middle- and high-SES groups. However, the impact of larger amounts of instructional time on low-SES children was negative. Maximum time produced lower gains than did minimum time for low-SES children in comprehension, as measured by the Sequential Test of Educational Progress (Table 7.8). For

TABLE 7.8

Percentile Scores on the STEP for Sixth-Grade Regular Programs Under Different Instructional Time and SES Categories

	Minimum			Maximum		
	Fall	*Spring*	*Change*	*Fall*	*Spring*	*Change*
SES						
High	53	56	+3	59	60	+1
Medium	53	53	0	50	53	+3
Low	47	53	+6	42	33	−9

low-SES children, minimum instructional time produced a gain of 6 percentile points; but maximum instructional time produced a loss of 9 percentile points for middle- and high-SES,with the changes in percentile points ranging from 0 to 3. It should be noted that the low-SES children in minimum instructional time were slightly lower in the fall percentile points than were low-SES children in maximum instructional time. It should also be noted that this was not a statistically significant difference. Under both conditions of instructional time, low-SES children had lower achievement entering sixth grade than did middle- and high-SES groups.

One possible reason for this interaction is that if a teacher commits a large amount of time to formal reading instruction and the low-SES children in the class have difficulty coping with the materials and activities, they learn very little. This may be due to the fact that the instructional demands exceed their capacity for performance and make learning difficult. Likewise, it is possible that under minimum instructional time, low-SES children may be able to direct themselves to interesting materials at an appropriate difficulty level from which they may learn at least something of reading comprehension.

The kind of interaction between instructional time and socioeconomic status described in the previous paragraph also occurred for the MAT reading subtest. However, in this case, the precondition of equal populations was violated. On the pretest, the low-SES children in maximum time conditions had a lower mean score than did low-SES children in minimum time conditions or middle-and high-SES children in maximum time conditions. They also showed the least amount of gain from pretest to posttest. Consequently, the low gains of the low-SES children in maximum time cannot be attributable to either time or previous achievement taken separately.

Finally, there was a significant interaction between instructional conditions and socioeconomic level on the MAT reading subtest. The degree of emphasis on skills interacted with SES, accounting for 2% of the variance ($p < .009$). For low-SES children, a high skill emphasis was superior to a low skill emphasis in producing gains in comprehension. However, skill emphasis did not differentially affect middle-SES and high-SES groups. In this case, as in others, instructional variation appeared to influence achievement of low-SES children, but it seemed to have less impact on middle- and high-SES groups.

Qualifications

A primary limitation of the findings of this study is the precision of the independent variables. Instructional time and emphasis were based on teacher self-reports and were not verified by independent observers. This may increase random error, but it probably does not bias the results. The items from the questionnaire on which these variables were based were relatively few in number and lacking in detail. With more precise observations of these instructional characterstics, stronger relationships to achievement are likely to be observed.

For both second and sixth grades, there were two tests that provided measures of reading comprehension. In second grade, the MAT reading subtest and the Cooperative Primary Reading Test were used; in sixth grade, the MAT reading subtest and the Sequential Test of Educational Progress were used. Effects of instructional variables were sometimes noted on one measure of comprehension for a given grade and sometimes on the other measure of comprehension; and in some cases, the effects occurred for both measures. We do not have an explanation for why an instructional effect should occur on one test of comprehension but not on a different test. From a conservative viewpoint, this indicates that an effect could not be replicated and consequently should not be seriously regarded. From a less conservative perspective, it indicates that comprehension tests may vary in their demands on children and that the nature of the measures and their sensitivity to instructional impacts should be studied closely. Furthermore, even though these tests are widely accepted measures of reading, they do not contain a heavy reliance on critical thinking nor do they assess functional uses of reading, nor attitudes toward reading. There are many important goals of reading instruction that are not measured by these tests.

The use of percentage of variance as a primary vehicle for reporting the outcomes seemed to be the most appropriate technique available, but some caveats regarding this procedure are in order. As indicated previously, any estimate of percentage of variance accounted for by a given independent variable is influenced by the range of values, the distributions of scores, the stratification system, and the particular formula used to estimate this statistic. For example, we compared instructional time that represented the upper 25% of the distribution against instructional time that represented the bottom 25% of the distribution. This was justified on the grounds that the two levels that were included—that is, about 45 minutes a day or more and about 5 minutes a day or less—represent realistic variations in instructional programs. Had we stratified this independent variable in a different manner, the percentage of variance that it accounted for might have been slightly different.

Finally, the magnitude of the instructional effects observed in this investigation was moderate. We could account for about 3% to 9% of the variance in reading achievement over the course of 1 year by instructional characterstics of reading programs. Notwithstanding variance that is attributable to pupil characteristics and error of measurement, there are bound to be other instructional qualities that influence achievement. However, the impact of instructional time as it occurred alone, in combination with instructional emphasis, and in combination with socioeconomic level was noteworthy. It seems that these variables have a place in the psychology of reading instruction and in the development of reading programs for the benefit of elementary school children.

Conclusions

At the outset of the study, two major problems were posed: (a) To what degree do characteristics of instructional programs such as emphasis on skills and language or amount of instructional time influence achievement of pupils? (b) To what degree do these effects depend on previous achievement, age, SES, reading level, and sex of the pupils?

Within the constraints of the present investigation, instructional characteristics of reading programs were observed to have an impact on reading achievement. The findings suggest that time in formal reading instruction is likely to increase achievement in reading. Maximum instructional time influenced some types of children more than others. Instructional time in formal reading instruction had the greatest impact on children in second-grade compensatory programs. The impact of time on achievement appeared to be greater in second than in sixth grade and greater in compensatory than in regular reading programs.

Instructional time seemed to influence low-SES children more than middle- and high-SES children at the sixth-grade level. At second grade, the combination of time and SES was not important. Among sixth graders, low-SES children benefited from larger amounts of instructional time, but time did not have an impact on achievement for middle- and high-SES groups. Although this effect occurred for compensatory programs, a different interaction occurred in regular reading programs. In that condition, larger amounts of instructional time had a slightly negative effect on achievement of low-SES children and a negligible impact on middle- and high-SES groups.

The types of instructional emphasis that are provided in reading programs had less impact on achievement than did the amount of instructional time. However, in second-grade compensatory reading programs, low instructional emphasis on skills combined with a maximum amount of time produced larger gains in comprehension than did a high instructional emphasis on skills combined with the maximum amount of instructional time.

Pupil characteristics of socioeconomic level and sex did not influence gains over the course of 1 year. Exceptions to this occurred only in terms of the interactions with program characteristics that we described previously. Considered apart from instructional characteristics, sex and socioeconomic level did not influence gains in achievement over 1 year. From this investigation, it appears that instructional characteristics have more impact than pupil characteristics on reading achievement; and instructional time is better invested in children who are relatively young and relatively low in reading achievement than in other groups. Among older children, instructional time had a positive impact on low-SES groups, but it did not influence middle- and high-SES children in reading achievement.

DISCUSSION

One of our findings was that the amount of formal instruction in reading that was given to children in compensatory reading programs at the second-grade level accounted for about 4% of the variance in achievement gains over 1 year. Compensatory reading programs in which 45 minutes per day or more were spent in teaching reading were clearly more effective than programs that spent 6 to 7 minutes per day. This outcome is consistent with the general model of schooling proposed by Wiley and Harnischfeger (1974), which holds that a high quantity of schooling increases achievement, especially for children with lower aptitudes. It also validated one feature of many exemplary reading programs, a considerable devotion of time to teaching the basics of reading. It should be recognized, however, that it is not time itself that influenced achievement; it was the events that occurred during that time. As Harris and Serwer (1966) have shown, instructional time influences reading achievement only if children are engaged specifically in reading activities. Time that is spent in management, general discussion, or such activities as art that are irrelevant to reading processes does not influence reading achievement.

Although the impact of instructional time on reading achievement appears to be generalizable across our national sample and is likely to be repeatable, the magnitude of the effect seems moderate. The importance of the relationship between instructional time and achievement may be considered from several viewpoints. First, instructional time is one component of a multicomponent system. As reflected in a variety of reports of exemplary reading programs, there are many components of successful programs, including strong leadership, clear objectives, structured curricula, individualization of instruction, administrative support, a variety of materials, and support personnel, as well as the investment of substantial amounts of time teaching reading. Although instructional time is not the only ingredient of a good program, it is clearly one that should not be neglected.

The magnitude of these results may be compared to an analysis of classroom instruction in Follow-Through programs. In one study of 30 first-grade classrooms, it was found that controlling for initial ability, 16% of the variance in reading and math achievement at the end of first grade was explained by classroom process variables (Cooley & Emrick, 1974). The process variables included: time spent on reading and math, praise and encouragement from the teacher, amount of individual instruction, and amount of teacher–pupil interaction. Our finding that 4% to 9% of the variance in reading achievement was attributable to instructional time is consistent with that study.

Time is most likely to be related to reading achievement in terms of student learning. That is, the amount of time students spend actively engaged in reading is more critical than the amount of time allocated to reading by the teacher. The correlation between learning time and reading achievement has been documented repeatedly (Lahaderne, 1968; Rosenshine & Berliner, 1978; Samuels & Turnure, 1974). It stands to reason that learning time is limited by the amount of time set aside (or allotted) by the teacher for learning. Although there is no evidence, we can speculate that there is a high correlation between instructional time in reading and learning time in reading that permits the positive correlation between instructional time and achievement.

The impact of instruction on achievement may also be compared with the impact of SES on achievement. Jencks et al.(1972) reported that differences in socioeconomic status accounted for about 9% of the variance in achievement scores of sixth graders, whereas differences between schools accounted for about 2% to 3% of the variance in achievement scores. By his analysis, socioeconomic status plays a bigger part than schools do in producing achievement. However, it should be remembered that his analysis neglected important instructional events. He only examined the association of achievement tests given at one time with school characteristics such as size of the library and per-pupil expenditure. As a result, he underestimated, sometimes drastically, the role of instruction in reading achievement. We believe our results are more realistic and more positive for instruction.

Our findings were that the impact of socioeconomic status is less at second than at sixth grade. We found no influence of SES on gains during second grade for regular or compensatory groups and no interactions with instructional time. At sixth grade, however, we observed significant interactions between SES and instructional time, showing the increasing role of SES in achievement as children progress through school. We also found that in sixth-grade compensatory programs, amount of formal instruction in reading was related positively to reading achievement among low-SES groups but did not make a difference for middle- and high-SES groups. One possible explanation for this result is that the amount of time that middle-SES and high-SES children spend in reading activities outside of formal instruction is substantial. The amount of time spent reading and learning in formal reading classes is minor by contrast. However, for low-SES children, the amount of time reading outside of formal lessons is relatively low. Consequently, the necessary interactions between the child and written language, from which complex operations needed for reading may be acquired, occur for low-SES children primarily during formal instruction but occur for middle-SES children in other circumstances as well. The implication is that the investment of instructional time in reading at the sixth-grade level is particularly important for low-SES children. Apparently, a primary agent of change in reading achievement for older, low-achieving children from lower socioeconomic backgrounds is direct instruction in reading.

In the introduction we remarked that reading teachers and specialists implicitly assume that at least some form of direct reading instruction is likely to increase achievement. Our findings substantiate this belief in part. Teaching reading directly, as reflected in amount of formal instructional time, is valuable for young, primary-aged children who have not learned to read as proficiently as their peers. Direct instruction that is designed to impart reading skills is also beneficial for older elementary children from lower socioeconomic backgrounds. Indeed, we are compelled to draw the conclusion that what children learn about reading in 1 year is determined primarily by the quantity of instruction they receive.

REFERENCES

Ball, S., & Bogatz, G. A. Research on Sesame Street: Some implications for compensatory education. In J. Stanley (Ed.), *Compensatory education for children, ages 2 to 8*. Baltimore: Johns Hopkins University Press, 1973.

Bond, G. L., & Dykstra, R. The cooperative research program in first-grade reading. *Reading Research Quarterly*, 1967, *2*, 5–142.

Campbell, D. T., & Erlebacher, A. How regression artifacts in quasi-experimental evaluations can mistakenly make compensatory education harmful. In J. Hellmuth (Ed.), *The disadvantaged child* (Vol. 3). New York: Brunner/Mazel, 1971.

Chall, J. *Learning to read: The great debate*. New York: McGraw-Hill, 1967.

Coleman, J.S., with Campbell, E. Q., Hobson, C. J., McPortland, J., Mood, A. M., Weinfeld, F. D., & York, R. L. *Equality of educational opportunity*. Washington, D.C.: U.S. Government Printing Office, 1966.

Cooley, W. W., & Emrick, J. A. *A model of classroom differences which explains variation in classroom achievement*. Paper presented at the meeting of the American Educational Research Association, Chicago, April 1974.

Durkin, D. *Children who read early*. New York: Teachers College Press, 1966.

Finn, J. D. *A general model for multivariate analysis*. New York: Holt, Rinehart and Winston, 1974.

Glass, G. V., & Hakstian, A. R. Measures of association in comparative experiments: Their development and interpretation. *American Educational Research Journal*, 1969, *6*, 403–414.

Harris, A., & Serwer, B. The CRAFT project: Instructional time in reading research. *Reading Research Quarterly*, 1966, *2*, 27–57.

Huus, H. Innovations in reading instruction: At later levels. In H. Robinson (Ed.), *Innovation and change in reading instruction, The Sixty-seventh Yearbook of the National Society for the Study of Education*, 1968, *67* (Pt. 2), 126–158.

Jencks, C., Smith, M., Acland, H., Bane, M. J., Cohen, D., Gintis, H., Heyns, B., & Michelson, S. *Inequality: A reassessment of the effect of family and schooling in America*. New York: Basic Books, 1972.

Karweit, N. Quantity of schooling: A major educational factor? *Educational Researcher,* 1976, *5,* 15–17.

Kenny, D. A. A quasi-experimental approach to assessing treatment effects in the nonequivalent control group design. *Psychological Bulletin,* 1975, *83,* 345–362.

Lahaderne, H. M. Attitudinal and intellectual correlates of attention: A study of four sixth-grade classrooms. *Journal of Educational Psychology,* 1968, *59,* 320–324.

Rosenshine, B. V., & Berliner, D. C. Academic engaged time. *British Journal of Teacher Education,* 1978, *4,* 3–16.

Samuels, S. J., & Turnure, J. E. Attention and reading achievement in first grade boys and girls. *Journal of Educational Psychology,* 1974, *66,* 29–32.

Wiley, D. E., & Harnischfeger, A. Explosion of a myth: Quantity of schooling and exposure to instruction, major educational vehicles. *Educational Researcher,* 1974, *3,* 7–12.

Wittick, M. L. Innovations in reading instruction: For beginners. In H. Robinson (Ed.), *Innovation and change in reading instruction, The Sixth-seventh Yearbook of the National Society for the Study of Education,* 1968, *67* (Pt. 2), 72–125.

8 The ABD's of Reading: A Program for the Learning Disabled

Joanna Williams
Teachers College, Columbia University

This chapter describes an instructional program designed to teach decoding skills to learning disabled children. The program was developed to serve as a supplement to whatever reading program is used in the classroom, and it will probably be most useful in remedial instruction.

OVERVIEW

The first part of *The ABDs of Reading* focuses solely on auditory tasks. Children learn to analyze syllables and short words into phonemes and then to blend phonemes into syllables and words. Only after proficiency in these tasks is reached are letters introduced—first in the context of individual letter–sound correspondences. Then decoding is taught. This instructional sequence is based on a task analysis. Because this approach is well documented (see e.g., Gagne, 1974; Glaser, 1977; Resnick & Beck, 1976) and rather widely accepted at the present time, it needs no discussion here.

One major difference between this program and other programs that teach beginning decoding skills is that at the very beginning of instruction, certain tasks are introduced that are not usually taught in isolation: auditory analysis and auditory blending. Classroom observation and a review of the literature led us to the conclusion that a sharper focus on these particular auditory skills than is provided elsewhere would be of value to learning disabled children—a population not often considered explicitly until recently.

It should be noted that our goal is to develop a program that will be useful in the normal school situation. Classes of learning disabled children usually contain fewer pupils than do regular classrooms; but there are still at least 8 or 10 children per class, and these are children who are hyperactive, distractible, or otherwise difficult to manage. They are often not able to work independently. Many learning disabled classrooms are staffed by a teacher and a teacher's aide, but one cannot count on this; recent budget cuts have resulted in the elimination of many aides. Thus, we do not assume the availability of an aide to help instruct. Because we were concerned about cost-effectiveness, we decided not to work toward individualized instruction, even though that is highly effective. We chose to develop materials suitable for small group instruction. Much of the instruction in learning disabled classrooms is of that type, and it appears to work well in terms of both instruction and classroom management. We also kept the materials as inexpensive as possible, consonant with actual instructional requirements. For example, color cues are not used, because full-color production is so expensive.

We had another aim in addition to achieving cost-effectiveness—to develop a set materials that teachers would accept and use. We rejected the necessity of any extensive "selling" of a point of view or even extensive teacher-training procedures. We also rejected the notion that teachers should spend a large amount of time preparing lessons. No matter how enthusiastic teachers may be about an instructional approach, they simply do not have the time to prepare elaborately for class. We have developed a program that is complete and self-contained. Teachers can pick it up at the place where they left off and continue without previous preparation. Moreover, while teachers work with a small group of children, they should concentrate totally on instruction. Thus, we provide word lists, examples, and so on so that teachers are not distracted from monitoring the performance of their pupils.

The goal, then, is not to develop a program that is effective during development and evaluation when there is a large amount of support (funds and trained personnel) available. Instead, our goal is to develop a program that can stand by itself without such resources, for in the normal school situation there are no such supports.

THE LEARNING DISABLED CHILD

There are many children who cannot make progress in a regular school situation, even though presumably they have the intellectual capacity to do so. Nor do they have physical handicaps, emotional problems, or sensory loss; nor have they suffered any educational or cultural deprivation. In other words, they appear to have potential for achievement but nevertheless do not demonstrate adequate achievement. Until only recently, such children were often characterized in terms of "brain injury" or "minimal cerebral dysfunction." The notion that the difficulty was due to some sort of damage to the central nervous system (Strauss & Lehtinen, 1947) rarely could be corroborated with actual evidence of neurological impairment. The newer term, *learning disability,* acknowledges the fact that we do not know the reason for these children's difficulties.

These children may demonstrate any of a wide variety of problems. They may show poor performance in several school subjects, or they may demonstrate more specific disability in only one area, such as reading. Their aptitude test scores are likely to show uneven performance among subtests, with a substantial difference between verbal and performance abilities. They may be impaired in one or several of the following areas: perception, conceptualization, language, memory and control of attention, impulse, or motor function (Hallahan & Kauffman, 1976). Ross (1976) considers that a basic problem shared by many if not all learning disabled children is a difficulty in sustaining selective attention. It is this difficulty, he claims, that leads to other problems characteristic of this type of child—perseveration, distractibility, and poor memory—which in turn lead to inadequate school performance.

Although not all learning disabled children have trouble learning to read, this area does represent an important source of difficulty for many of them. Disabled readers are themselves not easily categorized; they may have difficulty in any or all of the components on which reading is based. They may exhibit disorders in visual and auditory discrimination or memory and sequencing as well as in the integration of auditory and visual perception (Samuels, 1973). Vellutino (1974) has discussed the myriad patterns of error that occur on reading tasks: reversals and transpositions, adding or dropping of phonemes or syllables, substituting one word for another with a similar meaning, confusing similar letter sounds, and/or failing to blend and analyze word parts. These are the same mistakes, of course, that any beginning reader might make; but the normally achieving child eventually ceases to make them, whereas the disabled reader persists.

It is certainly unrealistic to expect that one particular teaching approach or one specific set of instructional materials will be maximally effective with the wide variety of children clasified as "learning disabled" or even as "reading disabled." It seems likely that some further differentiation of types of children within this overall classification will have to be made before we can confidently make judgments about the specific educational approach to take with an individual child. Indeed, a great deal of research has been done with just this goal in mind. Not too much progress has been made, unfortunately. It is not easy to find instances in which one instructional method is superior to another for one group of children and a second is superior to the first for another group of children (Cronbach & Snow, 1977).

Most of the search for such disordinal interactions in the area of reading instruction has focused on the issue of modality. That is, attempts have been make to characterize children as either "eye oriented" (they have trouble with tasks involving auditory analysis) or "ear oriented" (they have trouble with visual perceptual tasks). Wepman (1968),for example, proposed that all early learning is modality bound and that some children have a discrepancy in the ease with which they can process and store information received through the eyes and ears. There is, however, no sound empirical foundation for the notion that different reading approaches are differentially effective for children characterized in these ways. Most studies have compared some variety of the whole-word approach, which requires little analysis of sounds, with a phonics approach. Neither classroom studies (Bateman, 1968; Robinson, 1972) nor laboratory analogues (Bruinicks, 1970; Ringler & Smith, 1973) have come up with convincing findings. It should also be pointed out that in these studies, children identified as "visiles" and "audiles" together comprise only about 15% to 20% of the sample.

It would probably be unwise to argue that matching instructional treatment to diagnostic category will never be shown to enhance learning. It may even be true that there are special methods of teaching reading that will work most effectively with specific types of children. But we have no evidence now, and to develop curriculum materials with such a focus at the present time is not reasonable.

THE PROGRAM RATIONALE

Slow learners, including the learning disabled, need simple, clear, and direct instruction. They do well with a structured approach; and the material should be presented at a slow pace, with each step carefully made explicit and with sufficient opportunity for practice. They should be active participants in the instructional process, and ample feedback should be provided about their performance. They should be kept motivated to achieve. These general principles need not be defended here (although I will say that the effective implementation of these principles is not always easy!).

Decoding is the central task of beginning reading instruction. It consists of learning the fundamental relationships between spoken language and written language, that is, the mapping of the grapheme–phoneme correspondences. The ability to decode, then, implies both the ability to isolate the phonemes that make up a word and ability to blend individual phonemes into whole words. The development of these abilities requires the use of complex conceptual strategies (Resnick & Beck, 1976; Vernon, 1957).

In the whole-word (sight) method of instruction and to some extent in linguistic methods, there is no direct instruction in analysis of a word or word part into its component sounds. Not all children can do this inductive analysis on their own; some children will succeed with this type of instruction and others will not. Those who do not succeed often do not make much progress in reading, because for them, this sort of instruction requires rote learning of a large number of specific words and letter patterns; and there is after all a limit to one's memory. Moreover, Liberman, Cooper, Shankweiler, and Studdert-Kennedy (1967) have shown that the acoustic characteristics of a phoneme are modified by the other phonemes in a word or syllable and that the cues for recognizing the phonemes in a word occur simultaneously as well as sequentially. Thus, the component sounds of a word as we sound it out (e.g., "c-a-t") are not actually segments of the spoken word; blending is an abstraction. For these reasons, the desirability of giving direct, explicit instruction in analysis and blending to the learning disabled child seemed obvious to us.

It is clear that progress in beginning reading is related to proficiency in those auditory skills that can be identified as components of the decoding process. Much of the literature is based on correlational evidence, to be sure. Monroe (1932), for example, found significant differences between children with reading disabilities and younger controls in both auditory discrimination and the acquisition of auditory-visual associations. Relationships between a variety of auditory tasks and either reading readiness or first- and second-grade reading achievement have been demonstrated over and over again (e.g., Dykstra, 1966; Harrington & Durrell, 1955). More recently, the importance of the specific abilities of blending and segmentation has also been emphasized (Elkonin, 1963; MacGinitie, 1967). Substantial correlations have been found between these tasks and either concurrent or later reading achievement (e.g., Calfee, Lindamood, & Lindamood, 1973; Chall, Roswell, & Blumenthal 1963; Liberman, 1973.)

Moreover, there have been several studies showing that training in auditory skills may have positive effects on reading. Durrell and Murphy (1953) evaluated the results of 11 studies and concluded that training children to notice sounds in words improved their reading scores. Children whose initial scores were very low made the greatest progress. This training, incidentally, consisted only of identification of initial consonants and of rhymes. Elkonin (1963) taught kindergarten children to identify sounds in words by using counters to represent each phoneme. Rosner's (1973, 1974) instructional program, which develops word analysis skills to a high level of proficiency, shows some transfer of these skills to the reading task.

Since our work on this program began, more and more studies have corroborated this point of view. For example, Goldstein (1976) found that kindergartners' segmentation ability predicted reading achievement one year later; he concluded that reading instruction was much less effective if a child's ability in sound analysis and synthesis was very low. Fox and Routh (1976) found that phonic blending training was effective only if children were already proficient in phonic analysis; however, it is possible that the children who at the beginning of the study were superior in ability to analyze words into phonemes were generally more able students.

All this evidence suggested that a highly structured program with emphasis on the development of auditory skills would prove successful. Underlying this was the fact that auditory deficits—difficulties in auditory discrimination, memory, sequencing ability, and especially analysis and synthesis—seem to be more characteristic of learning disabled children than are visual or inter-sensory problems (Zigmond, 1969).

For most children, it would not be necessary to introduce the segmentation and blending tasks as purely auditory tasks; letters could be introduced at the same time. But we introduced them separately in order to simplify the task; we considered this important for learning disabled children. Many learning disabled children have failed to learn to read, simply because they cannot handle the complexity of the task as it is usually presented. That is, they suffer from "sensory overload." Or they may have failed simply because of the lack of explicit emphasis on the auditory components of the task and extensive enough practice on these skills.

Several points should be noted here. First, all the studies that I have cited are concerned with auditory tasks that involve language and that are therefore closely related to reading. Second, the literature is convincing on the specificity of transfer and the dangers of relying on transfer in instruction (Gage & Berliner, 1975; Williams, 1975). Third, the results of the formerly popular visual–perceptual– motor reading readiness programs (e.g., Frostig & Horne, 1964; Kephart, 1960) have turned out to be very disappointing. These facts should serve as a clear warning that "auditory preceptual training" in and of itself will not improve reading achievement (the plethora of recently and hastily developed programs of this type notwithstanding). It is the emphasis on effective presentation of the auditory components of the reading task itself that is important.

Of course, the "need" for a particular instructional approach and the demand for it are not determined solely by evidence from research. The zeitgeist has to be right. The field of linguistics has had a major impact on educational thinking over the last decade or two, and the consequent reaffirmation of the idea that "reading is a language skill" has helped to foster the current emphasis on auditory skills in beginning reading. In addition, because of the recent acknowledgment of the ineffectiveness of visual–perceptual training—the focus many of the standard reading readiness and remedial reading methods (Williams, 1977)—people have been clamoring for something new and different. It is interesting to note that in her classic book, *Backwardness in Reading*, Vernon (1957) stressed the need for analysis of both the visual and auditory structures of words; yet for almost 20 years, most of the references to her work document the need for visual analysis and ignore the same need in the auditory modality.

DESCRIPTION OF THE PROGRAM

Introduction. In a short introductory section of the program, the child learns the concept of analysis—that is, that words can be broken down into parts. Both compound words and multisyllabic words are presented. At the end of this sequence, the children can analyze at the syllable level. That is, they can tell what syllable occupies the initial, medial and final positions in a whole word. This is a much easier task than that of segmenting into phonemes (Hardy, Stennitt, & Smythe, 1973; Liberman, Shankweiler, Fischer, & Carter, 1974). Indeed, it is an extremely simple task, and this introductory section moves very quickly. In addition to demonstrating the concept of analysis, there is a second reason for beginning the program with this material. Because the sequencing of sounds is a temporal phenomenon, it is wise to provide some sort of visual "marker" (Elkonin,1963;Kuenne & Williams, 1973). Movable wooden squares, which provide tactile and visual representation of sounds, are used to facilitate auditory analysis and synthesis. The children learn to identify auditorially first, middle, and last syllable (or word parts) and to associate them visually with markers. Thus, this visual representation is introduced on a task that represents very little challenge to the children and is therefore accomplished easily.

Phoneme Analysis.   In this section of the program, analysis is taught, again as a strictly auditory task. The squares now represent phonemes and aid in focusing attention on the number and order of sounds, which has been found to be a difficult task for children (Calfee, Lindamood, & Lindamood, 1973). Combinations of two phonemes are presented first, followed by combinations of three phonemes; these form both real words and nonsense syllables.

All this auditory analysis and sequencing practice is done with a limited number of phonemes. In choosing the initial set of nine phonemes (and therefore, later in the program, letters), we considered the following factors: (a) avoidance of auditory confusability; (b) avoidance of visual confusability; (c) ease of blendability of the phonemes in combination; (b) productivity of phonemes in creating real-word trigrams; (e) ability of children to produce sounds; (f) ease of learning grapheme–phoneme associations; and (g) regularity of phonemes in spelling patterns. Each of the seven considerations suggested a different set of "most appropriate letters" so compromises had to be made on some points. Because of the program's emphasis on auditory skills, we decided that visual considerations would be of relatively low priority and that avoiding auditory confusability would be our highest priority.

The short vowels (*a* and *o*) were selected because of their adherence to regular spelling rules in consonant–vowel–cononant (CVC) trigrams and secondarily because of their productivity. Long vowels, though more easily discriminable and blendable (Coleman, 1970), were ruled out because of the irregularity of long vowel spelling patterns in English. The selection of consonants proved to be at least as difficult as that of vowels. Miller and Nicely (1955) divided consonant phonemes into four basic groups; within each one, there is considerable potential for confusion in discrimination, whereas between groups there is little. Thus, for ease of discrimination, we chose one consonant from within each group, the one that best satisfied the requirements of: (a) production of many real-word trigrams, and (b) children's ability to produce the sound without error (Marsh & Sherman, 1971). The ease of sound–symbol association learning (Coleman, 1970) was also considered, and the letters chosen were acceptable in this respect. On this basis, the initial set consisted of *b, m, p,* and *s*. Then, in violation of several considerations but in order to provide enough real-word trigrams for meaningful instruction, the letters *c, g,* and *t* were added. Thus the nine letters are *a, o, b, m, p, s, c, g* and *t*.

The use of only a small number of phonemes that are chosen for maximum discriminability means that if a child moves ahead rapidly in analysis and synthesis and yet finds auditory discrimination difficult, he or she can still proceed in the program. Furthermore, the program may well improve his or her discrimination abilities as a side effect, because it works to increase attention to detail.

Phoneme Blending. The next section of the program presents blending of the same two-phoneme and three-phoneme (all CVC) units. The CVCs are divided at different points. Initially, only the last phoneme is separated from the rest of the word. Next, only the first phoneme is separated from the rest of the word; and later all three phonemes are presented separately. This sequence is based on work by Coleman (1970).

Letter–Sound Correspondences. After the basic instructional sequence on auditory analysis and synthesis, there is a section that teaches the letter–sound correspondences for the nine phonemes. Thus children will be thoroughly familiar with the correspondences they will need for the initial decoding section before they get to that point in the program.

Decoding. The next section of the program combines the auditory skills and the letter–phoneme correspondences that the children have been practicing. Here they must integrate the skills they have learned in isolation.

Again using wooden squares, which now have letters on them, the children learn to decode bigrams and trigrams (both meaningful words and nonsense syllables) made up of the familiar nine letters. They receive extensive practice in the manipulation of these letters, so that they can decode (read) and construct from letter squares (spell) all the possible CVC combinations. Through this extensive practice with limited content, the children learn to attend to the details required for accurate decoding. They also learn the fundamental processes and strategies that will enable them to apply decoding skills to other content.

Further Instruction.   In the next section of the program, six additional letter–sound correspondences (*f, h, i, l, n,* and *r*) are introduced. Then these are used in trigram decoding. Following this, all 15 letters are combined and recombined for additional decoding practice.

The final section of the program introduces, one by one, more complex units for decoding. First, CCVC patterns are decoded, followed by CVCC and then CCVCC patterns. Finally, two-syllable words made up of the same basic patterns are presented.

Organization of the Program

The instruction just outlined is organized into 12 units and a total of 41 objectives. Each unit begins with a story, to be read by the teacher. This story is designed to capture the children's interest, and it incorporates a demonstration of the skills to be mastered in the unit. For example, a child must guess the "magic word" that unlocks a secret door when the magician says the word broken into phonemes. The same cast of characters—Isabel, whose nickname is Wisebell because she is a little "know-it-all," along with her friends, Tom and Mac, and Sam, the janitor—appears throughout the program in stories and games and provides a continuing theme and focus of interest.

Following the story, a teaching procedure is presented for each objective. This consists of a complete and very explicit script for the teacher, along with as many appropriate examples as will be needed. The instruction always follows the same format: First the teacher demonstrates the task by modeling one example. Then he or she calls on an individual pupil, models another example, and has the child copy that example. Then he or she presents another example that a child must do independently. Errors are corrected by the teacher's providing the proper response and then having the child repeat it immediately afterward.

Each unit also contains a variety of materials for practice. At least one game is provided for practice on each objective. The games are simple, and there are only a few different game formats—of the sort ("Go Fish,"

"Concentration," etc.) that most children recognize. Their content varies, however. In one game, children must collect three cards, each of which represents a different after-the-movie snack; in another, three different bicycle parts. This type of variation is enough to make each game novel and interesting. The games can be played either competitively or not.

In addition, two worksheets are provided for each objective. As with the games, some of the worksheets are designed to be completed under the supervision of the teacher and others to be done independently. In actuality, however, the use of all program materials is directed by the teacher.

All the activities are designed to provide small groups of children with the opportunity for extensive practice of skills in a variety of contexts. They also provide for continuity and interest, in that they are based on the theme of the story presented at the beginning of the unit.

Comprehension

This is a decoding program, not a complete reading program. But it is important that pupils be able to apply their decoding skills in the context of actual reading. To insure this, the teacher provides a meaningful context for words immediately after they have been decoded (or blended, earlier in the program); he or she uses the word in a sentence or identifies it as a nonsense word. In addition, simple comprehension activities are provided. For example, in the second half of the program there are several "stories," each consisting of a series of four pictures with one or two short sentences under each picture.

A few simple words that are not easily decodable, like *is, to,* and *of,* are necessary for these comprehension activities. When the program is used remedially, it is possible that some children have enough of a sight-word vocabulary that they can read this material on their own. In other cases, this is not true, and the teacher and the pupil read the sentences together, the teacher supplying the words that do not lend themselves to a decoding strategy.

Individual Differences

It is obvious that individual differences exist in the degree to which some of these abilities are deficient and in the amount of training that will be required. The program is designed to be maximally flexible in dealing with these differences. For example, the letter–sound unit may be begun early or late; and it, or any of the units, may be extended for whatever length of time is required to attain competence. Some children may prefer competitive games, and others may achieve readily with individual activities. Worksheets appeal to some children (and teachers) and are of very low interest to others. The variety of materials that are provided allows options, and the teachers (and, when feasible, the children) can choose the most effective combination of alternatives.

EVALUATION IN THE FIELD

During 1975–76, the complete program was used in the field for the first time. (Prior to this, during the earlier stages of development, portions of the program had been administered to small groups of children or to one child at a time both by staff members and by classroom teachers.) The children were pupils in Health Conservation (HC-30) classrooms, which are administered by the New York City Board of Education's Bureau for the Education of the Physically Handicapped. All children in these classrooms are learning disabled. Any emotional overlay to their disabilities is slight, since children with more severe emotional disturbances are placed in other classes. Children are assigned to these (or other) special classrooms when they perform unsuccessfully in a regular classrom setting and only after extensive psychological and neurological assessment. All classrooms were in Title I schools in Central and North Harlem and on the Lower East Side. The ages of the children ranged from 7 to 12 years.

Our main focus for the year's work was on formative questions; we were interested primarily in making further refinements in the program on the basis of observation of actual teachers using the program in their normal classroom settings. Because of this orientation, we invited to work with us teachers who had been recommended as competent and cooperative (which indeed they proved to be). In November 1975 more than 150 pupils in eight schools were pretested. The pretest assessed competence in the specific skills covered in the program: auditory analysis and blending of both syllables and phonemes, letter–sound correspondences, and decoding. On the basis of the pretest results, we selected those children, three or four from each classroom, who were most likely to profit from the program. Seventeen instructional groups totaling 63 children were formed. We found that in almost every case, we had chosen the same children whom the teacher had had in mind for the program.

We also administered the pretest to another group of HC-30 children in comparable school districts within Manhattan. Using the same procedure that was used to choose the instructional population, 16 groups (64 pupils) were formed (and their pretest scores did not differ from those of the instructed groups). This was not a proper control group, but comparing these children with those who were instructed did give us some notion of the overall impact of the program. It also provided pilot data for the next year's evaluation.

Teachers were asked to use the program daily for approximately 20 minutes per session. Four teachers were observed every day. This close monitoring of instruction is especially important when working with learning disabled children, because their behavior is often extremely erratic. The other 13 classes were observed and the teachers interviewed once a week. Teachers were asked to work through the program exactly as it was presented, using all the games, worksheets, and so forth, so that we would have a firm basis for evaluation and possible revision. (This, of course, is not the way the program is to be used ordinarily.) No teacher dropped out of the study, and very few children dropped out of their classes (and therefore, the program) during the year.

The same test we had used as a pretest was readministered at the end of the academic year, after over 6 months of instruction. Posttest scores were higher than pretest scores on every subtest for all children. The posttest scores of the instructed group were significantly higher than those of the comparison group on all of the subtests except some of those on which scores for both groups had been very high on the pretest (syllable analysis and blending and the two easiest phoneme analysis tasks—indentifying initial and identifying final phoneme). The tasks on which the instructed group showed significantly more improvement were both of the letter–sound correspondence tasks, the two more difficult phoneme analysis tasks (identifying the middle phoneme and identifying all three phonemes in CVCs), phoneme blending, and decoding. On the test of decoding, which included both real and nonsense material and both bigrams and trigrams, the posttest score of the instructed group was double that of the comparison group.

Six months later, the posttest was administered again. (Most of these children remain in the same classroom with the same teacher for more than one year.) The instructed children's scores were still superior to those of the comparison children. However, they did not show gains on any of the subtests from their earlier posttest performance to this one.

The lack of additional improvement of the instructed children is regrettable; it is not uncommon where there is no specific attention given to planning the interface of an instructional program with subsequent instruction (as we shall do in this year's full-scale evaluation). It should also be noted that two teachers remarked that because the instructed children had gained so much in decoding skill, they were no longer spending as much time with those children on these skills.

It is premature to attempt to evaluate the effectiveness of the program, of course, but these very preliminary data do seem promising. First of all, the teachers liked using the materials—a limited criterion, to be sure, but an essential one. They felt that their children were making progress (which our data corroborated), and they also felt that the program was easy and comfortable to use. Indeed, the length of daily sessions averaged around 30 minutes instead of the 20 that we had requested.

Not all children made the same amount of progress. There were a few for whom the program was no more successful than any other procedure than their teacher had attempted. And there were a few children whose responsiveness to the instruction and mastery of decoding amazed their teachers. It seems fair to say that many of the instructed children grasped for the first time the notion that there is a correspondence between phoneme and letter and that systematic strategies can be used to decode words. These fundamental aspects of the reading task are often glossed over by comprehensive code-emphasis programs, for the simple reason that most children achieve these early concepts fairly easily. Most children start to have trouble only when irregular correspondences are introduced. Several of the newer programs provide adequate instruction at this point and in the more complex aspects of decoding. However, for the slow learners with whom we are concerned, only thorough and systematic instruction in the earliest phases of the reading task, as provided by a program like this one, can prepare such children to perform adequately in the comprehensive programs.

In October and November of 1976-77, we tested children in six New York City school districts in Manhattan, Brooklyn, and the Bronx. On the basis of pretest scores, we formed 46 small groups ($N = 164$). These groups were assigned randomly to instructional treatment or to control (no instruction). The teachers involved were not specifially chosen for participation in the study; instead, they represented all the teachers in the districts whose classes contained a suitable group of children. Those teachers who were assigned to the instructional treatment were asked to use the program regularly—three or four times per week—but were told that they should use the program in the way that was, in their opinion, most appropriate for their pupils. That is, they might skip certain objectives or even entire units, might eliminate all worksheets, and so forth. We will obtain a complete record of how the program is used in each classroom.

In addition to assessing improvement on the particular skills taught in the program, we will also assess the children's ability to use those skills in other reading situations. Thus, we will incorporate comprehension items on the posttest. In addition, we will interview the teachers to determine how they used the teaching strategies presented in the program in their other reading instruction.

We will also attempt to answer the question of whether or not children can learn to transfer the decoding strategies they acquire in the program and if so, to what extent they do so. There are very little relevant data available. Often, small-scale, laboratory-analogue studies do not demonstrate evidence of transfer, perhaps because the small amount of training usually given in such experiments is not sufficient to promote transfer. Sometimes, of course, it is a matter of inadequate design, so that what the subjects are learning is a series of rote associations and not strategies at all. There is also very little information relevant to this point based on actual classroom instruction, because it is difficult to monitor the instruction sufficiently. We are making an attempt to do this; the highly structured nature of our program makes it at least feasible to try.

DISCUSSION

A few comments on the place of research in the development of instructional programs seem in order. Although this program is research based, it is obvious that—as in most if not all instructional development (See Venezky, 1976)—we did not have sufficient empirical data to support all our design decisions. Moreover, it would not be feasible or sensible to try to collect such data. In those instances where the appropriate data were available, they did not provide conclusive evidence for the choices we had to make. One very simple example is described in this chapter: our selection of the limited set of phonemes to introduce at the beginning of the program. Data were available on many of the relevant questions but were conflicting in their implications, and compromises were necessary. Thus, some research findings were deliberately ignored. This is not an isolated case; indeed, it represents a substantial proportion of the decisions that were made.

It should also be noted that whereas programs of instruction can and must be based on general principles of learning and cognition (and must also not run counter to common sense), more detailed and specific research findings will not ordinarily be useful in their development. For example, there was sufficient evidence 5 years ago that instruction should include greater focus on auditory segmentation and blending as component skills of the decoding process. A great deal of research since then has served to corroborate that fact, but the further details that have been generated by recent experiments do not themselves contribute very much to program development. More to the point as far as empirical findings are concerned are the actual outcomes of trials of the program itself in the field. The developer must be prepared to modify this program. whether or not the changes seem to mesh well with findings from basic research. And he or she must, from the very beginning, design the program according to other, quite different, considerations: cost, ease of implementation, appeal, acceptability to school personnel, "fit" within the overall curriculum, and so forth. An instructional program must also be adaptable and flexible, so that it will not be put aside with the first modification of the classroom setting.

There are certain exceptions to this statement. One might be interested in determining how far and with what success certain principles apply or in demonstrating the maximum effectiveness of a particular technique. In these cases, one must work within a setting that is in some sense "ideal" and one that is certainly unusual. For example, most current computer-assisted instruction requires so much special support (hardware, personnel, training, etc.) that it is unreasonable to expect that just any school could take on such a program. But is is clearly important to find out how effective this new technology can be in instruction. In the same way, current management systems often require a tremendous investment of time and effort on assessment. Just how valuable is it for children to be evaluated so closely and so frequently? How much energy are teachers willing to expend on assessment? [Eds. note: See the Calfee and Drum chapter, Volume 2, this series, for a discussion of related issues.] Without establishing special educational setting, we shall never be able to assess the effectiveness of some of these innovative techniques and methods.

Yet it must be recognized that these special situations are far from typical. Instructional programs for today—that is, programs to be used in the schools as they actually exist and as they will exist for the next several years—are also needed. *The ABDs of Reading* is one of these.

It would be highly desirable to have a comprehensive program of instruction that covers all aspects of early reading and that interfaces effectively with the rest of the school curriculum. But there are also advantages to programs that are more limited in scope, including the fact that it is easier for individual schools or even individual teachers to elect to use them. Moreover, in this particular instance, some teachers who would resist using a comprehensive, structured approach to reading would be willing to provide supplemental instruction of this sort, thus allowing more children the opportunity of gaining the benefits of this approach.

The most important goal for a project such as this one is not that the program itself be used by large numbers of children all over the United States. One crucial goal is for some of the teaching strategies and techniques that have been developed to become, eventually, part of teachers' general repertoire of teaching skills. This general diffusion of new techniques is one of the most significant outcomes of recent federal research and development efforts. Now and in the near future, we hope, *The ABDs of Reading* will itself be useful, because the particular aspects of the reading task that this program addresses have long been ignored in instruction. Later, however, if it is shown that this program does indeed help children to master decoding skills, those aspects of instruction that we have focused on and those techniques that we have developed may come to be emphasized in "regular" reading instruction, so that specific remedial instruction will be less necessary.

ACKNOWLEDGMENTS

The work reported here was supported by the Bureau for the Education of the Handicapped, U.S. Office of Education. Many people have contributed to the development of the program. The assistance of Christine Ansell, Joyce French, Barbara Higgins, Meredith Kattke, Nancy Kozak, Mary Oestereicher, and Suzanne Weiner is gratefully acknowledged. In addition to contributing to the overall organization of the program, Nancy Kozak wrote all the Unit Stories and many of the games; she deserves special thanks.

REFERENCES

Bateman, B. The efficacy of an auditory and a visual method of first-grade reading instruction with auditory and visual learners. In H. K. Smith (Ed.), *Perception and reading.* Newark,Del.: International Reading Association, 1968.

Bruinicks, R. H. Teaching word recognition to disadvantaged boys. *Journal of Learning Disabilities,* 1970, *3,* 28–37.

Calfee, R. C., Lindamood, P., & Lindamood, C. Acoustic-phonetic skills and reading: K through 12. *Journal of Educational Psychology,* 1973, *64,* 293–298.

Chall, J. S., Roswell, F. G., & Blumenthal, S. H. Auditory blending ability: A factor in success in beginning reading. *The Reading Teacher,* 1963, *17,* 113–118.

Coleman, E. B. Collecting a data base for a reading technology. *Journal of Educational Psychology,* 1970, *61,* 1–23.

Cronbach, L. J., & Snow, R. E. *Aptitudes and instructional methods.* New York: Irvington, 1977.

Durrell, D., & Murphy, H. The auditory discrimination factor in reading readiness and reading disability. *Education,* 1953, *73,* 556–560.

Dykstra, R. Auditory discrimination abilities and beginning reading achievement. *Reading Research Quarterly,* 1966, *1,* 5–34.

Elkonin, D. B. The psychology of mastering the elements of reading. In B. Simon & J. Simon (Eds.), *Educational psychology in the U.S.S.R.* London: Routledge & Kegan Paul, 1963.

Fox, B., & Routh, D. K. Phonemic analysis and synthesis as word-attack skills. *Journal of Educational Psychology,* 1976, *68,* 70–74.

Frostig, M., & Horne, D. *The Frostig program for the development of visual perception.* Chicago: Follett, 1964.

Gage, N. L., & Berliner, D. C. *Educational psychology.* Skokie, Ill.: Rand McNally, 1975.

Gagne, R. M. *Essentials of learning for instruction.* Hinsdale, Ill.: Dryden, 1974.

Glaser, R. *Adaptive education: Individual diversity and learning.* New York: Holt, Rinehart & Winston, 1977.

Goldstein, D. M. Cognitive-linguistic functioning and learning to read in preschoolers. *Journal of Educational Psychology,* 1976, *68,* 680–688.

Hallahan, D. P., & Kauffman, J. M. *Introduction to learning disabilities: A psychobehavioral approach.* Englewood Cliffs, N.J.: Prentice-Hall, 1976.

Hardy, M., Stennitt, R. G., & Smythe, P. C. Auditory segmentation and auditory blending in relation to beginning reading. *Alberta Journal of Educational Research,* 1973, *19,* 144–158.

Harrington, S. M. J., & Durrell, D. Mental maturity vs. perceptual abilities in primary reading. *Journal of Educational Psychology,* 1955, *46,* 375–380.

Kephart, N. *The slow learner in the classroom.* Columbus, Ohio: Merrill, 1960.

Kuenne, J. B., & Williams, J. P. Auditory recognition cues in the primary grades. *Journal of Educational Psychology,* 1973, *64,* 241–246.

Liberman, A. M., Cooper, F. S., Shankweiler, D., & Studdert-Kennedy, M. Perception of the speech code. *Psychological Review,* 1967, *74,* 431–461.

Liberman, I. Y. Segmentation of the spoken word and reading acquisition. *Bulletin of the Orton Society,* 1973, *23,* 65–77.

Liberman, I. Y., Shankweiler, D., Fischer, F. W., & Carter, B. Explicit syllable and phoneme segmentation in the young child. *Journal of Experimental Child Psychology,* 1974, *18,* 201–212.

MacGinitie, W. Auditory perception in reading. *Education,* 1967, *87,* 532–538.

Marsh, G., & Sherman, M. *Kindergarten children's discrimination and production of phonemes in isolation and in words* (Tech. Memorandum No. TM-2-71-07). Denver, Colo.: Southwest Regional Laboratory, 1971.

Miller, G. A., & Nicely, P. E. An analysis of perceptual confusions among some English consonants. *Journal of the Acoustical Society of America,* 1955, *27,* 338–352.

Monroe, M. Children who cannot read. Chicago: University of Chicago Press, 1932.

Resnick, L. B., & Beck, I. L. Designing instruction in reading: Interaction of theory and practice. In J. T. Guthrie (Ed.), *Aspects of reading acquisition.* Baltimore, Md.: Johns Hopkins University Press, 1976.

Ringler, L., & Smith, I. Learning modality and word recognition of first grade children. *Journal of Learning Disabilities,* 1973, *6,* 307–312.

Robinson, H. M. Visual and auditory modalities related to methods for beginning reading. *Reading Research Quarterly,* 1972, *8,* 7–39.

Rosner, J. Language arts and arithmetic achievement, and specifically related perceptual skills. *American Educational Research Journal,* 1973, *10,* 59–68.

Rosner, J. Auditory analysis training with prereaders. *Reading Teacher,* 1974, *27,* 379–384.

Ross, A. O. *Psychological aspects of learning disabilities and reading disorders.* New York: McGraw-Hill, 1976.

Samuels, S. J. Success and failure in learning to read: A critique of the research. *Reading Research Quarterly,* 1973, *8,* 200–239.

Strauss, A., & Lehtinen, L. *Psychopathology and education of the brain-injured child* (Vol. 1). New York: Grune & Stratton, 1947.

Vellutino, F. R. *Psychological factors in reading disability.* Paper presented at the meeting of the American Educational Research Association, Chicago, April 1974.

Venezky, R. L. Prerequisites for learning to read. In J. R. Levin & V. L. Allen (Eds.), *Cognitive learning in children: Theories and strategies.* New York: Academic Press, 1976.

Vernon, M. D. *Backwardness in reading.* Cambridge, England: Cambridge University Press, 1957.

Wepman, J. M. The modality concept—including a statement of the perceptual and conceptual levels of learning. In H. K. Smith (Ed.). *Perception and reading.* Newark, Del.: International Reading Association, 1968.

Williams, J. P. Training children to copy and to discriminate letterlike forms. *Journal of Educational Psychology,* 1975, *67,* 790–795.

Williams, J. P. Building perceptual and cognitive strategies into a reading curriculum. In A. S. Reber & D. L. Scarborough (Eds.), *Toward a psychology of reading.* Hillsdale, N.J.: Lawrence Erlbaum Associates, 1977.

Zigmond, N. Auditory processes in children with learning disabilities, In L. Tarnopol (Ed.) *Learning disabilities: Introduction to educational and medical management.* Springfield, Ill.: Charles C. Thomas, 1969.

9 Helping Disadvantaged Children Learn to Read by Teaching Them Phoneme Identification Skills

Michael A. Wallach and Lise Wallach
Duke University

In our view, a major reason that so many poor children have trouble learning to read is that they lack certain prerequisite skills that middle-class children typically possess. We believe further that these skills can be provided by instruction and that when they are provided, the children in question learn basic reading on schedule.

Of particular importance are skills in the recognition and manipulation of basic speech sounds, or phonemes—for example, the ability to identify the common beginning and ending sounds in *bat* and *bit* or to understand that the *ee* after the sound *mm* makes the word *me*. We present evidence indicating that disadvantaged children are often seriously lacking in such skills, although not—as is sometimes supposed—in auditory discrimination ability as such. Readiness curricula, to be sure, often provide exercises with sounds, such as sound matching and sound identification. But when children are lacking in skills of phoneme recognition and manipulation, as we have found to be the case for large numbers of the disadvantaged, they are unable to perform such tasks and hence are quite incapable of benefiting from the material intended to help them. Customary readiness work on sounds presupposes the very skills these children need to develop!

Consider what the lack of these skills means for learning to read. Children who cannot recognize a sound in different contexts—who do not comprehend, for example, that *mother* and *man* start with the same sound— are deprived of the possibility of making any use of the relationships between letters and sounds when faced with the task of turning print into the spoken language with which they are already familiar. But without this possibility, little or no basis exists for transfer in learning to read. Each different word must then be learned as a separate symbol—a task inordinately dependent on sheer rote memorization and made even harder by the interference that eventuates from the same letters continually recurring as parts of the stimulus patterns in different words. As the number of words increases and their distinguishability becomes ever less, learning must become more and more difficult.

Some have at times written (e.g., Smith, 1973) as if knowledge of the relationships between letters and sounds were unimportant for learning to read, or even irrelevant. For a child who is incapable of recognizing sounds in words, knowledge of letter–sound relationships indeed is useless. But for a child who is able to make use of it, such knowledge will inevitably make a great deal of difference as a source of transfer. This is the case despite the fact that letters and phonemes—including patterns of letters and phonemes—are far from showing complete correspondence in written English. Perfect predictability from letters to sounds is not needed in order for letters to provide useful information about sounds. Combining information about the usual sounds that letters stand for with information from the other sources a child has available—the child's repertoire of spoken English, contextual clues, and memory of previous encounters with a word—can enable word recognition to occur when neither the letter–sound information nor the other sources of information would suffice alone.

The potential utility of a child's knowing letter–sound relationships also is not gainsaid by the fact—sometimes viewed as a matter of concern—that a child, when "figuring out" a word, may lose track of its meaning. That this can happen does not imply that the child would be better off not paying attention to sounds. Again, the child would then be left with practically no basis for transfer in learning. When the deciphering of words into letter–sound correspondences takes so much of a child's effort that attention to meaning suffers, additional practice at deciphering can be given until it goes more smoothly and the child becomes able to recognize the words more rapidly. As Chall (1967) has shown, even when comprehension seems to be the problem beginning readers are having, such difficulties can be overcome by helping them gain greater facility in decoding, not having them put less emphasis on the deciphering of words.

Making use in this way of the information about sounds that a word's letters can give is not possible, however, unless the child possesses whatever skills are necessary for identifying the phonemes of which words are composed. If poor children lack these skills, it should not surprise us that they often have trouble learning to read. Is there evidence, then, for a deficiency in these skills on the part of low-income children?

POOR CHILDREN FREQUENTLY LACK
PHONEME IDENTIFICATION SKILLS

We have direct evidence that children from disadvantaged backgrounds, as distinct from middle-class children, tend to have considerable difficulty analyzing words into phonemes (Wallach, Wallach, Dozier, & Kaplan, 1977). Further, our research shows that it is the specific ability to recognize phonemes in words that these children lack, rather than—as has sometimes been thought (e.g., Deutsch, 1964; Plumer, 1970)—the ability to hear phoneme differences. If the latter kind of auditory discrimination were the problem, the instructional outlook might be less promising than in fact is the case.

Our subjects were 146 children who were soon to be entering first grade. Of them, 76 were from six different kindergartens or day-care centers serving low-income families; the other 70 were from five middle-class kindergartens.

The children were given two different kinds of tasks. The first kind—auditory discrimination—assessed whether a child could hear the difference between spoken words that differed only in the phonemes with which they began, such as *lake* versus *rake, mail* versus *nail,* or *key* versus *tea.* The two phonemes in each pair were similar. The second kind of task—phoneme recognition—determined whether a child could correctly identify given phonemes at the start of a word—for example, whether the child would agree that *rake* and *rag* begin with /r/ but *lake* and *mail* do not.

For the auditory discrimination task, we used a procedure that has often been used before for this purpose (e.g., Goldman, Fristoe, & Woodcock, 1970; Templin, 1957) but with an additional control. The procedure is to show sets of pictures of things that have very similar names—for example, a lake and a rake—and to have the child try to point to one of the pictures when the tester, avoiding giving other possible cues, pronounces its name. A child who consistently points to the correct picture in a series of such choices must be able to hear the differences between the phonemes that differentiate the names.

In the usual procedure of this kind, however, a child might hear the names quite correctly but still not be able to point to the correct pictures. This would be the case if, because of vocabulary limitations, the child didn't know which names went with which pictures. To avoid such a problem, we always told the children what the pictures were to be called, repeating the names, if necessary, until the child could name each picture correctly without help. Of course, learning the correct names itself requires being able to hear the differences between names that are similar. That almost all the children needed very few, if any, repetitions of the names was evidence that auditory discrimination gives little trouble.

But the critical question was whether the children, after learning what the pictures were to be called, could point at the picture that the tester named. One of two pictures was to be pointed at in each of 16 different sets. Only three children out of the 146 failed to get at least 15 of the 16 correct—two from middle-class kindergartens and one from a low-income day-care center. Our data, thus, seem to show quite clearly that neither middle-class nor poor children at the age when they start school tend to have much trouble hearing the difference between different, related phonemes.

The situation is strikingly different, however, for phoneme recognition. Almost all the poor children had a great deal of trouble with phoneme recognition in a variety of different tasks, although most of the middle-class children could identify phonemes readily. The tasks were designed to be as easy as possible; immediate feedback was provided, and a few selected phonemes (/m/, /s/, and /r/) were worked on extensively one at a time.

In one kind of phoneme recognition task, the child was shown pairs of pictures (again we made sure the child could name them correctly), of which one did and the other did not have a name that began with a particular phoneme. The child was to say which picture had the name beginning with the phoneme in question. Before proceeding with the items for any given phoneme, the child listened to instances of words that begin with it. For example, in the case of /m/, the tester said, "Some words start with the sound /m/, like *Ma* or *mud* or *me.*" The child was shown a picture of a man and a picture of a house and was asked whether *man* or *house* starts with /m/. If the child said *"man,"* the child was told that was correct; if the child said *"house,"* the child was told, "No, *man* starts with /m/." Then the child was shown the next pair of pictures, a book and a mop, proceeding the same way; then a car and a mouse; and so on.

There were five such pairs of pictures for /m/, five for /s/, and five for /r/. Of the 70 middle-class children, 65 got 12 or more of these 15 correct; this was the case for only 9 of the 76 poor children, and 46 of them got 9 or less correct.

A second kind of phoneme recognition task was similar to the one just described except that the child was provided with a third picture in each set and was told that the name of this third picture started with the phoneme at issue. This third picture thus could be used for matching. The results were essentially the same as those without the third picture.

There was one further kind of phoneme recognition task. After preliminary training that was designed to make the task as clear as possible, the child was asked whether he or she could hear a particular phoneme in a series of spoken words, some beginning with this phoneme and others not containing it. The tester indicated whether the child was right or wrong, and whenever the child said he or she couldn't hear the phoneme in a word that did contain it, the tester repeated the word, emphasizing and elongating that phoneme. Although this task was somewhat harder overall, the differences between the two social-class groups were as striking as before. The task contained a total of 36 items; of the 70 middle-class children, 62 got 25 or more of the 36 correct, but this was the case for only 9 of the 76 poor children.

Most of the poor children, then, had a great deal of trouble with each of the three phoneme recognition tasks, although most of the middle-class children had very little difficulty with any of them. But the various phoneme recognition tasks just described are all relatively simple versions of the kinds of procedures used in those standard reading-readiness curricula that are concerned with sounds. Our data thus indicate that very large numbers of poor children lack the necessary ability to recognize phonemes that is presupposed by these procedures. Virtually all children starting school (except those with actual sensory impairment) are able to hear phoneme differences, but a great many poor children lack the competence at phoneme recognition that is needed in order to benefit from the instruction they receive.

PHONEME RECOGNITION IS TEACHABLE

The belief is widespread that the ability to recognize phonemes cannot be taught. According to the conventional wisdom, if a child is unable to perform the kinds of tasks with sounds that readiness curricula provide, then further maturation is necessary before the child will be in a position to acquire the needed skills. This belief often goes hand in hand with the proposal that reading instruction be deferred for the children in question "until their readiness matures." The consequence of waiting in this manner for readiness to mature is, of course, that these children—most often from low-income and frequently also from minority-group backgrounds—fall still further behind in learning to read.

An alternative proposal that is sometimes recommended in light of the foregoing belief is to teach reading without regard for letter–sound relationships, thus avoiding any need for competence at recognizing and dealing with phonemes. But we have already noted how difficult the task of learning to read becomes if a child cannot make use of the possibilities for transfer afforded by relations between letters and sounds. This approach too, therefore, means that the children who lack phoneme identification skills will fall still further behind.

It seems, in fact, quite inevitable that children who lack the prerequisite skills involved in learning to read are going to fall further and further behind unless provision is made for them to acquire these skills. If children who cannot recognize phonemes can be taught to do so, such instruction clearly ought to be provided. Contrary to the conventional wisdom on the subject, it is apparent now that basic phoneme identification skills can be successfully taught. There is some evidence to this effect from research in the Soviet Union described by Elkonin (1971) and from research at the Universities of Wisconsin and Pittsburgh described by Gibson and Levin (1975). In the work that we have done along these lines (L. Wallach & M. A. Wallach, 1976; M. A. Wallach & L. Wallach, 1976), we have found it possible to spell out a systematic sequence of instructional procedures that reliably establishes phoneme recognition skills in first graders who lack them. This sequence, administered by community tutors to a sample of low-readiness children in Chicago inner-city schools, resulted in every child's becoming able to identify phonemes.

In the next section, we give an overview of these instructional procedures and of the other aspects of the tutorial program that contains them. First, however, some background information should be provided on how we arrived at them and what influenced their development. Our first attempts at pilot tutoring involved tasks that were not too far removed from the methods to be found in some of the most systematic of readiness curricula, such as Durrell and Murphy (1964) or Stern and Gould (1963). The tasks were, thus, similar to the phoneme recognition tasks in our experiment described in the previous section, which was actually performed after this tutoring. Working on one phoneme at a time, we would present the children with spoken words (often using pictures of what the words depicted as well), some of which did and others that did not begin with the phoneme in question. The child was to indicate whether each word started with the phoneme at issue or not, and when errors were made they would be corrected. We rather quickly found, however—as the experiment that we did later also showed and as many teachers have known—that some children simply couldn't do this kind of task and that extended practice didn't result in their learning how to do it, either, despite the best of indications regarding the child's motivation to perform and rapport with the tutor. If, instead of giving children the kind of series of words just described, we gave them two words at a time, one of which started with a given phoneme and the other that did not, with the child to choose the word in each pair that started with the phoneme at issue, making correct choices became a little easier. But again, for many children, this task also was quite impossible to learn. Such children simply did not seem capable of recognizing the phoneme in the context of the word.

What these children appeared to need was some sort of a strategy they could apply to a word that would make the phoneme recognizable, something they could do with a word that would serve to extract the phoneme from its context. Having the child try to accentuate the initial phoneme in some way did not seem to help. We finally hit on an approach that did work, however— namely, getting the child to "break words up," to separate off the first sound from the remaining sounds by a pause. If a child can say "r-ake" and "p-ot," then it is not hard for the child to tell whether *rake* or *pot* starts with /r/. All the children were able to learn to break up words in this manner, first in direct imitation of the tutor and later on their own. And once a child could isolate an initial phoneme in a word this way, the child no longer had any trouble recognizing it. Working with phonemes in other positions than at the start of a word came easily thereafter, and so too did learning to read—but that is a part of the story to come later.

Our procedure of separating off critical phonemes by pauses is not very different, it turns out, from one that Zhurova (1963/1973) had earlier found some young children to use spontaneously for identifying the initial sound in a word, and that she also found was of help to others when she taught it to them. The child would repeat the initial sound several times before saying the word; for example, "*d-d-doggie*," "*b-b-bear*." Essentially the same function is served: The critical phoneme is separated off and pronounced, as it were, "by itself."

Of course, most consonant phonemes, such as /d/ and /b/, cannot really be pronounced by themselves; some sort of vowel sound, such as *uh*, always accompanies them. This seems to be, in fact, a major reason that there has not been more use of procedures like Zhurova's and ours—or indeed that there have been so few attempts to teach phoneme identification skills altogether. It is widely believed (e.g., Gibson & Levin, 1975; Gleitman & Rozin, 1973) that the extra vowel sounds that get added when words are overtly analyzed into their constituent phonemes and deleted when the phonemes are "blended" to form words will inevitably confuse the child. We found this problem in fact, however, to be a relatively minor one and not hard to overcome. Perhaps the reason it turns out to be minor is that the added vowel can, after all, be a single, unemphasized sound that remains constant for various consonants, thus providing a common feature from which abstracting the consonant sound is relatively easy. In any case, most of the low-readiness children with whom we have worked show by their performance that they grasp fairly rapidly what the segmentation strategy that we want them to use is all about. They become quite proficient at breaking words up in this way, treating the additional vowel sound as irrelevant. Some children take longer to learn than others, but none have failed to catch on.

There were two further procedures for helping children learn to identify phonemes in words that we also included, although these seemed much less critical than isolating a phoneme by pronouncing it separately from the rest of the word that contains it. One was to have the tutor say "tongue-twister" sentences in which the critical phoneme that the child was to learn to identify would keep recurring at the beginning of different words. In the case of /j/, for example, the sentence is, "John got juice and jelly on his jacket when Judy jumped on him." The relevant words in such sentences would then be broken up as described before, with first the tutor and then the child saying, "*John, J-ohn, juice, j-uice,*" and so on. The other procedure was this: For a child who said that a word started with a given phoneme when it didn't, we thought that hearing what the word would sound like if it did start with that phoneme might also be of help. Thus, for example, if the child said that *telephone* started with /j/, the tutor would say, "No. It's *telephone, not jelephone.*"

But the most important by far of these procedures for learning phoneme identification skills seems to be having first the tutor, and then the child, break words up, with the initial sound separated off by a pause and pronounced "by itself." Here was a strategy that children could use for disembedding a phoneme from its word context—and could learn, after sufficient imitation, to apply on their own.

These three procedures for acquiring phoneme identification skills were built into an explicit and systematically sequenced program aimed at beginning first graders (L. Wallach & M. A. Wallach, 1976) that nonprofessionals could carry out as tutors with low-readiness children. All such children tutored by community adults with this program in our field research (see M. A. Wallach & L. Wallach, 1976) successfully learned phoneme concepts and letter–phoneme associations to rigorous criteria of mastery for every letter of the alphabet. Furthermore, 90% of these low-readiness children did so in approximately 2 1/2 months on the basis of a 30-minute tutoring session per school day. Those who took longer were children who had missed large numbers of tutoring sessions. Clearly, then, phoneme recognition can be taught, in a relatively short period of time, and to children whose low scores on readiness tests mean that they are expected to have a difficult time learning to read.

ARE THERE PRACTICAL MEANS FOR PROVIDING HELP TO THE CHILDREN WHO NEED IT?

On the basis of such considerations as the foregoing, we have developed a practical instructional program that establishes phoneme identification skills and builds systematically from them to basic reading competence. The program can be successfully applied by community adults without educational credentials as tutors under appropriate supervision. It is designed to bring most low-readiness first graders to mastery of basic reading within the first-grade year on the basis of a 30-minute tutoring session each school day.

Three key attributes characterize our tutorial program: It makes sure that a child will learn phoneme recognition and manipulation skills and apply them in reading; it uses the principle of cumulative mastery throughout—always assuring prior mastery of any needed prerequisites and always indicating what the tutor is to do in order to enable a child to master a step if that step is failed initially; and it is fully concrete and specific, so that successful application depends only on carrying out instructional routines that are spelled out in complete detail. An important means used for guaranteeing mastery of tasks in the program has been to build in the requirement that the child apply what is learned already to the task, rather than leaving such transfer up to the child. In this section, we first give an overview of the program's components (see L. Wallach & M. A. Wallach, 1976, for the complete program; and M. A. Wallach & L. Wallach, 1976, for a full description of its background and use) and then briefly review evidence that we have gathered testifying to its effectiveness under regular operating conditions in the field (see M. A. Wallach & L. Wallach, 1976, for a full presentation of this evidence).

In the first of the program's three parts, which takes about 2 1/2 months for low-readiness children, the child learns to recognize starting phonemes in words, to recognize leter shapes, and to connect the letter shapes with their phonemes. In the second part of the program, which takes about 2 or 3 weeks for low-readiness children, the child learns to blend phonemes to form words, gaining practice in the course of this at recognizing and manipulating phonemes in any position in a word. And in the third part, which runs for the rest of the academic year, the child meets stringent mastery criteria for reading with comprehension the regular classroom reading materials, learning whatever further words are needed by a process that assures use of prior knowledge of letter–phoneme relationships and of blending.

Part 1—Letters and Sounds

Part 1 of the program teaches the most typical sound for each consonant letter and the short vowel sound for each vowel, proceeding in alphabetical order and using only lowercase letters at this point. Such choices as these were determined by the principle that the program be kept as simple to use as was consistent with the goal of delivering reading competence to any child. A sequence of 10 steps is followed for each letter in turn.

Step 1, "introduction to the sound," introduces the phoneme in question with a "tongue-twister" sentence containing many words that start with it. For example, in the case of the phoneme for h, the sentence is, "Harry had a horrible headache and hated to hear Henry howl." The tutor has the child repeat after him or her each word that has /h/ as its starting sound in this sentence—first in the usual way and then with its starting sound separated off by a pause from the rest of the word.

Step 2, "the two-picture game," presents pairs of "game-pictures" to the child—line drawings depicting objects, the names of which start with the phonemes for the various letters. Of the two game-pictures in each pair, the name of one starts with the phoneme at issue, and the name of the other with any of a variety of possible phonemes. The child's task is to name the game-pictures and say which member of the pair starts with the phoneme being worked on, proceeding with successive pairs until the stringent criterion of seven correct choices in a row is met. If the child chooses the wrong picture—for example, selects *violin* instead of *window* as starting with /w/—the tutor follows a specific correction procedure, saying: "No. It's *violin*, not *wiolin*." Then, pointing to the window picture , the tutor says, "*Window* starts with /w/. Say w-indow." And the child repeats the word with its starting sound segregated off in this manner. If the child still finds the task too difficult, a further routine is added. After the child names the two pictures but before a choice is made, the tutor says the name of each picture with a pause between its starting sound and the rest of the word and has the child do likewise, only then permitting the child to choose.

Step 3, "the yes–no game," is harder than Step 2. Now game-pictures are presented one at a time. Half of them, in random order, have names starting with the critical phoneme, and the other half, names starting with various other phonemes that are different from the contrast phonemes used in Step 2. The child is to name each picture and say whether or not its name starts with the critical phoneme. In Step 2 the child decides which of two instances better fits the phoneme at issue; in Step 3 the child carries out the more demanding task of considering the phoneme's boundaries and deciding whether each instance falls within them or not. Again the rigorous criterion of seven correct answers in a row must be met. If the child calls a false positive, the tutor's correction procedure indicates what the word would sound like if it did start with the critical phoneme; if the child calls a false negative, the correction procedure lets the child hear the word with its starting sound segregated by a pause from the rest of the word. Again, if the child has too much difficulty, further practice is given in breaking words up as follows. After the child names a picture but before saying whether or not its name starts with the critical phoneme, first the tutor and then the child repeat the name with a pause after its starting sound.

Step 4, "letter tracing," introduces the letter shape for the phoneme in question through an "alpha-picture"—a picture that contains the letter form as an integral part of its design and depicts an object whose name starts with the critical phoneme. In the case of *d*, for example, the alpha-picture is a door. The round part of the *d* forms the doorknob, and the straight part is worked into the door's edge. Such embedding of the letter provides a cue that helps the child recollect what sound the letter is for. The tutor has the child say the name the normal way, say it with its starting sound isolated by a pause from the rest of the word, and say the starting sound alone. Practice then follows in tracing the letter's form on dotted outlines of the letter, using a sheet that also contains the alpha-picture.

Step 5, "letter drawing," is similar to Step 4, but now the child practices forming the letter without dotted outlines for tracing but only horizontal guidelines on the practice sheet. Again the sheet also contains the alpha-picture. Both steps together are to aid in the discrimination of the letter shape and its association with the critical phoneme.

Step 6, "the picture-matching game with the letter-drawing sheets," presents a series of game-pictures to be matched with one of three alpha-pictures according to the starting sounds of the game-pictures' names. The phoneme being worked on is contrasted with two others so chosen as to provide useful practice at discriminating similar letters and similar phonemes, as well as sufficient rehearsal of letter–phoneme linkages already learned. Various routines make sure the child knows what sounds the letters in the alpha-pictures represent and, as each game-picture is presented for matching to an alpha-picture, what sound the game-picture's name starts with. Matching errors are followed by correction procedures. The learning criterion again is a rigorous one of seven errorless matchings in a row. Further help is added to simplify the task if at first the child has too much trouble. For example, if the child has difficulty giving the correct starting sounds for the names of the game-pictures, a routine is inserted that provides additional practice at separating off the name's starting phoneme from the rest of the word by a pause.

Steps 7, 8, and 9 are further games for matching sounds to letters. Each game again contrasts the phoneme and letter at issue with two other phonemes and their corresponding letters—different ones in the case of each game—and calls for learning to a criterion of seven correct matchings in a row. Step 7 provides the added help of having the letters embedded in their alpha-pictures, but Steps 8 and 9 present the letters alone. In Steps 7 and 9, the tutor tells the child words from specified lists, with the child to give each word's starting sound and point to the appropriate letter. In Step 8, game-pictures are used again. The pool of spoken words and game-pictures for Steps 6 through 9 is large enough to preclude the child's learning these tasks by sheer rote memorization of what is to be done with individual game-pictures or words. As in Step 6, specific routines are followed for insuring correction of any of the possible kinds of errors that can occur and for simplifying the task if at first it is too hard.

Step 10, "giving the sounds for the letters," is the capstone of the sequence of steps for each letter and a continual review of all letters worked on already. All letters worked on thus far are presented singly, in scrambled sequence, with the child to give the letter's phoneme and a word that starts with it. Further practice is provided if necessary. Then the child returns to Step 1 for the next letter.

Part 2—Simple Words

After all 10 steps have been gone through for the last letter, z, the child begins Part 2 of the program. In this part, the child blends phonemes into words and reads short, regularly spelled words by sounding them out. In the process, the child gains facility at moving from phonemes to letters and back again at different positions in a word. Unlike the steps in Part 1, which are gone through for each letter in turn, here each step is completed for various sets of words before moving on to the next step. There are three steps in all.

Step 1, "the which-picture game," uses various triads of game-pictures. The three pictures in each set all have short names starting with the same phoneme. For example, the first set is *ball, bed,* and *bus.* The tutor says the name of one of the pictures sound by sound, and the child is to guess which picture it is. If the child has trouble, the tutor provides help by means of a graded series of routines that supply increasingly more of the needed blending and end, if necessary, with the word spoken normally. Then the tutor begins with separate sounds again for another picture in the set. This procedure continues until the child meets the criterion of correctly identifying all three pictures in the set from hearing their separate sounds alone. Then work begins on the next triad of game-pictures. After criterion is reached on the seventh such triad, the child moves on to Step 2. Since the members of a given triad share the same starting phoneme, the child, in making his or her identifications, is forced to consider later phonemes in the word and the relations between these phonemes as spoken separately and as blended.

Step 2, "building and reading the names of some game-pictures," again uses triads of game-pictures but also uses "letter-cards"—cards with lowercase letters on them—for all the letters needed to make the names of the three pictures in each set. For example, the first set of game-pictures is *hat, map,* and *yam;* and the letter-cards for *h, a, t, m, p,* and *y* are shuffled and presented as well. Placing one of the pictures before the child, the tutor has the child name it. The tutor, after repeating the name, then says it sound by sound. The child now tries to build the name by finding and assembling in sequence the letter-cards for the appropriate sounds, with help from the tutor as needed. Then the tutor, while pointing to the letters in sequence, has the child say the appropriate sound for each. After that, the tutor moves his or her finger progressively faster across the letters, saying the sounds more and more blended together until the name is said normally, and then has the child say it normally too. This routine is carried out with each of the three pictures in the set. Next, the tutor builds the name of one of the pictures in the set and has the child try to read it, giving help in sounding out and blending if necessary. This procedure is repeated with each of the three names, in varying orders, until the child meets the criterion of reading each name correctly without help. Finally, the child builds the names, receiving help if still needed. After completing these tasks for one triad of game-pictures, they all are repeated with the next. Step 2 comprises five triads in all. The names are consonant–vowel–consonant combinations in every case, the members of any triad have the same vowel, and all spelling conforms to the letter–phoneme linkages taught in Part 1. From Step 2 the child starts comprehending how a word's letters correspond in their visual sequence to the temporal sequence of phonemes in the word as spoken.

Step 3, "building and reading some more simple words," is similar to Step 2 but uses 22 new triads of words. Now only letter-cards are involved—the words are just spoken instead of being the names of game-pictures. When first introduced, the tutor uses each word in context. The words are analogous in form to those of Step 2, but the words within each set are closely similar. For instance, the first set of words is *pan, man,* and *fan*. To emphasize letter–sound correspondences, letter-cards that remain the same from one word to the next in a set are left in place, and only the changing ones are moved. For example, only the *p* and *m* are switched when working on *man* after working on *pan*. As before, the child meets the criterion of reading each word in a set correctly without help after the tutor builds it from letter-cards.

Part 3—Reading

After the prescribed tasks have been completed with the last of the 22 triads of words used in Step 3, the child proceeds to Part 3 of the program. In this part, the tutor works with the classroom reading materials, first teaching separately each page's new words according to explicit routines that assure transfer from what was learned in Parts 1 and 2 of the program. The tutor prepares a word-card for each vocabulary entry, noting the page on which it first occurs in the reader. Words are printed twice on the card—all letters in lowercase and again with the first letter capitalized (except for words always capitalized, such as names, which are printed only that way). The tutor has the child read the word-cards, going through them in the order of the words' first appearance in the reader. Part 3 is begun with that story in which the child's cumulative total of missed words reaches three.

For each page of a story, the tutor has the child read the word-cards for all words whose first occurrence is on that page. If a word is read incorrectly, the tutor moves into an explicit four-step routine for teaching words, stopping it at any point before the end if the child gets the word right. In Step A, if the word is composed of simpler words (e.g., *something*), these are shown to the child, and the remaining routines are followed with each simpler constituent first. In Step B, the tutor gives the sound for any letters whose sound differs from the letter–sound correspondences already learned. In Step C, the tutor, pointing to the letters in sequence, has the child give each letter's sound. A chart of the alpha-pictures can be looked at if the child needs a reminder of the sound that was learned for a letter. Where letters have sounds that differ from what was learned before, the tutor again gives the sound and then has the child repeat it. In Step D, if the child still can't read the word, the tutor sounds it out while pointing to the letters in sequence. If that doesn't result in the child's getting the word, the tutor then blends the first sounds together while pointing to the appropriate letters (e.g., for *father, "fa"*); if necessary, blends further into the word (e.g., *"fath"*); and so on until, if necessary, giving the entire word.

The tutor goes through the word-cards for all new words on a page, following the foregoing four-step routine for a word whenever needed and shuffling the cards after each run-through, until the child meets the criterion of reading all words correctly twice in a row without any help. Then reading of the page ensues, with the four-step routine for teaching words used for any words that the child can't get. The tutor discusses the story's meaning as the page is read, and if the child seems not to understand something, it is read again and discussed further. After the page has been read with understanding, the words that were missed are gone over the way the word-cards were before—to the same criterion of getting all words correct twice in a row without help. Then all word-cards for that page are gone through again to that same criterion. If the child, in reading the page, missed more than two words or read with difficulty, this whole cycle of reading the page, working on missed words, and working on word-cards is repeated until the child meets the criterion of reading the page smoothly and missing no more than two words.

This procedure now is repeated for the next page—once again starting with word-cards for all new words on the page, then reading the page, and so on. After all a story's pages have been gone through with this procedure, further review procedures follow. The entire process is repeated for a given story until the child satisfies the criterion of missing no more than seven different words in the story and reading it smoothly. Then work begins on the first page of the next story. Additional review procedures also are included. In all this, the four-step routine for teaching words is used wherever needed, and stringent mastery criteria must be met for moving from page to page and story to story.

Effectiveness of the Program

With our tutorial program now outlined, we turn next to the question of its effectiveness. The *Metropolitan Readiness Tests* (Hildreth, Griffiths, & McGauvran, 1966, 1969) were administered to 268 children (mostly first graders, with a few "slow-learner" second graders added) at two predominantly black inner-city public schools on Chicago's South Side at the start of the school year. Those 98 children scoring within the bottom 40% on national norms for beginning first graders defined the target group of "low-academic readiness" children for the research—children likely not to learn to read in first grade. Their median fell at the 25th percentile of the national norms. A random subset of these children, spread across eight classrooms in proportion to the incidence of low-readiness children in those classrooms, were tutored with the program by community adults—black mothers. The tutors were hired on the basis of no requirements other than reliability, working well with children, patience, and of course literacy. Selection and treatment of children and tutors were carried out in ways typical of what could be expected to occur in the program's normal operation.

Looking first at evidence internal to the tutorial program, 86% of the low-readiness children who were tutored showed a high level of reading competence before the end of the school year. They were reading on the order of 20 pages every 5 tutoring sessions or better in standard first-grade texts whose vocabularies started at about 80 to 100 words and kept rising. Indeed, 69% of the tutored children had been reading at this rate for 2 months or more before the year ended. One should keep in mind that this rather rapid rate of progress was displayed despite the very high mastery criteria imposed for moving forward in the texts. The other 14% of the tutored children were progressing too, but at slower rates.

What about comparisons between experimentals and controls? Recall that the children from the low-readiness target group found in each of the eight classrooms of the study were randomly assigned to tutored and control conditions on a proportionate basis reflecting their numbers in each classroom. Any teacher differences thus were taken into account. An extensive battery of tests were administered to the target children after an average of about 30 weeks of tutoring—somewhat before the end of the academic year. If anything, the test comparisons are conservative, since they pertain to less than the full amount of tutoring that the school year can accommodate. The testing was conducted on an individual basis by an examiner blind to whether children had been tutored or not. The spectrum of tests administered was intended to provide a representative assessment of what basic reading competence concerns—the reading of sentences and passages with understanding as well as the reading of words.

Some of the tests used were developed by us and drew on the vocabulary entries in the classroom texts; others were standardized tests of reading achievement that had been formulated independently of the classroom texts. The tests that we devised dealt with word recognition and sentence reading. The word recognition list and the series of sentences in these tests drew upon increasingly difficult classroom text vocabulary as they progressed. And although the sentences made use of vocabulary entries from the classroom texts, the sentences themselves were, insofar as possible, constructed so as to be new to the children. To pass the items on the sentence reading test, comprehension questions had to be successfully answered.

The standardized tests of reading achievement used were from Spache's *Diagnostic Reading Scales* (Spache, 1963a, 1963b, 1963c, 1972a, 1972b, 1972c). Again both word recognition and the reading of unfamiliar prose with understanding of its meaning were assessed. This time, the materials had no connection at all to the classroom texts. Spache's word recognition lists contain words graduated in difficulty. Spache's reading passages, also sequenced for increasing difficulty, require that the reading of a passage meet or exceed certain standards in regard both to reading facility and quality of comprehension in order for the child to pass to the next most difficult passage in the series.

Turning now to the results of these evaluations, consider first the findings of the tests that we developed. Because of the manner in which our word recognition list was constructed, we were able to estimate, on the basis of the children's scores, the absolute numbers of words they could read. According to these estimates, the median child in the experimental group could recognize about 150 words; the median child in the control group, a bit over 50. Regarding our sentence reading test, with its increasingly difficult sentences as the series progressses, the maximum possible score was 25 comprehension questions answered correctly. For the median child in the experimental group, the score was 19.5 of those comprehension questions correct; the score for the median child in the control group was less than half that. Large numbers of the experimentals read and comprehended even the more difficult of the sentences, but large numbers of the controls showed little comprehension at all.

Moving on to Spache's tests, the median child in the experimental group read 26 words correctly on the word recognition lists devised by Spache, and the median child in the control group read 8 or 9. Applying Spache's grade-level norms for performance on the lists, the proportions of the experimentals and controls performing near grade level or better at the word recognition task were about two-thirds and one-third, respectively. Spache's reading passages, in turn, gave results indicating that half of the experimental group, but only about one-sixth of the control group, performed near grade level or better. Recall that comprehension as well as reading facility had to be demonstrated for credit on this test.

We should add that the various effects described in these comparisons of experimentals and controls were found to be quite consistent across tutors and schools. The effects were highly significant statistically, of course, but more to the point, they were sufficiently large in their magnitudes to be important in practical terms. Children low in academic readiness at the start of the school year tended not to learn to read by the following spring with conventional instruction; but such children showed substantial reading competence by that time if tutored by nonprofessionals with our program under conditions that approximated what its normal intended usage would be like.

As a final point in regard to evaluating our program's effectiveness, note that work similar to ours in all respects except for the instructional program used was carried out by Ellson, Harris, and Barber (1968). In that work, community adults once again tutored first-grade children for 30 minutes each school day through the school year. Some of the tutors used procedures developed by Ellson and his associates that involved reading whole words in prose material from the beginning; others used procedures adapted by an experienced reading specialist from the classroom activities. No matter which one of these kinds of tutoring was used, little difference was found between tutored and untutored children on standardized tests of reading achievement. That, by contrast, children tutored with our program showed marked gains on tests of this kind thus does not seem likely to be a result of tutoring as such, but rather of tutoring with the specific content of our program.

CONCLUDING OBSERVATIONS

In closing, certain general observations seem in order. Although the point of departure for our program has been the problems disadvantaged children experience in learning to read, its applicability is by no means limited to poor children. The program also should be of help to middle-class children who have reading difficulties—especially if, as is often the case, these difficulties include trouble with phonemes.

The type of skill analysis exemplified by our work has been a highly empirical enterprise—not, as sometimes is done, merely the a priori devising of a logical-seeming task sequence. Thus, we had no idea how difficult phoneme identification could be for some children until we observed them trying to grapple with what we thought would be simple tasks and failing again and again to perform them correctly. Our emphasis on training phoneme identification skills is a direct outgrowth of these observations, and of our observations of the children's success after training was introduced. As another example, our belief in the importance of carefully establishing knowledge of letter–sound regularities was based on our observing that children often do not induce these regularities spontaneously. It was supported further by our finding that exceptions to such regularities did not seem to pose much difficulty for children; instead, knowing the regularities seemed to make the exceptions distinctive and hence recognizable as such. The need is for extensive pilot development aimed at empirically identifying whatever trouble spots may occur in a child's learning and building in ways of successfully coping with them.

As we see it, those with a cognitive outlook on education, in their zeal to counteract the stimulus–response views so recently ascendant in that field, are now overemphasizing the importance of children learning things "on their own," by discovery. To be sure, those interpreting education in cognitive terms have made significant contributions in pointing out that children are constantly picking up information spontaneously and that instruction will not help if a child does not see the relevance of what the instruction concerns. These points do not imply, however, that information—or, for that matter, strategies of processing information—cannot also be provided by instruction, or that learning is not real unless arrived at by spontaneous induction. One should not lose sight of what it is possible for instruction to accomplish—as when, for example, Gibson and Levin (1975) noted repeated evidence of children's failures to make discoveries of regularities by themselves but, in their opposition to a stimulus–response viewpoint, failed to draw what would seem the obvious implication, that instruction would be useful here.

There is no need to let a stimulus–response outlook preempt the topic of instruction. What one child is in a position to discover spontaneously, another child can be taught. And if a child does not know letter–sound regularities or how to identify phonemes when the child is expected to learn to read, then instruction in these matters is called for. Again, if a child cannot see how to use or apply something in further learning, we need not wait for spontaneous discovery to occur but can provide instruction in whatever will bring the child to such an understanding. Thus, for example, we found that children who knew letter–sound regularities but could not decipher words needed instruction in how to use for this purpose the knowledge they already possessed. When they were taught a transfer strategy for applying their knowledge of letter–sound regularities to the task of figuring out words, this task became feasible for them. Reliance on spontaneous discovery inevitably means that children who are lacking necessary skills will fall further and further behind. Rather than eschewing instruction in favor of spontaneous discovery, then, it is time for instruction to be taken much more seriously than it ever has before.

REFERENCES

Chall, J. S. *Learning to read: The great debate.* New York: McGraw-Hill, 1967.

Deutsch, C. P. Auditory discrimination and learning: Social factors. *Merrill–Palmer Quarterly,* 1964, *10,* 277–296.

Durrell, D. D., & Murphy, H. A. *Speech-to-print phonics.* New York: Harcourt, Brace & World, 1964.

Elkonin, D. B. Development of speech. In A. V. Zaporozhets & D. B. Elkonin (Eds.), *The psychology of preschool children.* Cambridge, Mass.: MIT Press, 1971.

Ellson, D. G., Harris, P., & Barber, L. A field test of programmed and directed tutoring. *Reading Research Quarterly,* 1968, *3,* 307–367.

Gibson, E. J., & Levin, H. *The psychology of reading.* Cambridge, Mass.: MIT Press, 1975.

Gleitman, L. R., & Rozin, P. Teaching reading by use of a syllabary. *Reading Research Quarterly,* 1973, *8,* 447–483.

Goldman, R., Fristoe, M., & Woodcock, R. W. *Test of auditory discrimination.* Circle Pines, Minn.: American Guidance Service, 1970.

Hildreth, G. H., Griffiths, N. L., & McGauvran, M. E. *Metropolitan readiness tests, form B.* New York: Harcourt, Brace & World, 1966.

Hildreth, G. H., Griffiths, N. L., & McGauvran, M. E. *Manual of directions: Metropolitan readiness tests, forms A and B.* New York: Harcourt, Brace & World, 1969.

Plumer, D. A summary of environmentalist views and some educational implications. In F. Williams (Ed.), *Language and poverty: Perspectives on a theme*. Chicago: Markham, 1970.

Smith, F. *Psycholinguistics and reading*. New York: Holt, Rinehart & Winston, 1973.

Spache, G.D. *Diagnostic reading scales: Examiner's manual*. Monterey, Calif.: CTB/McGraw-Hill, 1963. (a)

Spache, G. D. *Diagnostic reading scales: Examiner's record booklet*. Monterey, Calif.: CTB/McGraw-Hill, 1963. (b)

Spache, G. D. *Diagnostic reading scales: Test book*. Monterey, Calif.: CTB/McGraw-Hill, 1963. (c)

Spache, G. D. *Diagnostic reading scales: Examiner's manual* (Rev. ed.). Monterey, Calif.: CTB/McGraw-Hill, 1972. (a)

Spache, G. D. *Diagnostic reading scales: Examiner's record booklet* (Rev. ed.). Monterey, Calif.: CTB/McGraw-Hill, 1972. (b)

Spache, G. D. *Diagnostic reading scales: Test Book* (Rev. ed.). Monterey, Calif.: CTB/McGraw-Hill, 1972. (c)

Stern, C., & Gould, T. S. *Chidren discover reading*. Syracuse, N.Y.: Random House/Singer, 1963.

Templin, M. C. *Certain language skills in children: Their Development and interrelationships*. Minneapolis: University of Minnesota Press, 1957.

Wallach, L., & Wallach, M. A. *The teaching all children to read kit*. Chicago: University of Chicago Press, 1976.

Wallach, L., Wallach, M. A., Dozier, M. G., & Kaplan, N. E. Poor children learning to read do not have trouble with auditory discrimination but do have trouble with phoneme recognition. *Journal of Educational Psychology*, 1977, *69*, 36–39.

Wallach, M. A., & Wallach, L. *Teaching all children to read*. Chicago: University of Chicago Press, 1976.

Zhurova, L. E. The development of analysis of words into their sounds by preschool children. In C. A. Ferguson & D. I. Slobin (Eds.), *Studies of child language development*. New York: Holt, Rinehart & Winston, 1973. (Originally published, 1963.)

10

Two Approaches to Initial Reading Instruction: An Analysis of the *Reading Unlimited Program* and the *New Primary Grades Reading System*

Helen Mitchell Popp
Harvard University

The materials and methods of instruction for two beginning reading programs are analyzed in this chapter. The programs, the *Reading Unlimited Program* (Scott, Foresman, 1976) and the *New Primary Grades Reading System* (Learning Research and Development Center, 1974), provide maximal contrasts in materials and teaching strategies. Authors of both programs agree that the ultimate goal is to gain meaning from print, to comprehend written messages; but there are differences in the sequences of instruction and in the strategies taught to beginning readers. The instructional strategies in Scott, Foresman (SF) are analytic and inductive, whereas those in New Reading Systems (NRS) are mostly synthetic; and whereas SF begins instruction with the focus on syntactic and semantic information, NRS initially emphasizes graphemic information and letter–sound correspondences.

This chapter systematically compares the two programs and evaluates how each meets its stated objectives. I outline the scope of the two programs and the materials included in each, examine specific teaching/learning strategies and their organization in each program, ask how well each testing program evaluates the children's use of these strategies, look at the content and other motivational aspects of the programs, and estimate the extent of individualization possible under each program.

SCOPE

The *Reading Unlimited Program,* a revision of Scott, Foresman's 1972 *Reading Systems,* packages the components in a less cumbersome manner and better coordinates the management of the system. The SF program specifies two major goals: "to help children learn how to read and to communicate to children the rewards of reading [Teacher's Edition, p. 10]." Toward achieving these goals, the program combines a variety of teaching techniques to help children get meaning from print and incorporates a rich and varied content in the readers. Both of these aspects are discussed later in the chapter; however, Table 10.1 gives an indication of the materials available.

Beck and Mitroff (1972), in describing NRS, give as their underlying definition of reading that stated by Carroll (1964): "the perception and comprehension of written messages in a manner paralleling that of the corresponding spoken messages [p. 336]." NRS emphasizes individualization of student rate and uses adaptive strategies for teaching. The materials included in NRS are displayed in Table 10.1. Prior to commercial publication, NRS may be revised and consolidated somewhat, but my analysis includes the components listed in Table 10.1.

The analysis of program materials is confined to those levels most often used in first and second grades. Table 10.2 displays the distribution of the levels on a time line across grades 1 and 2 and indicates how many books are read at each level.

An overview of both programs reveals gross differences, differences that would be immediately obvious to the most casual visitor in classrooms implementing the programs. In the classrooms I visited using SF, I found, even in grade one, art projects, samples of creative writing, scenes for dramatic play, and books for the children to read that were correlated to the stories being read in the pupils' readers at that time. Some programs give suggestions to the teacher for such activities. SF goes beyond suggesting in several ways: Many art and craft projects are initiated in the pupils' readers and/or in their studybooks; selections, stories, and poems for the teacher to read to the children are in the teacher's editions; and boxes of trade books appropriate for each level may be purchased from the publishers.

Creative projects stemming from NRS are more apt to be teacher designed. There is no reason that activities similar to those in SF classrooms might not be found in NRS classrooms, but they are not an intergral part of the program. I observed NRS in a classroom for "learning disabled" children, and such activities were not evident. In another NRS classroom, arts and crafts were under way, but their relatedness to NRS was not obvious. Games that are specified for the various levels of NRS were very much in evidence in these rooms, and youngsters were actively engaged with each other, with the

TABLE 10.1
Materials Included in Scott, Foresman's, *Reading Unlimited Program* (SF) and
LRDC's *New Primary Grades Reading System* (NRS)

SF	*NRS*
Teacher's editions (all levels)	Teacher's manuals (Levels 1, 2, 3)
Magneboard and magnepiece file (for use with Levels 1–3)	Scope and sequence chart (Levels 4–14) Game presentation guide Alternative strategies booklet
Pupil's books (All levels have one book, except Level 2, which has 3. Available as smaller booklets at lowest levels.)	Blending booklet Read-Alone story booklets (about 8 each at 14 levels) Group readers (two at each level)
Studybook (one for each level) [Independent practice book] [Duplicating masters]	Workbook Audio-cassette instruction recorders, earphones
[End-of-level tests][a]	Progress check
[Skills Assessment tests][a]	
[A variety of other materials are available: Practice books for further pupil reading, puzzles, alphabet records and cards, picture dictionaries, storybook box with cassettes.][a]	Games (Correlated vocabulary at each level; 17 types, 10 per level) Flip-a-Words (word pattern manipulable)
	Management aids: Recording booklet for games and stories Progress-check booklet Prescription pages in workbooks

[a]Supplementary materials.

teachers, and with visitors who happpened by. Games, which are not included in SF, are an important component of the NRS program and appear to be highly motivating.

What are some other readily observable differences between NRS and SF classrooms that are attributable to program variation? Certainly the role of the teacher varies, and the children's behavior varies. Instruction for the SF pupil is very much directed by the teacher. Groups of students gather daily to

TABLE 10.2

Sequence of Levels of Instruction and Pupil Materials for SF and NRS through Second Grade

Grade level	1					2		
SF Levels	1	2	3	4	5	6	7	8
Number of pupil books	5	9	5	8	1	1	1	1

NRS levels	1	2	3	4	5	6	7	8	9	10	11	12	13	14
Number of pupil books														
Read-Alones	6	8	8	8	8	8	8	8	8	8	8	8	5	5
Group Stories	2	2	2	2	2	2	2	2	2	2	2	2	2	2

be motivated and guided in their story reading in their SF readers. Explicit directions are given in the teacher's editions for building background concepts and interest and for giving the pupils a purpose for reading. Each page of text then can be read independently or with the guidance of teacher questioning and direction. Those pupils not reading with the teacher work in their workbooks, sometimes as a group with the teacher's aide; work on projects or activities, as described earlier; read trade books; or engage in some other math or science work. In one first-grade classroom I visited, the involvement of one group with an extra workbook, not included in the program, caught my attention. The children were completing exercises in letter–sound relationships. When I asked about the material they were using, I was told that it was supplementary material purchased from Scott, Foresman, because the teachers found it "extremely valuable for teaching consonant and vowel sounds which the children do need more practice on." I realized once again that attempting research that correlates children's achievement with specific program components only, rather than observing what materials are actually used in the classrooms, is a delusion.

In the NRS classroom, five or six pupils are seated at listening stations, complete with earphones, responding in their workbooks to the audio-cassette instructions. The remainder are on the floor playing relevant games or at their seats working in their workbooks. A few may be found at a library table, each reading an appropriate paper back "Read-Alone" story. The teacher's aid and the teacher travel among the students, responding to their questions, initiating dialogue about workbook pages, and/or listening to individual pupils read their "Progress Check" page. The teacher has a significant management role: making individual assignments, checking on the progress of each pupil individually, and reading with the children. The teacher's role is well defined, and the material is well organized, so that these various tasks were easily managed in the classroom I saw. Although not seen the day I visited the classroom, the NRS teacher also gathers three or more children together for a group story for which they previously have signed up. They sign up when they come to a pink page in their workbooks directing them to make a mark beside a specific story name on a class chart. Two such pink pages appear at each level, and the teacher assembles a group whenever several pupils have marked the chart for any given story. Because of individual pacing, there could be a wait of a few days between the time that one student signed up and two others were ready. Each child reads at least one group story every two weeks; all other reading is relatively independent.

The view just given of the NRS classroom is found only after children have completed Levels 1 and 2. The lessons of Levels 1 and 2 consist of "teacher-led small-group instruction, with provision for one-to-one teaching when necessary [Teacher's Edition, Level, p. 5]." In these first two levels, children learn the mechanics and conventions of NRS for the remaining 12 levels and develop self-management skills and reading strategies.

I have followed the format of Beck and Block (see Chapter 11, Volume 1, this series) to outline typical lessons in NRS and SF. Figures 10.1 and 10.2 and the descriptions already given should give a flavor of the manner in which teaching occurs in SF and NRS, the role of the teacher, and the pupils' interaction with the materials.

TEACHING/LEARNING STRATEGIES

A simplified schema of the interrelationships among certain dimensions of reading behaviors is presented in Fig. 10.3. Differences in the way the developers of the two programs view the teaching of reading can be illustrated by tracking instruction along the various sides of the triangle in Fig. 10.3.

Developers of the programs agree that their major objective is to teach children to get from *a* (print) to A (meaning), but they disagree on how that should be done. SF begins with meaning (A); and meaning may be derived from pictures, the children's knowledge of the world and of the language, and explicit information provided by the teacher. From the very beginning levels, teachers focus on meaning to elicit oral sentences (or teachers may actually give the sentences) that will match those printed on the page. The children are than asked to "read" the print orally ("a"). The goal of the early program segments is for children to "reconstruct the meaning of the written language [Teacher's Edition, Level 2, p.25]" and to "understand that the print tells the story: the pictures help, but the print supplies the meaning [Teacher's Edition, Level 2, p. 30]." Therefore, SF states, "A substitution which makes sense as the child reads is acceptable [Teacher's Edition, Level 2, p. 89]." For example, "fruit" is acceptable for *bananas* or "grocery" for *supermarket*. It would seem that a child must know the meaning before such a substitution could be made; therefore, the child is not getting the meaning from the print but from experiences, picture cues, and teacher prompts. Nevertheless, after the print is read orally ("a"), a check for meaning (A) follows.

If we were to draw arrows on the diagram in Fig. 10.3 to represent this sequence, they would be from the top (A, or meaning), down the right side to speech ("a"), over to print (*a*), and back the same route to meaning. The goal, however, for early instruction is to go back and forth from print to meaning, or up and down the left side of the triangle, as the child uses meaning to predict print and print to elicit further meaning. Practice appears to be in another direction.

NRS begins with the print (*a*); the child is given an associated oral response ("a") to that unit of print, and there is practice on the association of print to speech. Then that oral response is associated with meaning (A). Their stated

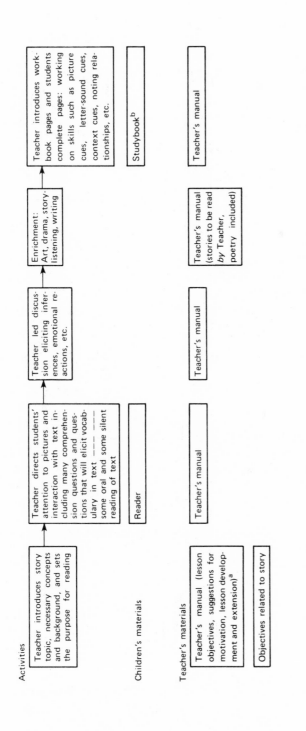

Activities

Teacher introduces story topic, necessary concepts and background, and sets the purpose for reading → Teacher directs students' attention to pictures and interaction with text including many comprehension questions and questions that will elicit vocabulary in text ——— some oral and some silent reading of text → Teacher led discussion eliciting inferences, emotional reactions, etc. → Enrichment: Art, drama, story-listening, writing → Teacher introduces workbook pages and students complete pages: working on skills such as picture cues, letter-sound cues, context cues, noting relationships, etc.

Children's materials

Reader

Studybook[b]

Teacher's materials

Teacher's manual (lesson objectives, suggestions for motivation, lesson development and extension)[a]

Objectives related to story

Teacher's manual

Teacher's manual (stories to be read by Teacher, poetry included)

Teacher's manual

Teacher's manual

[a] Magneboard picture, word, and letter cards are used extensively through levels 1 and 2 and somewhat in level 3.

[b] Independent practice books and masters are available supplementary materials.

FIG. 10.1. General flow of a typical lesson in SF (Level 3).

223

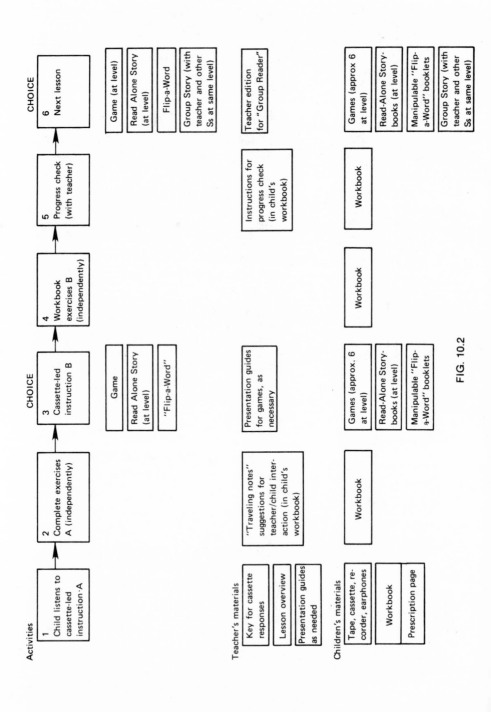

FIG. 10.2

224

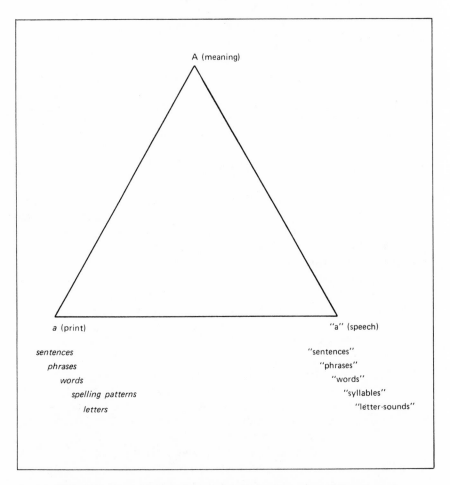

FIG. 10.3. A model of the interrelationships among relevant dimensions of reading behavior. (Adapted from a schema developed by Hively, Popp, & Porter and given full explanation in Hively, 1966.)

goal for early instruction is that a child "be able to read and demonstrate understanding....(Beck & Mitroff, 1972, p. 10)" and "NRS follows a 'code breaking' approach as the primary instructional means to that goal....[p. 12];" that is, across the bottom of the diagram to speech and up to meaning. Therefore the direction of teaching/learning in NRS is consistent with these statements.

It is important to remember that I am referring only to the initial stages of each program: The sequence of strategies, as well as the skills taught, are

FIG. 10.2. (*opposite page*) General flow of a typical lesson in NRS (does not include possible review exercises).

different for the two programs, and the skills emphasized vary at different points within each program.

Print-to-Speech Units Taught

Both programs call attention to different units of writing and speech at different points in their programs. During the first levels of the programs, the children spend varying amounts of time going from print to speech. Instruction includes work on letters, spelling patterns, words, sentences, and stories, with different input from meaning.

Letter–Sound Associations.   The intent in the SF program is to teach the children to use semantic, syntactic, and, in a minimal way, graphemic cues in reading for meaning. The ability to use oral semantic and syntactic cues is assumed to be in the pupils' repertoires, a part of their skill with language. Therefore, students are taught to use them to read. In Levels 2–5, students are also prompted to use semantic and syntactic cues to discover that graphemic cues are available and to discover what they are. In Level 2, graphemic cues are limited to initial consonant letter–sound cues. Semantic knowledge is used to predict what an unlearned word might be in context, and then knowledge of initial letter cues might be used to confirm this prediction as reading proceeds.

The inductive approach is used in SF to teach letter–sound associations to aid the student in understanding a story. The teaching strategy begins with meaning. For example, beginning with a discussion of a picture of a boy in a boat, the teacher prompts the reading of a sentence written beside it: "The boy is in the boat." Attention is then directed to *boy* and *boat;* their oral recodings, "boy" and "boat", and the picture of each to maintain the meaning. Next, the teacher queries students about the first letter of each word (both are *b*'s). The isolated letter is presented under each word, and children are asked if the words "begin with the same sound" (a task for which they've had much prior practice). This sound is referred to as the *b* ("bee," not "buh") sound. Other objects are found whose names begin with the *b* sound, they are written in a list, and attention is drawn to the letter *b* and the *b* sound at the beginning of the words. In studybook exercises following such teaching, the child is asked to select one of two sentences that tells about a picture. The only difference between the two sentences is a key word in each, a word that begins with the recently taught letters *b* or *g*. For example: "The goat is in the garden" and "The bird is in the garden [Studybook, Level 2, p. 4]."

I did not find in the Teacher's Edition of Level 2 any explicit statement that children are to be told that a letter stands for a specific sound until page 177: "Both the letter *c* and the letter *k* stand for the *k* sound at the beginning of these words." However, one assumes the children do, in fact, learn that each letter stands for a specific sound, as these associations are pointed out and worked on in the studybooks. The expected learning is that *b* represents the various allophones of the phoneme /b/ found in the initial position of words.[1] Consonant letter–sound correspondences are taught initially as one-letter-to-one-sound relationships. At Level 3, probably past midyear in first grade, SF introduces vowel letter–sound correspondences.

The concept that a vowel letter can stand for more than one vowel sound is taught very quickly. Picture cues and oral and written context cues (syntax and semantics) are used to read the words, and then attention is called to the vowel sounds. After matching vowel sounds with the associated letters, explanation is offered that the letter *a,* for instance, "followed by one consonant letter and final *e* stands for the vowel sound heard in *ate, lake, game, make,* and *cakes.* The letter *a* followed by one or more consonant letters stands for the vowel sound heard in *at, sat, and, Ann,* and *Jan* [Teacher's Edition, Level 3, p. 72]." In the next lesson, the children learn that "the letter *a* followed by *r* usually stands for the vowel sound heard in *park, car, jar,* and *shark* [Teacher's Edition, Level 3, p. 77]." It is relevant to note, however, that the simultaneous presentation of one-vowel-letter-to-several-sounds associations is not the children's introduction to recoding these vowels. Quite to the contrary, for at this point in the program, early in first grade, the children are analyzing words they have been reading in their books. The program uses these known words as examples to call attention to the fact that the letter *a* stands for several vowel sounds.

In SF when the child is taught that "the letter *a* stands for the vowel sounds in *at* and *ate,"* the term *vowel sound* is used; and in the explanation of this concept, the term *consonant letter* is used (i.e., "the letter *a* followed by one consonant letter...," [Teacher's Edition, Level 3, p. 72]. These terms are also used in the study books. However, there is no explanation given, nor is discovery prompted, of which letters are vowels and which are consonants. Because the program is so fastidious in teaching the concept of words and the concept of association of oral to written language, it is difficult to understand why these more difficult concepts are not taught as the words are used in a critical manner.

Studybook exercises are offered wherein the child reads words (from context or picture cues) and decides whether the vowel *a* stands for the same or different sound as that in a stimulus word. Other suggestions for extended work in skills ask the child to apply his or her knowledge of graphemic cues, but always in the presence of semantic and/or syntactic cues as well. (See Table 10.3 for letter–sound associations taught in Levels 2 through 5.)

---

[1]Throughout the chapter, phonemes are presented between slash marks. Short vowels are represented by the vowel letter only (e.g., /a/ not /ae/); long vowels are marked with a bar (e.g., /ā/ not /ey/).

In NRS, teachers are trained to use a basic script for presenting letter–sound relationships. The children are asked to listen and watch while the isolated sound is given by the teacher, children say it together with the teacher mouthing it, individual children say the sound, the letter is shown, the sound is given by the teacher, the sound is repeated by the children several times as the teacher points to the letter, and finally the children point to the letter and say its sound. This explicit sequence of 10 steps is followed for the introduction of the letter–sound relationships by the teacher until further along in Level 1 when audio-cassette instruction begins. Nearly 100

TABLE 10.3

Sequence of Letter-Sound Correspondences in Levels 1–14 in LRDC's *New Primary Grades Reading System* and in Scott Foresman's *Reading Unlimited*, Levels 1–5

			NRS		
Level		5.	v		ie (pie)
1.	m, t, s, c, a—/a/		es	10.	ou (couch)
	sh		th		un, re, dis
	n		ar		air, are
	e—/e/		y (try)		ea (bread)
	b		o—/ō/		-tion
	ā ¢ (as in āte)		er, ur, ir		ie (chief)
2.	f		u—/ū/	11.	ow (brown)
	ee, ea—/ē/	6.	wh		ui (fruit)
	i—/i/		y (funny)		au (August)
	ff, ss, tt, ing		j		-ture
	p		ay, ai		o (front)
	patterns: at, it		x		e pre (eleven)
3.	ch		est	12.	oe (toe)
	o	7.	z		silent h (echo)
	l		le		mis
	patterns: et, it, ot, op,		qu		y (gym)
	ep, ap		-ed		al (calm)
	r		-old		ear, or (earth, worm)
	g		oo (book)		-ous
	h	8.	ear	13.	ei (reindeer)
	patterns: og, eg, ag, ig		c (city)		silent t (fasten)
4.	d		a (across)		o, ou (lose, cougar)
	u—/u/		ew, ue (few, blue)		ought
	patterns: ut, up, us, un, ug		-ly		-sion
	k		oa, ow		ey (key)
	patterns: ack, uck,		igh		u (bush)
	ock, ick, eck		kn	14.	y (yard)
	all	9.	g (giant)		silent b, n, c, l
	w		oy, oi		i (gasoline)
	i—/ī/		aw (saw)		ou, oo (cousin, flood)
	or, or¢, oor		ful, less		gu (guard)
					oar (board)
					ei (ceiling)

TABLE 10.3 *(continued)*

	SF		
	Level		
1.	—		o— /o/ (corn)
2.	b, g		u— /u/, /ü/, /yu/, (cup, flute, cube)
	f, h, r		u— /ë/ (fur)
	t, l		e— /e/, ee—/e/
	m, s	4.	igh—/i/
	br, fl, fr, gr, st		oa—/ō/
	d, n		ai—/ā/, a—/ô/
	p, w		ay—/ā/, aw—/ô/
	c, k		oy—/oi/, y—/ī/
	j, v, y, z		ew—/ü/ or /yu/, ea/ē/
	cl, cr, cr, pl, sk, sn		ow—/ō/, /ou/
	gl, pr, sp, str, sw, tr		kn—/n/ wr-/r/
3.	ch,sh, th	5.	ea—/e/
	qu		oo—/ú/ oo—/ü/
	c—/k/ and /s/, g—/g/ and /j/		ou—/ou/
	a—/a/, /ā/, and /ä/		ou—/ü/
	i—/i/, /ī/		ow—/ou/
	i—/ė/ (bird)		
	o— /o/, /ō/		New correspondences taught in levels 6–8 are minimal.

consonants, consonant blends, vowels, consonant digraphs, and vowel digraph associations are explicitly taught (see Table 10.3), though not all in this specific manner.

NRS introduces *a,* teaches the children that it "has the /a/ sound," and then teaches them to blend consonant-/a/-consonant words. Only five lessons later, NRS presents the *a*-/ā/ correspondence in *aCȼ* pattern words and marks both letters (*āCȼ*). What does research have to say about multiple letter–sound correspondences? Is it better to teach single-letter-to-single-sound correspondences, multiple-letters-to-single-sound correspondences, single-letter-to-multiple-sounds correspondences, or multiple-letter-to-multiple-sounds correspondences? Studies by Levin and Watson (1963) and Williams (1968) led to the popularization of the "set for diversity" theory. Levin and Watson concluded that "when a graphic symbol stands for two or more sounds, it should be learned and transferred more readily when the variations are learned together than when they are learned separately [p. 21]." However, Blackman, Marston, and Reinhardt (1973) called attention to problems with the research in terms of: (a) the age of the subjects (always older readers); (b) the design of the word lists using an artificial orthography; (c) the use of trigrams or single letters rather than words in context; (d) the validity of equating the experimental task with the learning task confronting the 6-year-old beginning reader; and (e) the validity of equating an experimental method with regular classroom instruction. A modified paired-associate task giving successive or concurrent one-letter-to-several-sounds is the experimental task, whereas in actual teaching a second association to a given letter would rarely be taught without reference to an earlier learned association. These critics concluded that the basic question about training multiple correspondences successively or concurrently remains unanswered.

The methodology of the Levin and Williams research does not approximate the teaching strategies in either SF or NRS. And if one were posing a research question concerning multiple or one-to-one associations, the same question would not be appropriate to both NRS training and SF training. NRS teaches letter–sound correspondences to recode print to oral speech, but SF analyzes already known words to indicate that there is a systematic relationship between letters and sounds. If the nature of these two tasks is taken into account in trying to generalize from research results with yet a different experimental task, I do not believe it is possible to draw any meaningful implications.

Table 10.3 presents the sequence of letter–sound associations taught in NRS as well as in SF. The list is quite extensive for NRS, and the program developers expect that many second graders will learn all these elements. Another question to which research has not offered an answer has to do with the usefulness of extended phonic teaching.

Spelling Patterns.   Among others, Fletcher (1973) commented rather astutely about some of the disadvantages accruing when one uses spelling patterns for beginning reading instruction:

> In initial reading, the use of spelling patterns encounters several practical difficulties, one of which is the strained vocabulary that results in choosing words to illustrate the regular spelling patterns being presented, and another of which is the pronunciation of an orthographically regular utterance in ordinary discourse. Both of these difficulties are illustrated by Bloomfield's prototypal "NAN CAN FAN DAN." The sentence appears strained because Nan is not a particularly familiar name and because who can fan whom is not a concern of moment to initial readers. Further, the sentence may contain grapheme–irregularities in ordinary discourse. For instance, CAN in this sentence would be ordinarily pronounced /ken/ or /kin/ in American dialects [p. 9].

It is interesting to note that when SF calls attention to words that rhyme, it is in the context of other words, and the spelling patterns are found by the pupils in a manner consistent with their other analytic procedures. For instance, pupils are to underline the words in their workbooks that rhyme with *fat* and *pig* in the following: "A *fat* little cat went to sleep on a mat. He dreamed of a *pig* in a wig who was dancing a jig [Level 3, p. 34]."

NRS introduces the *at* and *in* spelling patterns in Level 2 by using words in isolation and dramatizing them with a manipulable booklet called "Flip-a-

Word" with which the children form words by changing the initial consonant that appears before the pattern. These same words are presented in the workbook in isolation and in sentences. Rarely do the sentences use several words with the same spelling pattern, and the pattern itself is emphasized on only two pages (pp. 123 and 124) of the Workbook where "The fat cat sat," "Tap can nap in a cap," "ten men," and "Nan can fan" appear. There is a new set of patterns in Level 3, and "Nop the cop is tasting pop [p. 145]" illustrates one of the infrequent uses of words with the same spelling pattern in a sentence.

Both programs work with spelling patterns; however, they are not the major focus of either program. The usual difficulties are not apparent in SF at all, and in NRS they are lessened somewhat by the use of other words and by the limited emphasis on spelling patterns.

Words.   Instruction that will lead to recognition of individual words is given much more attention in NRS than in SF. In a promotional brochure for SF, it is stated that *"reading is meaning centered, not word centered.* . . . Emphasis is upon getting beyond individual words to the ideas encompassed in them. . . . *Printed words are a symbol system that has no meaning unless the reader brings meaning to it."* With this philosophy, it is not surprising that individual words are not given much attention in SF. Color name words are isolated on one page in the studybook at Level 1, but they are used as directions for coloring balloons. Occasionally at Level 2, less than midway in first grade, choices for answering studybook questions are words, but most often they are preceded by an article. Rarely in either the studybook or the pupil's book are there isolated words, even for instruction. The exception is when instruction is being directed toward letter-sound correspondences and words are isolated prior to isolating letters. However, I return to a consideration of teaching words in SF when I consider the teaching/learning of sentences.

The attention given to the concept of a word in SF is very significant. In levels 1 and 2, there are pages in the studybook designed to give the child an understanding of where a word begins and ends and of the fact that a sentence is composed of a number of words. For example, the child is asked to draw a line between the words in a sentence and pictures printed in the workbook and then to circle a specific word after the sentence is read aloud by the teacher (see Fig. 10.4).

NRS introduces 11 grapheme–phoneme correspondences in Level 1, including some digraphs, and these are immediately incorporated into a synthetic approach for recoding printed words to oral words. A blending procedure is established. In this procedure of "successive" blending, "as soon as two sounds are produced, they are blended, and successive phonemes are incorporated in the blends as they are pronounced (Resnick & Beck, 1975, p.

Which Word?

Monkeys are funny.

See the balloon.

Donna is running.

Ed and Sue are here.

Pat is riding with Ann.

Tom likes his new bike.

FIG. 10.4. Item from SF Study-book, Level 1, on using word boundaries. (Material reprinted from Scott, Foresman and Company's *Reading Unlimited Program.* © 1976, Scott, Foresman and Company, is used with permission of the publisher.)

6)." For instance, with their first word, *sat,* the children are taught through very explicit teacher instruction and modeling to proceed thusly: /s/, /a/, /sa/; /sa/, /t/, /sat/; ending with the final decoding of the word *sat.* Each child uses a blending booklet with manipulable letters during this very structured teaching/learning sequence. Later, blending is taught by audio-cassettes. The traveling teacher who oversees workbook activity encourages and reinforces the pupil for using the blending procedure to decode new or unfamiliar words.

In the NRS classroom I visited in the spring, children who had started on NRS in September would, without the slightest hesitation, blend a word on cue from the teacher (or me). I also saw a few children spontaneously using the technique. In every case where the pupil knew the component sounds, it "worked." Several youngsters were still having a problem with a few vowel letter–sound correspondences they had not mastered, but once the individual elements had been established (and the children seemed to know enough to ask if they did not know them), the confidence with which they attacked the words was very impressive. Children are encouraged to remember words they have learned and are reinforced for responding to the whole word once they get under way with their workbook exercises.

The words taught in Level 1 are used in phrases and sentences in Level 2, and new letter–sound correspondences are taught. The new vocabulary is controlled by and generated from these taught correspondences. In addition, a few sight words are incorporated in paragraphs and the first group story at the end of Level 2. Letter–sound correspondences and the blending procedure are the major emphases in these early NRS ·lessons. However, this phonics instruction is not devoid of attention to the meaning aspect of reading. After letter–sound correspondences are taught and words are blended, those words appear in a context that requires the children to respond to the meaning of the print. For example, in the first lessons, children are expected to match pictures and words or phrases in one of several formats, and the children must read and understand the words in order to make the required responses (see Fig. 10.5). Level 2 introduces eight "sight words" taught as whole words, and these are helpful in creating meaningful text.

NRS focuses on recoding letters into sounds, blending those sounds into words, and then verifying the oral word by questioning meaning. The blending process is conditioned, and the child is prompted to use it for all unknown words. As the repertoire of decoding words becomes larger, the blending procedure is relied on less and less, even though new letter–sound associations are introduced. For many students this is so because semantic and syntactic contextual cues are available to aid the decoding process. When unknown words are not prompted by picture cues or discussion and are presented in isolation, recoding into the oral word depends on graphemic cues only. SF understandably avoids presenting words in isolation, since the students would not have sufficient phonic skills to decode them. The structure

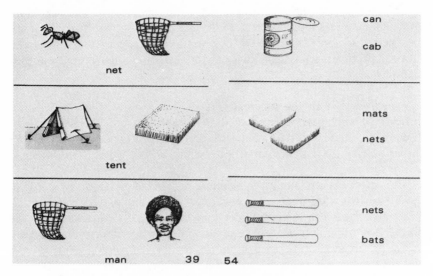

FIG. 10.5.   Items from two pages of NRS Workbook, Level 1. (Reproduced with permission of the Learning Research and Development Center, University of Pittsburgh. All rights reserved.)

of NRS has assured that graphemic cues are salient and that students are well practiced in using them and the blending procedure. In the NRS classroom, I listened to all ten children read, and virtually every one of them who blended an unknown word in context began with the practiced method. They did, however, often stop short of blending the final letter and give a correct whole-word response based on the first few blended sounds and the context.

Kintsch (Chapter 12, Volume 1, this series) proposed that we might research the question: Is meaning achieved before the oral reading of the word in context? Educators who carefully observe the child learning to read could suggest an experiment where the hypothesis could not be rejected. They could also suggest one that would spell its doom. For example, take the case of successful beginning readers learning from a carefully sequenced program like NRS. Given an uncommon, unknown word that contains previously taught graphemic elements and that is presented in an uninformative context, such children will blend the elements of the word, pronounce it, and acquire its meaning. Children who have learned only initial consonant letter–sound cues in a program similar to Scott, Foresman's, where the major emphasis is on using semantic and syntactic cues, may begin to give the initial sound. However, chances are that they will draw on every other available cue to find a meaningful completion to the phrase or sentence, and then they will utter a word. I believe that theory has to allow for both possibilities: pronunciation first, then meaning and vice versa. Likewise, both may occur for the more competent reader under certain circumstances. Secure in our knowledge of how we read and often of how we think we learned to read, we are too eager, it seems to me, to posit either/or hypotheses. The very fact that we can conjure up such hypotheses should alert us to the fact that the same answer ought not be expected to apply equally to all beginning readers, particularly not to all "at risk" beginners whose cognitive capabilities are changing rapidly as they mature.

Sentences.   Given the differences in their approach to words, it is not difficult to anticipate differences in the approach to sentences. In SF, discussion is used prior to asking children to read sentences. In the very earliest stories, the sentence patterns to be read are elicited prior to reading to assure success.

NRS, after having taught the blending procedure, moves from words to Level 1 to two-word phrases, three-word phrases, and sentences in Level 2. The teacher reads the phrase under a picture, and the children repeat the phrase. A workbook format for responding to a choice of pictures for a given phrase or sentence, or a choice of phrases for a given picture, is introduced; and the teacher continues to read the phrases with the children for several pages before independent work is assigned for these same phrases. Similar models are provided for sentence reading, and the same workbook procedure is followed. The game "Sentence Lotto" is introduced to support sentence reading.

Strategies for Story Reading

As the students move toward reading more context in both programs, strategies change. In SF, the first strategy uses the teacher's telling a story as children follow pictures in their books. She or he asks inference questions and questions that can be answered from the pictures. Then print appears in the chilren's books within the framework of the story, and children are guided by the storytelling to read the print. For instance, in the pupil's book *Balloons* (see Fig. 10.6), the teacher tells the story of Mr. Burton selling his balloons at the zoo and of how he accidentally let go of the balloons. The students look at the first five pages of related pictures and discuss questions asked by the teacher. The first print, "Here is the yellow one," appears on the next page, and the teacher reads what one of the girls in the story says as she catches one of Mr. Burton's balloons. The teacher then asks the children to read what Janet called. The same procedure is repeated for the next page when Danny finds a balloon and calls, "Here is the blue one." Seven more balloons, each of a different color, are found by seven different children, and the same sentence is printed on each page, with the appropriate color name used to match the color of the balloon in each picture. The teacher continues to tell the story and asks the children to "read" what each child in the story said as he or she found a balloon. Children are thus reading sentences that fit into the context of the story, not from a "sight word" approach at all, but instead from a total meaning approach, and they predict the text based on teacher comments and picture cues.

Throughout Level 1 and somewhat into Level 2, the teacher continues to provide a rich story context for the students. Such prompting is gradually faded as children's attention is directed toward the pictures and toward their own anticipation of the story events. For those children who need guidance in their reading, the teacher continues to comment and to elicit phrases that the children read in the text. The use of redundant phrases and/or sentence patterns is prevalent. In fact, verbal cues are still being given in Level 3. For instance, the teacher reads the title of "The Great Big Enormous Turnip" and says, "The old man talked to the turnip he had planted and told it to grow sweet and strong." The children are then asked to read the story: "The old man said, 'Grow, grow little turnip. Grow sweet. Grow, grow little turnip. Grow strong.'" The students who listen to the teacher are given strong cues for reading.

By Level 4 (end of grade 1) these cues are dropped, and teacher-guided reading consists of literal and inferential comprehension questions and some statements to set a purpose for reading. For some stories at Level 5, the

Page 2 Teacher tells story:
Every morning Mr. Burton got up very early to blow up his balloons. Then he took them to the zoo to sell.

Page 3 Teacher tells:
Mr. Burton was at the zoo with his balloons before the animals were awake.
Teacher asks:
How can you tell that it is early in the morning? How do you think Mr. Burton might blow up his balloons? Can anyone tell what kind of animals are sleeping here?

FIG. 10.6. Selected pages from Teacher's Edition of SF story, Level 1. (Material reprinted from Scott, Foresman and Company's *Reading Unlimited Program,* © 1976, Scott, Foresman and Company, is used with permission of the publisher.)

236

Page 4 Teacher tells:
Today there weren't many people at the zoo. When the bus arrived, a woman and some children got off. Mr. Burton was still sleepy, so he didn't hear the children coming to buy his balloons.
Teacher asks:
What made Mr. Burton jump? How many children do you see? Where is Mr. Burton?

Page 5 Teacher tells:
He was so surprised that he let go of the balloons, and they floated away from him.
Teacher asks:
How do you think the children feel now? What do you think will happen next?

FIG. 10.6 *(cont.)*

Page 6   Teacher tells:
Quickly, the boys and girls scrambled around trying to help Mr. Burton catch the balloons.

Here is the yellow one.

Page 7   Teacher tells:
Janet grabbed one as it flew by her face. She called, "Here is the yellow one."
Teacher asks:
Look at the sentence on this page. Who thinks they can read what Janet called?
Children read:
Here is the yellow one.

FIG. 10.6 *(cont.)*

Here is the blue one.

8

Page 8 Teacher tells:
Danny found one by the fence. He shouted, "Here is the blue one."
Teacher asks:
Who can read what he shouted?
Children read:
Here is the blue one.

Here is the red one.

9

Page 9 Teacher asks:
Where did Debbie find a balloon?
Teacher asks:
What did Debbie yell from the tree?
Children read:
Here is the red one.

FIG. 10.6 *(cont.)*

Here is the orange one.

Page 10 Teacher asks:
What did Ken say?
Children read:
Here is the orange one.
Teacher asks:
Does anyone know what animal Ken found the balloon by?

Here is the black one.

Page 11 Teacher tells:
Yoshi tried to catch one as it floated over a flower bed. She grabbed for the balloon and tried not to step on the flowers. Then she called...
Children read:
Here is the black one.

FIG. 10.6 (cont.)

240

Here is the white one.

12

Page 12   Teacher tells:
Mr. Burton caught two balloons. Stretch-
ing for the first one, he said...
Children read:
Here is the white one.

Here is the brown one.

13

Page 13   Teacher tells:
Then he saw the second one, grabbed for
it with his other hand, and called...
Children read:
Here is the brown one.

FIG. 10.6 *(cont.)*

Here is the purple one.

14

Page 14 Teacher tells:
Carlos really had to run to catch his balloon. It kept getting away from him. But finally he caught up with it. As he reached for it, he shouted...
Children read:
Here is the purple one.

Here is the green one.

15

Page 15 Teacher tells:
Then they all heard a voice calling from near the peanut stand. It was Elena. She had found the last balloon and was yelling...
Children read:
Here is the green one.

FIG. 10.6 *(cont.)*

Page 16 Teacher tells:
Mr. Burton thanked the children for helping him and offered to give each of them a balloon. But the children were sorry they had startled him and they wanted to buy the balloons. So Janet got the yellow one, Danny got the blue one, Debbie got the red one, Ken got the orange one, Yoshi got the black one, Carlos got the purple one, and Elena got the green one.
Teacher asks:
How does Mr. Burton look now that he has all the balloons back? How do you think the children felt at the end of the story?

Teacher's Edition suggests that "children will benefit from reading and discussing the first two pages of the story before continuing independently [p.35]." For other stories, the suggestion is to "encourage children to read [the whole story], "The Man and The Donkey." If there are some who need help in the initial reading, use some or all of the guidance that follows [p. 84]." Guidance at this level usually consists of key questions posed by the teacher. At the end of every story, suggestions to the teacher are given for checking comprehension and for providing students an opportunity to react to the story.

In NRS most of the stories are Read-Alones, and the provision for teacher involvement with them is minimal. At each level eight Read-Alone Books are available from which the students select as many as they wish to read. In the learning disabilities classroom I visited, I noticed that these books, along with the games, tended to be assigned rather than selected. I expect this would vary from one classroom situation to another. The books are written using a restricted vocabulary and controlled sentence structures. There are no comprehension questions asked following the reading. Figure 10.7 gives an example of a Read-Alone at Level 2.

The children are expected to approach the task of reading a story in a manner similar to the way they previously have been guided to do so by audio-cassette instruction or the teacher. That is, they are expected to read stories

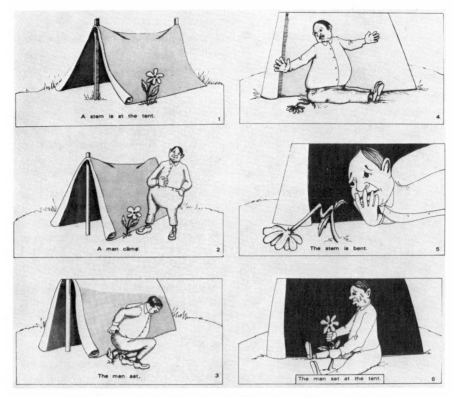

FIG. 10.7. NRS Read-Alone, Level 2. (Reproduced with permission of the Learning Research and Development Center, University of Pittsburgh. All rights reserved.)

for meaning, responding to familar and frequent words as whole words and approaching unknown words with the blending technique and the use of contextual cues. This approach is practiced in the Group Stories which are prescribed, two per level, throughout the 14 levels. The teacher/group interaction scheme for the first of these early stories differs somewhat from SF's early story reading. There is very little teacher modeling, but the teacher guides the children to read the sentences on each page. Comprehension questions on the text and pictures are asked, and both silent and oral reading is required. For instance, in *Sasha* (Level 2), the fifth page of the story includes a picture and the two sentences—*Sam came* and *Sasha is Sam's*. The interaction suggested for the page is as follows:

Teacher: Who came to visit Nan and Ben?
(Reinforce Sam or a boy and a dog.)
Read the first sentence for us, *(child)*.

Point to the word Sasha on the page. Now say the word out loud. Now you know who Sasha is. Sasha is a dog. Read the second sentence to yourself to find out who Sasha belongs to.

(child), read the second sentence for us.

In NRS, the story line is expected to be carried more by the printed text than by the teacher's explanation. In NRS the teacher asks questions that the text will answer, whereas in SF, the teacher enriches the context to cue reading the text.

By Level 7 of NRS, near the end of first grade, in the group reading situation, the teacher introduces the characters, sets a purpose for silent reading, orally reads some of the sentences and paragraphs, and asks for oral reading by the children of specific sentences to answer questions. The emphasis in the group story reading in NRS is on using contextual cues. The approach expected of the child after the first few levels is not significantly different as we view NRS group stories and SF pupil's books. However, an important difference is that all students, including the poorer readers, are expected to be able to read the Read-Alone Books in NRS independently, whereas only the better readers will be able to read independently in SF. This independence has been structured into the NRS program from the beginning. The Read-Alones are composed of only vocabulary for which the program has prepared the child. The books are intended to serve as a bridge between workbook activities, teacher-guided group reading, and trade books in the real world. In contrast to this, SF pays little attention to the development of reading vocabulary or word recognition skills. Thus, the guidance of the teacher continues to be a necessary part of instruction for the less able children.

Differences in the use of NRS workbooks and SF studybooks also affect independent mastery. I briefly examine this aspect of the two programs in the next section and give particular attention to the behaviors required of the student in responding.

Studybooks and Workbooks

The studybooks of SF are used as an introduction to skills helpful in reading a new story, as a follow-up of concepts or skills used in the story, or as a complete lesson itself. At the bottom of every page of the SF studybooks, the emphasized skill is stated. These skills tend to support the emphasis given in the teacher's edition. The content of the studybooks is attractive, and the format is not difficult. Responses in Levels 1–4 include: underlining the correct choice or sentence in a passage, mark an X in an answer square, and circling a word. Levels 5–8 add responses of writing in words, phrases, and

FIG. 10.8. Exercise from SF Studybook, Level 2, on associating letters and sounds. (Material reprinted from Scott, Foresman and Company's *Reading Unlimited Program,* © 1976, Scott, Foresman and Company, is used with permission of the publisher.)

sentences; selecting a choice—A, B, or C—for each of eight or more questions; numbering sentences in sequence; and drawing lines to indicate matches.

A random selection of pages was sampled to analyze the extent to which the stated objectives were apt to be met by the responses required of the students. "Associating letters and sounds" is one such objective. The teacher is to guide the students in underlining the word choice that begins with the sound of the letter (see Fig. 10.8). A sentence emphasizing the sound is included.

If the teacher guides the reading on the entire page, students will likely read it all. However, if teacher guidance is omitted, students are apt not to read all the print included. They can simply underline the word that begins with the letter given in the same row as a stimulus, and they may or may not attempt to read the word that is pictured. There is no reason to read the sentences.

"Using letter–sound cues" is another stated objective of Level 2. The children are to name the picture, read the sentence, read the words, and mark an X in the answer square beside the word that begins with the same sound as the picture (see Fig. 10.9). Responses can be made without reading anything on the page if the children know the initial sound–letter association.

In "recognizing story problems," the intent is for children to read an entire story and then go back to underline the problem. However, they can underline the problem by reading only until the sentence that relates to the problem is reached (see Fig. 10.10). Some pages on "story problems" also include "solutions," and then more actual reading is required.

It is suggested that pages designed to teach children to "recognize time relationships" incorporate guided reading (Level 4), but students may read

Consonant Review

1. The ____ is on the table.

   dish ☐   book ☐   pie ☐

2. The ____ is behind the tree.

   lion ☐   camel ☐   horse ☐

3. The boy is looking at a ____.

   bear ☐   seal ☐   duck ☐

FIG. 10.9. Exercise from SF Studybook, Level 2, on using letter–sound cues. (Material reprinted from Scott, Foresman and Company's *Reading Unlimited Program*, © 1976, Scott, Foresman and Company is used with permisssion of the publisher.)

Once a baby woodpecker flew through the hole of a birdhouse.
But it grew too big to go out that hole.
So it began to peck around the hole.
Soon the hole was big enough for the bird to get out.

Draw a line under the sentence that tells what the problem is.

FIG. 10.10. Exercise from SF Studybook, Level 4, on recognizing story problems. (Material reprinted from Scott, Foresman and Company's *Reading Unlimited Program*, © 1976, Scott, Foresman and Company, is used with permission of the publisher.)

Miss Grant's class was going to the
Science Museum to see baby chicks
hatch. The children made name tags.
Miss Grant hired a bus.

When they got inside the museum, the
children walked toward the sign
marked Baby Chicks. Everyone liked
watching the chicks. The chicks
worked very hard to get out of
their shells.

When the children got back to
school, they drew pictures of
what they had seen. Everyone
wanted to go to the museum again.

1. When did the children make name tags?
   before the trip ☐   during the trip ☐   after the trip ☐

2. When did the children see the eggs hatch?
   before the trip ☐   during the trip ☐   after the trip ☐

3. When did the children draw pictures?
   before the trip ☐   during the trip ☐   after the trip ☐

FIG. 10.11. Exercise from SF Studybook, Level 4, on recognizing time
relationships. (Material reprinted from Scott, Foresman and Company's
Reading Unlimited Program © 1976, Scott, Foresman and Company, is used
with permission of the publisher.)

the page independently. Questions following the selection are "when"
questions, and on some pages the answers might easily be guessed without
reading the selection (see Fig. 10.11).

In "using context cues," the children are expected to select a word from
those at the top of the page on the basis of sentence context (see Fig. 10.12).
They must read; there is no other way they could select the correct word. It is
a good test of reading and using context cues.

As is the case with most workbooks, the SF studybooks are directed toward
specific objectives, but in some instances the responses may be made with
less reading than the authors intend. Most pages test a skill rather than teach
it, and practice is provided on the skills designated on each page.

NRS workbooks are also designed to teach specific skills. A variety of
formats are introduced by the teacher in Levels 1 and 2 and the teacher guides
the students through the exercises, asking them to read all the material
presented. Beginning at Level 3, the audio-cassette becomes the mode of

stilts   lantern   grape   harp   wizard   otter

A _____ is a small fruit that
grows on a vine.

A light that can be carried is

called a _____ .

Long poles used to walk on for fun are

called _____ .

A _____ is a large musical
instrument with strings.

An _____ is a playful water animal.

A storybook man who uses magic

is a _____ .

Using context cues (word meaning)

FIG. 10.12.   Exercise from SF Studybook, Level 6, on using context cues.
(Material reprinted from Scott, Foresman and Company's *Reading Unlimited
Program,* © 1976, Scott, Foresman and Company, is used with permisssion of
the publisher.)

instruction for introductory pages of each lesson, and the student is required
to do several pages independently for each lesson. Formats include selecting a
word that corresponds to a picture, selecting a picture that corresponds to
a printed word or sentence, underlining letters in words that correspond to
isolated phonemes or spelling patterns, selecting words or sentences that
correspond to pictures, yes–no responses, and selecting words to go in blanks.

The objective for each page is not specifically stated in NRS workbooks;
therefore, an analysis of objectives similar to that done for SF is not feasible.
However, inspection of pages from NRS workbooks suggests that NRS is
more successful than SF in posing questions or exercises that require reading
of the text. Often questions are asked that must be answered by examining a

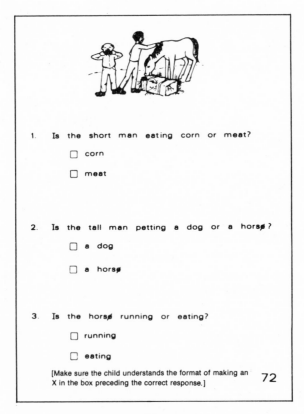

1. Is the short man eating corn or meat?

   ☐ corn

   ☐ meat

2. Is the tall man petting a dog or a horse?

   ☐ a dog

   ☐ a horse

3. Is the horse running or eating?

   ☐ running

   ☐ eating

[Make sure the child understands the format of making an X in the box preceding the correct response.] 72

FIG. 10.13. Exercise from NRS Workbook, Level 4. (Reproduced with permission of the Learning Research and Development Center, University of Pittsburgh. All rights reserved.)

picture. The questions themselves and the response selections must be read to complete the page successfully (see Fig. 10.13). Other formats such as sentence completion also require reading.

Occasionally, children can respond to questions without reading the entire page. In the example in Fig. 10.14, children may respond to the questions by reasoning instead of reading if they wish. They must, of course, read the questions in either case.

At levels most apt to be used in the second grade, two or three pages may relate to one story, and the questions posed are similar to comprehension questions asked by teachers about stories in the readers in SF (see Fig. 10.15). The questions posed often require more accurate and careful reading than those in SF, which are devised to conform to one specific objective or another.

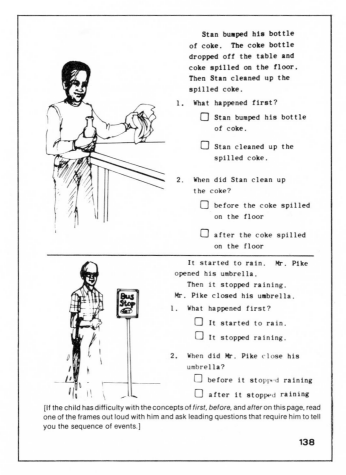

Stan bumped his bottle
of coke. The coke bottle
dropped off the table and
coke spilled on the floor.
Then Stan cleaned up the
spilled coke.

1. What happened first?

☐ Stan bumped his bottle
of coke.

☐ Stan cleaned up the
spilled coke.

2. When did Stan clean up
the coke?

☐ before the coke spilled
on the floor

☐ after the coke spilled
on the floor

It started to rain. Mr. Pike
opened his umbrella.
Then it stopped raining.
Mr. Pike closed his umbrella.

1. What happened first?

☐ It started to rain.

☐ It stopped raining.

2. When did Mr. Pike close his
umbrella?

☐ before it stopped raining

☐ after it stopped raining

[If the child has difficulty with the concepts of *first, before,* and *after* on this page, read
one of the frames out loud with him and ask leading questions that require him to tell
you the sequence of events.]

138

FIG. 10.14. Exercise from NRS Workbook, Level 7. (Reproduced with
permission of the Learning Research and Development Center, University of
Pittsburgh. All rights reserved.)

Persistent Questions

There are some persistent and relevant questions about the programs that
could be answered by research. In SF, what are the expectancies set up in the
child by having the teacher play such a large role in guiding the reading,
including eliciting exact oral language patterns that are then presented in
print? What strategies do the children actually learn? Do they learn to ask
their own questions and set their own purposes? The children use what they

Read this story:

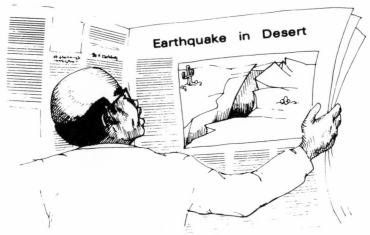

An Earthquake in the News

One day, Mr. Pike was reading his newspaper. He read that there had been an earthquake out in the desert.

The newspaper story said that the earthquake had made a large fault in the crust of the earth, and that the earth had vibrated for many miles in all directions during the earthquake. But luckily, there were no people living near the place where the earthquake occurred. No one had gotten hurt.

Mr. Pike also read that many scientists had been able to predict that the earthquake was going to occur. They had studied their seismographs in their seismic observatories, and they had seen the seismographs start to draw wavy lines. If there had been people living near where the earthquake was going to occur, the scientists would have had time to warn the people and to tell them to go to a place where there would have been no damage.

57

FIG. 10.15. Exercise from NRS Workbook, Level 11. (Reproduced with permission of the Learning Research and Development Center, University of Pittsburgh. All rights reserved.)

Answer these questions about An Earthquake in the News:

1. Where was the earthquake that Mr. Pike read about?

☐ in the woods

☐ in the sea

☐ in the desert

2. What had the earthquake done to the crust of the earth?

☐ It had made a large fault in the crust of the earth.

☐ It had made a large mountain in the crust of the earth.

3. Had scientists been able to predict that the earthquake was going to occur?

yes   no

4. The scientists had studied their
| telephones. |
| seismographs. |

5. The scientists
| would |
| would not |
have had time to warn people that the earthquake was going to occur.

[If there are any errors, turn back to the story on page 57 and show the child the paragraph in which a particular answer is found. Have him read that paragraph until he finds the information that will answer the question. Then have him correct his error.]

58

FIG. 10.15 (cont.)

1. I am thinking of a machine which can measure how much
   pressure is being pushed through the earth. This
   machine is on a piece of wood which is attached to the
   earth. What is the name of the machine I am thinking of?

   ☐ a telescope

   ☐ a washing machine

   ☐ a seismograph

2. I am thinking of the building where scientists who study
   earthquakes work. This building is found near the
   fault from an old earthquake. What is this building
   that I am thinking of called?

   ☐ a seismic observatory

   ☐ a pharmacy

   ☐ a skyscraper

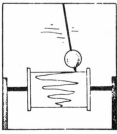

Pretend that you are a scientist
who studies earthquakes. You are
working in your seismic observatory
and the seismograph starts to draw
wavy lines.

1. What could the wavy lines on the seismograph mean?

   ☐ that there is a lot of pressure being pushed through
   the earth and that there might be an earthquake soon

   ☐ that there is not much pressure being pushed through
   the earth and that there is no danger of an earthquake

59

FIG. 10.15 (cont.)

know of the world and their language to understand what the print means, and they then use that "message" to inductively learn letter–sound associations. But do they learn to use letter–sound knowledge to recode printed words into oral words in order to understand the meaning of the print? Correspondences taught are not put in a context where it is necessary to use them to decode. How do the children then learn that the knowledge of letter–sound correspondences is useful in reading?

Because of the tight structure of NRS and the relatively greater control of student behavior, much of their material is suitable for research questions. A few that come to mind immediately are: (a) Can all children be led successfully through the detailed blending process? (b) How might one determine, in the context of the program, the optimal number of letter–sound associations for any individual student; that is, when does context efficiently "take over?" How much phonics is enough, too little, or too much? (c) Does marking the long vowel and the final silent *e* prompt children to attend to these cues rather than to the spelling pattern? (d) Which lessons are relatively more difficult? Why? Researching such questions would, admittedly, keep the program "in the lab" for several more years, and it may be more important now to have it published and follow its use in schools, but the questions are tantalizing.

I am troubled by some of the elaborate and slowly paced teaching in NRS. For many children, much of this is unnecessary. Although the developers say that the more capable students go through the NRS program more rapidly, certain questions remain. If children are capable of coming closer to the desired mature reading behavior early in their reading instruction, does it affect their understanding and positive response to reading if they are forced to go through specific tasks? Of course, the attitude of the teacher and the classroom climate will exert a significant influence.

Summary.   A way to display some of the major differences between the two programs is presented in Fig. 10.16, which is an adaptation of Shuy's (1975) acquisitional sequence of the "language accesses" in reading.

The lines are tentative at best, but for future program evaluations, one might consider having the program developers estimate the slope of each line. These then could be verified by reviewers. Such a scheme portrays the major emphasis of each program and helps the evaluator keep in mind the direction of the program.

TESTING

An examination of tests in a reading program allows us to determine which abilities the developers believe should be formally checked in children. One would assume that the abilities tested would have been assigned the greatest

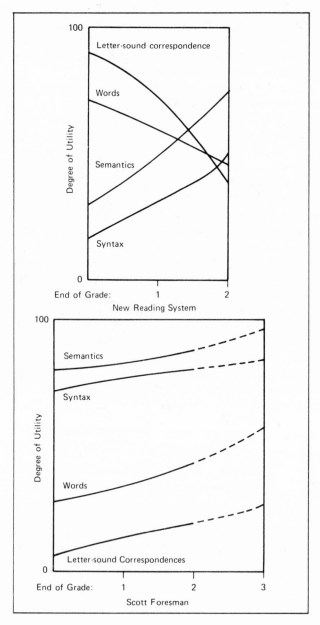

FIG. 10.16. Proportion of language skills used in initial "reading" as taught by NRS and SF. (See Shuy, 1975.)

significance, or they would not be tested. The following analysis of the content of an End-of-Level Test (Level 3, late in first grade) and a Skills Assessment Test (Level 2, midway in first grade) from SF and the content of several Progress Checks from NRS gives a slightly different flavor for the emphasis implied in each program's design.

End-of-Level Test (SF, Level 3)

Throughout this test a set of items presents a stimulus with three-choice responses. The first 23 items are in the format shown in Fig. 10.17. The correct alternatives for these 23 items contain only 9 words that are indexed as having been used more than once in the pupils' books, Levels 1 to 3; 8 of these and eleven more (or 19 response words) are used in the corresponding studybooks. The students then must rely on letter–sound correspondences to respond correctly to the remaining four items, and they may, in fact, use the strategy to respond to the others as well. As all initial letter–sound correspondences have been taught by the end of Level 3, that strategy for word identification would be a possible choice. For the first 12 items, it is an efficient strategy: Only the correct choice has an initial letter that matches the sound in the stimulus item. However, for items 12–23, the students must use a strategy that focuses on the medial vowel if they do not recognize the whole word. All three choices for each of these items have the same initial consonant. If the child could label the picture correctly, hear the vowel sound in that word, and find its representation among the alternatives, he or she would be successful. It is possible, because all the vowel representations used in the correct choices have been taught.

Incidentally, it is entirely unnecessary to read the entire sentence containing that picture as a rebus for the missing word. Sentence reading is of no more help than picture–word matching in selecting the correct response. This format of selecting the correct word using either the whole word or the letter–sound cues strategy is not found in the studybooks.

Items 24–29 and 30–34 are two sets of "wh" questions, each of which follows a story and has a three-choice response format. This format is a familiar exercise in the studybooks. Test questions of this type vary in difficulty and may be answered by various means. In a somewhat simplified

The _____ is on the bench.

ruler [a]
razor [b]
ranger [c]

FIG. 10.17.   An example of one item test format from SF End-of-Level Test, Level 3. (Material reprinted from Scott, Foresman and Company's *Reading Unlimited Program*, © 1976, Scott, Foresman and Company, is used with permission of the publisher.)

The dog has a huge <u>bone</u>.

hop [a]
horn [b]
hope [c]

FIG. 10.18.   An example of item test format from SF End-of-Level Test, Level 3, focused on vowel letter–sound correspondences. (Material reprinted from Scott, Foresman and Company's *Reading Unlimited Program,* © 1976, Scott, Foresman and Company, is used with permission of the publisher.)

categorization, these items are of the following types (the numbers in parentheses indicate the number of items for each type): (a) can be answered merely by looking at pictures (2); (b) can be answered with minimal reading and the pictures (1); (c) reading—facts present (6); and (d) reading—inference necessary (2).

One story is the "everyday" type and one is a fantasy; the vocabulary and language patterns are similar to what the children have been reading in their books. These 11 items seem to reflect the stated emphasis of the program.

Items 35–50 focus on vowel letter–sound correspondences, and the children are required to select the correct response from three alternatives. They are to choose the printed word containing the vowel sound that is the same as that found in a picture and a word printed in isolation for items 35–45 and in a picture and a word printed in context for items 46–50 (see Fig. 10.18). Reading the context, or sentences, in items 46–50 will help the child to read the underlined target word (which may be necessary because of ambigious pictures), but it is possible to respond correctly by reading only the target word or by correctly identifying the picture. Children may avoid reading the sentence if they so desire. All three alternatives in each response set have the same vowel letter present but in different spelling contexts. For instance, the choices for /a/ might be words with *a* followed by a consonant (s), followed by *r,* or followed by a consonant and final *e.* Thus the children must know that the letter *a* represents different sounds in different spelling contexts, and they must know how to identify these contexts. This is a format familiar to them from their studybook exercises.

In summary, in this End-of-Level Test, 11 of 50 items focus directly on meaning, on using context, and on reading larger chunks of materials; these 11 thus reflect the stated primary objectives of the program. The other 39 items focus on letter–sound associations, not particularly as cues to meaning, but more as a skill.

The Skills Assessment Test (SF, Level 2)

Twelve skill areas are defined (one for each subtest), seven of which use particular initial consonant letter–sound cues and consonant blends. An analysis of the items in each subtest of using letter–sound cues reveals that knowledge of those cues is necessary for making correct responses and that having that skill is sufficient, that is, reading the context is not necessary.

In other subtests, the circling of specific words in sentences tests word boundaries; "why" questions test cause–effect; sorting pictures tests distinguishing real from fanciful content; and answering comprehension questions following a reading selection tests the effective use of picture, context, and letter–sound cues.

The purposes for which these subtests were designed—periodic diagnostic testing of skills—seem to be adequately met, judging from the one available for examination at Level 2. These skills are taught in SF to achieve meaningful reading, but meaningful reading per se constitutes a minimal part of the testing program. However, another testing technique, the teacher's use of the miscue analysis outlined in the teacher's edition, is a direct attempt to determine if the child is using syntactic and semantic cues in reading and therefore, by inference, in comprehending.

NRS Progress Checks

From the very first lessons in NRS, the progress checks occur after almost every one of ten lessons at each level. They consist of one page of oral reading by the children, and the teacher scores the correctness of their responses to only selected key words (see Fig. 10.19). I analyzed the words scored, and they consistently include the element(s) taught in the preceding lesson. For instance (see Fig. 10.20), /ū/ and the words words *bear*(s)('s), *play*(s)(ing)(er)(ers), and *does* are taught in Lesson 9 at Level 5 (late in first grade). Beginning at Level 5, a few items that require choice answers by the students are included to check on comprehension.

The students in NRS (a program in which initial emphasis is on phonics) read sentences and short stories individually to their teacher, who scores them on specific words to determine if they have "mastered the element taught." In SF (a meaning-emphasis program) most test items require little contextual reading, and specific skills are tested to determine if the children are able to "read for meaning." In the case of NRS, the context could prompt the correct reading of the key words rather than mastery of the elements; and in SF, mastery of the elements could in many cases provide correct responses without contextual reading. One has to pause and reflect on this for its implications for both theory and practice.

CONTENT

Although most youngsters have a high degree of motivation for learning to read, the content of the reading program itself may provide further motivation. Some subjective judgments may be made about motivational

hen	has

1. **The hen has an egg.**

hatching	

2. **The egg is hatching.**

me	hit

3. **Stan said, "See me hit the can.**

she	

4. **Mom is singing.**

   She is singing to Ben.

hopping		
he	hopping	hill

5. **Sam is hopping.**

   He is hopping on a hill.

his	hat

6. **Ben sees his hat on the table.**

Total Points	Child's Score
12	

FIG. 10.19. NRS Progress Check, Level 3, Lesson 9. (Reproduced with
permission of the Learning Research and Development Center, University of
Pittsburgh. All rights reserved.)

Name _____ Date _____

Progress Check 5-9

Directions: Have the child read each sentence aloud. The words in
the sentence that are scored are listed in the box(es) at the end of
each sentence. Place a ✔ above the word in the box if the child reads
that word in the sentence correctly. Place a 0 above the word in the
box if the child misreads that word in the sentence.

bear	cute

1. The bear cubs are cūte.

bear	use
play	music

2. The big bear can ūse the drum

to play mūsic.

mule	

3. A mūle kicks with his back legs.

tube	

4. The tūbe has cream in it.

*Note: Have the child read the sentence by numeral 5
aloud. Then, direct him to make an X in the box in
front of the right answer. Count 1 point for the
correct answer to question 5.*

5. Where does Ben tāke a bath?

☐ in a tub

☐ in a tūbe

where	does
tube	1 point for correct answer

Total Points   Child's Score

12	

Scoring Procedure: Only the words in the boxes are scored. Give one
point for the correct reading of each of those words and one point for
the correct answer to question 5. If a child's score is 7 points or
more, his next prescription is cassette 5-9-P. If the child's score
is less than 7 points, his next assignment is the review cassette,
5-9-R.

FIG. 10.20. NRS Progress Check, Level 5, Lesson 9. (Reproduced with
permission of the Learning Research and Development Center, University of
Pittsburgh. All rights reserved.)

value by examining the format and story and picture content of the instructional materials.

Scott, Foresman Content

The books in the SF program are nothing short of delightful. They are appealing in design and very colorful. Beginning with the very easiest books, the content includes fanciful stories, common experiences of children, selections about animals, suggestions for craft projects, poetry, folk tales, and scientific selections. Children's art enhances each book's cover, and the illustrations within include diagrams; black and white and color photographs; realistic, fanciful, and surrealistic art; and a variety of media and styles. The print is clear, and the amount of print per page increases gradually over the eight levels analyzed. From level 7 on, there is a glossary of unfamiliar words and information on places referred to in the text.

Examples of stories from Level 1 and Level 4 of SF are included in Appendices A and B to give an indication of the content of these first-grade books. Although the story content of these can be replicated here, certainly the flavor of the books themselves cannot. Illustrations and other format characteristics that provide interest are missing. One notices immediately the literary quality that can be achieved in these early stories when vocabulary is not restricted by the number of new words introduced or the regularity of letter-to-sound relationships. If there are controls over the syntactic structures used, they are not obvious. At Level 4, end of first grade, the following complex sentence structure appears in a story: "The dragon was happy because no one was afraid of him, and he had lots of friends" (*The Little Knight*, p. 24; see Appendix B). The rhythm and tempo of the selections, the "flow" of the language, are quite natural. Sensitive to the fact that on trial runs, children's miscues of reading errors arose mostly from the use of unfamiliar language or from difficult concepts, these early stories use natural language patterns and familiar concepts in a manner designed to elicit correct reading responses.

From the point of view of appeal, the SF readers are quite superior and very much like the wider world of children's literature. That is in keeping with the program objectives to introduce the students to literature and to motivate them to read. It is important to note that although some children may be able to read *The Little Knight*, the instructional procedure includes a great deal of guidance from the teacher, with suggested motivating comprehension and discussion questions for children who are not able to read it independently.

New Primary Grades Reading System Content

NRS is still in experimental form, and it is with some reservations that I comment on its eye appeal. Although the illustrations are very good, they all are done in the same style in black and white for trial use. I assume these features will change with commercial publication. The literary forms incorporated in the series of Read-Alone Books for Levels 2–8 include many realistic fiction or personal interest selections and fantasy selections, a few informational articles, and some poetry. Many of the personal interest stories are oriented toward city youngsters. The number of words per page increases gradually over the eight levels of Read-Alone Books reviewed.

The authors state that new sentence structures are first introduced in the group story situation rather than in the Read-Alones and that "NRS slowly increases the complexity of sentence structure under the guidance of the teacher" (Beck & Mitroff, 1972, p. 76). The intent is to assist the students in transferring their oral/aural knowledge of structure to the printed language. An example of a group story for Level 7, end of first grade, is presented in Appendix C. Vocabulary in these group readers is controlled to include mostly words with phonic relationships that have been taught. Therefore, at the earliest levels, it is difficult to avoid some awkward language patterns.

However, at the end of first grade in the Read-Alone Books (Level 7), there are such complex sentences as: "The foxes were so glad to be free that they went back and had fun at the winter party" (*Boxes of Foxes*, p.19; see Appendix D). It takes a great deal of imagination to create stories with a vocabulary restricted to certain letter–sound correspondences and a limited number of sight words, and NRS has done well. However, the result, of necessity, includes restricted story lines and language patterns that are not entirely natural or literary. The authors intended that these books be read alone by all students who have advanced to the assigned level, and no teacher-guided reading is expected. This expectation that children be able to read alone has exerted a strong influence on the content of these readers. A careful analysis indicates that if the phonic elements and sight words taught are mastered, one would expect the books to be mastered as well. It would be interesting to know if children impose their own language patterns in these stories that are written so that the children can master the printed word. And would such reading behavior be considered good or bad by the program developers?

For the highly successful student, independent reading is possible in SF and NRS, and the content of SF intuitively has more appeal. The less successful students are apt to need guidance, either from the teacher or the structure of a controlled vocabulary. Guidance from the teacher is provided for the less able SF students who cannot and do not read alone. The NRS students are able and required to read alone, and the content is structured for them to do so. If there is motivation in interaction with the teacher and one's peers, SF provides that as the group reads their stories together. If there is intrinsic motivation for children in mastering and in knowing they have mastered a skill,the content in NRS is more apt to provide that form of motivation, even for the less able students.

OTHER MOTIVATIONAL FEATURES

One senses motivation for reading the selections themselves in the SF readers and motivation for mastering the reading skill and being able to read the content in the NRS readers. As for other motivational aspects of the program, they are beyond the scope of this chapter, but I would like briefly to note some features of each program that might be particularly motivating.

SF encourages projects associated with the children's reading and prestory discussions of their experiences. Reading tends to focus much of the activity in the classrooms. Another motivational aspect is the occasional letter sent home to the parents informing them of what reading experiences the children are having in their classroom.

The extensive use of manipulables in NRS is striking: games, Flip-a-Words, audio-cassettes and recorders with headphones, and the Read-Alone storybooks are available for independent use. Individual and personal attention from the teacher at regular intervals and the frequent mastery checks are also motivating factors.

Motivation and attention are no small part of beginning reading. A more complete program analysis ought to include how attention is captured and reinforced in reading programs and how that reinforcement is faded. We should note how the cluster of behaviors we call attention is first taught and then how it comes to be the intent of the reader rather than the teacher.

INDIVIDUALIZATION

Surely there are a multitude of problems when one attempts to adapt an educational program to individual differences. To my knowledge, none of the current theories of the acquisition of reading skills has incorporated parameters of individual differences. With or without theoretical rationale, the desire to design instructional systems that take into account individual differences is very evident. The literature on new programs is laden with assurances that these programs provide for individual differences. Such is the case with the reading programs analyzed in this chapter. The program announcement of SF says that "materials in Reading Unlimited can be combined to accommodate differences in children, their timing, and your classroom organization." And Beck and Mitroff (1972) wrote:

> NRS is described as an individualized-adaptive system. It is individualized in that it permits children to progress at various rates, it allows for different routes to the mastery of an objective, and it is organized so that a teacher can monitor a classroom of children doing different things at different times. It is adaptive in that alternative teaching strategies are available to meet the needs of different children and for the requirements of different tasks [p. 35].

Lesson plans in SF offer ideas for "personalizing instruction" that may relate to additional work on specific skills, extending the reading to more difficult selections and so on. Each teacher's edition contains an explanation of and directions for miscue analysis (developed by Kenneth Goodman, one of the program's authors). An analysis of the "variations from the text" made in oral reading may be conducted to estimate how well a student uses syntactic cues or graphic cues and to note whether the student self-corrects the miscues that alter the meaning of the text. In addition, private conferences with the children to discuss their progress, as well as the story content, are highly recommended by Helen Robinson, another program author.

The extent of individualization in SF then is dependent on the teacher's initiative in adapting to variations in children's performance and on his or her willingness to incorporate the many suggestions given. However, specific suggestions that offer an alternative to the basic approach to instruction are not evident in the program. As I've mentioned, the authors of SF espouse an inductive methodology that emphasizes the meaning of the passages in the pupil's books. The hierarchy of skills taught/learned is from the largest meaningful units down to letter–sound relationships, and no provision is made for children who are unable to cope with this strategy.

In an SF classroom, the teacher assembles groups of children to read and discuss stories together. One assumes that the first-grade teacher will make judgments about the students' readiness for reading and then group them accordingly. End-of-level tests and criterion-referenced skills assessment tests help in deciding whether a pace is too fast for an indvidual and whether or not review is necessary, and one assumes that adjustments in group assignments are made accordingly.

NRS, on the other hand, is definitely designed for individualized pacing. Only the first two levels of the program are taught to groups of students. At these levels, each group moves at a pace geared to its facility with the program. During this time, self-management schemes are taught, and then, beginning at Level 3 (early in first grade), the teacher makes a daily assignment, or prescription, for every individual. Because review work is necessary for some children, and because the assignments may vary in the amount of work expected, students are very soon working on different segments and at different levels according to their individual needs and progress.

Different routes are available for the child in terms of games and other manipulables, but the road is pretty well charted through the cassette-led instruction and the workbooks. The built-in review sequences for students who do not achieve mastery on the progress checks at the end of each lesson are "more of," rather than "different from," the instruction already given; that is, the basic approach remains the same. Later, the techniques offered as alternative teaching strategies (after a child has failed at least two times to master the skill in the prescribed manner) include first, tutoring the child following the same basic procedures in moving through the several levels of difficulty for letter-sound correspondences. In addition, tracing the letter is a further suggestion. The procedure for blending is altered, and instead of blending sounds into words, the strategy is to begin with the whole word, break it into its component sounds, and then blend them into the whole word.

Although these alternatives are suggested, the instructional method underlying the program does not change. The hierarchy of skills is from the lowest of discernible units—the letter-to-sound relationships—up to words, sentences, and meaningful reading of continuous text; and little provision is made for children who are unable to cope with this strategy.

All 11 students in the learning disabilities classroom I visited were progressing in NRS. Because it is still an "in-house" program, I asked whether or not any children in other NRS classrooms had been given an alternate program with an entirely different structure. Although the answer was that they had, the authors obviously felt that alternate programs might not be necessary once teachers gain experience and become effective in teaching NRS to children with a wide range of skills and abilities. The opportunities for individualization that are present in the program are greater than in other programs I am familiar with, and the authors may be correct in their assumption that it is enough. At least they should be given credit for moving significantly in this important direction.

Beginning readers are different. Their behavioral repertoires are different, their strategies for thinking about their world are different, and their personality characteristics are different (Durkin, 1972; Jansky & de Hirsch, 1972). The fact that they all learned language in a similar way, although possibly on a different time line, does not necessarily mean that they will all learn to read in the same way. At the most obvious level, instruction in the first grade has to be geared toward children whose chronological ages range over a full year. The provisions made for individualization of instruction, particularly those that go beyond pacing, appear to me to be crucial for a successful first-grade experience. And the success of that experience is crucial for ego and scholarly development. Procedures that might be introduced to individualize effectively initial reading instruction are still absent from beginning programs. However, more research is needed prior to prescriptive methodologies.

SUMMARY AND CONCLUSIONS

This examination of two very different approaches to initial reading instruction began with a presentation of the scope of each program and an overview of obvious differences between them. A comparison was then made of the teaching/learning strategies related to various linguistic units (graphemes/phonemes, spelling patterns, words, sentences, and stories), and the workbooks were analyzed. Testing in each program was examined in relation to the objectives of the program. The content of the students' books and other motivational aspects of each program were discussed, and the extent of individualization possible under each program was examined. Analyses similar to this one, covering the same aspects of other programs, might allow educators to know what options are available for initial instruction in reading. Further, such analyses suggest areas for further research.

Hypotheses about how children learn to read need to be formulated and tested by studying children who are taught in various ways. Systems similar to the two investigated in this chapter and other systems ought to be included. There seems to be more than one way to learn to read; the mere fact that children have learned under systems as different as SF and NRS suggests that this is so. The challenge to research and pedagogy is that children have failed to learn under different kinds of instruction. Beginning readers soon fall into one of several categories; They learn what we teach them, they learn in spite of what we teach them, or they do not learn. That fact influences the child's future success in reading and other academic as well as emotional areas. For this reason, research in beginning reading instruction ought to continue.

There is general consensus that there has been a rise in the mean achievement on standardized tests in first and second grades. Some have attributed that improvement to the shift toward the inclusion of a phonics component at the earliest levels of instruction (although that has not been proven, to my knowledge). However, does this information help us to select programs for our "at risk" children? Does any of the research focus on the lower 50% of the children and ask what is more effective with them or if they also are now better achievers? Are there differences within this group in learning strategies? One might hypothesize that the differences in achievement that have occurred are largely a function of raising the scores of children in the upper end of the continuum rather than the lower. However, to my knowledge, no data have been analyzed to address that hypothesis. There appears to be a need to reconsider the implications of data that have been accumulated.

We consciously need to relate our research in beginning reading instruction to theory. Would it not be possible to tap behaviors of young children to determine where they are in their cognitive development and to research initial strategies in beginning reading in an attempt to make a match between child characteristics and program characteristics? We need to be asking what abilities are necessary for success in different types of programs: Sight-word approaches, with their straight stimulus–response, almost paired-associate type learning, may require strategies different from those required in programs in which there is recoding from letters to sounds and then to words and sentences that must be remembered until meaning is attained (as in NRS). And both these types of programs may require skills different from the skills needed in SF, which moves from meaning, through language, to print, and back again. Young children, especially immature children, may find it difficult in the beginning to attend to syntactic, semantic, and graphic information all at the same time. Different programs emphasize different aspects, and I believe the challenge is to know for whom each is most appropriate—the way a very wise first-grade teacher knows. Can research and theory building tolerate different processes for different children? Close observation of teachers and children, along with program analyses, may move us closer to some answers.

REFERENCES

Beck, I. L., & Mitroff, D. D. *The rationale and design of a primary grades reading system for an individualized classroom.* Pittsburgh: University of Pittsburgh, Learning Research and Development Center, 1972 (Publication No. 1972/4). (ERIC Document Reproduction Service No. ED 063 100)

Blackman, B., Marston, E., & Reinhardt, M. *Simultaneous and successive training and trasnsfer: An examination of the research.* Unpublished manuscript, Harvard University, 1973.

Carroll, J. B. The analysis of reading instruction: Perspectives from psychology and linguistics. *Sixty-Third Yearbook of the National Society for the Study of Education,* 1964, *63,* 336–353.

Durkin, D. *Teaching young children to read.* Boston: Allyn & Bacon, 1972.

Fletcher, J. D. *Transfer from alternative presentations of spelling patterns in initial reading* (Tech. Rep. No. 216). Stanford, Calif.: Stanford University, 1973.

Hively, W. A framework for the analysis of elementary reading behavior. *American Educational Research Journal,* 1966, *3,* 89–103.

Jansky, J., & de Hirsch, K. *Preventing reading failure* New York: Harper & Row, 1972.

Learning Research and Development Center. *New primary grades reading system.* Pittsburgh: University of Pittsburgh, Learning Research and Development Center, 1974.

Levin, H., & Watson, J. The learning of variable grapheme-to-phoneme correspondences. In H. Levin & E. J. Gibson (Eds.), *A basic research program on reading* (U.S. Office of Education Cooperative Research Project No. 639). Ithaca, N.Y.: Cornell University, 1963. (ERIC Document Reproduction Service No. ED 002 967)

Resnick, L.B., & Beck, I. L. *Designing instruction in reading: Interaction of theory and practice.* Pittsburgh: University of Pittsburgh, Learning Research and Development Center, 1975 (Publication No. 1975/25). Also in J. T. Gutherie (Ed.), *Aspects of reading acquisition.* Baltimore: Johns Hopkins University Press, 1976.

Scott, Foresman & Co. *Reading unlimited program.* Glenview, Ill.: Scott, Foresman, 1976.

Shuy, R. Pragmatics: Still another contribution of linguistics to reading. In S. Smiley & J. Twoner (Eds.), *Language and reading.* Bellingham, Wash.: Western Washington State College, 1975.

Williams, J. P. Successive vs. concurrent presentation of multiple grapheme–phoneme correspondences. *Journal of Educational Psychology,* 1968, *59,* 309–314.

APPENDIX A

The Bus Ride
(Scott, Foresman, Level 1)

A girl got on the bus.

2

Then the bus went fast.

3

A boy got on the bus.

4

Then the bus went fast.

A fox got on the bus.

6

Then the bus went fast.

7

A hippopotamus got on the bus.

8

Then the bus went fast.

9

270

A goat got on the bus.

10

Then the bus went fast.

11

A rhinoceros got on the bus.

12

Then the bus went fast.

13

271

A fish got on the bus.

14

Then the bus went fast.

15

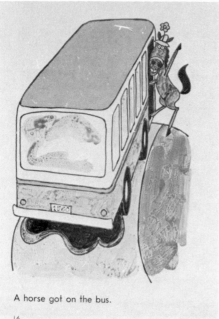

A horse got on the bus.

16

Then the bus went fast.

17

A rabbit got on the bus.

18

Then the bus went fast.

19

A bee got on the bus.

Then!

273

The rabbit got off the bus.

The horse got off the bus.

The fish got off the bus.

The rhinoceros got off the bus.

The goat got off the bus.

The hippopotamus got off the bus.

The fox got off the bus.

The boy got off the bus.

The girl got off the bus.

22

Then they all ran fast.

23

Who got on the bus?

a bee   a boy   a fish

a fox   a girl   a goat

a horse   a book   a rabbit

a rhinoceros   a hippopotamus

APPENDIX B

The Little Knight
by Anne Rowe
(Scott, Foresman, Level 4)

Page 2

Once upon a time a king and a queen lived in a big old castle.

Page 3

The king and the queen were sad because their castle was so cold. Sometimes the queen had to put on a blanket to keep warm. And the king had to put on an old rug. Then they didn't look like a king and a queen.

Page 4

Something else made the king and queen sad. They couldn't sleep because a dragon kept them awake.

Page 5

Every night the dragon sat in his cave on the top of the hill. And he roared and roared and roared.

Page 6

The king and queen didn't know it, but the dragon was sad too. Everybody was afraid of him. No one came to see him. He was always alone. That's why he was sad. That's why he roared. Sometimes he was so sad he cried.

Page 8

One day the king sent for his knights. There were four big knights and one little knight. The king was mad. "I can't get any sleep," he said. "Do something about that dragon!"

Page 9

"What should we do?" asked one of the big knights. "I don't care what you do!" said the king. "But do it fast!"

Page 10

So the knights left the castle to do something about the dragon.

Page 11

They started to go up the hill to the dragon's cave.

Page 12

Just then the dragon roared. The big knights turned and ran.

Page 13

But the little knight kept on going. He was a brave little knight who wasn't afraid of any old dragon. He kept on going up the hill until he got to the dragon's cave.

Page 14

The little knight tiptoed into the cave. He saw the dragon. The dragon was crying. The knight asked, "Why are you crying?"

Page 15

"I'm crying because everybody is afraid of me," said the dragon. "No one comes to see me. I don't have any friends." The little knight said, "I came to see you. I'll be your friend."

Page 16

The dragon gave a happy snort. Fire came out of his nose. The fire made the cave nice and warm. Soon the little knight was warm. Then he thought of something.

Page 18

The little knight said, "Why don't you come and live at the castle? The castle is always cold. You could keep it warm, and you'd have lots of friends. Blow your nose and come with me."

Page 20

The king and queen were afraid when they saw the dragon.

Page 21

The little knight said, "He won't hurt you. He's going to live with us and keep the castle warm. He'll be very quiet."

Page 22

The dragon made fire come out of his nose. The castle began to get warm. The king took off his rug, and the queen took off her blanket. Then they looked like a king and a queen again.

APPENDIX C

Rumplestiltskin
(NRS Group Story, Level 7)

Page 17

Once upon a time, a miller and his daughter lived in a tiny house. The miller was not a rich man. He had to work hard just so he and his daughter could live.

One day, the king was passing by and the miller wanted to impress the king. So the miller ran and told the king that his daughter could do a fine trick. He told the king that she could spin weeds into gold on her spinning wheel.

Page 18

The greedy king began to think.

He said, "If you have told me the truth, miller, then your daughter would please me very much. Bring her to the castle tomorrow and I will see if she really can turn weeds into gold."

Page 19

The next morning, the king led the girl into a room that was full of weeds.

He gave her a spinning wheel and he said, "You must spin these weeds into gold by tomorrow. If you do not, I will have you killed."

And then the king left.

Page 20

The girl looked around the room at all the weeds. She really couldn't spin weeds into gold. That was just a story that her father had told the king. She began to cry.

All at once the door opened, and in stepped an ugly little man.

"Good day, miller's daughter," said the man. "Why are you crying?"

"Oh," said the girl. "The king wants me to spin these weeds into gold and I can't. If this room is not filled with gold by tomorrow, he is going to have me killed."

Page 23

Then the ugly little man said, "What will you give me if I spin it for you?"

"I will give you the ring from my finger," said the girl.

The ugly little man took the ring and sat down at the spinning wheel.

Whirr-whirr, three times round and the bobbin was full of gold. Then he took another bobbin and, whirr-whirr, three times round and that bobbin was full too.

He went on spinning until morning. When all the weeds were spun, and all the bobbins were full of gold, he went away.

Page 24

The king came into the room, and he was very happy to see all the gold. The king wanted the girl to make him the richest man who ever lived. He was starting to like the miller's daughter too.

So he said, "This pleases me very much. But I am going to test you one more time. I am going to put you in a bigger room full of weeds. If you spin those weeds into gold, then you will become my wife."

When the girl was left alone in the big room, the ugly little man came in and said, "What will you give me this time if I spin the weeds for you?"

Page 25

The girl said, "I have nothing left to give."

"Then you must give me the first baby you have after you are queen," said the little man.

Then the man sat down and he began to spin. He spun until all the weeds were gold.

And in the morning when the king came and saw that all the weeds were turned into gold, he ordered the wedding to be held at once. The miller's daughter became the queen.

Page 26

After a year's time, the queen had a fine child. She did not think once of the ugly little man.

But soon after the baby was born, the man came into her room and said, "Now give me the child as you said you would."

Page 27

The queen wanted to keep her baby, so she offered the ugly little man all the riches of the kingdom, if only he would leave the child with her.

But the ugly little man wouldn't listen. He wanted the baby.

He said, "I will give you three days. If at the end of that time you cannot tell me my name, you must give me the child."

Page 28

The queen spent all of her time thinking of what the man's name could be. She even sent a friend to ask far and wide for all the names her people could think of.

And when the ugly little man came the next day, she repeated all the names she could think of.

But after each name, the little man said, "That is not my name."

The same thing happened on the second day.

On the third day her friend went by a hut in the woods. Someone was singing so she peeked inside the hut. There was the ugly little man singing a song and jumping up and down.

The song went like this:
"Rumplestiltskin is my name.
She'll never get my little game."

Page 30

The friend went back to the queen and told her what she had seen. The queen smiled.

"Rumplestiltskin," said the queen. "So that's his name."

Page 31

And when the ugly little man came back later that day, the queen said, "Is your name Alfred?"

"No," said the man.

"Is it Martin?" asked the queen.

"No," said the man.

"Well, then, I bet it's Rumplestiltskin," said the queen.

Page 32

"The devil told you that! The devil told you that," said the ugly little man.

He was so mad that he stamped his foot so hard it got stuck in the floor. Then he grabbed his other foot with both hands and pulled so hard that he split in two.

And that was the end of Rumplestiltskin.

APPENDIX D

Boxes of Foxes
(NRS Read Alone, Level 7)

Page 1

Last week, something bad happened in the forest. It happened the day the foxes were having a winter party.

Page 2

It was winter and the foxes were having a winter party in the forest. The sun was shining and all the foxes were happy.

Page 3

Suddenly, one of the little foxes said, "What is that thing over there?"

All the foxes began to look at what the little fox saw.

Page 4

It was a wagon. And it was the biggest wagon that the foxes had ever seen.

Page 5

The driver got off the wagon. He was the biggest man the foxes had ever seen.

Page 6

Then the man said, "Hurry, hurry. Today I am giving away free jelly beans. Come inside my wagon and get your free jelly beans."

Page 7

All the foxes got in a line by the door of the wagon. One by one they went in to get some jelly beans.

Page 8

As each fox went in, the big man would grab it and put a rope around its legs. Then he would drop the fox on the floor of the wagon.

Page 9

Soon all the foxes were in a big pile. They were all feeling sad.

"What will that man do with us?" they said.

Page 10

The man was laughing.

Then he said, "I am going to put all of you in boxes. Then I will have boxes of foxes. I will use your fur to make jackets. Then I will sell the fur jackets and get rich."

Page 11

The man put all of the foxes in boxes. There were boxes of foxes all over. By that time all the foxes were so sad that they began to cry.

Page 12

First one fox was crying. Then three foxes were crying. Then ten foxes were crying. But one fox was not crying.

Page 13

The baby fox was not crying. He was getting away.

Page 14

When the man went away, the baby fox went around to take all the locks off all the boxes.

Page 15

First one fox was free. Then three foxes were free. Then ten foxes were free. In a little while, all the foxes were free, and that made them stop crying.

Page 16

When the man came back, he said, "How did you get the locks off the boxes?"

Page 17

"We will never tell," said the foxes. "But now we are going to chase you away."

Page 18

"Oh, no!" said the man, running as fast as he could.

The man ran and ran until the foxes could not see him any more.

Page 19

The foxes were so glad to be free that they went back and had fun at the winter party. And the baby fox was made king for the day.

IV DISCUSSION

11

Reflections on Reading about Reading

Tom Trabasso
University of Chicago

Discussants have essentially three choices as to the kind of commentary they write. One choice is to write yet another chapter related to the theme of the volume but on one's own work or set of interests. A second choice is to pay slightly more attention to the chapters but to present one's comments in a general way. The third choice is to deal more directly with the chapters and to react to what the authors write in a candid and frank manner with a willingness to provoke discussion. I have decided on the third approach, partly because I do not have another chapter to write, partly because I am not very apt at making generalizations, and partly because I would like to provide an overview of the chapters. My comments are, I hope, both substantive and prescriptive, with the goal of provoking further discussion.

In surveying the chapters, one can discern four main themes: (a) theories of the reading process; (b) problems in acquisition of reading by, or in teaching reading to, poor, retarded, or bilingual persons; (c) systematic programs for early reading instruction; and (d) evaluation and effectiveness of instruction.

THEORY

Each of us adheres to some implicit or, at times, explicit notion of the nature of the reading process. The prevailing view in this volume pictures the act of reading as a linear, "bottom-up" process analogous to speech perception. In both, recognition is followed by comprehension; however, reading has the added initial problem of rendering the print into speech. Both the theory and practice of beginning reading instruction assume that the process order dictates the instructional order; hence, the stress on the decoding process of translating print into sound.

The widespread use of oral reading to assess comprehension appears to be consistent with this view, since when children render the print into acceptable sound, they can be said to "read." Danks and Fears, in their examination of what transpires in oral reading, adopt a two-stage linear model against which to assess whether oral reading involves one or both stages. I think that it should be made clear that this analysis treats the oral production as a "dependent measure," that is, an outcome that is observed or recorded in an experiment. The stages are hypothetical events assumed to occur prior to and/or during the outcome observed. By definition, decoding has to be involved, and the central question is whether or not understanding of what has been read or what one is about to read influences one's oral production.

After surveying the literature, Danks and Fears leave us with a rather unsatisfactory conclusion: One can, in some circumstances and under special conditions, demonstrate that comprehension occurs in oral reading. What does this mean for the teacher? What does this imply for practice? Their conclusion certainly does not imply that comprehension is necessary for oral reading or that it is a characteristic found in the early reader.

What seems to be required is more direct way of studying the question. Danks and Fears (see also McConkie) discuss procedures for advanced readers that could be adapted for use with younger subjects. In those, one deliberately manipulates syntactic and/or semantic relations within the sentence, so that if the reader is using the preceding text to predict what he or she is about to read, violations of the relations would lead to a disruption of the on-line reading performance. This method is consistent, in part, with procedures used in cognitive psychology to assess stages of processing (Sternberg, 1969) where one manipulates a variable, A, that is known to affect Stage 1 and a second variable, B, that is known to affect Stage 2. If Stages 1 and 2 are independent, then the effects of factors A and B "add" in the treatment of the data. What Danks and Fears need to complete their approach is to manipulate another factor that clearly affects decoding (say, for example, clarity of print or acoustic confusions among words). If they can show additive effects, then their general model is supported; at least the assumption of two independent stages is supported. However, the stages need not be linear or sequential; they could be parallel or overlapping. Nonadditivity would suggest an interactive ("bottom-down"? "top-up"?) model.

Thus, Danks and Fears raise an interesting theoretical issue. The existing literature and experiments, however, are not adequate to answer it. As far as practice is concerned, if the teacher accepts the child's oral production as a reasonable approximation to the text, and if the teacher is not prescriptive about how the child says what he or she reads, and if the teacher does not stress adherence to a particular phonological expression of language, then it would appear that oral reading is a useful method of assessing reading comprehension.

In a similar but more explicit view, LaBerge (Chapter 1) provides a microanalysis of the decoding process. He also adopts a "bottom-up" model where analysis goes from unspecified features to letters to clusters to words on the visual side and from corresponding phonemes to syllables to morphemes and words on the acoustic side. His main concern is with the questions: How do we recognize a word? How do we acquire the necessary structures to do so? The latter question predominates.

The value of LaBerge's approach is that it is analytic. One can break down the visual stimulus into components and then speculate about what the reader must consequently do to perceive and interpret that stimulus as a word. The focus of the approach is on the reader's unit of analysis. These units, sometimes referred to as "codes" when they are represented internally, have to become structured or linked within and across modalities. That is, a word must be visually decomposable into letters (and lower-level features), and these units must have some structural relations corresponding to those of their acoustic counterparts. LaBerge summarizes through diagrams several possible relational structures within the visual system. He argues strongly for the development of "contextual" nodes that allow the reader to perform the analysis at different levels of unitizing. He omits, however, the relations between the visual and acoustic nodes, so much the concern of those who teach sight–sound correspondence.

LaBerge's model shares the problems of any general feature model (see Gibson & Levin, 1975). What are the basic units, and how can they be identified? How are the units represented internally? How are they analyzed and acquired? How do they become combined? These questions and their answers represent only a small part of the more general problem of how we recognize objects or patterns. To be complete as a model, a feature analysis requires something like an analysis-by-synthesis model (Chomsky & Halle, 1968; Neisser, 1967).

The appeal of the feature approach is that one can, by contrasting minimal pairs, show that letters or words differ by certain features. The question arises as to whether these contrasts are necessary or are made in reading or word recognition. The success of the whole-word method of instruction and other forms of visual recognition may very well rest on the fact that any visual configuration, independent of contrast, can be perceived, identified, and subsequently labeled as a configuration per se.

There are two other aspects of LaBerge's chapter on which I would like to remark. First, contextual nodes play a role akin to "control processes" whereby the child can, at will, direct his or her attention to units of varying size. LaBerge assumes that such nodes have to be established as a prerequisite for the later unitization of letters into clusters and words. The postulation of the context node, however, seems to make the unit more mysterious. It remains unclear to me what these contextual nodes are, how they work, and from where they arise.

A second, related point is that children already have highly developed speech by the time reading occurs. Contrary to LaBerge's claim, children do not perceive the speech of another as an undifferentiated stream (speech spectrograms do, though). They can segment words and produce them as in, "Say, 'dog,' Johnny." If segmentation did not occur, how could Johnny say "dog"? In addition, Williams (Chapter 8, this volume) has shown that children who are poor learners in general can isolate syllables from words quite readily, and this skill apparently can be used to facilitate learning segmentation strategies for the isolation of initial word consonants (which Wallach and Wallach [Chapter 9] imply is impossible). It may be that the higher-order units are already available in the acoustic domain and that by Gestalt principles of grouping and spacing of letters, letter configurations can be assimilated to these units. Finally, the co-occurrence of some combinations of letters more frequently than others must play a role. One can specify a set of rules for combining consonants and consonant clusters plus vowels—for example, STR + vowel or Sp + (r,l) + vowel—and children presumably derive them by noticing spelling patterns that conform to them.

In striking contrast to LaBerge's microanalysis is the macroanalysis of reading by Gregg and Farnham–Diggory (Chapter 2), who valiantly try to meet a request for an information-processing approach to the task. One has to agree with their goal of producing explicit models. The problem with a comprehensive model, especially of something as complex as reading, is that there are too many options within the framework.

The model they propose is also linear, a string of past models developed for different purposes in cognitive psychology and artificial intelligence and dealing with different problems: attention, short-term memory, semantic memory, and so on. Each of these in turn is but one representative of several alternative models, only some of which are verifiable. This linear string of linear processes faithfully reflects some of the better approaches in cognitive "boxology," but the inherent sequentiality fails to capture the interactions that must occur between the systems.

I wish that Gregg and Farnham–Diggory had dwelled more on their briefly presented taxonomy of reading tasks rather than on the model. One could argue that analyses of the reading task and of the resources and skill of the reader are prerequisites of the development of an information-processing model. As it now stands, the model they present could exist if reading never occurred; it is a model of a general information processor.

Their table summarizing the taxonomy seems to be more than two-dimensional. It contains an implicit developmental model moving from pre-to skilled reading levels, thus classifying the overall state of the reader. The sight–sound correspondences are analogous to those mentioned previously, except that at each level there is the useful addition of a set of rules for the use and combination of the stored feature, letter, or word list. Task complexity is another feature; and examples are given in which the child is asked just to read a letter versus reading with feeling (add prosodic features), asked to recognize a figure versus providing a diagram of it (recognition versus reconstruction or recall), asked to find the meaning of a single word versus reasoning through a logical proposition, asked to find the meaning of a word versus the meaning of a longer narrative. Each of these tasks demands a model in its own right, but they sensitize us to what is being asked of the reader and force us to begin to wonder about how each of these is accomplished. A further description would be most welcome and more in the spirit of an information-processing analysis.

Of the three chapters on theory, LaBerge (Chapter 1) is alone in addressing the problem of acquisition of skill. I am afraid that practitioners are going to be disappointed with the present offerings. For some reason, current theoretical work in cognitive psychology and information processing seems preoccupied with detailed description of the underlying mechanisms, operations, or processes by which a person solves a problem task rather than with the mechanisms by which the knowledge and skills required to solve the problem are learned. Knowledge—often in the form of list structures—is given, not derived. This is probably because computers, the main analogy for most information-processing models, operate on data but do not acquire either the data or the operations. Another reason is historical—learning was closely identified with the now unpopular behaviorist tradition. This continued neglect, however, by modern cognitive psychologists may prove to be one of the major stumbling blocks in their path to answering their questions successfully. One value of returning to a learning orientation, regardless of ideology, is that one seeks to know the conditions under which learning is promoted as well as the possible mechanisms for its operation. Even in LaBerge's account, too much is left to "automaticity" and unspecified ways of change. There is a serious need for a revival of instructional and learning theory here.

McConkie (Chapter 3) reflects this lament with a series of disturbing questions regarding our assumptions about skilled and beginning readers and our general lack of real knowledge about them. McConkie's solution, however, is decidedly empirical: One can, he asserts, learn much about reading by measuring eye movements during its occurence. However, this approach, thus far, seems to be restricted to the more advanced and older, skilled reader. The question is: Can one, as in the Danks and Fears on-line procedure, adapt the method for use in the study of the beginning reader? Is the eye the pathway to the mind of the reader?

In McConkie's empirical approach, one studies the act of reading by studying eye movements; its product is studied later. The problem is that even empirical observation must be guided by some theoretical orientation; even the choice of variables to be manipulated must be so guided. One needs to examine the reasons for one's selection of variables, both independent and dependent. McConkie's contribution should not be underrated, however. He and his colleagues have developed reliable on-line methods for studying how much information can be taken in during fixations and saccades by a computer-controlled procedure where changes in the material being read are made contingent on eye movements. His finding that fixations increase in the face of semantic change indicates that comprehension processing occurs during the fixation. However, his finding that manipulation of the size of the perceptual span was unrelated to the subsequent retention of the material would have led me to conclude that eye movements, or at least perceptual span, are unrelated to reading comprehension. Apparently, readers are flexible in the strategies they use and can overcome some limitations imposed on them.

PROBLEMS

Reading problems are not the province of the individual reader or the classroom. They are, as Natalicio (Chapter 6) so clearly indicates, linguistic, social, and political. Natalicio and Simons (Chapter 5) treat current social and political issues having to do with how minority populations can achieve literacy comparable to that of members of the middle-class, white American society. In Natalicio's chapter, the central question is whether or not literacy should first be achieved in the child's native language. There are several problems here. There appears to be no homogeneous group of Spanish or Black English speakers in the United States. If one taught the native language, one would be adopting a standard, codified Spanish or Black English at variance with the speaker's dialect. Furthermore, it is unclear whether there would be positive transfer between the reading achievements of the first and second languages. Given the need to make a readjustment in the sight–sound correspondence (since the alphabet is not a syllabary for either), one might well anticipate interference.

Natalicio's analysis is based on the assumption that the training would be sequential—learning to read first in one's native language followed by learning to read in one's second language. But there is an alternative: parallel training, where children learn to read in each language according to their respective competence. The training is done simultaneously but separately. By keeping the training separate, one can achieve independent bilingualism (see Riegel & Freedle, 1976, who discuss different kinds of bilingualism) and minimize negative transfer. In keeping with good educational practice, regardless of whether the child is to learn to read in either one or two languages, what the child knows linguistically will have to be taken into account. If there were general language arts training in each language, reading would be a natural part of the curriculum and hardly revolutionary. One need not be so pessimistic as Natalicio's careful and complete discussion of the issues leads one to be.

Simons puts the problem more in the role of the speaker of the nonstandard dialect. He asks whether speaking Black English vernacular "interferes" with the acquisition of reading. His answer is that there is little or no evidence to support the idea that a mismatch between one's language and the standard language interferes. Although he may be correct, one would like to have seen experiments that were more sensitively designed. That is, one would have to define precisely what the mismatches are; select materials to be read or learned that are representative samples of these mismatches; explain by a psychological process model why one would expect to see interference; and test for its occurrence, including control items that should not interfere. From Simons' review, I do not believe that much of the research met these stringent, but minimal, criteria. because the most obvious differences between speakers of Black English and those of standard English appear to be phonological. Black English speakers may have the most difficulty in having their oral reading product accepted by the teacher (see Danks & Fears, Chapter 4, this volume). This puts the problem elsewhere than in the reader's head.

In discussions of Black English, writers often fail to distinguish between standard English as it is codified and written and "standard" English as a preferred spoken form—ostensibly that used by radio and television broadcasters (who frequently read aloud reports, advertisements, etc.) or by elementary school teachers. If the speaker of a Black English dialect is criticized for his or her pronunciation, then the interference is not internal to the reader but external in the teacher/child interaction. Hence, Simons' shift to the dialogue analysis as a source of ideas about what takes place in the classroom and beginning reading instruction is very reasonable. In these kinds of observations, one can find sources of miscommunication and failure to accept dialect variation.

Cazden, in her commentary (Chapter 12), discusses this approach at length, and I want to add briefly to it. These investigations of communicative strategies enable us to "take a walk in the classroom" and see what goes on. If one is interested in the acquisition process or in didactic effectiveness, it would seem to be useful to look at teachers' strategies in accepting or rejecting the child's oral production (Nelson, 1973) as well as at other reinforcement or modeling behaviors on the part of the teacher. The emerging emphasis on teacher/child or mother/child interaction in communicative settings tends to yield highly detailed description but lacks economical data reduction and theoretical force. One needs to have some a priori guidance on what to observe and on how to reduce the potential mass of observational data obtained from this descriptive-analytic approach. Can one find protocols of good and successful teacher/child interchange? Can one compare these with poor protocols? Would such contrasts help teachers learn better teaching and communicating strategies? Are shared knowledge and assumptions as critical as Simons would have us believe? Teaching situations are ones where knowledge is not yet shared, and the game is transmission to achieve sharing. It seems less a matter of sharing knowledge or assumptions than of teacher's being more sensitive to and accepting of the child's attempts.

PROGRAMS

I recognize that to construct and implement a reading program represents a considerable undertaking, and I temper my critical remarks because of this consideration. In this volume, four programs are described—two that are prereading or supplemental (those of the Wallachs and of Williams) and two that are complete programs. Of these, the first two and the *New Primary Grades Reading System* (reviewed by Popp (Chapter 10) are "bottom-up" approaches and emphasize decoding skills. The fourth, Scott, Foresman's *Reading Unlimited Program* (also reviewed by Popp), is a "top-down" approach, emphasizing the use of the child's knowledge of the context in which the stories occur. The programs are sufficiently complex and varied so as to virtually defy any simple contrasts. Popp's informative comparisons and criticism represent a genuine service.

Perhaps the strongest claims are those made by Wallach and Wallach (Chapter 9). They argue that phoneme identification skills are a prerequisite of learning to read. If a reading program emphasizes decoding and phonemic skills, then they may be correct. However, it is hard to see how this claim holds for a program such as the one developed by Scott, Foresman. Perhaps the Wallachs' basis for their claim rests with the baseline against which they began and the success their tutors had with a difficult sample of potential readers. The problem with accepting their claim is quite simple, however: Because the phonemic identification training is but one part of a larger program and there is no control comparison, one cannot decide what led to the success they claim. This problem, namely, what control comparisons are necessary to decide that a program is what it claims to be, holds for all programs and is not unique to the Wallachs.'

One reason that phoneme identification or segmentation is difficult, both for adults and children, is that the phoneme is not a basic, psychological unit. Williams' review and procedures suggest that one can more readily segment and identify syllables and that such training can be used to get across the notion of segmentation of sounds within words. Williams' program uses visual aids as mnemonic supports and physically demonstrates the idea of segmentation via blocks that can be moved together and apart. LaBerge might discover by analogy how to relate the visual and acoustic systems by an examination of how segmentation and blending are achieved with the nonprint visual and acoustic cues used in this program.

Another reason for the difficulty of the phoneme identification task is that there is not a close correspondence between phonemes in isolation and those segmented from a word. The initial consonant of *b-at* sounds like "buh" not /b/. Furthermore, the English alphabet is not a syllabary, and the letter names and sounds differ from the phonemes. These differences could be an additional source of confusion to the child. The difficulty may be further compounded when phonemes are "blended" into words, because they change when combined with other phonemes so that they are no longer clearly recognizable.

Given these sources of difficulty, it is impressive indeed that the Wallachs succeeded. Thirty-six weeks of tutoring strikes me as rather extensive and intensive, and one must wonder whether that much training is both necessary and worth it. The Wallachs' report of success is hard to judge, because they report proportions passing at some percentile level without controls. The evaluation is done, not on reading performance, but on standardized, reading-readiness tests. How well do the children do when they are taught to read?

Williams, in contrast to the Wallachs, is more modest in her claims and program (Chapter 8). She worked with children who already had records of learning problems, whereas the Wallachs' children were chosen according to class. Williams offers a stronger experimental rationale for her choice of procedures and materials. Her program was developed as an alternative to the discredited perceptual-motor training approach. She was cognizant of the literature on phonics and recognized the problems associated with phoneme segregation and blending and, as a consequence, adopted the easier syllable segmentation procedure. She also used efficiency criteria for training phoneme discrimination, analysis, and segmentation—such as avoiding acoustic and visual confusions, ease of blending, and use of short words such as trigrams (*cat, boy,* etc), all of which have a basis in the research literature. The main problems have to do with how well her program blends into existing ones, whether her students show transfer, and evaluation of what she accomplished.

The *New Primary Grades Reading System* developed at the Learning Research and Development Center is a highly structured, full phonics-oriented program. It is clearly a "bottom-up" approach, adhering closely in principle to the basic theory subscribed to by most of the authors in this volume. It is quite apparent from Popp's review that meaning is minimized, although it would seem that meaning must occur in the workbooks, read-along books, and so on. If the materials and procedures place such a heavy stress on basic phonic skills, I wonder what would sustain children's interest through such a program. The proof is in the pudding. If the children move from this program into the middle grades and show good reading achievement, then some kind of fundamental basis was laid. Popp could have provided us with some evaluation evidence (or perhaps it is too soon?).

Popp (Chapter 10) provides less in the way of critical commentary on the *New Primary Grades Reading System* than she does for the Scott, Foresman program, although she also praises the latter more. The examples she provides—especially those of fairy tales,—certainly suggest that the Scott, Foresman program would be the more interesting one to participate in as a student. It is unfortunate that those who designed the *Reading Unlimited Program* were not careful in the construction of drill and test items so that both reading and comprehension are assured. Pop's criticisms of these items are worthy of study and should be of use to the test construction people at Scott, Foresman.

Aside from the *Reading Unlimited Program,* this volume does not address the question of "context." Context has several meanings, and contexts have an influence on reading. One context is the word. It is well known that letters are more easily identified when they occur in words than when they occur in nonword letter strings or alone, the so-called word superiority effect. Another context is the sentence. Here, the other words and the meaningful relations among them allow the reader to anticipate something about the remaining words to be read. This idea, in part, is contained in the *Reading Unlimited Program.* Selectional restrictions on verbs can play a role as in the following:

1. The farmer plowed the———.
2. The farmer fed the———.

In 1, the verb *plow* takes an inanimate object, whereas in 2, *fed* most likely has an animate object.

Another context is across sentences. Consider the following three pairs of sentences that Dave Nicholas, one of my students at Princeton, developed (Nicholas & Trabasso, 1980):

3. Mary had a little lamb. Its fleece was white as snow.
4. Mary had a little lamb. She spilled gravy and mint jelly on her dress.
5. Mary had a little lamb. The delivery was a difficult one, and afterwards, the vet needed a drink.

In 3, *Mary* refers to a nursery rhyme character, a little girl who is followed about by her pet lamb; *had* alludes to ownership, and the animal is alive and well in this context. The sheep does not fare so well in 4. Here, Mary is probably human and female (the new dress allows this inference as well); she may be a child (having spilled food). The references to gravy and mint jelly, however, indicate that the lamb is a meal, not a pet, only a small portion of which Mary ate. Finally, in 5, the references to a veterinarian and a difficult delivery suggest that Mary has given birth to a small lamb and is herself a mature ewe. The vet is probably an adult human being whose profession is to tend to sick animals; the drink, presumably, is an alcoholic beverage intended to enable the vet to relax after the difficult delivery of the lamb.

This cursory analysis reveals that a considerable amount of knowledge—about nursery rhymes, ownership, pets, little girls, sheep, food, animal births, veterinarians, and alcohol—must be brought to bear in order to understand sentences 3, 4, and 5.

Another context, again one that is used by the *Reading Unlimited Program,* is the knowledge of the world that the reader has at his or her disposal to interpret the meaning of the print. Consider the following passage taken from a study on comprehension and memory by Bransford and Johnson (1973). Read over the passage, and see if you can understand what it is about:

> The procedure is actually quite simple. First, you arrange things into different groups. Of course, one pile may be sufficient depending upon how much there is to do. If you have to go somewhere else due to lack of facilities that is the next step, otherwise you are pretty well set. It is important not to overdo things. That is, it is better to do too few things at once than too many. In the short run, this may not seem important, but complications can easily arise. A mistake can be expensive as well. At first the whole procedure will seem complicated. Soon, however, it will become just another facet of life. It is difficult to foresee any end to the necessity for this task in the immediate future, but then one can never tell. After the procedure is completed, one arranges the materials into different groups again. Then they can be put into their appropriate places. Eventually, they will be used once more and the whole cycle will then have to be repeated. However, that is part of life [p. 400].

If you have not already figured out what is being referred to in this passage, let me tell you: washing clothes. Now does it make sense? Bransford and Johnson showed that if a person had the context given prior to reading the passage, recall was much greater. This result suggests that the context words allow the reader to bring into working memory information about what is to be read and to assimilate the newly read information into an existing structure. If the reader can assimilate what is being read, then the process continues smoothly; if not, the reader might lose motivation and "tune out." There is an analogy here: It is virtually impossible to continue to listen to a conversation in a language you do not understand or of which you have little understanding. Speech perception in the sense of hearing and sensing the stream of words is not enough. Comprehension is a part of speech perception and reading.

EVALUATION AND EFFECTIVENESS

Of the chapters in this volume, only one is explicitly concerned with answering a question of evaluation—namely, the chapter by Guthrie, Martuza, and Seifert (Chapter 7). Others—Wallach and Wallach, Popp, and Williams—present some data or consider it as a part of their contribution, but it is safe to say that evaluation is not a central theme. It should be, or at least we should expect it to be more so in the future. I've been told that evaluation gets so little consideration because after you have spent 2 or 3 years developing, implementing, and improving on a reading program, in addition to writing about it and publicizing it, you are too exhausted to do an evaluation. This is understandable. Perhaps the consumers should then take on the responsibility.

The responsibility is not an easy one, as Guthrie and his colleagues found out. They began their quest with a sensible and simple set of questions, questions to which all of us would like to know the answers: Do children need formal reading instruction to learn how to read? If so, how much instruction is beneficial, and what kind or kinds of instruction are most beneficial? Do some children benefit more from one kind of reading instruction than from other kinds? Does instruction benefit low achievers in reading? All are reasonable questions.

The surprising but disappointing result is that we do not have an adequate set of data to provide answers to any of these questions! Guthrie and his colleagues took what was available from an elaborate questionnaire study carried out by the Educational Testing Service (ETS) for apparently other purposes. Guthrie et al. hoped to be able to use these data to answer some, if not all, of the above questions. Using mean scores of groups of children, they carried out a correlational study using analysis of variance and covariance procedures. They could have, and perhaps should have, used existing multiple-regression procedures, because they could have obtained the same information on main affects and interactions, treated their variables as continuous rather than discontinuous or even dichotomous, and obtained regression weights or percentages of variance accounted for by the several factors under examination. The finding most disturbing to me is that the tests used for assessing reading skill by ETS did not show the same significant effects or interactions. Either the tests measure different aspects of reading, or they measure different aspects of something unknown. The low intercorrelations among tests purporting to measure the same abilities are of concern. Of course, we do not know how accurate the teacher/principal questionnaire data are anyway, so part of the unreliability of measures may reside in misclassified scores for the independent variables.

The Guthrie et al. study is a good example of where a small, well-designed, representative, well-planned, and well-executed experiment would have yielded more reliable information at considerably less cost than the massive questionnaire-correlational procedure. The value of the experimental approach would seem to be that more care is taken in consideration and manipulation of the independent variables (e.g., what the teachers actually do) and in selection of the dependent variables (e.g., what the child does). The reliance on self-reports may represent a first approximation to what goes on, but it is at least one step removed from what goes on.

I wish I could say something more positive about evaluation than I have said. I clearly think we need more; I clearly expect there will be more.

In conclusion, although I do not know how representative the volume is of work on theory and practice of early reading, I do know that I learned a great deal from each of the contributors. I suspect that several of these contributors are on the leading edge of the field, that research and programs on decoding are just coming into vogue, and that their effectiveness will be felt during the next decade. I appreciate the opportunity to comment on what has happened and will be happening.

ACKNOWLEDGMENT

The preparation of this paper was supported in part by research grant MH 29365 to T. Trabasso from the National Institutes of Mental Health.

REFERENCES

Bransford, J., & Johnson, M. Considerations of some problems of comprehension. In W. G. Chase (Ed.), *Visual information processing*. New York: Academic Press, 1973.

Chomsky, N., & Halle, M. *The sound patterns of English*. New York: Harper & Row, 1968.

Gibson, E. J., & Levin, H. *The psychology of reading*. Cambridge, Mass.: M.I.T. Press, 1975.

Neisser, U. *Cognitive psychology*. New York: Appleton-Century-Crofts, 1967.

Nelson, K. Structure and strategy in learning to talk. *Monographs of the Society for Research in Child Development*, 1973, *38* (1–2, Serial No. 149).

Nicholas, D. W., & Trabasso, T. Towards a taxonomy of inferences. In F. Wilkening, J. Becker, & T. Trabasso (Eds.), *Information integration by children*. Hillsdale, N.J.: Lawrence Erlbaum Associates, 1980.

Riegel, K., & Freedle, R. Bilingualism. In D. Harrison & T. Trabasso (Eds.), *Black English: A seminar*. Hillsdale, N.J.: Lawrence Erlbaum Associates, 1976.

Sternberg, S. Memory-scanning: Mental processes revealed by reaction-time experiments. *Ameican Scientist*, 1969, *57*, 421–457.

12 Learning to Read in Classroom Interaction

Courtney B. Cazden
Harvard University

In the second of these volumes, Sheldon White (Chapter 13) wrote that a new way to bring research and practice together is for researchers to take a walk,— a walk out of their laboratories and offices and into school classrooms. He wrote about the new problems that such walks produce. But they also bring some new information,—information that I think is underrepresented in these volumes: information on what is actually happening in classrooms where children are or are not learning to read.

The volumes include chapters about the microlevel of eye movements, hemisphere dominance, and information processing. There is at least one chapter at the macrolevel of statistical sureveys. And in between there are chapters on specific curriculum materials. But except for Clay's and Simons' chapters in these volumes, there is very little about what goes on in classrooms where teachers and children come together around the materials and behave in ways that get counted and statistically analyzed in reading research.

In this chapter I attempt to fill this gap and report some observational research by myself and others on learning to read in classroom interaction. Trabasso (this volume) mentions that speech act theories have become fashionable in linguistics, and observational research is again fashionable in psychology. Together, the two have resulted in the relatively recent sociolinguistic or ethnographic research in classroom settings. Not much of this research to date has focused on reading, but it easily could. Reading, after all, is itself a language performance, even an oral performance in the beginning school years. That performance and the interactions in which it is embedded—between teacher and child or among children—can easily be monitored by audio- or videotape. My hope is that from such research we will learn something about effective environments for learning to read and also that it will be a productive point of intersection between sociolinguistic analyses of how language is used interpersonally and cognitive psychological analyses of what people do with language in their heads. We are a long way from understanding that relationship now. (We do not even have many theoretically based hypotheses that could shift observational research from a "bottom-up" to a more "top-down" enterprise.) But we do know that at least for some cognitive tasks, such relationships to the language environment do exist. Perhaps the clearest example is the effect of immersion in an environment where a language is spoken that one once knew but thought had been totally forgotten for 5, 10, or even 20 years. Somehow, one's memory of that language, or access to it, is changed dramatically within hours of getting off the plane.

I know of no indication that ability to read can be affected so sharply by shifts from one environment to another. But we do have studies that point up some of the environmental influences on that more prosaic but important variable of time engaged in reading tasks. Two, by Hess and Takanishi (1974) and Cazden (1973), are more traditional studies in which observers did on-the-spot coding. Two others, by Piestrup (1973) and McDermott (1976, 1977), are socio linguistic and ethnographic analyses of audio- or videotaped segments of verbal and nonverbal behaviors.

TIME ON TASK

Hess and Takanishi observed student "engagement" in eight 30-minute observations in 39 elementary school classrooms in low-income communities to find out what teachers did to "turn on" their students to academic work in mathematics and language arts. Overall, they found that student engagement was strongly and consistently related to teacher behavior but not to classroom architecture or to student characteristics such as sex and ethnicity. Two demonstrations of intrateacher consistency in their data are impressive. First, two teachers were observed during two consecutive years. Although they had completely different classes and reported that they felt large differences between the two years, the mean level of engagement in their classes remained almost identical. Second, during the second year of the study, an entire school being observed moved from a self-contained classroom building to one with open-space architecture. The overall level of engagement across these very different physical environments was identical (82% and 83%), and when the teachers were ranked according to the percent engagement in their classrooms in each environment, the correlation between the two rank orders was .85.

Contrary to expectations, Hess and Takanishi found that these levels of student engagement were not consistently related across teachers to "specific teacher strategies" such as the frequency of specific questions or of feedback. Instead, they were strongly related to more "global instructional strategies" such as instructional group size (more engagement in small groups) and direction of student attention (more engagement when directed toward the teacher than toward other students or materials alone). The authors concluded with a recommendation that teacher-training programs concentrate on skills in classroom social organization rather than on more specific teaching behaviors. This is an important caution for competency-based training as it is usually conceptualized.

Several years ago, at the request of Children's Television Workshop, I (Cazden, 1973) conducted an observational study that also measured children's engagement—or attention as we called it. We wanted to find out what environmental variables affected the viewing behavior of children watching "The Electric Company" in their elementary school classrooms. Viewing behavior was defined as both visual attention and verbalization. We observed 10 primary—grade classrooms during the 30-minute show 5 or 6 times each. Two independent measures of attention were used: a scan of the entire class at 30-second intervals to count those visually oriented toward the TV screens, and continuous monitoring and recording of the visual attention of individual students on an event-recorder. (This instrument makes possible the continuous recording of binary information—e.g., attention to the screen or not—by a pen on graph paper on a revolving drum.) Monitoring individual attention on the event-recorder was extremely reliable (.94 interobserver agreement), and group attention averages from the 30-second scans had high validity (average within-classroom correlation coefficients of .94 between measures of group and individual attention).[1] Coding verbalizations was more difficult (interobserver reliability attained only .84).[2] The 10 classrooms were selected to represent a range in classroom "structure" on a continuum from classrooms where attention to the show was expected and enforced by the teacher ("high" structure) to classrooms where a variety of competing activities was available ("low" structure). As expected, we found that classroom structure was positively related to both group attention ($r = .87$) and individual attention ($r = .95$). High structure affected all children,

---

[1]Interobserver agreement was computed on the basis of the following formula:

$$\frac{\text{no. of seconds in agreement}}{\text{total no. of seconds observed}} \times 100$$

[2]Interobserver agreement was computed on the basis of the following formula:

$$\frac{\text{no. of codings in agreement}}{\text{no. of codings}} \times 100$$

increasing their attentiveness and responsiveness to *"The Electric Company,"* so that poor readers in high-structure classrooms had higher attention scores than better readers in low-structure classrooms.

With the exception of one classroom, structure also correlated highly with average number of reading responses (r = .90 for 9 classes but only .38 for all 10). In the one exception, the most highly structured classroom, the amount of attention paid by the students was highest, but the average number of reading responses was lowest. Since there was nothing in the level of reading ability in the classroom that would explain this anomaly, we think that some aspect of this teacher's classroom control (which we could not understand from our limited observations) discouraged overt reading responses.

Because *"The Electric Company"* is designed especially for children reading below grade level, we were also interested in the relationship between viewing behavior and reading level. Children's reading ability can be categorized according to their relative standing in their class (high, middle, or low reading group) or ranked more absolutely according to standardized test scores. Average attention of children in the lowest quartile of achievement test scores was 79.1%. Although this was not as high as the 86.5% and 90.2% attention of the two middle quartiles, it was higher than the 65.8% attention of the best readers, encouraging evidence that the show was reaching its intended audience. More interesting and surprising was a finding that without exception, children of the same tested reading level showed less attention and more fluctuations in their attention (more distractions) when they were among the lowest readers in their classroom than when they were in relatively higher reading groups. These data are shown in Table 12.1 for the six second-grade classrooms for which fall standardized test scores were available.

TABLE 12.1
Attention and Fluctuation of Children in High and Low Reading Groups

Class Standing	Comprehension Quartiles[a]			
	1–25	26–50	51–76	76–100
	Percent attention			
High	0. (0)	89.5 (10)	90.9 (9)	73.2 (11)
Low	79.1 (20)	79.0 (4)	87.3 (2)	49.4 (5)
	Number of fluctuations			
High	0. (0)	51.2 (10)	30.6 (9)	44.4 (11)
Low	50.6 (20)	58.6 (4)	57.5 (2)	64.6 (5)

Note. The data are from Cazden, 1973.
[a]Numbers in parentheses indicate the number of children in each cell.

Because our sample was not designed for matching numbers of children in each of these cells, firm conclusions cannot be drawn. But in these admittedly limited data, lower relative standing in class (in terms of reading group assignments) adversely affects children's attention to televised reading material. Seen in this way, a variable such as reading level, which is usually considered a child variable in its absolute sense, becomes an environmental variable as well through the child's relative standing in the classroom group. This phenomenon deserves further research.

Piestrup's (1973) research on sources of interference between the language of Black children and their teacher's was referred to in Simons' chapter (this volume). In an analysis of 104 reading instruction episodes audiotaped in 14 first-grade classrooms with predominantly Black children, Piestrup identified two kinds of interference that she labeled structural and functional. Whether the mismatch is only a temporary misunderstanding or a more serious barrier depends on the teacher's understanding of the problem and response to it. In the following episode about a workbook lesson, the teacher explicitly and effectively dealt with a structural (dialect) conflict (Piestrup, 1973):

T   ... how would you harm the colt?
C_1 Tear it.
T   Huh?
C_1 Tear it.
T   Th—th—Oh! Do you, do you know what a colt is, now?
C_1 Oh, kill it, kill it!
T   No, what's a colt?
C_1 Somethin' you wear.
T   There's an "l" in it. "Coat" is c-o-a-ah—don't laugh, that's all right. "Colt" is very hard for city children, because they haven't been out on the farm, and they don't know about it. It's a baby, a baby colt.
C_3 A baby colt.
C_1 Oh yeah!
T   Remember the story? an' it's a c-o-l-t. "Coat" is c-o-a-t, and it's no "l" in it, but listen to—Keisha—colt, colt, colt. Now do you know what a colt is?
C_4 Yeah, I know.
T   What is it?
C_2 A baby horse.
T   Yes, uh-huh, how could you harm a baby horse? [pp. 3–5]

Interference is termed functional rather than structural when the mismatch comes from the functions language is used for rather than from structural features of the language itself. In the following excerpt from oral reading, the children shift away from discussion of remote content to verbal play; the teacher is ignored and fails to get their attention back to the reading task (Piestrups 1973):

T   "Off"
C₁   "Off to the—
T   Ok. It says "wood."
C₁   "— wood."
T   We would say "woods"—this book was written in England.
C₁   Now, I'm through. I ain't gonna read this page again.
T   Ok. Well, we're gonna turn the page and we're just gonna read the next page.
C₁   Uh uh! Darren 'sposed to be first.
T   Well, I'm waiting for Darren to come back. Come on, Darren.
C₂   He just playin' aroun'——— (not clear)
C₁   He crack his knuckles, in the buckles.
C₃   Uh-uh.
T   Ok, Zip and Wendy ran to the woods, and here's the—
C₁   I got a tow truck. My mama bought me one.
T   — father.
C₁   An' I got me a car to hook it on. It got a hook— [pp. 6-7]

Out of the group of 14, the 2 teachers who were able to accommodate their instruction for both structural and functional sources of interference had teaching episodes that were both lively and focused on reading, and their children had the highest reading scores at the end of first grade. Piestrup's conclusion that "the ways teachers communicate in the classroom are crucial to children's success in learning to read [p. 170]" is worthy of more extended sociolinguistic research.

McDermott (1976, 1977) has done an intensive frame-by-frame microanalysis of videotapes of two 30-minute reading groups (top group and bottom group) in one first-grade classroom. During these 30 minutes around the reading table, children in the top group spent three times as much time on task as did children in the bottom group, and McDermott has tried to understand how this happened. First, the procedure for allocating turns to read was different in the two groups. In the top group, the number of pages in the story was allocated equally among the children, and each child read his or her share in order around the table. In the bottom group, there was no fixed order, and each turn was negotiated according to who requested a turn and who the teacher thought could read the page in question. Interruptions were more frequent in the bottom group (40 vs. 2 for top group) and more disruptive because continuation of reading was more dependent on the teacher for assigning the next turn. Some of these interruptions were even initiated by the teacher herself (McDermott, 1977):

On one occasion, for example, she organizes the children to call for a turn to read their new books, "Raise your hands if you can read page 4." The children straighten themselves up in their chairs, form neat lines along the sides of the reading table, and either raise their hands for a turn or at least look at their books or the teacher. As their hands reach their highest point, the teacher looks away from the reading group to the back of the room. She yells at one child in the top group, and then another child in the top group. The three children in the bottom group who raised their hands, lower them to the table. Another little boy who didn't have his hand raised thrusts his chair back away from the reading table and the teacher and balances it on its two back legs. The other two children in the group simply look down at their books. The teacher returns and says, "nobody can read page 4? Why not?" Eventually the children recover, and someone gets a turn. But it all takes time [pp. 25–26].

How does this contrast come about? Possibly the teacher has been told somewhere that calling on the children in a random order helps keep the attention of potentially more disorderly children (as recommended, for example, in the program analyzed by Bartlett in Volume 2 of this series). More importantly, McDermott (1977) suggested:

What is driving this whole system? I don't think it is the negative expectations of the teacher. Rather, the children in the bottom group represent pedagogical and instructional problems for the teacher. Pedagogically, there is no doubt that it is easier for the teacher to practice reading with the children in the top group than to struggle with the process of teaching decoding to the children in the bottom group. And interactionally, there is the pressure of the competition between the groups and the scarred identities of the children in the bottom group. Even within the bottom group we hear claims of one child against another. ("Oh, you can't read". "Better than you.") Or we can point to a child in the bottom group who constantly calls for turns to read while, at the same time, appears to struggle to make sure that she does not get eye contact with the teacher.

In response to all these problems, the teacher and the children in the bottom group make adaptations. In response to all these pressures they struggle to solve the pedagogical and interactional problems of coming to school not knowing how to read, of having a teacher who expects them to know how to read, of having a teacher who doesn't know how to overcome that they do not know how to read while she has twenty other children walking around the room, and of overcoming the pressure of having the other children taunt them for their performances. In response to all this, they make very specific adaptations. One adaptation is to make sure that no one child is isolated to read something too difficult. So the teacher uses the two different turn-taking systems with the different groups, and this adaptation has the consequences already explicated [pp. 27–28].

McDermott concluded:

Success in learning is best predicted by the time a child spends on a task; some may learn faster than others, but with time, almost any child can learn what has to be learned in school, if there are the proper organizational constraints for getting the child on task for the necessary amount of time. The question of why some children achieve more than others has been transformed into a question about the environments in terms of which some children get consistently organized to attend to school tasks in classrooms while others do not...

Certain children, who, for whatever reasons come to school behind their peers in the development of classroom skills, constitute both pedagogical and interactional problems for most teachers. Most teachers say of them that they are harder to teach; part of that reaction is that they need more of the teacher's time if they are to catch up with their peers. In addition, they must learn under the pressure of knowing that they are behind, generally in a classroom which allocates status in part on the basis of the children's intellectual ranking in the classroom...

Thus, the small differences between children in the early years of school expand quickly to the drastic forms of differential performance which become obvious in later years. At the root of these differences is not so much the extreme complexity of the school tasks, nor the differences in the learning potentials of the different children, but the differential environments we offer the children for getting organized and on task so that learning can take place [pp. 11–12].

I think we have to acknowledge that what McDermott has exposed would probably be found elsewhere if we dared to take as close a look.

FOCUS OF ATTENTION

Time on task is a powerful variable, but it is not the only one. A more qualitative variable is where the attention of children and teacher is focused. The simplest contrast here is decoding skills versus meaning. We know we cannot tell what actually happens from the manuals on a teacher's desk or the methods she or he professes to use. For example, in one of the first-grade reading studies supported by the Office of Education Cooperative Research Project, Chall and Feldman (1966) went behind "method A versus method B" comparisons to examine what teachers actually did to implement those methods. Observational studies of teachers showed no significant relationship between the ranking of the teacher's professed method emphasis (whether "sound-symbol" or "meaning") and the method emphasis observed in the classroom (p. 573). Popp (Chapter 10, this volume) makes a similar point in her contrastive analysis of curriculum materials.

McDermott's research suggests that the focus may vary from one group in a classroom to another.

Occasionally, the children create problems by word calling instead of reading for meaning, and the teacher's main pedagogical task is to convince the children that there is living language complete with propositions with illocutionary force on the page. Thus, one child reads, "But Ricky said his mother..." in a dull monotone, and the teacher corrects her, "Let's read it this way, 'But Ricky, said his mother'."

With the bottom group, the teacher has rather different problems. Accordingly, the teacher and the children constitute rather different environments for each other in the different groups. The children in the bottom group do not read as well as the children in the top group, and the teacher attends less to the language on the book's pages and more to the phonics skills needed to interpret any given word in the text. Thus, there are many more stopping places in the children's reading, and the story line which is to hold the lesson together is seldom alluded to and never developed [pp. 22–23].

These alternative foci of attention—story line or phonic skills—may also be distributed throughout different parts of the school day. As part of a larger study of children's functional language competence in kindergarten and the primary grades being conducted at the Center for Applied Linguistics, Griffin (1977) has isolated a set of reading event contexts that differ in the kinds of interaction that take place. She presented a pilot analysis of two events in one first-grade classroom: the traditional reading group and the teacher reading a story to the entire class. In the latter, teacher questions were all "comprehension" questions, in this case primarily of anticipated meaning: "What do you think will happen then?" In the reading group, by contrast, teacher comments and questions were about decoding, about units no larger than a word. Evidently, this pattern was so pervasive that definite expectations about appropriate responses had been learned by the children. When the teacher at one point shifted and asked about meaning in the reading group, the child responding gave an incorrect decoding-type answer. At least in this first-grade classroom, there was a division of teacher attention and therefore of child attention as well, such that decoding and comprehension were taught in entirely separate contexts.

At first thought, such a separation may seem detrimental to learning. Intuitively, it seems harder for children to get decoding and comprehending together in a single mental act if they are taught separately in different parts of the school day. On the other hand, maybe a clear and consistent focus of attention is helpful, especially for beginning learners. A student paper (Dickinson, Kozak, Nelson, & Epstein, 1977) raised this question in a new way.

Dickinson et al. described differences in single versus multiple foci and attendant differences in time spent off task in a math lesson and a reading group lesson with first-grade children in a single, combined kindergarten-first-grade classroom. In the math lesson, the children were individually manipulating attribute blocks into intersecting sets. There was a repeated and therefore predictable sequence of teacher directives about placement of the blocks, questions to the children about what they had done, and finally a concluding statement about what they had found out. In successive sequences, the two parts of each directive (e.g., "Place the blue blocks in this circle" and "Place the yellow blocks in this circle") were spoken with decreasing intervening time, and successive questions to the children elicited progressively more information. In the reading group, in contrast, this interactional simplification did not occur. There were more variation and less predictability in both the focus of attention and the interactional structure. The teacher asked individual children to take turns reading aloud; but talk about the book title, table of contents, page numbers, and capital versus lowercase letters was interspersed in seemingly unpatterned ways.

There were so many other differences between the two groups that no firm conclusions can be drawn—differences in activity, group size, and whether all children were present or only a subset. Although the reading group was smaller, it did not include all the children in the room at the time and so was more subject to interruptions and divided teacher attention. It would take more controlled research to determine how much the interactional simplification of the math group alone contributed to the greater on-task engagement.

The possible instructional value of such interactional simplification is not a new idea. Some of the success of *Distar* (described in Bartlett's chapter in Volume 2 of this series and Bateman's chapter in Volume 1 of this series) may be due to this feature. Recently, such simplification has been advocated anew in a discussion of the design of "Sesame Street" (Gibbon, Palmer, & Fowles, 1975). A familiar example of holding the instructional frame constant while varying the content is the "Sesame Street" categorization game, "One of these things is not like the other." Gibbon et al explained the reason for this design:

Varying the content while keeping the format constant promotes familiarity with format conventions that are potentially useful for instructional purposes. The format of any program segment functions as a kind of "frame" for the instructional content, a complex of auditory and visual conventions that the child can master through repeated exposure. For example, the viewer can learn to expect that a particular format will usually deal with a particular category of stimulus (letter, word number, concept) and with a particular intellectual activity (memorizing, sorting or classifying, guessing, combining). A particular sequence of events or types of events will reliably occur; a particular type of feedback to the viewer's implicit or explicit responses will be delivered. Moreover, a viewer's familiarity with a given format can help him determine at what point in the presentation the important information will come, how much of it there will be, perhaps even whether it is likely to be too easy, too difficult, or about right for him. Among the main instructional advantages afforded by these various forms of cueing is that they will entice the viewing child to attend to what is new in each succeeding application of the format, since it will "stand out" against the familiar background more than if the entire presentation were novel. As a result, learning and concept formation are enhanced [pp. 225–226].

CONCLUSION

Reading groups as traditionally enacted in primary-grade classrooms are inherently complex in content and interactional structure. Learning to read requires many different kinds of learnings about the nested levels of organization of a written text—letter–sound correspondences, unusual word order, punctuation, layout on a page and in chapters, and so on. We need interactional analyses of alternative organizations of reading events in which these learnings can be separated or combined. Such analyses should investigate the effect of different organizations on both the quantity of time children spend on task and the qualitative aspects of foci of attention of teachers and students. Brophy, Anderson, Greenhalgh, Ogden, and Selig (1976) provide a useful set of 22 principles for managing instruction in first-grade reading groups (of which no. 8 is: "The teacher should call on children in order rather than randomly!"). These principles should increase time on task by their use alone. But they take for granted the traditional reading group structure for all aspects of beginning reading instruction. At least as a research venture, we should try out other possibilities—combinations of reading events that differ in focus and in the most appropriate size and interactional structure for each.

REFERENCES

Brophy, J. E., Anderson, L. M., Greenhalgh, C., Ogden, J., & Selig, H. *An instructional model for first grade reading groups* (Rep. No. 76-7). Austin, Tex.: University of Texas at Austin, Research and Development Center for Teacher Education, 1976.

Cazden, C. B. *Watching children watch "The Electric Company": An observational study in ten classrooms* (Final report to Children's Television Workshop). Cambridge, Mass.: Harvard Graduate School of Education, 1973. (ERIC Document Reproduction service No. ED 125 861)

Chall, J., & Feldman, S. A study in depth of first-grade reading: An analysis of the interactions of proposed methods, teacher implementation and child background (Cooperative Research Project No. 2728, U. S. Office of Education). *The Reading Teacher,* 1966, *19,* 269–275.

Dickinson, D., Kozak, N., Nelson, E., & Epstein, M. *Examination of differences in the dynamics of small and large group instruction.* Unpublished term paper, Harvard Graduate School of Education, 1977.

Gibbon, S. Y., Jr., Palmer, E. L., & Fowles, B. R. Sesame Street, the Electric Company and reading. In J. B. Carroll & J. S. Chall (Eds.), *Towards a literate society.* New York: McGraw-Hill, 1975.

Griffin, P. Presentation at a symposium on *Studies of the social organization of the classroom.* Presented at the meeting of the American Educational Association, San Francisco, April 1977.

Hess, R. D., & Takanishi, R. *The relationship of teacher behavior and school characteristics in student engagement* (Tech. Rep. No. 42). Stanford, Calif.: Stanford Center for Research and Development in Teaching, 1974.

McDermott, R. P.   *Kids make sense: An ethnographic account of the interactional management of success and failure in one first-grade classroom.* Unpublished doctoral dissertation, Stanford University, 1976.

McDermott, R. P. *Pirandello in the classroom: On the possibility of equal educational opportunity in American culture.* Paper presented at a conference on Issues Relating to the Future of Special Education, University of Minnesota, April 1977.

Piestrup, A. M.   Black dialect interference and accommodation of reading instruction in first grade. *Monographs of the Language Behavior Research Laboratory,* University of California, Berkeley, 1973, (No. 4).

13

Observations on Research and Practice in Beginning Reading

Robert Glaser
University of Pittsburgh

My comments on this impressive assembly of work in the field of reading have two objectives: to present my reactions to the main thrusts of the work, and to speculate on what some of the findings and issues imply for future research and practice in reading. My remarks can be considered best as transition notes between the chapters in these volumes and more integrative summary reviews.

USING WHAT WE KNOW

The three volumes focus predominantly on the basic skills of reading. The experimental work reported includes investigations of letter discrimination, orthographic regularities, phoneme identification, acoustical analysis, mapping sound to print, and orthography and phonics training. At more complex levels, the work reported considers the transition from elementary units to context influences, lexical access, and the relationships between decoding and comprehension. The more practical chapters on the construction and use of reading programs and the chapters that analyze completed and published programs are also concerned with the development of the early basic skills.

I consider this concentration of effort on beginning reading as a charge to the future. We appear to know quite a bit about these early basic skills, even though we have debates about their detailed characteristics and about different theories that explain how children perform them. My current belief is that it is time to shift our emphasis from descriptive research concerned with explaining how things work to normative research concerned with making things work. While new investigations in cognitive psychology, artificial intelligence, and so forth, come along behind the scene and further add to our theoretical and practical understanding, we do know something, and we ought to use it now.

It is important to concentrate now on optimization-oriented, prescriptive research. This work, as Trabasso (this volume) points out, needs to be generated by a problem base that is convenient not only for theory, but also for other applications. In this prescriptive enterprise, we should try to get away from the attitude of my former garage mechanic. When I went to this garage mechanic and asked, "What is wrong with my car and what does it need," he would say, "Well, you know how a carburetor works," and then he would start to tell me all the things he knew about how a carburetor works. All the while, what I wanted to know was his prescription for fixing my car.

I am certainly not talking about abandoning basic research, but I am suggesting a shift in tactics given what we know about beginning skills. Since we do not have the large engineering resources in psychology and education that other fields have, we have to attend to this aspect ourselves, at least for the time being. In other words, we must turn to the problems of design, prescription, and optimization of learning and instructional procedures. I would like, for example, to see LaBerge (this volume) do further work facilitating the transition between units of processing. He should try not only to understand the phenomenon, but also attempt to produce it. The attempt to produce it will in turn contribute to its further understanding.

The instructional, prescriptive experimentation we begin in the laboratory needs to continue into the school system, in partnership with educators. This latter work requires serious attention to the management and design of school and classroom structures so that what we do know about acoustical processing and teaching decoding will be implemented appropriately. It is up to research psychologists to see to it that our ideas are understood, and that criteria we believe to be adequate are used to assess student performance.

For many laboratory scientists, this change in emphasis requires a change in motivation and prestige values. We cannot remain content to say, with Gregg and Farnham-Diggory (this volume), that we are going to continue to do simulation modeling because it has paid off in the past for our theoretical work; nor should we feel comfortable, as many of the authors in these volumes do, with a statement like "My real objective in doing this work is to develop new hypotheses for experimentation." Especially where the processes of beginning reading are concerned, attention to practice can be useful in its own right and also as a means of correcting theory.

In the area of higher level aspects of reading comprehension, however, there is still a need for descriptive research, as the smaller number of findings reported in these volumes demonstrates. There are chapters on discourse processing, making inferences, and reasoning from text.In these areas, there is active theoretical debate, as witnessed in the chapters by Gregg and Farnham-Diggory (this volume), Frederiksen (Volume 1), Smith (Volume 2), and Perfetti and Lesgold (Volume 1). Of particular importance for study are the interactive relationships between low level processes such as phonemic decoding and word recognition and higher level comprehension processes. Future work on the cognitive processes of text comprehension should proceed strongly in the descriptive research tradition. Current theories and experimental findings in developmental psychology and information processing offer promissory notes for interesting investigations that may have very significant implictions. The knowledge we gain from this new research will eventually change the kind of prescriptive research that we will be able to do.

PHYSIOLOGICAL RESEARCH AND CLINICAL INVESTIGATIONS

There are two chapters in these volumes on physiological functioning and biological structures. Fisher's chapter (Volume 1) on visual periphery dysfunction indicates that this kind of dysfunction precludes eye movements of long durations and affects reading. Johnson (Volume 2) reviews brain damage and clinical research. These studies recommend two kinds of research—laboratory research and analytical clinical work. I find this work important in the context of research on reading because it offers, among its other contributions, a corrective element to highly speculative cognitive theorizing by providing parameters based on structural limitations and functioning.

CURRICULUM ANALYSIS

The editors of these volumes thoughtfully included the very interesting venture of curriculum program analysis, and there are three good examples. Popp (this volume) contrasts two programs—one with an "initial meaning" emphasis and one with an "initial decoding" emphasis. Beck and Block (Volume 1) analyze two programs, contrasting different procedures of phonics instruction. Bartlett (Volume 2) also considers two curricula, offers the very interesting observation that "meaning curricula" tend to be for rich children and "decoding curricula" for disadvantaged children, and speculates on the implications of these observations.

Curriculum analyses are useful for a number of reasons. First, they give the teacher more detailed information about the nature of, and reasoning behind, an instructional program than is usually given in the short descriptions that are written in teachers' curriculum manuals. With such information, teachers can select programs—if indeed they have a choice—on a more rational basis than is usually possible. Second, these curriculum analyses give researchers ideas for conducting studies on how reading is learned. Knowing how these programs were designed and what their characteristics are raises questions regarding the differential effectiveness of instructional methods. Curriculum analyses begin to dissect global program ideas; and if these ideas can be filtered down into manageable research studies, then questions about why they work can be answered.

Curriculum analyses are also useful because they can lead to more flexible use of programs. Detailed understanding of the component parts of a program could allow teachers to break out of the rigidity of total-program approaches that lock them into a single reading series for all instruction. It is to be hoped that the analytical description of different reading programs starts a trend toward the design of programs that have more interchangeable parts. If programs were described in such a way that their various instructional components were well understood, if they were built in such a way that they were less monolithic, then they could be more adaptively used to accommodate different children (see Glaser, 1977).

Another comment related to curriculum analysis refers to Williams' chapter (this volume). Trabasso (this volume) commends her for trying to look at the rules of psychological knowledge and then attempting to build them into her program. But Williams makes the comment, "Well, as I did these things, I had to ignore psychological rules, cast them aside, or modify them." These remarks prompt me to comment on how I believe psychological knowledge is to be used in program design. Psychological principles are to be understood on a heuristic level and then applied in an artistic way. Programs that are designed and built solely from algorithmic interpretations of principles are generally quite dull. A program designer needs to take principles and bend and twist them; that is the required artistry for design. And one can take pride in this artistry without feeling obliged to apologize for "not using psychology very well."

TESTING PRACTICES

Calfee and Drum (Volume 2) emphasize the importance of carefully training teachers in the use and interpretation of testing instruments and of developing kinds of testing instruments that are more useful for teaching reading and reading comprehension. A number of issues are important in considering future directions in this work. One is that testing and teaching are part of the same enterprise. We tend to think of tests as "outside" evaluation devices rather than as sources of information required for teaching. Students should conceive of test information as being valuable for themselves as well as for their teachers. Testing and teaching are part of the same system, should be attitudinally conceived so, and should be so considered in program development.

For effective instruction, characterization and diagnosis of the capabilities of the learner must be made in terms that are relevant to educational decision making. Tests given only at the beginning of a period of schooling are not enough; a more continuous assessment process is required. It is necessary to describe changes in the learner's capabilities as instruction progresses and to consider this updated description of abilities in making decisions regarding the sequence of instructional activities.

What this implies is that there is a need for tests of the details of discourse-processing skills. This is a research task. Throughout these volumes, it is said that teachers want to know "where the child is coming from." As you teach a child who has difficulty learning, a major frustration is in not knowing how to get this child to advance. There is a need for information. What should I know about this child to be able to teach appropriately? There is a need for tests that give us much more information about language capabilities, letter discrimination, acoustical abilities, and in general, an analysis of generalized readiness skills.

In undertaking test design work for instruction, we should consider analyzing readiness and the aptitude-like processes basic to reading skills using notions from cognitive psychology. Research is now being carried out that attempts to analyze school tasks, such as reading, in terms of the demands that the tasks place on the child's memory, perceptual abilities, and capabilities for new learning. If the cognitive processes that underlie these task demands can be identified, information might be provided that could be used as a basis for instruction.

TEACHING PRACTICES

In a number of chapters (Clay, Volume 2; Natalicio, this volume; F. Smith, Volume 2), the authors say essentially that teachers should be flexible and proceed from what children know. The implication of this statement is that schools should be capable of adapting readily to the progress of children. Some work is required for enhancing the capability of the school and the teacher to do this.

One thing that I hope can be derived from these volumes is a set of heuristics for teachers about teaching reading. Teachers need some kind of a theory, not only rules. What I mean by this has been discussed by Broudy (1972). He observes that like many other large systems, school systems and the teachers in them tend to live by rules that are supposed to take care of standard cases, with only slight adjustments allowed for departures from standard cases. There are, for example, rules that organize the educational continuum into grades; and for each grade, there are prescriptions concerning the kinds of information and skills to be covered in the course of the school year. There are also rules about the logistics of living in the school environment that pertain to attendance, time periods, and movement through the building. Of course, no complex system can do without certain accepted rules of conduct. What is important to observe, however, is not just the presence of rules but a preoccupation with the rules and standard procedures. In order to correct this imbalance, principles that provide general guides to action and that free teachers from the narrow specificity of standard operating procedures should be articulated. Workbooks, manuals, and other materials for teachers frequently have "cookbooky" formats that indicate a belief by the authors and an expectation by teachers that teachers need specific, standard operating procedures that cover most anticipated events in the classroom. Excessively rule-ridden operations and practices attest to a lack of professionalism. Broudy points out that frequently the teacher's autonomy is restricted to trivialities; a teacher is expected to make only minor adaptations in a program of study, in instructional procedures, or in teaching style.

I am sure this is not uniformly true, but the attitude is reported frequently, and I would like to see whether we can derive from these volumes a set of heuristics related to teaching the basic skills of reading and communicate this to teachers. Information would be required about reading theories—for example, our understanding of how decoding works and what influences it, the consequences of an overemphasis on decoding, the influence of a child's stage of development, and so on. This would provide teachers with a problem-solving framework in which to place good judgments of how to use their curricula and make effective instructional decisions. Such a theory for teachers would be a fascinating thing to develop. To a significant extent, these volumes contain the practical and experimental knowledge necessary for beginning to build such a theory.

FIELD AND CLASSROOM RESEARCH

Field research studies—for example, the work by Guthrie, Martuza, and Seifert (this volume)—show trends that must be accounted for. The implications of their work have already been presented by other discussants, especially the need to analyze and use data that are collected in the classroom. However, there are two further points that can be made. One is the need for analytical models—models by which one can assess what actually occurs in the classroom. Such models would include the assessment of initial student performance, achievement at the end of instruction, and—between these two—various components of the processes' that characterize classroom practices. The variance attributable to the influence of these different factors could then be assessed. Combined with Cazden's (this volume) concern for the dynamics of the classroom process, these analytical models of the influences on achievement will be useful for improving teaching. Such models are beginning to be developed by Cooley and others (Cooley & Leinhardt, 1975; Cooley & Lohnes, 1976; Wiley & Harnischfeger, 1974). Some years ago, Carroll (1963) introduced a model from which many present notions arise.

In relation to the foregoing, there is another point that is important to mention. There is need for a framework in which to systematize the data collected from survey and field research. A way is needed to store the information, and it seems to me that some kind of organizing scheme should be articulated by the people who reflect on these volumes—a scheme that helps to focus the collection of field data and that uses language that connects with theories of learning and performance. If a connecting language (words that mean the same thing to field researchers and laboratory researchers) could serve as a framework for collecting field information, then data describing what is happening in a classroom could begin to be related to concepts in a theory of learning.

LEARNING AND ACQUISITION

I am concerned, as is Trabasso (this volume), about the omission or neglect of chapters on learning and acquisition. With the exception of the chapter by Holland (Volume 1) on what responses are being controlled from an operant point of view and the chapter by Wallach and Wallach (this volume), who discuss some notions about the transfer of learning, there are no chapters on the variables that influence learning and acquisition; no theory of acquisition is expressed. This probably reflects the present emphasis of cognitive theories on describing performance and development.

My guess is that as we do a better job teaching the early basic skills of reading and look for the kind of learning principles to use, we will use what we already seem to know. At the present time, this consists of what we have learned about reinforcement and verbal learning in the stimulus–response (S–R) tradition. However, we cannot describe complex competence very well with the tools of older S–R theories of learning. The more modern information-processing notions give us a richer structure for describing human performance. Perhaps eventually, the work on cognitive processes, and particularly on cognition in reading comprehension, will suggest not only what to teach but also how to teach it and how to design environments that better allow learning and growth to occur. Our research over the next few years should focus on the acquisition of complex behavior and on theories that describe how competent performance and skilled behavior are acquired (Glaser, 1976). But at the moment, we should not hesitate to rely on what we already know about learning.

We must consider not only what reading specialists and teachers do to help children learn, but also what children do to teach themselves. Under what conditions of instruction do children learn how to learn? Of significant interest in this regard are the studies of metacognition (Brown, 1978) and self-reinforcement (Bandura, 1971). The development of learning skills, competence in self-management, and the ability to modify one's own environment for effective learning are very significant aspects to be considered in any attempt to understand and improve learning in schools.

STAGES OF PROFICIENCY

A "levels of proficiency" theory, something like a stage theory, is needed to guide our work, and instructional theories must be formulated in terms of levels of increasing competence. These stages of skill in reading performance should be described in terms somewhere between the detailed units of cognitive-processing experiments and the grosser measurements of field-assessment studies.

Chall presents some notions about these levels in the first volume of this series. The first level is primarily concerned with decoding skills. In a later stage, an individual reads things he or she knows in order to develop fluency in reading and to confirm existing knowledge. A third stage is reading for new knowledge, where one learns to connect old knowledge to new. At advanced stages, reading is critical and reflective and specialized. People learn to have one kind of text structure in mind when they read a novel and another kind of text structure in mind when they read a scientific article. The reader also is able to use printed materials selectively and to decide what to read to obtain knowledge of interest.

A crude stage model would be very useful. Perhaps we can learn from the kind of stage theory that is used in the field of child development. My hunch is that the microgenetic changes that occur in skill learning are similar to macrogenetic developmental changes. Whether or not this is the case, work should proceed to identify the nature of competent performance at progressive levels of proficiency.

As I said at the beginning of my remarks, most immediately we can and should move strongly on teaching decoding skills. In the future, however, there is going to be a change in what we know about complex processes, and this knowledge will change the ways in which we teach. Twenty-five years from now, when we know more about human cognition, the emphasis will be on producing skilled thinkers at the same time as we are producing skilled readers. That is the real challenge of the future, and it is part of our more immediate challenge of getting most people to be skilled readers.

READING AS A GENERAL PROBLEM OF ACQUIRING SKILL

In concluding these observations, I would like to console those who are discouraged by the amount of work left to do by showing that our problems are not ours alone. For this purpose, I would like to discuss a little book I received in the mail recently. It is called *Acquiring Ball Skill* (Whiting, 1969), and in it, the author discusses what psychologists know about acquiring skill in ball games. I indicate what the state of knowledge is in that field because it has direct relevance to one of the major themes of these volumes—the "bottom-up" versus "top-down" approaches to the teaching of reading: in other words, a decoding versus a meaning emphasis in reading instruction.

The author asks: "how do people start off to acquire ball skill(s)?" He describes three methods used in the field. The first is

> comparatively free experimentation with a variety of striking implements (bats, racquets, clubs, etc.), balls and players in an attempt to exploit their potentialities in a wide variety of situations. Under such circumstances, the person performing would generally set the criterion of success, although particular objectives might be defined by the teacher/coach who might also give knowledge of results. This type of approach might well be used in the initial stages of ball skill experience.... In such a procedure, specificity of skilled action is usually less important than diversity of experience [p.73].
>
> [Technique two is] a development which precedes from the specific to the general. Ball games are broken down into a series of skills, subskills and tactical situations. These are then practiced in isolation or in small groups and the game is gradually built up from the isolated skill level to the composite game. As progress is made, more complex skill sequences involving groups of players may be taken out of the game situation and practiced as a unit with the idea that when later fitted back into the game there will be a carry over from the practice situation [p.73]. [That was the bottom-up technique.]
>
> [The third technique is top-down—] an almost reverse procedure which progresses from the general to the specific. In this situation, the players are introduced to the game more or less immediately and specific skills are acquired during the game itself. Any coaching which takes place is always in the game situation and it is considered unnecessary to abstract patterns of play for practice in isolation [pp. 73–74].

The author dismisses the first method because it is of limited applicability and states that the superiority of either the second or the third is yet to be established: "Both have their committed adherents, and both have resulted in the production of highly skilled games players. There have been few comparative studies between the two approaches and it is difficult to see how such investigations could be established with adequate controls [p.74]." However, he says that

> if anything, there has been a discernible move towards methods which span those outlined in...[techniques] 2 and 3 such that skills considered to be too complex to be acquired during a game are practiced in isolation while the more simple skills are acquired during play. It still must be recalled that when skills are learned outside the game situation itself, there is still necessity for experiencing the perceptual cues which are necessary for bringing the...action in to play at the *right* time [p. 74].

Ergo, perhaps the debate about top-down versus bottom-up is a straw man. Certainly both kinds of learning are involved—specific to general and general to specific—in the development of skilled performance. An effective balance between the two is a function of individual differences in the learner, differences in teacher skills, and available instructional procedures. We seek the combination of these elements that results in highly skilled players of the game.

REFERENCES

Bandura, A. Vicarious and self-reinforcement processes. In R. Glaser (Ed.), *The nature of reinforcement*. New York: Academic Press, 1971.

Broudy, H. S. *The real world of the public schools*. New York: Harcourt Brace Jovanovich, 1972.

Brown, A. L. Knowing when, where, and how to remember: A problem of metacognition. In R. Glaser (Ed.), *Advances in instructional psychology* (Vol. 1.). Hillsdale, N.J.: Lawrence Erlbaum Associates, 1978.

Carroll, J. B. A model of school learning *Teachers College Record*, 1963, *64*, 723-733.

Cooley, W. W., & Leinhardt, G. *The application of a model for investigating classroom processes*. Pittsburgh: University of Pittsburgh, Learning Research and Development Center, 1975. (Publication No. 1975/24)

Cooley, W. W., & Lohnes, P. R. *Evaluation research in education*. New York: Irvington Publishers, 1976.

Glaser, R. Components of a psychology of instruction: Toward a science of design. *Review of Educational Research*, 1976, *46*, 1-24.

Glaser, R. *Adaptive education: Individual diversity and learning*. New York: Holt, Rinehart & Winston, 1977.

Whiting, H. T. A. *Acquiring ball skill: A psychological interpretation*. Philadelphia: Lea & Febiger, 1969.

Wiley, D. E., & Harnischfeger, A. Explosion of a myth: Quantity of schooling and exposure to instruction, major educational vehicles. *Educational Researcher*, 1974, *3* 7-12.

14

Has the Reel Reeding Prablum Bin Lade Bear? Summary Comments on the Theory and Practice of Early Reading[1]

John B. Carroll
Marsha Walton
University of North Carolina at Chapel Hill

Of all the young people going through the nation's school system at any one time, a certain percentage—about 15% overall—have distinct trouble in learning to read or, for one reason or another, fail to learn to read beyond a very simple level. Percentages are higher in some groups of the population, such as poor blacks and bilingual speakers. Although these percentages are relatively small, the actual numbers of students who do not progress normally in learning to read are staggering—ranging into the hundreds of thousands or perhaps into the millions. These facts are the basis for what is often called "the reading problem"—a problem that is rightfully seen as very large and serious.

The volumes on the *Theory and Practice of Early Reading* were organized with the hope of their editors that some solutions to this reading problem might come forth, based on sound theories about processes in reading and learning to read. There was a reasonable expectation that if some of the country's leading theorists and researchers in the field of reading could be brought together, they might be able to arrive at some consensus on the needed theories and agree on some guidelines for actions that would significantly reduce the numbers of children failing to learn to read in their

---

[1]In preparing these comments, the authors have responded mainly to the written materials that came out of the series of conferences on the relationships between theory and practice in beginning reading instruction—that is, the formal papers published in these volumes and the transcriptions of the open discussions that took place. They have also consulted and referred to current literature on the teaching of reading and examined a number of widely used published reading programs. The first author (Carroll) attended two of the conferences—the first and the third—and was thus able to profit from witnessing and hearing the presentations and discussions at those conferences.

early schooling. The inclusion of applied researchers and reading curriculum developers among the contributors was believed to be desirable because it would allow theorists and researchers to avail themselves of the insights that these individuals might have into the practical circumstances of reading instruction and encourage the theorists and researchers to be more realistic in their assumptions and recommendations than might otherwise be the case. There was to be an emphasis on the problems of *early* reading instruction— that is, instruction up to the third or fourth grade of school—because the editors thought that the problems are most serious in these early stages and that theories of the reading process could make their greatest contribution at this level by helping to ensure that young learners get the right start.

In the organization of this effort, there was provision for periodic summaries and commentaries on the chapters in each volume. There was also provision in the total plan for final summaries and critiques to be written about the chapters in all three volumes. In preparing one of these final summarizing chapters, we recognize that we have a serious responsibility to put forward an interpretation that will adequately reflect the achievements of the volumes and be meaningful, useful, and helpful to teachers, parents, researchers, and others concerned with the teaching of beginning reading.

The senior author has practically lost count of the number of major enterprises concerning reading—conferences, committees, publications, and the like—that he has contributed to or assisted in, enterprises all with much the same aim—to solve "the reading problem." His memory goes back to a conference that the late James B. Conant organized, in 1961, in an effort to resolve the then raging controversy over "phonic" versus "look–say" methods of reading instruction—a controversy that had been precipitated by the publication of Flesch's (1955) *Why Johnny Can't Read.* Conant hoped to allay some of the concerns of the public about the prevalence of "look–say" methods and the alleged lack of emphasis on "phonics." The conference resulted in the publication and wide circulation, in 1962, of a brief report (Conant, n.d.) that attempted to effect a judicious compromise between opposing points of view and to reassure its readers that then-current teaching methods did indeed include adequate attention to phonics.

Whether this little pamphlet, the most interesting part of which was a vigorous minority report, had any impact on the teaching of reading or on solving the reading problem, there is no way of telling; but, for sure, the reading problem did not go away. In 1968, the then Secretary of the Department of Health, Education, and Welfare, Wilbur J. Cohen, set up a National Advisory Committee on Dyslexia and Related Reading Disorders, again to find a solution to the national "reading problem"; after a year-long series of meetings that took place in various parts of the country, this distinguished advisory group issued a small report (National Advisory Committee on Dyslexia and Related Disorders, 1970) that recommended against the use of the term *dyslexia* and made a number of suggestions about what should be done to improve the teaching of reading, including the training of teachers.

Next was the National Academy of Education Committee on Literacy, called together in 1970 to respond to Commissioner of Education James E. Allen, Jr.'s request for guidance on how his proposed Right-to-Read campaign should be conducted. The middle-of-the-road report (Carroll & Chall, 1975) that eventually resulted from the conference conducted by the committee has been termed "boring" by one reviewer (Olson, 1975) and "disappointing" by another (Petty, 1977).

Then there was the supreme effort by George Miller and his colleagues to help the National Institute of Education to formulate a program of effective research on reading; a 3-week conference brought numerous reading experts and researchers together at a pleasant location on Cape Cod, Massachusetts, and resulted in still another report (Miller, 1973).

The history would not be complete without mention of several other conferences and the resultant published volumes (e.g., see Kavanagh & Mattingly, 1972; Reber & Scarborough, 1977) that had as their principal goal the exchange of ideas among researchers in reading, linguistics, psycholinguistics, and other relevant specialties in order to make a contribution to the solution of the reading problem.

Thus the volumes of the series *Theory and Practice of Early Reading* may be considered as part of long series of such efforts that have addressed the same general goal—the solution of the "reading problem." Is there any reason to hope that the present report can have any major impact on the teaching of reading in the nation?

We can only say that we are perennial optimists. We believe that the dissemination of information, ideas, and judgments from scientific enterprises such as these can have effects on practice that are real and beneficial even if they are not easily discernible. Publications such as these are read widely by teachers and teacher trainees. The present volumes can have an impact—insofar as the issues are phrased succinctly, intelligibly, and convincingly. We do our utmost to make clear what we think the significant issues are and to integrate these issues with ideas from current research and writing in the field of reading.

The national "reading problem" has changed little since Conant's conference in 1961. If anything, it has grown in magnitude and seriousness. Its full scope has been better perceived, as encompassing not only the problems of white middle-class children in suburbia who appear to be "dyslexic" but also the problems of children who are poor, inner-city and rural Blacks, Chicanos, Puerto Ricans, American Indians, or members of other minority groups. Further, the extent of illiteracy among adults is more widely recognized. The argumentation about "the nature of the reading process" has not changed much, however. Still with us are questions about whether reading should be taught with a "meaning emphasis" or a "decoding emphasis" and to what extent reading involves language competence and cognitive skills. These questions are raised anew and discussed extensively in these volumes.

Looking back over the last decade or so, however, we sense that some things have definitely changed. Problems are now perceived with greater sophistication, and there is much more research knowledge available to support discussion. The linguistic and psycholinguistic considerations that underlie learning to read are better understood, and we know much more about processes of grapheme discrimination, word perception, and language comprehension. There has been real progress. Numbers of competent psychological and educational researchers have turned their attention to the study of reading behavior, and these people have been, in general, amply supported in their efforts by funds from government and foundation sources. The effects of all these trends are much in evidence in the chapters in these volumes.

Also, in the last decade or so, the problems of teaching reading in the schools have been approached with greater realism by researchers. While much of their work has been conducted in the laboratory—raising the perennial question of the ecological validity of such research as applied to instruction—reading researchers have also spent much time working in the schools to observe teaching practices and to assess the effects of these practices. A significant feature of the volumes is the group of chapters on actual instructional programs and those on the effects of such variables as instructional time.

Three principal themes are addressed in the volumes:

1. What is reading, particularly as it occurs in the beginning phases of instruction, and what are the separate skills and processes involved?
2. How is early reading instruction currently being conducted, and how well do programs of instruction reflect theory and knowledge about the reading process and about learning to read?
3. Why do some children have trouble learning to read, and how can these children be helped?

A major amount of space is devoted to the first of these themes—the analysis of the information processing activity that we call *reading*. Results of recent research into exactly what processes occur as the child or adult reads, or learns to read, are presented and discussed at length, and several different theories of reading behavior are offered. Given the purpose of the volumes, this emphasis on theory and analytical research can easily be defended, for we must know what reading is, and what it involves and requires in the way of psychological processes, before we can be confident in giving advice on how reading should be taught or make an adequate diagnosis of why children fail in learning to read.

The second of these themes is addressed by the inclusion of descriptions and critiques of a number of current reading programs, in the chapters by Bartlett (Vol. 2), Beck and Block (Vol. 1), Fletcher (Vol. 2), Holland (Vol. 1), Popp (Vol. 3), Wallach and Wallach (Vol. 3), and Williams (Vol. 3). Nevertheless, a thorough integration among these chapters and those having to do with the nature of reading is missing. Perhaps such an integration could not have been expected, given the fact that the writers of the program description chapters had little opportunity to benefit in advance from reading the more technically oriented chapters.

Issues about why some children have trouble learning to read and how they can be helped are considered in only a few of the chapters—for example, those of Fisher (Vol. 1), Johnson (Vol. 2), and Rosner (Vol. 2). One finishes reading the individual chapters with the feeling that these issues are far from resolved, despite the fact that a number of promising suggestions are offered.

Only occasionally touched on, in the formal chapters and in the discussion chapters, are many other themes that might have been addressed more fully: the organization and administration of reading instruction, the training of teachers of reading, the kinds of interactions and understandings between teachers and pupils that make for effective learning, and the social implications of different policies and strategies of reading instruction.

This three-volume series offers much enlightenment concerning central issues in the planning of reading instruction—issues that should be addressed prior to considerations of logistics, teacher training, classroom procedure, and social policy. In the sections of our comments that follow, we attempt to single out the areas of agreement that emerge from the chapters and to offer certain compromise solutions for problems on which the contributors differ in their opinions. In the discussion of current reading programs, we endeavor to apply the results of theoretical discussion and research to their assessment in a way and to an extent that is not otherwise done in the volumes.

THE NATURE OF READING

It was a token of the increased sophistication of the contributors here over that of contributors in some earlier works that there is general agreement that the characteristic purpose of reading is getting meaning from print or writing. There are none of the dreary and interminable arguments that one used to hear to the effect that reading is *just* being able to convert print to speech, or that reading is *just* getting meaning. It is recognized that reading is not just one process but many processes, depending on the nature of the material being read, the reader's purposes, and the reader's maturity. As Perfetti and Lesgold (Vol. 1) remark, reading is "highly flexible."

Authors who regard themselves as "cognitive psychologists"—in effect, nearly all the psychologists included in the series—see reading as constituting a variety of very complex behaviors that are amenable to study from an information-processing point of view. This is the point of view that the apprehension of speech codes and/or meanings from print involves a series of detailed steps or processes, such as: the identification of features in the visual perception of print; the use of these features in recognizing letters, syllables, and words; the further recognition of these units by referring them to a long-term memory store; the use of language knowledge to interpret units in their particular contexts; and the use of "real-world" and other kinds of knowledge to arrive at appropriate semantic interpretations. Cognitive psychologists believe that they now have theories and technologies that are sufficiently well developed to permit studying the detailed operation of such information-conversion processes. Many chapters offer illustrations of research, nearly always conducted in the psychological laboratory, that was designed to reveal the operation of such processes.

There are, to be sure, many arguments about the details of reading behavior. Subsequently in these comments, we discuss some of the issues, particularly those issues that might have some bearing on how one goes about teaching reading in the early phases. The theoretical argumentation concerning these issues must necessarily be on a relatively high plane of abstraction. It concerns the "reader in general," or, if you will, the "typical" child who learns to read in the "normal" way, or the "typical" skilled adult reader. Exactly how this line of thinking applies to the "retarded" or "disabled" learner, or, for example, to the bilingual child, is not yet clear. The researcher's strategy, it appears, is to try to understand the normal and typical course of reading development and behavior before turning attention to the pathologies or special variations of that development. On the other hand, it may be pointed out that a number of the chapters are written by researchers who have concerned themselves specifically with pathologies and special cases (e.g., Bateman, Fisher, Vol. 1: Johnson, Rosner, Vol. 2; Wallach & Wallach, Williams, Vol. 3).

It should also be recognized that the researchers' apparent lack of closure and agreement on a general theory of reading, thus far, should not lead to despair over the outcomes of reading research. There has been definite progress, over the last decade or so, in our understanding of the reading process, and a start can be made in using this understanding to make effective recommendations about the teaching of reading. There are frequent remarks to the effect that "there does not yet exist any adequate theory of reading" and that the lack of such a theory puts certain limits on the researcher's ability to recommend effective teaching techniques (e.g., Venezky, Vol. 2; Trabasso,

Vol. 3). Nevertheless, several authors (e.g., Gregg & Farnham-Diggory, Vol. 3) make commendable attempts to propose outlines of a theory of reading. Posner (Vol. 1) feels that an adequate theory would inform teachers by giving them a language to talk about reading behavior and its teaching on a more rigorous and scientific basis than previously. It would be our judgment, however, that no general theory such as those proposed or discussed in these volumes is going to say much to teachers unless it is framed in such a way as to speak directly to particular issues and procedures in teaching. Teachers are not disposed to think of reading in terms of flow diagrams and cognitive decision nodes, and there is little likelihood that many of them can or should be brought to the point of doing so. Teachers can, however, benefit from theories of reading if those theories refer to specific and concrete phenomena that can be observed in the classroom.

The theoretical controversies that arise in the study of reading should not be taken, furthermore, as an indication that we know nothing about how to teach reading, or that we know nothing about how children learn to read. In fact, at one point in the discussions during the conferences on which these volumes are based, a participant (Bateman, Vol. 1) wanted it put in the record that, "while we sit here accurately recognizing that our theories are incomplete and that our data are incomplete, we, nonetheless, know enough to teach kids to read, and we are not doing it." Continuing, she insisted that, "it is very important that, in addition to sitting here, we also recommend that somebody get out there and teach kids to read, because we all need it—*kids* need it, and *we* need it." To which Kenneth Goodman (see Goodman & Goodman, Vol. 1) rejoined, "For the record also: Cancer is a disease, too, but you are not going to let every quack out there try to cure people, just because people are dying every day." This exchange, it seems to us, epitomizes the present status of the theory and practice of reading: We know a great deal about how to teach kids to read, and in fact most kids do learn to read—to varying degrees of mastery, of course, and at different times in the course of their schooling—but there is promise that theory and research will help us teach more effectively and enable kids to learn more easily and rapidly and to higher levels of mastery.

We now discuss some of the particular theoretical issues bearing on the teaching of reading that are prominently treated in the chapters of these volumes.

"Inside-out" Versus "Outside-in" Theories of Reading

Throughout the volumes, there is an undercurrent of basic disagreement among the researchers and theorists as to the nature of the reading process—a disagreement that occasionally surfaces in almost acrimonious debate. The issue—actually consisting of a number of interrelated issues—is put forward by F. Smith (Vol. 2) in the form of a contrast between what he calls "outside-in" and "inside-out" theories of reading.

Proponents of "outside-in" theories, according to Smith, see reading as a process that is stimulated by print on a page, that translates the written symbols to speech symbols or codes, and that then translates the speech codes into a meaningful representation or interpretation "in the head." Outside-in theorists, Smith complained, have dominated research and theory in the field of reading; one can agree with Smith, in fact, that they dominate the discussions in these volumes. Smith asserts that "outside-in" theories are wrong. First, he claims, they lead to research that lacks ecological validity and relevance. For example, research on the perception of isolated words presented tachistoscopically has little if any bearing on how the reader perceives words in the normal process of reading. Second, he suggests that "outside-in" theories lead to incorrect recommendations about how reading should be taught, because they suggest that the learner should be taught to "decode" print into speech rather than to extract meaning directly from print, without the mediation of speech.

In Smith's view, decoding of print into some form of speech—either covert or overt—is generally unnecessary and undesirable. In an "inside-out" theory, it is postulated that reading begins with intention and purpose and proceeds by using print only to the extent necessary to "resolve uncertainty" among the various alternatives that the reader is presumed to be able to have in mind. According to this theory, reading is a process that begins "in the head." Starting from his intentions and purposes in reading, the reader "makes predictions" of what the meaning may be, using print only to confirm or disconfirm these predictions.

The reader may refer to Smith's chapter (Vol. 2) to gain a more adequate idea of his "inside-out" theory of reading which, at the extreme, almost reduces to the absurd view that one might be able to read a text without opening one's eyes. Smith admits that the theory is vague and that it could not specify particular procedures of teaching. He thinks that its benefits could come through orienting teachers to a "different view of their trade." He also appeals to Rumelhart's suggestion (1977) that reading is a performance in which "top–down" (i.e., inside-out) processes interact with "bottom–up" (i.e., outside-in) processes. Thus even Smith seems to agree that reading involves some "outside-in" processes.

The one major virtue of the "inside-out" theory, we think, is that it draws attention to those processes in reading in which the ongoing apprehension of the total meaning of a text plays a role in facilitating the apprehension of particular parts of the text, or further stretches of it, and in cuing the interpretation of words and other text elements whose readings and meanings might otherwise be ambigous. There are many kinds of observations and experiments that suggest the operation of such processes. For example, texts

whose words and ideas are linked by common and frequent associations are easier to understand and remember than texts with words and ideas whose associations are more remote (Rosenberg, 1968). For another example, if a certain number of words are deliberately omitted from a text and replaced by blanks, as in the testing of reading comprehension by the "cloze procedure" (Taylor, 1953), skilled readers can accurately guess a large proportion of the omitted words. Thus they can get a large part of the meaning of a text from limited cues, presumably deriving that meaning by making maximal use of whatever cues are present, in conjunction with their general language competence, their knowledge of the world, and their capacities for making inferences.

One may, however, question the ecological validity of experiments with the cloze procedure, regardless of how valuable and valid the cloze procedure may be for certain purposes. One does not ordinarily have to read text with a proportion of the words omitted. Simply because skilled readers can guess the identities of words omitted from a text does not necessarily mean that they guess or "make predictions" when they do not have to do so in reading normal textual materials. Moreover, "inside-out" processes in reading "cloze procedure" texts can operate well only when the reader can make maximal use of "outside-in" processes—that is, correctly responding to the stimuli that are actually present in such texts.

Therefore, to put forward an "inside-out" theory that leaves no room for the necessary "outside-in" processes seems to us to be woefully neglectful of the stimulus value of the printed word and its role in cuing a language response. It is all very well for Smith to write about the reader's "intentions" and "purposes" and their role in motivating a reader's efforts to gain meanings, but it is hard to believe that a skilled reader puts any serious reliance on the "predictions" he or she might make about the words and meanings in a text, except perhaps in the limited sense that the context of a word, when properly apprehended, often helps the reader to determine how that word (that might otherwise be ambiguous as to its grammatical, lexical, or semantic content) is to be read. There *must* be an "outside-in" process in reading whereby an external stimulus (a word, a text, etc.) cues the apprehension of meaning. Although we acknowledge that there can be "inside-out" processes in reading, we believe that "outside-in" processes must occur if the "inside-out" processes are to occur at all. And these "outside-in" processes must be taught. One cannot expect them necessarily to arise spontaneously as a result of the operation of "inside-out" processes.

At the same time, there is undoubtedly a place for the teaching of "inside-out" processes. Especially in the early phases of reading instruction, the child is somewhat in the same position as a skilled reader of a "cloze procedure" text in which the reader must guess the words that have been replaced by blanks: The difference is that, for the child, the words are all there, but he or

she fails to recognize some of them or is not sure what words they are. It is a legitimate strategy to encourage the child to make guesses at these words—provided that the guesses are based primarily on the cues (phonic or otherwise) in the words themselves and only secondarily on the total context surrounding the words that have to be guessed at. Furthermore, at some early point in beginning reading instruction, the child must somehow be made aware of the feature of English whereby a given word can have a different content or meaning depending on the total context. The child must be taught to rely essentially on "inside-out" processes in order to use the total context to arrive at the intended interpretation of such words.

Our conclusion on the "inside-out" versus "outside-in" controversy is that it presents a false contrast. Normal reading behavior involves both "inside-out" and "outside-in" processes. In the teaching of reading, it is mistake to neglect either kind of process.

"Decoding" and the Relation of Reading to Speech

Some of the argumentation involved in the discussion of an "inside-out" theory of reading leads directly to various issues having to do with the relation of reading to speech. One of F. Smith's claims is that it is possible to extract meaning from print without the mediation of speech and that therefore there is no point in teaching children to render print into speech. In some of his other writings, Smith (1973) derides what he calls "the great decoding fallacy," denying or minimizing the usefulness of teaching children to respond specifically to what are often called "phonic cues" in printed words—that is, the representations of sound patterns that are contained in particular letters and combinations of letters. Like some other authors (e.g., Clymer, 1962–1963), Smith cites what he believes to be a large degree of irregularity in English spelling–sound correspondences as the basis for arguing that phonic cues are not sufficiently useful in learning to read, and, to the extent that they are useful at all, that they are too difficult to learn.

As we can see, there are two basic issues here:

1. Is there a proper role, in reading or in learning to read, of processes in which printed representations of language are converted to corresponding speech codes, either in overt or covert form, to facilitate the apprehension of meaning on the part of the reader?
2. In case of languages (like English) that use an alphabetic principle in their writing systems, is there a proper role, in reading or in learning to read, of processes in which the reader responds to "phonic" cues in words?

The term *decoding,* in its application to reading, was popularized by Chall (1967) in her analysis of "the great debate" about "phonic" as opposed to "look–say" methods of teaching reading. In Chall's usage, the term was intended to refer chiefly to the use of phonic cues in determining speech–sound representations of words, but the term can also have the more general meaning of referring to *any* translation of print to speech (or some other form of language) whether it depends on phonic cues or not. Therefore, "decoding" can refer to either of the two basic issues that we have just identified.

The chapters and discussions in these volumes never arrive at a clear consensus on the issues that can arise under the rubric of "decoding," in either of its senses, but from them perhaps we can piece together an integrated view.

First, can meaning be extracted from print without mediation of some sort of speech code? Almost undoubtedly, this *can* occur. Animals without speech can be conditioned to make meaningful responses to arbitrary symbols, and human beings who for some reason do not posess speech capabilities (e.g., in case of severe deafness) can derive meaning from print without the mediation of a speech code (they may, however, use some other type of language code; see Frumkin & Anisfeld, 1977). The question therefore changes to one of whether normal children *should* be taught to extract meaning from print without mediation of a speech code.

The answer to this latter question depends on answers to questions such as: Is reading learned faster if speech code mediation is avoided? Is skilled reading faster and more efficient if it does not include speech-code mediation? Can individuals who are taught to use phonological mediation (or come to use it naturally) learn to drop its use when they approach high levels of skill in reading?

None of these questions is directly addressed in any of the research reported in these volumes. Evidence is presented, however, suggesting that many readers do normally use speech-code mediation, or at least that extraction of meaning from print is normally accompanied by some form of phonological mediation (Juola, Schadler, Chabot, McCaughey, & Wait, Vol. 2; LaBerge, Vol. 3; Perfetti & Lesgold, Vol. 1; and Smith & Kleiman, Vol. 2). Thus meaning extraction and speech-code rendering may be processes that can operate simultaneously—in parallel, if not sequentially. Nevertheless, research is not yet clear as to whether a phonological coding of the printed stimulus is necessary for access to the internal lexicon (i.e., to retrieve the meaning of a word). Nor is it clear as to whether any form of phonological coding takes place in reading that is much more rapid than to appear to permit such speech coding. It is difficult to arrange experimental settings that would reveal clear answers to such questions. Furthermore, it would be difficult to control the past experience of the reader—that is, to take account of the degree to which the reader has used speech coding at any time in learning to read, and the degree to which he or she has learned to avoid phonological mediation processes in extremely rapid reading. The fact is that most readers will have made at least some use of speech coding in the early stages of learning to read, even if it is only when they are required to read "out loud."

Nevertheless, all these questions may be vacuous and unrealistic with respect to the teaching of reading in its early phases. Regardless of whether meaning can under any circumstances and at any level of reading skill be extracted from print without phonological mediation, it would seem that teaching the child to render print into some form of speech representation helps the child to use, in comprehending print, those habits of language comprehension that have been learned in acquiring the understanding of spoken language. It is inefficient to ignore whatever competence of that sort the child has already attained, and it is probably futile to try to make the child avoid any form of speech coding. Most children will tend to form speech-code representations anyway, as they must when required to read aloud, and as they appear to do naturally even in silent reading. There is at least no evidence that use of speech mediation in early reading impedes the acquisition, at a later stage, of fast reading skills in which use of speech-code representations may virtually disappear.

Our conclusion, therefore, with respect to the general issue of "decoding" in the sense of translating print to some form of speech-code representation is this: There is no reason to discourage the teaching of this form of decoding in the early phases of reading instruction. On the contrary, we believe that the weight of evidence favors the positive recommendation that children should explicitly be taught to convert print into speech in beginning reading instruction. It also recommends that they be taught with the expectation that this will help them in getting meanings from print and with the further expectation that as reading becomes more skilled and automatized, speech-code representations will play an increasingly diminished role in the reading process. Obviously, requiring a child to read aloud is one way that the teacher has at his or her disposal to assess the child's skill in accurately rendering print into speech, whereas in later phases of instruction the child's skills are better tested by having the child respond to comprehension questions on the basis of rapid silent reading.

Let us now turn to the other issue suggested by the term *decoding:* What role should teaching play in enabling learners to respond to "phonic" cues— that is, to make use of letter–sound correspondences to help in identifying the spoken words represented by a sequence of letters? If such teaching has any role at all, how should it be done? Again, the volumes do not give clear, explicit answers. One must make inferences from the array of chapters that are included.

We must start with some basic considerations about the goals of reading and the nature of the task to be learned. It seems to us that one of the basic goals of reading is to teach the child to make full use of the characteristic of English orthography whereby sounds are indeed represented, although not at all perfectly, in spelling. The ways in which letters and letter combinations cue sound patterns in English spelling are probabilistic rather than deterministic (as they virtually are in some languages). Still, they must somehow be learned if new or unfamiliar words, particularly proper names, are to be recognized and pronounced. Although it can properly be claimed that there is no known limitation to the number of words that a person could learn to recognize without using any letter–sound cues, greater efficiency in learning and performance can be achieved if these cues are in fact used when a new word is first encountered and even for some time after that. (This is not to deny, of course, the usefulness of many other types of cues, generally referred to under the rubric of "context"; the role of such cues has been discussed in our treatment of "inside-out" theories of reading.)

There is no intention here of suggesting that a child who is early taught to employ phonic cues in recognizing words will necessarily continue to use them regularly, or have to use them always, in later stages of attaining reading skill. In time, and with repeated use, habits of responding to phonic cues can become so highly automatized that they no longer have any critical function in recognizing words. Nevertheless, if they are well learned, they are always available for use—as in recognizing and pronouncing an unfamiliar word. There is evidence (Baron & Strawson, 1976) that many skilled readers do in fact make latent and unconscious use of phonic cues even in pronouncing words that are highly familiar, in that these readers read aloud irregularly spelled words with slightly less facility than they read regularly spelled words. There is no evidence, however, that such readers are impeded by phonic-cue responses in normal silent reading.

Many children have trouble in learning the use of phonic cues. The possible reasons for the trouble are varied. Poor instruction, inappropriate instructional materials, affective responses, inherent constitutional defects in the child, and many other factors could be at its root. Two important factors are emphasized in chapters included in the volumes. The first of these concerns the child's lacking in awareness of the feature of segmentation in language and its representation in print (Chall, Vol. 1; Chomsky, Liberman, & Shankweiler, Vol. 2; Wallach & Wallach, Williams, Vol. 3). That is, children will have trouble, it seems, if in the early stages of instruction in phonics they have not come to recognize that spoken sentences are composed of segments we call words, or, at later stages, that words are segmented into syllables, and syllables into distinct phonemes, and if, further, they fail to recognize that all these types of segmentation are represented in the system of writing. For example, word segmentation is usually represented by the spaces between words in print, whereas phoneme segmentation is represented, albeit in complex ways, by the use of distinct letters placed in sequence.

Evidence is presented in these volumes that segmentation skills can be critical in learning to use phonic cues and that they are quite easily taught to nearly all children.[2] It has occurred to us that if this is true, as we are prepared to believe, much of the research comparing "phonic" and "look–say"(whole-word) methods of instruction—usually concluding that the methods do not materially differ in their effectiveness—may be flawed by the fact that the degree to which the subjects in these experiments possessed the prerequisite segmentation skills was not adequately controlled. We would expect that if children were taught segmentation skills before being exposed to either phonic or whole-word methods of instruction, phonic methods might show greater effectiveness. (It is even possible that prior exposure to instruction in segmentation skills might benefit children given "whole-word" instruction.)

The second major factor implicated in the difficulty some children have in learning phonic cues is an inability of the child to maintain selective attention to critical features of the instructional setting (see especially Bateman, Vol. 1). Ross (1976) reviewed evidence that the ability to inhibit stimuli irrelevant to the task at hand and to focus attention on relevant stimuli is a skill that develops with age and that at least some of the children who are unable to learn to read simply may have not yet developed this prerequisite skill. Very simple techniques can be used to assess selective attention. Typically, children are asked to watch a small screen and to push a button every time a red light (or some such stimulus) appears. Children with high error scores on such a task may be immature in the sense of being unable to attend selectively to the critical aspects of a task. Ross suggested that various behavioral techniques be employed with such children—that tasks be analyzed into specific components, that teachers be very explicit about where the child's attention should be focused, and that responses entailing selective attention be reinforced. Bateman's chapter points out that children who have attentional problems present a special challenge to educators and may require more systematic and detailed instruction.

Even if children possess adequate segmentation skills and are relatively mature in their ability to attend selectively, the learning of letter–sound correspondences can be difficult if the children are not given materials that exemplify, draw attention to, and contrast these correspondences in a fairly

---

[2]Actually, although many chapters stressed the importance of segmentation skills, little attention was given to the teaching of such skills. Wallach and Wallach (Vol. 3) described procedures they found useful, and their description is expanded in their book (Wallach & Wallach, 1976). Other useful procedures are mentioned, for example, by Gibson and Levin (1975, pp. 119–121; 259–261).

systematic way. It is probably not necessary that children be given materials that present letter–sound correspondences in a totally systematic way—progressing from those correspondences that are completely regular to those that show irregularity and variation, but the material needs to be characterized by enough regularity and system to permit the children to induce enough to begin figuring out how letters and letter combinations represent sounds. To a large degree, this is something the children indeed will have to figure out for themselves; they will have to notice the cases where exceptions occur, because these exceptions are too numerous to be made specific objects of instruction. In any event, we believe—along with the Wallachs (Vol. 3) and several other authors—that the best way to solve "the reading problem" for many children is to draw attention, gently but firmly, to the way in which letters and letter sequences represent the sounds of spoken words. Perhaps our belief is a bit trite and old-fashioned, but it is worth being forcefully stated nevertheless.

Teaching a child to become aware of and use phonic cues is a very subtle matter, however. As Chomsky (Vol. 2) remarked, it should be borne in mind that the child learning to read will in most cases already know the language. Teaching him or her to use letters and letter combinations as cues is a matter of first making the child realize that there is some sort of connection between the way words are spelled and the way they are sounded and that the letters will help the child to recognize most of the words in a primer text as old friends that are already known in spoken form. One does not want to insist on having the child try to "sound out" words by some rigid series of pronunciation rules. The rules will not always work well; they will not always, by themselves, lead to the correct pronunciation. Other cues must be used—the meanings of the other parts of the sentence, or even cues in pictures, if they are present—as long as the child does not learn to rely on pictures alone. Nevertheless, the essential and critical cues remain in the words themselves and the letters that compose them. The letters in a word are the child's starting point for making a guess as to how the word is to be sounded. If the first guess does not work, or make sense, it is all right to make another guess. In most cases, the child can correct himself or herself as Clay observed (Vol. 2). As the child gains more and more experience in guessing words, and gets more and more practice in recognizing words in this way, the words will become more familiar and their recognition will become more automatic.

If this is the kind of "guessing" and "hypothesis making" that Smith (Vol. 2) and Goodman and Goodman (Vol. 1) refer to in their "inside-out" theory of reading, we approve of it. We insist, however, that the theory depends on certain "outside-in" processes whereby the child knows at least something about the possible cue values of the letters in a word and uses them as the basis for the guesses.

Automaticity

In our discussion of speech-code representation as well as that of phonic skills, we have implied that the very specific skills that must be taught in early reading instruction can and should become so automatic that they no longer remain as problems—and even seem to vanish or become nonfunctional—in later phases of reading instruction. The process of automatization is somewhat mysterious, and it may take a long time to develop fully. As far as we know, it occurs only through repeated use, practice, and reinforcement of the relevant skills. But it can and does occur. Thus it can happen that in later stages of reading-skill attainment, words and their meanings are instantly recognized with no apparent reference to speech-code representations or to phonic skills. Experimental research on mature readers, as reported in several chapters in the volumes, makes it clear that in these readers the basic skills of word recognition were highly automatized (LaBerge, Vol. 3; Perfetti & Lesgold, Vol. 1; Samuels, Vol. 1). Even in the case of quite common and familiar words, skilled readers had faster recognition skills than poor readers. The simplest hypothesis to explain a lack of automatization on the part of the poor readers would be that the less skilled readers had had less exposure and practice with these basic skills. At least, we are not aware of any evidence presented in the volumes that would rule out this hypothesis. Although the results of Guthrie, Martuza, and Seifert's (Vol. 3) study of the effect of instructional time and "time on task" were mixed, they do not rule out the interpretation that time on task is indeed an important variable for many children, particularly for those whose home and educational backgrounds suggest that they need more time to learn and practice basic skills. This possibility raises a problem of how such students can be motivated to spend the extra time they need to learn, but the simple fact that they need to acquire these basic skills, and that they need more time to master them, is clear.

Stages of Progress in Attaining Reading Skills

The notion that the various skills involved in reading preferably are learned and mastered in a distinct order, and that after they are mastered they can become automatic and no longer critical in reading behavior, fits in well with the notion of stages of progress in attaining reading skills. We think that Chall (Vol. 1) is correct in her labeling of the earliest stage as one of mastering elementary "decoding" skills—provided that it is recognized, as she herself would doubtless agree, that the decoding stage would start with the attainment of prerequisite skills of segmentation.

In later stages, the push would be toward comprehension and "reading to learn," much more so than in earlier stages. But even in earlier stages there is no reason to ignore or neglect the need for the child to comprehend meaning. It could be a mistake, for example, to give drills in early stages that are concerned solely with learning phonic skills—that is, without reading for comprehension, although children who are otherwise highly motivated might profit from such drills.

We end this section with a reaffirmation of our belief that the essential characteristic of reading behavior is reading to get meaning. Nothing we have said is intended to controvert this belief.

PROGRAMS OF
BEGINNING READING INSTRUCTION

Having spelled out what we consider to be the basic theoretical issues that are connected with the teaching of reading, we now want to see how these issues are handled in current programs of beginning reading instruction. Several of the currently available programs were examined in some detail by various authors (Bartlett, Vol. 2; Beck & Block, Vol. 1; Fletcher, Vol. 3; Popp, Vol. 3; and Wallach & Wallach, Vol. 3). Here we attempt to extend the analysis to a number of other programs, and we look at all of them from the perspective of the issues in the preceding section.[3] We ask the question: How much have curriculum designers tried to take into account theories of reading and the research findings that support them, and how well have they succeeded in translating these theories and findings into instructional practice? Ultimately, we would like to provide a guide that educators might use in assessing the various reading programs and selecting the ones that are most appropriate for particular groups of children. Armed with a list of specific points to consider about the available programs, the educator can more easily analyze the strengths and weaknesses of individual programs and compensate for any weaknesses found in the program that is eventually chosen.

We address three questions that a teacher or administrator selecting a reading program ought to ask: (1) What model of the reading process does the program assume? (2) How does the program go about teaching the component skills involved in reading? and (3) How does the program deal with special problems of both the teacher and the student?

---

[3]In addition to the reading programs described in chapters [*Open Court Reading Program* (1975), *Distar Reading* (1974), *Reading 720* (1976), *New Primary Grades Reading System* (1972), *The Palo Alto Reading Program* (1973), *Reading Unlimited* (1976), and the Wallachs' tutorial program], a number of other programs were surveyed. Complete citations for all these programs are included in the list of references. An effort was made to survey as many programs as possible that were not included in Popp's (1975) survey.

Theoretical Underpinnings of Reading Programs

Finding out what model of the reading process is assumed by a reading program requires a careful consideration of the entire program. This is easier to do for some programs than for others. Some authors publish material in the teachers' manuals that explicitly describes their beliefs about the reading process. For example, Harper and Row's *Design for Reading* (1973) claims a Piagetian orientation, whereas Science Research Associates' (SRA) *Distar Reading* (1974) purports to represent a learning-theory approach. Many other programs are much less explicit, and their theoretical underpinnings must be inferred from the instructional techniques and material they recommend. This inference can be quite difficult to make, because a given theoretical perspective may be expressed in a number of quite distinct practical techniques. Very different theoretical orientations may seem more similar than different when one examines the particular exercises and instructional devices employed in a reading program. Inferring the authors' points of view on theoretical questions generally requires examination of the sequencing and relative amounts of attention paid to particular types of instructional tasks.

There are two major aspects of a reading program from which the theoretical leanings of the authors can be inferred. First, one can look at the extent to which it emphasizes decoding skills—that is, the learning of letter–sound correspondences and other orthographic regularities. Reading programs whose authors are more on the side of an "inside-out" theory (for example, Macmillan's *Bank Street Readers,* 1973) stress reading for a purpose, gaining information from pictorial and other contextual cues, and whole-word recognition. Programs whose authors favor "outside-in" theories (for example, the *Macmillan Reading Program,* 1974) spend more time on explicit instruction in letter–sound correspondences and word–attack skills. Actually, neither of these examples and few published reading programs fall at the extremes of this dimension. Most programs pay at least some attention to the development of decoding skills, although they differ in the timing and the explicitness of this instruction. Almost all reading programs spend some amount of time on comprehension skills, but there are a variety of approaches to the development of comprehension. Because most published reading programs do not seem to see reading as either solely an "inside-out" or solely an "outside-in" process, the educator selecting a program usually has to decide on the relative amounts of emphasis put on decoding and comprehension skills and on the timing of such instruction. Programs leaning toward the "inside-out" viewpoint stress comprehension skills early, adding letter–sound instruction somewhat later and often making it supplemental to the basic instruction. Letter–sound correspondence instruction occurs early in a program whose authors favor "outside-in" processes and is a vital part of the child's reading experience.

As we mentioned earlier, some "inside-out" theories recommend instructional plans that consider decoding skills a liability and therefore do not teach them at all (Goodman & Goodman, Vol. 1; Smith, Vol. 2). As the Goodmans state in their chapter, such an orientation does not lend itself to the development of an instructional program based on skill sequences and learning hierarchies. It depends much more on the ingenuity and skill of individual teachers than on lesson plans and materials published for widespread use. The Goodmans' chapter describes some aspects of an instructional program that follows this extreme "inside-out" orientation. Although the activities they propose seem excellent for increasing and supporting the child's motivation to read, we think it omits some important instructional objectives. For reasons discussed earlier, we hesitate to recommend such programs for widespread use, although they may be satisfactory for teaching certain highly motivated and capable students who enter instruction with the prerequisite segmentation skills already well-developed and who can be trusted to work out decoding skills on their own.

In contrast, some programs give minimal attention to comprehension skills and thus appear to favor extreme "outside-in" theories of reading. An example of such a program is SRA's *Basic Reading Series* (1970). Teachers using this program are advised as follows: "Remember that lengthy discussions slow up the lesson and questions about meaning suggest that you doubt the child's ability to understand. . . . When an occasional question of content or interpretation does arise, accept any reasonable answer that a child offers." (*Teaching Guide to Level A,* p. 10). Just as we are reluctant to recommend a program that relies entirely on teaching comprehension skills to the exclusion of word–attack skills, we hesitate to approve a program that deliberately ignores comprehension skills in early phases of instruction. Such a program may be quite satisfactory for teaching motivated and capable students, but it may risk unnecessary failures if used in a class that covers a range of abilities.

The second aspect of a reading program that reflects theoretical assumptions of its authors concerns the sequencing of different components of the program. On the basis of their model of the reading process and their beliefs about how children learn, developers of a reading curriculum decide which skills are prerequisite to learning other skills. The chapters in these volumes, especially the one by Chall (Vol. 1) on a stage theory of reading development, suggest that in prereading phases of instruction there should be a major emphasis on the development of certain skills, such as the ability to segment spoken language into words, syllables, and phonemes, that are regarded as prerequisite to learning word–attack skills based on phonics instruction during the first phase of actual reading instruction. Chall proposes that this first phase of actual reading instruction, in which the child learns word–attack skills, should be followed by a "firming-up" phase in which extensive exposure to familiar materials will facilitate automatization of decoding skills. According to Chall's model, only after this automatization occurs can extensive progress be made in establishing higher-level comprehension skills and reading flexibility. In the following section, we consider the teaching of basic component skills in various reading programs, in the light of Chall's stage model.

Teaching Component Skills: The Prereading Curriculum

Most reading programs offer a prereading curriculum that is designed to establish and strengthen the skills that are considered prerequisite to reading. There are four areas of development that prereading programs address to varying extents and in different ways: (1) language development; (2) segmentation skills; (3) grapheme discrimination; and (4) desire to learn to read.

Language Development.   Before beginning to learn to read in a particular language (such as English, which is the language we are most concerned with here), the child typically will have attained considerable skill in understanding the spoken form of the language. Most reading programs assume that the children starting work in their preprimers have already attained the language competence required for learning to read. Indeed, most 5-year-olds have acquired syntactic structures and vocabularies considerably more complex than those presented in their early readers.

Children for whom English is a second language present a special problem, however, and some programs make suggestions about how to instruct these students. SRA's *Basic Reading Series* (1970), for example, suggests that reading instruction for these children be delayed until their command of English is adequate. Natalicio, in her chapter (Vol. 3) on reading instruction for bilingual children, calls this the "direct approach." The alternative, according to her, is to teach reading in the child's native language while teaching English as a second language—the "native-language approach." This latter is the method advocated by the *Macmillan Reading Program* (1974), which publishes special materials for Spanish-speaking children. Natalicio reviews a number of studies comparing the effectiveness of these two approaches; although the studies do not permit making a definitive conclusion, it is her impression that the evidence tends to favor the "direct approach," whereby reading instruction of any kind is deferred while the child gains an adequate command of English. Although there are many passionate advocates of the native-language approach, we believe that Natalicio's thoughtful discussion should lead to serious consideration of the possible merits of the direct approach in many situations.

Even for children who have learned English as their native language, there are ways in which inadequate language and communication skills may interfere with learning to read. One skill whose importance is easily overlooked, and the lack of which may be quite critical in a child's failure to progress normally, is the ability to attend to and understand the stories that are a part of most instructional programs. Children can enter school with ability adequate to understand English at the sentence level and in ordinary conversation but with inadequate ability to comprehend longer discourse. The difficulty may stem in part from problems with attention and concentration as the child listens to a story, but it can also arise from the child's unfamiliarity with what we may call the *conventions of storytelling*. Here we refer to such conventions as the following: A story is typically told from the viewpoint of a particular narrator, whose role or lack of role in the story must be understood; dialogue can be reported in either direct or indirect modes, and there are conventions as to how the various speakers are identified; there are ways of establishing a time frame for the story or of indicating changes in the time frame; and in telling a story, the narrator is permitted to give the hearer information that may be unavailable to the story characters. It is probable that many children will have no trouble grasping these conventions, particularly if they are frequently read to at home, but some children may not catch on to these conventions easily. Many reading programs pay little attention to the development of story-understanding skills. Examples of programs that do give attention to these skills are Allyn and Bacon's *Sheldon Basic Reading Series* (1973) (which provides preprimer lessons in recognizing narration and dialogue), American Book Company's *Reading Experience and Development (READ) Series* (1968), Harper and Row's *Design for Reading* (1973), SRA's *Distar Reading* (1974), and several others.

Another language difficulty that arises for some children is inadequate comprehension of the "language of instruction"—that is, the particular words and phrases that have to be used in teaching reading. The most immediate examples that come to mind are the very words *word* and *read*. A prereading program that assumes that children already know what these words mean is probably assuming too much. American Book Company's *READ Series* is a good example of a program that attempts to teach these concepts early on. The series starts from the assumption that comprehension of the language of reading instruction is the first prerequisite for learning to read, and it concentrates on developing this comprehension in the three preprimers that begin the series.

There are even subtler aspects of the way in which language is used in instruction that may cause problems for some children. Some of these aspects are discussed in the volumes. The language of the classroom may be different from the language used at home in ways that are difficult to specify. The teacher may use "indirect speech acts" whose meaning and intent is unfamiliar to the child. For example, a teacher's request for the repetition of a response, such as "Again?" may be intended to mean that the original response was incorrect, but it might be interpreted by the child as an indication that the teacher didn't hear the first time, with the result that the child repeats the same wrong answer, perhaps in a louder voice. This, in turn, may be interpreted by the teacher as an indication of the child's inability to formulate another answer, or even as an expression of defiance. Although this example may seem trivial, the amount of damage to teacher–child relations and to overall progress in reading caused by misunderstandings of this type can be serious. We are not aware of any reading programs that discuss this type of problem in their teachers' manuals.

According to Shuy (Vol. 1) and Simon (Vol. 3), problems of this sort, stemming from sociolinguistic differences between teachers and students, constitute the major way in which Black English dialect appears to interfere with learning to read. (Neither Shuy nor Simons feel that Black English dialect per se poses much of a problem in the mechanics of letter–sound correspondences in reading.) A teacher whose class contains children from different social classes or subcultures from his or her own would certainly have to be sensitive to these problems. Unfortunately, such sensitivity cannot be written easily into a program of reading instruction. Many programs include exhortations to teachers to be sensitive to dialect differences; among such programs are the *Macmillan Reading Program* (1974), the *Bank Street Readers* (1973), and SRA's *Basic Reading Series* (1970). Most of these, however, stress acceptance of pronunciation and syntax differences as opposed to the sociolinguistic differences discussed by Shuy or by Simons. The *Macmillan Reading Program*, for example, recommends that teachers of students who speak Black English make an effort to learn the regularities of that dialect, in order to be able to tell whether children's errors are true errors or merely stem from dialect differences. Shuy reports in his chapter that teaching Black English to teachers has had limited success and is probably not necessary. Similarly, both Shuy and Simon conclude from the evidence they review that it is not necessary to teach black children Standard English (as recommended by the authors of the *Bank Street Readers*) or to teach black children with materials written in Black English dialect (as advocated by Baratz, 1969).

To summarize, the readiness program of a reading curriculum should include attention to certain aspects of language and communicative skill development. Children who are not fluent in English need specialized instruction designed to improve their mastery of English. Children who have adequate mastery of English may still need help in understanding the words and concepts that are introduced in the process of reading instruction and in attending to stories with adequate comprehension of the conventions of storytelling. Children who speak dialects that are considerably different from Standard English and come from backgrounds that do not prepare them to understand "school language" may suffer because of subtle misunderstandings, due to linguistic and sociolinguistic differences, that can arise between them and their teachers. Although it is not possible to take care of every eventuality by specific prescriptions in reading programs, teachers should be made aware that subtle differences in patterns of language use may hamper communication and rapport with students from different backgrounds.

Segmentation Skills. A linguistic skill that is now considered by many as crucial to learning to read is the ability to recognize how the stream of speech can be segmented into linguistic units of various sizes—phrases, words, syllables, and distinctive sounds (phonemes). This skill requires the child not only to know the language he or she is going to read but also to engage in a kind of critical analysis to become aware of how the language is put together. For this reason, we can call this "segmentation skill" a *metalinguistic* skill.

Although we now recognize the importance of this skill and know that it can be successfully taught to most children (from the work of the Wallachs [Vol. 3], and from several other sources), most of the currently available reading programs were designed before its importance and "teachability" had become evident. Therefore, few programs make any systematic attempt to determine which children lack this skill or to provide instruction in it for those who need it. If a child enters school with segmentation skills already developed or very nearly developed, the chances are that he or she will be exposed to tasks that strengthen this skill. Most prereading programs include games involving rhyming and alliteration that make use of the metalinguistic skills to which we are referring here. The *Macmillan Reading Program* (1974), for example, was one of the best programs examined in terms of its recognition of the importance of segmentation. In addition to suggesting tasks that involve play with word sounds, its teachers' manuals frequently remind the instructor that a failure to progress may stem from a difficulty at this point. However, the recommendations offered for children who seem to be stuck at this point are additional exposure to the rhyming and alliteration games. As Wallach and Wallach (Vol. 3) point out, the child who cannot segment at all is not in a good position to benefit from these tasks.

Because most reading programs do not provide either prereading training in segmenting skills or diagnostic aids for discovering which children are in need of such training, we suggest that educators supplement such programs. Easily administered tests are available that can identify children who need special help in segmentation (Fox & Routh, 1975; Rosner & Simon, 1971). It is critical that these children be given the needed extra help before starting serious instruction in the use of phonic cues. The tutorial techniques developed by the Wallachs have been shown to be effective in establishing segmentation skills and permitting the transfer of students to regular classroom materials after 3 to 4 months of 30-minute daily sessions.

Grapheme Discrimination. The third skill that needs to be developed during the prereading phase of instruction is letter discrimination—that is, the ability to distinguish among letters of the alphabet and other graphemic symbols. Virtually all published instructional programs attend to this aspect of development in the early stages of instruction, and the techniques used to teach the letters of the alphabet do not differ much from program to program. Tracing, coloring, and matching tasks all seem to be effective. Programs differ in the sequence in which the letters are taught and in other details of instruction, but graphemic discrimination does not appear to be a serious problem for most students, regardless of the mode of instruction (Gibson & Levin, 1975, p. 246).

Desire To Learn To Read. A good prereading curriculum should establish in the child a desire to learn to read or should reinforce whatever motivation the child may already have. As suggested in the Goodman and Goodman chapter (Vol. 1), the preschool or kindergarten classroom should be a "literate environment," full of things to be read—even if they are only signs and labels. The child needs to be brought to recognize that a great deal of useful and interesting information and entertainment is available to those who know how to read.

Most curriculum materials do attempt to establish this motivation to learn. One might suspect that the kinds of materials and techniques that would be most motivating would differ with various characteristics of the population of children (for example, socioeconomic class, urban versus rural environment, etc.). This certainly should be taken into account in the selection of a program for a particular group of children.

Desiderata in the Prereading Program: Summary. We have suggested that a prereading curriculum should: (1) make sure that the student is prepared with an adequate language competence and an understanding of the special ways in which language is used in teaching reading; (2) make sure that the student can segment spoken language into words, syllables, and phonemes; (3) make sure that the student can discriminate among and recognize the letters of the alphabet; and (4) help the student to establish a motivation to learn to read. These are the skills to be established in what Chall (Vol. 1) refers to as "Stage Zero" of the reading program.

Teaching Component Skills: Instruction in Decoding

Development of word–attack skills, according to Chall, should be the major focus of the early phase of reading instruction. As we said earlier, there are two issues involved here. The first and most basic concerns whether children should learn to translate printed language into spoken language, or whether an attempt should be made to teach the child to access meaning directly from print, without phonological mediation. This may be more interesting theoretically than pragmatically because of the impracticality of providing the child with the meaning of a passage without exposing him or her to a phonological representation of it. Even if the student never reads orally, his or her earliest reading experiences must surely involve being read to. Without such experience, we could predict that learning to read would be very difficult indeed—rather like deciphering the Egyptian hieroglyphics without the aid of the Rosetta Stone.

Although no reading instructional program that we know of has attempted to avoid phonological mediation altogether, there have been efforts to prevent the student from producing an oral representation of printed material (see the discussion of the work of McDade and of Buswell on a "nonoral hypothesis" and a "nonoral" reading program, cited in Anderson & Dearborn, 1952, pp. 152-157). None of the reading programs surveyed for this investigation forbids oral reading by students, but they do differ in the extent to which they stress silent reading. Macmillan's *Bank Street Readers* (1973) appeared to be the most cautious about oral reading, warning teachers of the dangers of "word calling" (oral reading without comprehension). Danks and Fears (Vol. 3) express some skepticism about the existence of true "word callers," concluding that if such cases exist they are probably extremely rare. Nevertheless, the authors of the *Bank Street Readers* have minimized students' opportunity to read orally without comprehension by requiring that all oral reading be in response to particular questions (with the exception of certain poems and plays that are specifically provided for the purpose of developing "dramatic" reading skills, which are deemed to be quite separate from more basic reading ability).

Betts' Basic Readers (1963) and the *Triple "I" Series* (1970), although they do not express reservations about oral reading, are both attentive to the development of silent reading skills at the earliest stages. The Betts program is especially concerned with the early development of good silent reading habits, warning teachers to watch children carefully as they read. Children are not to move their lips or their heads, nor should they point to words with their fingers as they read along. Although we agree that children might benefit from early opportunities to read independently, to themselves, we suspect that saddling a new reader with the additional requirements of keeping head and lips and fingers still may be just too much additional work for the student who really ought to be directing all concentration on deriving meaning from the text. Nevertheless, there is little research evidence that can be brought to bear on the question of the effect of early instructional experiences of this type on the development of silent reading ability.

Most of the programs we examined did not emphasize silent reading in early reading instruction. Although we have clearly sided with those who believe that phonological mediation is important in early reading (and perhaps in later reading as well), we also believe that children should begin to read silently early in the reading instruction program. An instructional sequence in which children first read a passage independently and then read the same passage orally has the advantage of allowing practice in silent reading and of increasing confidence and fluency in oral reading.

The second major issue to be confronted in the decoding stage of reading instruction applies only if one concludes, as we have, that there is a proper role of phonological mediation in learning to read. This second issue concerns whether and how to teach the alphabetic principle upon which our writing system is based. Even one who believes that meaning is accessed through phonological mediation could conceivably believe that phonics should not be taught as a part of reading instruction. One could hold this belief either on the ground that the English writing system is not regular enough for such learning to be of much use, or on the ground that a child is well equipped to induce the regularities without explicit instruction. We were not able to find any reading programs that avoid phonics instructions on either of these grounds.[4] There were, however, wide differences among the programs in the extent to which students were expected to induce the orthographic regularities on their own.

Several aspects of an instructional program are relevant to the question of how much orthographic regularity is to be inferred by the student and how much is to be taught directly. The first of these has to do with the timing of letter–sound correspondence instruction. Many programs introduce letter–sound relationships in the earliest phases of instruction, as the children are first learning their letters (for example, the *Bookmark Reading Program,* 1970; *Houghton Mifflin Readers,* 1974; *Macmillan Reading Program,* 1974). An alternate procedure, followed by *Betts' Basic Readers* (1963), SRA's *Basic Reading Series* (1970), and Scott Foresman's *Reading Unlimited* (1976), points out letter–sound relationships only in words that the children have already learned by sight. This method gives the children an opportunity to induce the regularities before explicit instruction is given. The former method

---

[4]The two programs that did not provide for phonics instruction, the *Triple "I" Series* (1970) and *Language Experiences in Reading* (1970), did not seem to be opposed to phonics instruction. Each suggested that the program could be supplemented with a phonics program if the teacher felt that systematic instruction would be helpful.

has the advantage of allowing the children to use decoding skills in their earliest reading experiences. Because children are reading before they have learned all the correspondences, we do not feel that this instructional method robs them of an opportunity for independent learning. It does introduce early the notion that letters represent sounds, and by doing so it may even facilitate the child's natural tendency to search for other such regularities and independently induce letter–sound relationships that have not yet been explicitly taught. At any rate, we see no reason to believe that learning a rule verbally, as a result of instruction, should prevent a child from "discovering" the regularity as a result of experience with printed materials. Students and practitioners of all ages frequently have the experience of "discovering" through experience something they had previously known only as a result of "book learning." Often the book learning is a necessary forerunner to the discovery.

Related to the issue of when to teach letter–sound correspondences is the question of how to introduce new words. As noted previously, some reading programs teach new words by memorization, allowing regularities to be pointed out in the words after they are learned. Alternatively, children can be allowed to practice decoding skills on new words. *Houghton Mifflin Readers* (1974) and the *Macmillan Reading Program* (1974) illustrate what we consider to be an appropriate method for introducing new words. Some of the new words that are presented either are not regular or are not decodable using only the skills the students have developed so far. These words are presented before they are encountered in reading and learned as sight words. Without them, the language of early readers would be much less natural, and students would be given the impression of great regularity in the writing system. Words that the children ought to be able to decode are not reviewed before they are encountered in the reading materials. The first time they are presented they occur in a highly constrained context, and the children are given an opportunity to practice their word–attack skills—not only phonic analysis skills but also skills using semantics and syntax to aid recognition of new words. After the students have had this chance to discover the new word on their own, the teacher may review the phonic and structural analysis skills involved in decoding it.

Another curriculum design decision related to the issue of implicit versus explicit phonics instruction concerns the vocabulary selected for early readers. SRA's *Basic Reading Series* (1970) and American Book Company's *READ Series* (1968) were the most extreme among the programs we examined in selecting a vocabulary of regular words for the children to encounter in their early reading. Children in these programs learn words that fit into "pattern boxes," and the stories contain a large number of rhyming words and words containing the same initial and/or final consonant. In the *Basic Reading Series* program, teachers are never to pronounce the sound that a letter represents, so letter–sound instruction proceeds entirely by filling in and reciting words in pattern boxes. Irregularities are avoided for as long as possible in both programs and are introduced only after the students can be expected to have a strong grasp of the rules. This bombardment of the child with regular words is expected to facilitate the child's inferencing about orthographic regularities.

At the other extreme are programs like *Language Experiences in Reading* (1970), in which the early reading vocabulary is not in any way controlled by the designers or the teachers. Children learn to read their own stories, and teachers help them to spell any word they want to use. Because many of the highest-frequency words in English are irregular, one might expect such a program to result in exposure to a large number of irregularities.

Houghton Mifflin Readers (1974) provide still another criterion for selecting a reading vocabulary. A survey of literature written for primary-grade children was used, and an attempt was made to introduce as many of the high-frequency words as early as possible, with the additional constraint that the children be exposed to words that give them an opportunity to try out the decoding skills as they learn them. This method approximates what we have recommended as a "gentle" handling of the problem of irregularity. Children are exposed to a good dose of words they can decode, a number of regular words that they cannot yet decode, and a few irregular words.

Perhaps the most difficult decision related to phonics instruction concerns which orthographic regularities to present when. This decision is related to the decision about vocabulary selection, of course, because children typically are taught the phonics rules that will be most useful for recognizing the words used in their readers. Usually, children start reading after learning only a few of the correspondences, and, by the time they get around to learning the more complex, context-dependent rules, it can be considered more legitimately a part of their spelling lesson than a part of learning to read.

The *Bookmark Reading Program* (1970), *Houghton Mifflin Readers* (1974), the *Macmillan Reading Program* (1974), and *Reading Unlimited* (1976) all use some variation of what seems to us to be a reasonable sequence of phonics instruction. Children first are taught letter–sound relationships for the most common sounds made by each consonant in initial position. In their earliest reading, they are encouraged to use what they know about the initial sounds along with semantic and syntactic cues to help to identify words. As they progress, they learn to identify the final and then the medial consonant sounds in words, and they learn to use that information in conjunction with context. Vowel sounds are not introduced until later when children have already mastered most of the consonant letter–sound relationships, including some consonant digraphs, and when they are already reading with some skill. By this time, the students will have induced some of the more regular vowel sounds, and because of greater maturity and confidence they should be better prepared to learn the more difficult context-dependent rules that govern vowel sounds.

We consider this a sensible procedure for several reasons. First, it is compatible with the observation that English print can be rather easily deciphered when vowel letters are replaced with an arbitrary symbol such as a hyphen, as in the following excerpt from a child's reader that we have treated in this way:

_ f_t m_n L_k_d t_ g_ f_st. H_ w_nt f_st _n h_s c_r. H_ w_lk_d f_st _nd h_ r_n f_st. H_ _v_n t_lk_d f_st. H_s w_f_ d_d n_t L_k_ h_m t_ g_ s_ f_st. B_t h_ w_nt f_st.

H_ s_t d_wn t_ __t _n _gg _nd _ c_k_ _nd _ p__. B_t h_ _t_ s_ f_st th_t th_ _gg sL_pp_d _nd f_ll _n h_s f__t.

H_ b_nt d_wn f_st _nd h_s n_s_ w_nt _nt_ th_ c_k_. H_ w_nt t_ w_p_ h_s n_s_ f_st _nd h_ h_t th_ p__. Th_ p__ h_t h_s w_f_.

Because vowel letters are considerably less regular in their sound correspondence than consonant letters, and because the rules governing their use are so much more complex, there seems to be no reason to burden new readers with these complexities if they can identify words without them. (Of course, a more mature reader, who will begin to encounter words in reading that are not in his or her speaking vocabulary, will need to know such rules in order to discover how to pronounce new words. Such rules are also useful in spelling.)

Second, we think this procedure meets the major criticism leveled by "inside-out" theorists against phonics instruction: the criticism that children who are directed to sound out words end up laboriously picking apart the pieces of unfamiliar words and lose sight of the real goal of reading—to extract meaning from print. The kind of phonics instruction developed in these programs encourages children to use only those phonic cues that are needed in conjunction with context clues to recognize words. On the other hand, children do get exposure to the idea that our alphabet uses letters to represent sounds—an idea that may stimulate many of them to search for phonic patterns not yet introduced in explicit instruction.

A final note about phonics instruction is a reiteration of the problem of segmentation skills discussed in the section on prereading. Children who cannot segment will benefit from phonics instruction only with great difficulty. A child who is not progressing at this stage of reading instruction should be tested for segmentation skills. Such skills should be developed before the child is put through the frustration of lessons from which he or she cannot benefit.

Development of Automatization

Chall's (Vol. 1) model of the sequence of reading development suggests that after students attain an insight into the way an alphabetic writing system operates, they should be exposed to large amounts of familiar reading materials. Not having to expend much effort on obtaining information from the text, the child can learn to recognize and make use of the redundancies in written language. As a result of this exposure, the decoding skills that were developed in Stage One will become so well practiced as to become automatic.

The development of automaticity is one of the most frequently discussed issues in these volumes. It is the development of automaticity that marks the transition from beginning reading to skilled reading. Many contributors assume, as does Chall (Vol. 1), that automaticity comes through practice and frequency of exposure, and several advocate the use of old-fashioned drill methods of instruction to attain the overlearning required for automaticity (Fletcher, Vol. 2; Perfetti & Lesgold, Vol. 1). Virtually all reading programs examined provide drills and practice exercises, and most provide a large enough variety of such exercises to allow students who need extra work to practice the same skills in several different tasks. Some programs remind teachers that students should practice skills until they become automatic. For example, in the *READ Series* (1968), it is recommended that children who finish the self-instructional units early should repeat them to establish necessary overlearning. The obvious difficulty with this is that only the faster students end up getting the extra practice; it is probably the slower students who need it most. SRA's *Basic Reading Series* (1970) introduces the concept of automaticity in the earliest teachers' guide. It recommends that students make a game of repeating drills, each time a little faster. This emphasis on speed is supposed to develop automaticity. The problem with drills and with extensive exposure to already familiar materials is that neither is very motivating. This produces a challenging dilemma. We are proposing that children who have difficulty with learning to read are most in need of extra exposure and practice. On the other hand, it has often been pointed out that these same children seriously lack motivation to learn or to achieve in school. Is it practical to suggest that the children who seem to have the least intrinsic motivation ought to be given extra doses of the least motivating instructional techniques?

There may be a solution to this problem in the use of such behavioral techniques as positive reinforcement or response cost. A recent study by Brent and Routh (1978), for instance, showed that the performance of poor readers on a word-recognition task increased significantly when tokens were taken away from the students for incorrect responses. Haring and Hauck (1969) described a successful remedial reading program implemented in Seattle that used behavioral techniques to keep students diligently working on practice materials.

The use of behavioral techniques in reading instruction has been criticized on the ground that they may weaken the intrinsic value of reading (Gibson & Levin, 1975). This notion is supported by a series of studies carried out by Lepper and several colleagues (e.g., Lepper, Greene, & Nisbett, 1973). Typically, in these studies, children participated in an activity that had been established through pretesting to be enjoyable for that age group. Some of the children were told that they would be rewarded for this play; others were rewarded unexpectedly, after playing; still others received no reward. Some time later, the children were observed in a free-play setting in which they could participate in the same activity or in a number of different ones. Children who had earlier expected a reward for participating in the selected activity spent less time in that activity than children who had not expected rewards. These studies have been interpreted in terms of self-attributional processes. The child who was to be rewarded for coloring with magic markers presumably said, "I'm doing this in order to get that reward." Children who did not expect a reward were thinking, "I'm doing this because I like to do it." Those who made the latter attribution were more likely to participate voluntarily in the activity at a later time. Applying this research to reading instruction, one might conclude that children should not be rewarded for reading (or for other academic performance) lest they lose their intrinsic motivation to read.

There are a number of reasons that this line of research might not apply directly to problems in reading instruction. Ross (1977) pointed out that children in this type of attribution study were rewarded simply for participating in an activity, and the rewards were in no way contingent on quality of performance. Clearly, in most educational settings, rewards should be contingent not on engaging in an activity but on quality of performance. Ross described three studies that showed that intrinsic motivation is not reduced by the expectation of rewards that are contingent upon quality of performance and may in fact be increased in such situations.

Based on this evidence, and on the success reported by Haring and Hauck (1969), we conclude that the use of tangible rewards may be a very useful way of ensuring the necessary repetitive practice needed for some children to attain automaticity. Because children differ in the amount of practice they need for a response to become automatic, a good reading program should contain ample opportunity for drill and practice, which can be skipped over by children who do not need such help. Assessment techniques should be provided to help teachers determine which children need to spend more time in this area. Perfetti and Lesgold (Vol. 1) suggest that reaction-time measures be used in the classroom in order to monitor the development of automaticity.

Chall's theory would suggest that automaticity should develop after basic decoding skills have been mastered—not so much by drills as by practice in reading familiar materials. Several programs recommend reading each passage twice, once silently and once orally, and the *Macmillan Reading Program* (1974), in an effort to promote confidence and fluency, frequently presents reading passages that contain no new words. Classrooms are also provided with a set of "Discovery Books," which children are encouraged to read on their own. A number of other publishers provide similar short, easy-to-read books to supplement readers. Efforts that have been made to provide disadvantaged children with books of their own may well serve the purpose of encouraging rereading of familiar materials.

In spite of all the materials available for use in a "firming-up" stage, the critical variables here may be the amount of classroom time devoted to "free" or "independent" reading and the amount of encouragement and aid given to the child in selecting and reading books on familiar and interesting topics.

Development of Comprehension Skills

As noted earlier, there are no programs of reading instruction that ignore comprehension. Even the most extreme "outside-in" theorist agrees that comprehension is the essential goal of reading instruction. There are differences in the level of comprehension assessed, however. Whereas SRA's *Basic Reading Series* (1970) briefly assesses children's ability to understand and remember events and details from a passage, American Book Company's *Triple "I" Series* (1970) probes for more critical evaluation, with questions such as, "Should the little boy have done that?" and "What would you do if you were there?" Bartlett's (Vol. 2) evaluation of the *Open Court Reading Program* (1975) and *Distar Reading* (1974) contrasts the two along this dimension of depth of comprehension required. She expresses the belief that children should be exposed to good literature and encouraged to evaluate reading materials critically from the earliest stages of reading instruction. This would seem to be at odds with Chall's suggestion that children begin to read for information and critically evaluate reading materials only after they have well-established, automatized decoding skills. We would concur with Chall that the most important development in the early stages of reading is the establishment and sharpening of decoding skills. But learning and enjoyment should also come from reading at the earliest stages. We agree with Bartlett that probing discussions and challenging questions about the stories are good ways to encourage the development of some very good habits—critical, thoughtful reading. Although this aspect of development should take preeminence only after decoding has been mastered, some work in this area is probably appropriate from the beginning of reading instruction.

Besides considering the comprehension questions asked about the stories in a reading primer, it is important to consider the comprehensibility of the stories for young readers. Generally, the stories offered in the earliest primers are not stories at all: They are simply a few very short sentences made up of the few words that the children are able to read. As the reading vocabulary grows, however, the stories become more complex, and complete understanding may require some rather sophisticated inferences. Of course, there are many levels of understanding of a good story, and interest can be maintained in stories that are not completely understood (as witnessed by the enthusiasm young children show for detective programs on television). Nevertheless, it seems probable that a story will be most successful if it is written in such a way as to be understandable but not too simple for its audience. The work of Frederiksen (Vol. 1) and Gregg and Farnham-Diggory (Vol. 3) addresses this issue. They are attempting to discover more about the kinds of inferences children will and will not make at various ages. Meanwhile, it is not difficult to see that some of the stories we offer to young children are simply not going to be comprehensible at the deeper levels. For instance, the Scott, Foresman *Reading Unlimited* (1976) program reviewed in Popp's (Vol. 3) chapter presents first graders with a short version of the Grimms' fairy tale, *Rumplestiltskin,* in which a greedy king locks a helpless maiden in a room with instructions to spin straw into gold or else be killed. A little man comes along and helps the maiden in distress, and she promises to give him her first child. The maiden marries the king, has a child, and refuses to honor her promise to the little man, who becomes so distressed that he pounds his foot into the floor and splits himself in two. The greedy king and the queen who broke her promise live happily ever after. Clearly, this is not the kind of story that can help a first grader to learn more about the social world. Young children need a lot more help than this story or the accompanying activities in the teachers' manual could provide in identifying motives and plans and in generating explanations for the behavior of other people.

FINAL COMMENTS

We have seen our task in preparing this chapter as having several aspects. First, we wanted to assess whether the volumes brought out a well-rounded discussion of what research and theory claim to say about the nature of the reading process and about how beginning reading should be taught. Second, and related to this, we wanted to examine whether the contributors to the series identified significant areas for further research in reading and its teaching. Third, we wanted to try to assess the "ecological validity" of reading theory and research—that is, whether its assumptions as to what problems are significant are correct in terms of the actual problems and decisions that appear to have been faced by authors of curricular materials for the teaching of beginning reading. But fourth, we wanted to look at the other side of this coin—that is, whether authors of instructional materials have adequately perceived what their real problems are and whether they could profit from considering the theories and findings of theorists and researchers.

On the first of these questions, it immediately became obvious, on inspecting the variety of chapters in the three volumes, that the participants addressed a wide range of basic and central issues on the nature of the reading process and the ways in which reading behavior is learned. Considering the chapters in the aggregate, we found thorough coverage of what we regard as important and crucial problems in the design of prereading programs, procedures for teaching decoding skills, and ways of promoting skill automatization and meaning comprehension. Although there seem to be disagreements about the nature of the reading process, these disagreements turn out to be on matters of emphasis. For example, in the contrast between "inside-out" and "outside-in" theories of the reading process, theorists seem to feel that there must be both "outside-in" processes involving stimulation by print and "inside-out" processes involving interpretation of stimuli through the use of the readers' knowledge of the language and knowledge of the world; they disagree as to which processes are more important and should be given priority in teaching reading. We ourselves conclude that in early stages, "inside-out" and motivational processes are very important but that even more important is the teaching of "outside-in" processes, whereby the child is taught what print stimuli represent so that he or she can learn to use "inside-out" processes to interpret those stimuli.

One of the most important ideas we found stressed in the chapters and discussions is the importance of segmentation skills as prerequisites to instruction in phonic cues. The evidence tentatively offered suggests that possession of these skills might make all the difference in whether a child succeeds in acquiring adequate decoding skills and that attention to these prerequisite skills might be crucial, therefore, in resolving the question of whether decoding skills are to be addressed in early reading instruction. Obviously, further research is needed to firm up this speculation; research on the importance of segmentation skills in early reading indeed becomes a most significant area for further study in reading research.

Inspection of actual reading programs and instructional materials could lead a reading theorist and researcher to a certain amount of despair. One could feel that these materials are developed without any consideration whatsoever of the results of reading research and theoretical formulations; teachers' manuals and general informational literature about programs do not often make any explicit mention of research findings and theories.

Probably this impression—that reading programs do not take adequate account of research and advances in theory—would be incorrect. There is evidence that authors of reading programs are cognizant of reading research; some of these authors are themselves researchers. Furthermore, we note that currently available programs do put more emphasis on reading research and theory than they used to; for example, it appears that current programs lay more stress on decoding skills than previously—partly in response, we believe, to pronouncements and writings of people like Chall who have indicated the importance of those skills. Thus, authors and publishers of reading programs are to a considerable extent sensitive to research findings— at least to the writings of leaders in the field who try to summarize and integrate these findings.

We have fairly high hopes for the impact of the present series of volumes on future work in the design of instructional programs. For example, it is conceivable that more programs will begin to make provisions for teaching segmentation skills in early phases of reading instruction. Likewise, more programs may develop more systematic instruction in phonic cues and their uses in early stages of instruction, and programs may begin to introduce more adequate techniques of promoting motivation, better procedures for ensuring automatization of word-recognition skills, and better programs for increasing comprehension as the child proceeds through the reading program.

Much of the current effort to describe reading in terms of cognitive processes is probably not directly relevant to the development of instructional programs—it feeds theoretical discussion more than it finds application in the details of teaching procedures. This does not mean that such research is unimportant. Clarifying the component processes in mature reading and in the attainment of maturity in reading will help to support decisions as to what is most important to emphasize at various stages of learning. For example, the finding that many students at the high-school level who have trouble in reading have that trouble because of inadequate word-recognition skills indicates that stress should be put on the attainment of rapid word-recognition skills, perhaps more than on comprehension skills. Similarly, a finding that poor comprehension skills are primarily traceable to deficits in vocabulary and information rather than to difficulties in understanding syntax would lead to greater emphasis on teaching vocabulary and information (if indeed this were to be the finding). The present technology of research in reading promises to give much more revealing answers to problems of this sort than research of the past that has depended primarily on static correlational analyses. One has the feeling that in view of the enormous amount of research that has been done on reading over the past five decades, we have long ago identified most of the variables that are relevant to reading, but we do not know which of these variables are most important, either in individual cases or over groups of individuals.

In raising the question of whether authors of reading materials have taken adequate account of research findings, and whether they have correctly identified what problems they should address, we note that instructional programs and materials vary widely with respect to their emphases. Some emphasize decoding and other "outside-in" processes, whereas others emphasize comprehension and other "inside-out" processes. It would seem that many programs have overlooked problems of segmentation and selective attention. These observations suggest that authors of instructional programs do indeed need guidance from research that indicates what approaches are more effective and what problems need to be addressed.

We come around to trying to answer the question posed in the title of this chapter, which was couched in an orthography that was intended to suggest an answer. Note that a reader trained only in "decoding" processes might in the extreme case not be able to understand the title except as a string of spoken words whose meanings would confuse him or her. And a reader trained only in "inside-out" processes would have even more trouble, hardly being able to guess the meaning intended because he or she would have trouble decoding the words in the first place. The theories and research reviewed in these volumes suggest, however, that beginning readers given adequate teaching in both "outside-in" and "inside-out" processes would be able to state the question and give its answer: Yes, the real reading problem has been laid bare.

REFERENCES

Anderson, I. R., & Dearborn, W. F. *The psychology of teaching reading.* New York: Ronald, 1952.

Baratz, J. C. Teaching reading in an urban Negro school system. In J. C. Baratz & R. Shuy (Eds.), *Teaching black children to read.* Washington, D. C.: Center for Applied Linguistics, 1969.

Baron, J., & Strawson, C. Use of orthographic and word-specific knowledge in reading words aloud. *Journal of Experimental Psychology: Human Perception and Performance,* 1976, *2,* 386–393.

Brent, D. E., & Routh, D. K. Response cost and impulsive word recognition errors in reading-disabled children. *Journal of Abnormal Child Psychology,* 1978, *6,* 211–219.

Carroll, J. B., & Chall, J. S. (Eds.). *Toward a literate society: The report of the commitee on reading of the National Academy of Education.* New York: McGraw-Hill, 1975.

Chall, J. S. *Learning to read: The great debate.* New York: McGraw-Hill, 1967.

Clymer, T. The utility of phonemic generalizations in the primary grades. *Reading Teacher,* 1962–1963, *16*(4), 252–258.

Conant, J. B. *Learning to read: A report of a conference of reading experts.* Princeton, N.J.: Educational Testing Service, n.d. (Published in 1962.)

Flesch, R. *Why Johnny can't read and what you can do about it.* New York: Harper, 1955.

Fox, B., & Routh, D. K. Analyzing spoken language into words, syllables, and phonemes: A developmental study. *Journal of Psycholinguistic Research,* 1975, *4,* 331–342.

Frumkin, B., & Anisfeld, M. Semantic and surface codes in the memory of deaf children. *Cognitive Psychology,* 1977, *9,* 475–493.

Gibson, E. J., & Levin, H. *The psychology of reading.* Cambridge, Mass.: MIT Press, 1975.

Haring, N. G., & Hauck, M. A. Improved learning conditions in the establishment of reading skills with disabled readers. *Exceptional Children,* 1969, *35,* 341–352.

Kavanagh, J. F., & Mattingly, I. *Language by ear and by eye: The relationships between speech and reading.* Cambridge, Mass.: MIT Press, 1972.

Lepper, M. R., Greene, D., & Nisbett, R. E. Undermining chidren's intrinsic interest with extrinsic reward: A test of the "overjustification" hypothesis. *Journal of Personality and Social Psychology,* 1973, *28,* 129–137.

Miller, G. A. (Ed.). *Linguistic communication: Perspectives for research* (Report of the study group on linguistic communication to the National Institute of Education). Newark, Del.: International Reading Association, 1973.

National Advisory Committee on Dyslexia and Related Reading Disorders. *Reading disorders in the United States.* Chicago: Developmental Learning Materials, 1970.

Olson, D. R. Review of Carroll and Chall's *Toward a literate society: The report of the Commitee on Reading of the National Academy of Education. Proceedings of the National Academy of Education,* 1975, *2,* 109–178.

Petty, W. T. Review of Carroll and Chall's *Toward a literate society: The report of the Committee on Reading of the National Academy of Education. Research in the Teaching of English,* 1977, *11,* 68–70.

Popp, H. M. Current practices in the teaching of beginning reading. In J. B. Carroll & J. S. Chall (Eds.), *Toward a literate society: The report of the Committee on Reading of the National Academy of Education.* New York: McGraw-Hill, 1975.

Reber, A. S., & Scarborough, D. L. *Toward a psychology of reading: The proceedings of the CUNY conferences.* Hillsdale, N.J.: Lawrence Erlbaum Associates, 1977.

Rosenberg, S. Association and phrase structure in sentence recall. *Journal of Verbal Learning & Verbal Behavior,* 1968, *7,* 1077–1081.

Rosner, J., & Simon, D. The auditory analysis test: An initial report. *Journal of Learning Disabilities,* 1971, *4,* 383–392.

Ross, A. O. *Psychological aspects of learning disabilities and reading disorders.* New York: McGraw-Hill, 1976.

Ross, M. The self-perception of intrinsic motivation. In J. H. Harvey, W. J. Ickes, & R. F. Kidd (Eds.), *New directions in attribution research* (Vol. 1). Hillsdale, N.J.: Lawrence Erlbaum Associates, 1977.

Rumelhart, D. E. Toward an interactive model of reading. In S. Dornič (Ed.), *Attention and performance VI.* Hillsdale, N.J.: Lawrence Erlbaum Associates, 1977.

Smith, F. Decoding: The great fallacy. In F. Smith (Ed.), *Psycholinguistics and reading.* New York: Holt, Rinehart & Winston, 1973.

Taylor, W. L. Cloze procedure: A new tool for measuring readability. *Journalism Quarterly,* 1953, *30,* 415–433.

Wallach, M. A., & Wallach, L. *Teaching all children to read.* Chicago: University of Chicago Press, 1976.

Reading Programs

Bank Street Readers. Bank Street College of Education. New York: Macmillan, 1973.

Basic Reading Series. D. Rasmussen & L. Goldberg. Chicago: Science Research Associates, 1970.

Betts' Basic Readers. E. A. Betts & C. M. Welch. New York: American Book Company, 1963.

Bookmark Reading Program. M. Early, E. K. Cooper, N. Santevsania, & M. Adell. New York: Harcourt Brace Jovanovich, 1970.

Design for Reading. Harper & Row. New York: Harper & Row, 1973.

Distar Reading. S. Engelmann & E. C. Bruner. Chicago: Science Research Associates, 1974.

Houghton Mifflin Readers. W. K. Durr, J. M. Lepere, & M. L. Alsin. Boston: Houghton Mifflin, 1974.

Language Experiences in Reading. R. Van Allen & C. Allen. Chicago: Encyclopedia Brittanica Educational Corporation, 1970.

Macmillan Reading Program. A. J. Harris & M. K. Clark. New York: Macmillan, 1974.

New Primary Grades Reading System. Beck, I. Pittsburgh: Learning Research and Development Center, 1972.

Open Court Reading Program. Open Court. LaSalle, Ill.: Open Court, 1975.

The Palo Alto Reading Program: Sequential Steps in Reading. T. E. Glim. New York: Harcourt Brace Jovanovich, 1973.

Reading Experience and Development (READ) Series. M. S. Johnson, R. A. Kress, & J. D. McNeil. New York: American Book Company, 1968.

Reading 720. Clymer, T., Christenson, B., & Brown, Y. Lexington, Mass.: Ginn, 1976.

Reading Unlimited. Scott, Foresman. Glenview, Ill.: Scott, Foresman, 1976.

Sheldon Basic Reading Series. W. D. Sheldon & Q. B. Mills. Boston: Allyn & Bacon, 1973.

Triple "I" Series. J. M. Franco & J. Kelley. New York: American Book Company, 1970.

15 Toward a Usable Psychology of Reading Instruction

Lauren B. Resnick
University of Pittsburgh

The last decade has witnessed a remarkable renewal of interest among psychologists in the psychology of reading processes. Major works have been devoted to the psychology of reading, and several psychologists have heralded a return, after 50 or so years of neglect, to active concern with describing the processes of reading (Gibson & Levin, 1975; Venezky, 1977). But even while celebrating this renewed attention to reading, certain cognitive psychologists have expressed doubt about whether basic research on reading will have much to say, in a direct way, about instruction. Gibson and Levin, whose book on the psychology of reading has done much to both mark and advance the growing interest of psychologists in reading, question whether their research can, "in the end, help children learn to read [p.xi]." The present volumes were specifically intended to explore and document the contributions of basic research in the psychology of reading to reading instruction. Yet, even here, doubts about the present and the possible contributions of psychological research are expressed, not only by the more practically oriented contributors (see, for example, the chapter by Clay, Vol. 2) but also by psychologists themselves (e.g., Kintsch, Vol. 1; Smith & Kleiman, and Venezky, Vol. 2). Why should it be the case that even those who have made a considerable contribution to understanding the processes of reading are so uncertain about the contributions of their own and their colleagues' work to reading instruction? Why is linking the theory-based research effort to the largely intuitively driven instructional effort so difficult?

Reviewing the various chapters of these volumes has led me to understand these difficulties better. The task has made it clear to me that the psychology of reading *instruction* cannot be simply the psychology of reading processes "applied" to education. Instead, the psychology of reading instruction has a set of questions of its own, questions that concern the ways in which the environmental interventions we call instruction interact with cognitive processes to modify competence. The bulk of the present chapter illustrates this point by presenting some of the questions a psychology of reading instruction must address and by considering how the attempt to answer these questions may require us to modify our traditional research approaches. Before turning to this task, however, it is worth pausing to consider the forces within the field of psychology that have contributed to its present difficulty in addressing questions of instruction in reading.

TWO STREAMS OF PSYCHOLOGICAL RESEARCH

When, in the early 1960s, American psychologists began once again to turn their attention to questions of education, two groups of psychologists—the "established" learning psychologists and the nascent cognitive psychologists—vied for preeminence. Learning psychologists (especially Skinner, and those who developed his interest in instructional technology) and the cognitive psychologists (Jerome Bruner and George Miller, for example) recommended very different prescriptions for improving educational practice and for conducting psychological research on instruction. But it is not often recognized that the two branches of psychology were actually addressing different sets of instructional issues.

Most research in cognitive psychology has been largely concerned with describing mental processes in what can be described as steady-state situations. In the growing body of cognitive task analyses (see Resnick, 1976, for an analysis of the forms that task analysis has taken in cognitive/instructional psychology), for example, what is modeled or described is typically a "snapshot" of task performance. Although temporally organized processes are recognized, models of cognitive performance assume that no important changes occur *during the period being modeled.* It is true that in many cognitive studies, data are examined for practice effects—that is, for the possibility that subjects perform differently in later than in earlier trials. However, evidence of a practice effect usually leads the cognitive psychologist to drop early trials from the data analysis (because they do not represent full competence) or, at best, to give separate descriptions of earlier and later performance. Thus, even when changes in processing in the course of performance have been recognized, there has usually been no attempt to describe the processes involved in the *transition* from one kind of processing to another.

This general characterization is as true of developmental studies of cognition as it is of studies of a single age group. Although developmental studies typically compare performances at different ages, the descriptions for any one age are steady-state descriptions. There is at the present time no well-developed theory of *acquisition* within developmental psychology, although cognitive psychologists have begun to note the need for theories of transition and thus of learning (e.g., Trabasso's chapter, Vol. 3; and Anderson, Kline, & Beasley, in press; Estes, 1976).

Cognitive psychology's lack of concern with transitions in competence must be contrasted with traditional learning psychology's pervasive interest in transitions. Learning theories had weak or nonexistent descriptions of what goes on, mentally, during a given performance, but they did develop detailed descriptions of external events that lead to changes in performance. In fact, learning was defined in these theories as a change in performance, and research attention was directed to what produced the changes (practice, timing, stimulus conditions, rewards, etc.). Some learning psychologies—particularly operant psychology—were especially concerned with arranging environmental events so as to enhance learning; these branches of psychology can appropriately be called *intervention sciences.*

We have within psychology, then, two kinds of thinking about instructional matters. In one, detailed attention is paid to what the processes of cognition are, but the transition from one level of competence to another is largely ignored. In the other, the conditions that produce transitions are described quite carefully, but the nature of the mental processes themselves is ignored. Recent research on reading processes is clearly rooted in cognitive rather than learning psychology. As a result, this research has for the most part been unable to address directly the general question of how reading skill is acquired, or the more particular question of how intervention can foster the acquisition of this skill. A psychology of instruction, in reading or any other subject matter, cannot neglect these questions; they lie at the heart of instructional psychology. On the other hand, we cannot simply return to the old learning psychology, for a psychology of instruction cannot omit, in the way that learning psychology did, detailed descriptions of skilled, novice, and intermediate levels of performance. Descriptions of performance provide, at the least, the landmarks by which instruction can be monitored—the eventual goals of instruction and some of the intermediate points en route. What is needed, then, for a viable and usable psychology of reading instruction is a joining of cognitive psychology and certain aspects of learning psychology to create a cognitive psychology of learning.

I attempt in the remainder of this chapter to consider: (1) what a psychology of reading instruction that joins these two lines of psychological thought might be like; and (2) where we stand with respect to its development. I do this in relation to a number of issues that seem to me to be promising, perhaps even essential, for a new instructional psychology of reading. These include: (1) the role of developmental research in elucidating the relationship between skilled performance and the acquisition of reading skill; (2) the relationship between individual differences and instruction in reading; and (3) the role of invention and discovery in learning to read. In the course of the discussion, I suggest how cognitive and learning psychology might draw upon each other in responding to these issues.

SKILLED PERFORMANCE AND ACQUISITION: THE QUESTION OF DEVELOPMENT

Much of the current research on reading processes focuses on skilled performance, and many chapters in these volumes reflect this predominant concern. Research is reported here on how information is acquired from the written text, how this new information is related to information already held by the individual, how strategies are used in interacting with a text, and so forth. The individuals studied in most of this research already know how to read, usually with considerable skill. Research of this kind can be thought of as psychological task analysis; it is designed to determine empirically how people actually perform aspects of a complex family of tasks that we call reading. Kintsch (Vol. 1) calls for an extension and elaboration of this kind of task analysis as a basis of instructional design, and this call is implicitly echoed in the comments and analyses of several other contributors. One can hardly disagree that the psychology of instruction must attend to the nature of skilled performance as a kind of target toward which instruction must work. Nevertheless, I do not believe that an understanding of skilled task performance will, by itself, produce the recommendations for instructional practice that we seek. Knowing how skilled readers read may not automatically tell us what should be taught to beginners. Instead, novices may need to proceed through stages of acquisition and development in which their performance is quite different from skilled performance.

Failure to distinguish between skilled performance and performances useful during acquisition and instruction is part of the reason that today's psychology of reading does not always illuminate questions of instruction. A good example is the debate, actively pursued in the pages of these volumes, over direct versus mediated access to meaning. The question generally posed is whether skilled readers translate printed material into a phonemic representation, which in turn allows them to recognize a meaningful word, or whether they directly access meaning from the print itself. It is sometimes assumed that resolution of the question with respect to skilled readers will prescribe the extent of instruction in "code-breaking" (translating print into sound) that beginning readers should recieve. An assumption is implicitly made, in other words, that performance during the acquisition of a skill is simply a less smooth version of skilled performance, and that what we teach the novice should match as directly as possible the processes that the expert will employ. But even if we suppose, for the sake of argument, that skilled readers access meaning directly from print, it does not necessarily mean that beginning readers will not profit from instruction in phonemic translation skills. In fact, it is quite possible that the only way to become a skilled reader—one who can bypass phonemic translation—is to learn the process of phonemic translation first.

Venezky and Massaro (Vol. 1) suggest how this might work. They argue that skilled readers respond directly to information carried in spelling patterns of the language, without any translation to phonemic form. This orthographic information, in other words, leads directly to meaning. Responding to orthographic information, however, requires the reader to attend to patterns of letter grouping and letter order—the same patterns that must be attended to in learning phonemic translation skills. On the basis of this analysis, Venezky and Massaro propose that an excellent, and perhaps the only, way of learning to use the orthographic information of the language is to learn phonemic decoding.

It is important to note that Venezky and Massaro's suggestion that code instruction, with its demands for phonemic translation, may assist people in acquiring the ability to access meaning directly from print is essentially an inference from analysis of skilled reading performance. They have not attempted to trace experimentally a course of development in which eventual skill in picking up orthographic information depends on having early experience in phonemic decoding. A developmental research program of this kind is what would be needed to establish empirically their claim that code or phonics instruction is an important step in developing skill in reading, even though skilled reading does not necessarily include phonemic translation of print.

It is perhaps not surprising that a new claim such as Venezky and Massaro's is not yet supported by developmental studies. What is surprising is how little developmental knowledge we have of *any* aspects of reading. Gibson and Levin (1975), in their detailed interpretive review of the literature on the psychology of reading, describe studies on the development of visual perception and general cognitive strategies but report few developmental studies of the reading process itself. Doehring's (1976) report of changes in word-processing skills between kindergarten and 11th grade probably represents the most extensive data base on the development of reading processes now in existence. In these volumes, only a few chapters directly address developmental concerns. Smith and Kleiman's (Vol. 2) extensive and thorough review of research on word-recognition processes, for example, touches hardly at all on how these processes develop. Only two chapters (Juola, Schadler, Chabot, McCaughey, & Wait, Vol. 2; Liberman & Shankweiler, Vol. 2) are explicitly concerned with the development of word-recognition skill. Juola et al. found that second graders were already performing like adults, and quite differently from the nonreading kindergartners, on a set of word-recognition and visual-search tasks. As these authors suggest, investigations of changes in word-recognition processes in the critical early months of learning to read are needed. Also needed is an extension of this kind of cross-age comparison to more complex processes that may show developmental shifts later in the learning process. Research of this kind is reported by Liberman and Shankweiler (Vol. 2), who found changes in specific kinds of oral-reading errors over the second- through fourth-grade period.

Cross-age comparisons such as these are an important first step toward a usable psychology of reading instruction. At the most global level, they serve to alert us to the fact that skilled readers do not spring forth "full-blown" at age 6 or 7 and that there are differences between the way beginners attack the task and the way skilled readers perform. They thus warn us against making the assumption that prescriptions for instruction can be derived directly from the characteristics of skilled performance—as the early advocates of whole-word recognition wanted it to do, and as some contributors to the present volumes (e.g., Goodman & Goodman, Vol. 1; Smith, Vol. 2) still appear to recommend. At a more detailed level, developmental studies of reading acquisition can suggest performance rules that may be directly taught or that may serve as a basis for diagnostic instruments for monitoring and guiding instruction. But cross-age comparisons alone cannot provide a firm foundation for instruction, because such studies can neither deal directly with transitions in competence nor establish reliably that observed stages of reading skill are characteristic of each *individual's* development.

Contrastive Studies of Good and Poor Readers. An approach that complements cross-age comparisons, by focusing on differences in skill rather than differences in age, is one that compares the reading processes of individuals of the same age whose reading ability differs. In these studies, good and poor readers are compared on various component processes of word recognition or text processing. This is a very common research strategy in the psychology of reading; a list of studies comparing good and poor readers could easily fill several pages. The work of Perfetti and Lesgold (Vol. 1) on "automaticity" of word recognition is an example of this research strategy. Perfetti and Lesgold show that people who do well on reading comprehension tests (good readers) recognize words more quickly than people who do poorly on comprehension tests (poor readers). Both groups can read the words correctly; yet a reliable difference in speed of recognition exists. Perfetti and Lesgold argue that the extra time needed by the poorer readers shows that they are using a more complicated and less automatic word-recognition strategy than the good readers. This complicated strategy creates a "bottleneck" in the poorer readers' working memory. That is, since working memory can accommodate only a limited number of operations at once, and since simply recognizing words involves many operations for the poorer readers, the poorer readers have less "space" left for comprehension work than the better, more "automatic" readers do. Lower scores on comprehension tests, the argument goes, are partly the consequence of this overcrowding of working memory.

The finding of automaticity differences, and its interpretation in terms of a working memory bottleneck, would seem to suggest that weaker readers' general reading skill could be improved by providing word-recognition drills in order to increase automaticity. This should free the individual for more comprehension work. This form of instruction has had at least a limited trial; in one study (Fleisher, Jenkins & Pany, 1978), it produced greater speed in word recognition but did not lead to increased comprehension performance. Further experiments are needed, however, before we can conclude that word drill does not foster comprehension. These experiments would need to ensure that the instructional treatment was quite substantial, not just a session or two of practice, as is often the case in laboratory training studies. Furthermore, the practice might be effective largely in helping people to benefit from subsequent *training* in comprehension, not in directly producing improved comprehension performance. Some form of transfer experiment would be needed to test for this kind of indirect effect.

Perfetti and Lesgold anticipated the possibility that automaticity training might not improve comprehension. In doing so, they acknowledged one weakness of contrastive studies: The data collected in such studies are essentially correlational and thus do not permit strong causal inferences. For example, automaticity might *come from* practice in reading meaningful material rather than *fostering* the ability to comprehend what is read. If so, other skills, unspecified in the Perfetti and Lesgold model but essential to effective comprehension, might also be acquired through practice in reading for meaning. In this case, automaticity in recognizing individual words would have to be interpreted as merely a signal that the whole process of learning to read is going well. Such an interpretation, and the instructional practice of providing many opportunities for reading for meaning, would fit well with Chall's (Vol. 1) proposal that a long period of reading familiar materials is required to develop fluency. It would undoubtedly also be congenial to the Goodmans (Vol. 1) and F. Smith (Vol. 2), who argue against any reading instruction that is not clearly oriented toward processing for meaning.

It is important to note in this context another fundamental difficulty in drawing instructional implications from contrastive data. Even when reliable differences in processing can be found, it cannot necessarily be assumed that the poorer readers are simply less advanced than better readers but are on the same developmental track. It is at least possible that good and poor readers are proceeding along different developmental tracks and that the processes observed or inferred for the less skilled are symptoms of generally less adaptive strategies rather than slower development. This would mean that instruction in any single subskill, such as automatic word recognition, would be unlikely by itself to change weak readers into strong ones, because the observed subskill differences are actually indicators of a whole "package" of differences between good and poor performers. Why some readers might adopt less efficient strategies than others is a question that has barely been raised, and I know of no research addressed directly to it. Some of the authors in these volumes, such as the Goodmans and F. Smith, suggest that too much insistence on overt decoding during early reading instruction may encourage an overly deliberate approach to reading and may actually interfere with the development of more efficient reading processes. To my knowledge, no direct evidence to support such a claim exists, but it is the kind of hypothesis that clearly bears investigation. Such investigations, however, cannot proceed within either a cross-age or a contrastive paradigm, because neither strategy permits direct observation of acquisition sequences. Instead, longitudinal research designs will be required.

Longitudinal Studies of Reading Development. Unlike cross-age and contrastive research, which examine reading processes in steady-state conditions, longitudinal research examines changes in reading processes as individuals, over time, become more competent readers. This approach allows for relatively direct observation of how reading skill develops and how processes such as automatic word recognition, semantic access, and the like are related to reading at various points in development. Longitudinal studies of reading development are rare, however, and it is difficult to find data on the cognitive processes underlying changes in reading performance. A research project currently underway at the Learning Research and Development Center in Pittsburgh may begin to fill this gap. Alan Lesgold, Isabel Beck, and I are conducting a longitudinal study of children in two quite different reading programs: a systematic decoding program developed by Beck (described here by Popp, Vol. 3) and a more eclectic but essentially "whole-word"-oriented basal reading program. When each child reaches a specified point in the instructional sequence, he or she is tested for general visual processing speed, speed of word recognition, and speed of semantic access for both words and sentences (e.g., how quickly the child can decide whether the word "rabbit" or "chair" shown on a screen is an animal). These tests use words drawn from the instructional program that the children have studied and from "transfer" words that conform to the same orthographic patterns as the program words. In addition to these reading process measures, the children's fluency in oral reading and the numbers and types of errors they make are measured, using texts made up of words they have been taught and transfer words. The time between tests is relatively short; children are usually tested every 2 months or so, depending on their rate of progress through the instructional programs. About 300 children are now being followed in this study. On the basis of this data, we expect to be able to describe individual children's sequences of acquisition in relation to their instructional program and to their progress within the program.

This study has potential for answering several long-debated questions concerning reading instruction. Consider, for example, the question of whether code-oriented instruction prompts children to ignore meaning as they read or, conversely, whether meaning-oriented instruction prompts children to ignore the code and guess at words indiscriminately. There is already some evidence (Barr, 1974-1975) that the reading errors made by children in code-oriented programs are different from those made by children in language-oriented programs. Children in code programs make errors based on orthographic similarity almost from the beginning of their reading instruction, whereas language-oriented learners make these errors later in their development. The Pittsburgh longitudinal study, conducted in two contrasting instructional contexts, will allow us to check on findings of this kind and to draw out their implications for instruction. If children in the Beck code-oriented program make context-based errors as early and to the same extent as children in the basal program (indicating that they are attending to context as much as the basal-taught children), then the claim that code approaches encourage children to ignore context would have to be abandoned. Conversely, if we find that children in the basal program attend to the orthographic structure of words in ways similar to the code-taught children, then the claim that language approaches encourage children to ignore orthography would have to be abandoned.

The general point to be made is that developmental research on reading— whether cross-age, contrastive, or longitudinal—needs to attend to the instructional context in which individuals learn to read. Virtually none of the developmental research on reading up to now has taken into account the nature of the instruction and practice that the individuals being tested have been exposed to. The instructional program is almost never even described (much less analyzed) in developmental studies of reading. Yet it seems quite likely that different instructional programs produce quite different acquisition sequences. To make developmental research more useful to the psychology of reading instruction, we need to relate changes in performance both to the general nature of instruction that children are undergoing and to the exact point they have reached in course of instruction. In other words, we need to treat instructional experience as a crucial independent variable in developmental research on reading.

INDIVIDUAL DIFFERENCES IN READING

Everyone agrees that children do not all learn to read in the same way. The literature on reading instruction is filled with the advice that instruction should be matched to individual differences. This principle seems virtually unassailable. No instruction that fails to take into acount what the learner already knows or does not know can possibly be optimal. But beyond the general advice that individual differences should be respected lies a series of largely unanswered questions that the psychology of reading instruction must try to address. Two general approaches to adapting instruction to individual differences can be identified. I call these the "readiness" approach and the "aptitude-matching" approach.

Readiness. A frequently proposed way of respecting the developmental status of the learner is to ensure that instruction is not offered until the learner is "ready" for some new demand or new concept. Nowhere in education is this notion more firmly established than in reading, where reading readiness tests are part of the standard armamentarium of placement and instructional practice at the beginning of school. Reading-readiness testing has traditionally been based on some estimate of general cognitive competence (many of the items on reading-readiness tests are very similar to those on intelligence tests, and the two kinds of tests tend to correlate rather well) and some measure of visual and auditory perceptual skill. The prevailing view has been that children who are not ready by these criteria will fail in learning to read. The evidence for this belief is largely correlational: Reading-readiness tests are reasonably good predictors of performance on reading tests a few years later. Earlier in the 20th century, the prescription for children who did not show adequate readiness had been to delay reading instruction. Thus the implicit definition of respecting developmental level had been that the instructor should simply wait until readiness appears.

Later, partly in response to readiness tests, many kindergartens in fact introduced programs to teach reading readiness. These programs typically taught children to perform the kinds of tasks that appeared on the readiness tests. This tendency to teach the components of readiness rather than wait for them to develop was reinforced by the social pressures and some of the psychological writing of the 1950s and 1960s. Teaching readiness, rather than just waiting for it to develop, was in keeping with the proposal, originally made by Hunt (1961), that matching instruction to developmental level should properly consist of presenting children with tasks that were slightly beyond their current level of competence—enough beyond to provide a challenge but not so far beyond as to provide no base for constructive cognitive activity.

But teaching readiness skills for reading will prove fruitful only if the skills taught are in fact important in learning to read. Readiness tests validated on the basis of how well they predict later success or failure may be misleading in this respect. Consider, for example, the ability to name the letters of the alphabet. This has traditionally been assessed by nearly all readiness tests, and it does predict later success in learning to read. But naming the letters is not needed for reading. Distinguishing one letter from another is needed, and so is knowing their sound values, but knowing their names is not. Knowing the names prior to entering first grade correlates with exposure to and discussion of printed material during the preschool years and probably for that reason predicts reading success. But teaching children the letter names in the absence of other attention to print and its uses might only marginally improve their chances of learning to read easily. Similarly, although the ability to make precise discriminations among nonspeech sounds (animal sounds, traffic noises) may predict how easily one will learn to read, this may be because the sound discriminations are learned earliest or best by those whose ability to acquire information quickly is greatest—that is, by those children whose general intelligence, by any measure, would test highest. Teaching sound discriminations, unless these discriminations are actually part of the reading process, might do little to improve reading acquisition.

What is needed to pursue successfully the readiness teaching approach is an analysis of the reading task itself in order to identify component or closely related abilities that may be directly instructable. Such task analysis has been undertaken during the past 10 years. Decoding has been analyzed, both logically and empirically, and the incidence of difficulty with particular components of the task has been examined. This line of work is well reflected in these volumes; indeed, certain chapters are models of instructionally relevant psychological research on readiness. Liberman and Shankweiler (Vol. 2), for example, have noted that learning the alphabetic code requires the mapping of graphemes to phonemes but that phonemes are a unit of speech smaller than that to which we normally attend. It seems likely, therefore, that many individuals—particularly young children—might have difficulty in segmenting the speech stream into phonemic units (e.g., hearing the *a* as a separate sound in the word *bat*). This indeed turns out to be the case (a finding echoed by other investigators including Calfee, Chapman, & Venezky, 1972; Rosner, Vol. 2; Wallach & Wallach, Vol. 3). Liberman and Shankweiler propose direct instruction in segmentation for individuals found to be weak at it; they describe one such instructional program, developed in the Soviet Union, and refer to other programs prepared with similar principles in mind.

What is required to complete this line of research and reasoning is to demonstrate that learning to segment does facilitate learning to read.

Preliminary evidence that such instruction can not only improve segmentation ability but transfer to learning to read is offered by a study of Rosner's (1971). Gleitman and Rozin (1973) proposed a less direct attack— one that begins reading instruction by requiring a mapping at the syllable level, and only later introducing a grapheme-by-grapheme (and therefore phoneme-by-phoneme) analysis. Others (for example, Beck & Block, Vol. 1; Wallach & Wallach, Vol. 3) propose that the same deficit can be dealt with by highly structured beginning reading instruction that explicitly associates phonemes with graphemes, thus providing curricular assistance to those children who would ordinarily have the most difficulty with segmentation. All of these approaches seem to be logical ways of addressing children's difficulties with segmenting the speech stream. From a theoretical point of view, separate instruction in segmentation that is then shown to transfer to reading is the most interesting approach, because it shows clearly that segmentation is a component of learning to read. From a strictly practical point of view, however, the three approaches are of equal potential interest, and decisions among them will have to be based on instructional simplicity, cost, and efficiency. Meanwhile, other aspects of readiness—especially those connected with general oral-language competence—need to be attended to with the same kind of experimental care that has characterized work on segmentation.

Aptitude Matching.   A second way of adapting to individual differences is to attempt to match a general instructional strategy to an individual's particular style or aptitude for learning. This approach assumes that individuals have characteristic differences in abilities or in approaches to learning that are sustained over time and across tasks. One adapts to these differences by seeking instructional methods that capitalize on strong points and minimize dependence on weaker abilities. Effective aptitude matching should produce interactions between measured aptitudes and instructional treatments: People with one set of aptitudes should do best under one instructional treatment; people with a different set of aptitudes should prosper most under a different instructional treatment.

There is notably little discussion in these volumes of aptitude-treatment interactions. Perhaps this is because so little of the psychological research on reading acquisition has proceeded in the context of known instructional treatments. For example, despite a traditional belief among reading specialists that children with "visual" styles of learning should be taught differently from those with "auditory" styles (see Bateman's discussion, Vol. 1, of work on modality differences), there appears to have been little empirical support for this notion over the years, and the issue is barely mentioned in these volumes. What is suggested in a number of the more applied chapters is that children with generally weak cognitive skills may profit particularly from structured code teaching in the initial grades, whereas for more generally competent children the method of teaching makes little difference. The general argument is that unstructured teaching, such as in language-experience approaches, depends heavily on prior learning, and we can therefore expect outcomes to be highly correlated with measured general intelligence; this correlation can reduced by use of a more structured and direct teaching approach. This suggestion is in general accord with Cronbach and Snow's (1977) careful review of a portion of the aptitiude-treatment interaction literature for reading. Although no single generalization holds for all studies they reviewed, language-experience methods generally showed the highest correlation with intelligence. Other than this rather general finding, the research literature has little to say about aptitude-treatment inter-actions. Defining aptitudes in terms of the processes known to be involved in reading and then exploring the interaction of these aptitudes with specific instructional methods is a future task for the psychology of reading instruction.

INVENTION AND DISCOVERY
IN LEARNING TO READ

The notion of aptitude-treatment may help us to deal more sensibly with an issue that often provokes heated argument among reading specialists but that is only rarely posed as a question related to individual differences. The issue involves the extent to which all aspects of reading must be taught directly. Several contributors to these volumes (e.g., Frederiksen, Vol. 1: Goodman & Goodman, Vol. l; Chomsky, Vol. 2; Smith, Vol. 2) argue that all or much of the alphabetic code can be learned without direct instruction. Others (e.g., Bateman, Vol. 1; Rosner, Vol. 2) believe that only direct instruction ensures that children will learn this essential aspect of reading. Almost everyone who has taught reading has encountered striking examples of children who appeared to "teach themselves." Exposed to a rich diet of written material, given the opportunity to play alphabet games in which sounds are associated with letters, and encouraged to ask questions about what words and letters "say" and how words are spelled, these children seem suddenly to be able to read. They acquire the code without anyone's having systematically taught it to them, and they quickly delve into reading for meaning and pleasure. Other children don't make such a startling breakthrough but do appear to catch on to it after some time in an instructional program that does not emphasize the code. It seems reasonable to say that these children are "inventing" or discovering reading processes. They are told or shown some of the principles of print–sound relationships; with this as a basis, they construct for themselves a system that can decipher most of the words they encounter. Once they catch on to the idea of orthographic and phonemic patterning in the written language, they don't need to be taught every orthographic pattern.

There seems to be little doubt that for many children learning to read is primarily an invention or discovery based on relatively small amounts of external direction. But to what extent can reading instruction afford to depend on children's inventions? This question lies at the heart of the psychology of reading instruction, because the answer to it will prescribe how much and what kinds of instruction must be offered to which kinds of children. To explore this question of direct instruction versus invention, we need to answer questions about what is invented and what prior knowledge enhances the likelihood of invention, as well as the central question of who is likely to be inventive.

What Is Invented?   Does what is invented in the course of learning to read vary idiosyncratically from child to child, or is there considerable regularity among children? Chomsky (Vol. 2) has collected evidence that some children invent systematic patterns of spelling even before they know how to read. Furthermore, there is striking regularity in the spelling conventions that these children adopt. How widespread is this phenomenon? Does it exist in other geographic regions and among other types of families than those Chomsky studied? Furthermore, is there the same regularity in the case of reading? Do children invent the same processing units, discover the same rules as one another? Do they develop the same strategies for recognizing words and for deriving meaning from the text, or are there large individual differences that might affect instructional decisions? These are some of the questions that the psychology of reading instruction needs to address.

What Kinds of Already Established Knowledge or Skill Enhance the Likelihood of Invention?   Is there some information about the code, some set of rules for analyzing print, that is relatively easy to teach and easy for the learner to transform into rules or processes that we know are part of the acquisition sequence? LaBerge (Vol 3), for example, suggests that learning "context nodes"—the size of units to look for—may prepare the learner to acquire the specific associations of graphemes to phonemes. We need instructional experiments that establish context nodes for learners and that study their effects. The point is that we may not need to teach all children everything about reading. Good teaching may be more a matter of drawing attention to certain characteristics of words or letters than of teaching exactly how to analyze them. An easily communicated rule that is not very efficient to use (e.g., soft *c* before *e* and *i*, hard *c* otherwise) may "set a child up" to invent a more efficient performance rule after enough practice. If we view learning as, in part, a process of invention, deciding what to teach becomes more complex than simply analyzing task performance. The job includes finding rules that invite further elaboration by the learner.

Who Is Likely To Invent and Who Seems To Need Very Explicit Instruction? This is clearly the most important issue in terms of current instructional applications. The question is whether there is a general tendency, differentially present in different children, to invent for oneself or not to do so, so that instruction can be matched in advance to this "trait." It is worth noting that many people argue that the central characteristic of the "hard to teach" (see especially Bateman, Vol. 1; Rosner, Vol. 2), including both compensatory populations (the poor and minority groups) and the learning disabled, is that they cannot be depended on to do much invention, but instead they require a great deal of direct instruction. This assumption seems to underlie the programs that have been most successful with both groups of children. It appears that the best way (statistically speaking) of teaching a child who is labeled compensatory, learning disabled, or mildly retarded to read is to use a direct-instruction code program. (See my review of the evidence for this claim in Vol. 2.) But can we not go beyond this kind of statistically based prescription and assess the need for direct instruction on a more individual basis?

In particular, I believe that we ought to question whether children from poor and minority families should be automatically treated as "hard to teach"—that is, as if they cannot invent much of the reading process for themselves and so, like special-education populations, must be slowly and patiently tutored in every component of the reading process. In recalling this question, it is useful to consider how the "hard-to-teach" label came to be applied to both compensatory and special-education populations. As Bateman (Vol. 1) points out, assessing the specific difficulties shown by children who do not learn to read on schedule suggests similar patterns in the special-education and compensatory groups: Both have difficulty with auditory blending and phonemic segmentation; both sometimes have difficulty forming phrases and sentences after painfully sounding out the individual words; and both seem to have difficulty using the alphabetic coding of the written language unless it is directly pointed out in the course of instruction. Thus both groups seem to be hard to teach, and in similar ways. From this observation, it seems a natural step to the assumption that compensatory populations and special-education populations (especially the learning disabled) should be treated in the same way.

But let us reconsider for a moment. If a child does poorly on a phonemic segmentation task at the age of 5 or 6, it may be because that child has had little exposure to the task before (few alphabet books at home; no sound analysis games around the dinner table, etc.), *or* it may be that, despite exposure, the child has failed to catch on to the basic principle. In the first case, we would expect the child to respond quickly to the opportunity to engage in these tasks; it would take relatively few "trials," to use a term from learning psychology, for him or her to learn the tasks, and transfer to new sounds or new phonemic contexts might be very fast. In the second case, learning would proceed slowly, many trials would be needed, and little transfer might occur. Two children might, in other words, start out in the same position, but one would show a steep learning curve, the other a flat and extended one. Both children could, with enough patient instruction and practice, reach "criterion," but we would not be likely to consider them equally difficult to teach. Similar differences in learning rates—for children who have virtually identical entering subskill profiles—might be found for learning new grapheme–phoneme correspondences, blending, recognizing phrase boundaries in order to segment a text meaningfully, and the like. Those who acquire each new aspect of reading quickly and who seem to transfer what they learn to new vocabulary or text with little or no direct instruction are probably children who lacked exposure but not learning ability. Such children are not hard to teach in the sense of not being able to invent. They are (if they can be shown to exist) simply children who have not yet been well taught.

The possibility exists, then, that the group we label compensatory may have within it both children who are truly hard to teach and children who are—in terms of ability—easy to teach but as yet untutored. Here, then, is another fundamental question for the psychology of reading instruction. Starting with a group of children who according to tests lack the same prerequisites of reading, can we develop measures of learning rate and learning processes that will distinguish between individuals who learn quickly once a principle is pointed out and minimal practice is provided and individuals who need extensive teacher-directed practice? If this kind of discrimination can be made for some component of reading, we will then be able to ask whether children who learn that component easily also tend to learn other aspects of reading easily. Do some children, in other words, possess a general ability to learn easily, even though they lack certain knowledge or skill at the beginning of instruction? If we can distinguish, within populations now labeled simply compensatory, those who learn quickly with minimal help from those who need long-term direct instruction in virtually every component of reading, we will have taken a giant step toward turning a socioeconomic definition of a population into a psychological one. In so doing, we will have opened the way for instruction that makes full use of individuals' learning abilities whatever their social group. To make such discriminations, however, we will have to turn from assessments of individuals' current capabilities to assessments that directly consider learning itself.

CONCLUSION: REUNITING COGNITIVE
AND LEARNING PSYCHOLOGY

In the preceding paragraphs I have quietly introduced some concepts and language that seem closer to the learning psychology of a decade or two ago than to the language and models of contemporary cognitive psychology. I spoke of learning curves and learning rates not to demonstrate that one *could* deal with questions of reading in these more traditional terms, but because these concepts seem *necessary* to answer critical questions concerning instruction. It is in the context of such instructional questions that the cognitive branch and the learning branch of psychological research can fruitfully interact. The resulting cognitive learning psychology, which is required if psychology is to prove useful for instruction, will need to attend to questions of the kind raised here.

We must, as I have suggested, learn a great deal more about the relationship between skilled performance in reading and patterns of its acquisition. Therefore we must enlarge and extend developmental research in reading. We must also—and this is both the larger and in many respects the newer question—learn how development is modified by certain kinds of environmental events, particularly those we call instruction. A view of learning that acknowledges the learner's role in constructing his or her own knowledge and skill must be joined with an analysis of the environmental events that can foster—or hinder—such constructions. We cannot choose between a constructive learner operating in an undifferentiated environment and a passive "receptacle" of knowledge whose environment is structured to provide all needed information. We must begin to take the notion of *interaction* between learner and environment quite seriously, specifying features of the environment that interact with characteristics of the learner's knowledge and processes to produce transitions in cognitive competence. Finally, the new psychology of reading instruction that I envisage will be highly attentive to individual differences, seeking to explain and predict the effects of instructional environments on individuals characterized in terms of their psychological processes of learning and their cognitive performance.

Sustained attention to questions of this kind will not only teach us about reading and reading instruction; it will also directly contribute to the development of a cognitive theory of learning. The new psychology of reading instruction, in other words, must be grounded in and part of cognitive, learning, and developmental psychology. It cannot simply apply to reading the established methods of those branches of psychology. Instead it must pursue the logic of its own questions. In the process, it may change the face of its parent disciplines.

ACKNOWLEDGMENTS

Work on this chapter was begun during the author's stay at the Center for Advanced Study in the Behavioral Sciences, where she was supported by a fellowship from the Spencer Foundation. Work was also supported by contract 400-75-0049 from the National Institute of Education.

REFERENCES

Anderson, J. F., Kline, P. J., & Beasley, C. M. Complex learning processes. In R. E. Snow, P. A. Federico, & W. E. Montague (Eds.), *Aptitude, learning, and instruction: Cognitive process analyses.* Hillsdale, N.J.: Lawrence Erlbaum Associates, in press.

Barr, R. The effect of instruction on pupil reading strategies. *Reading Research Quarterly,* 1974–1975, *10*(4), 555–582.

Calfee, R. C., Chapman, R. S., & Venezky, R. L. How a child needs to think to learn to read. In L. W. Gregg (Ed.), *Cognition in learning and memory.* New York: Wiley, 1972.

Cronbach, L. J., & Snow, R. E. *Aptitudes and instructional methods: A handbook for research on interactions.* New York: Irvington Publishers, 1977.

Doehring, D. G. Acquisition of rapid reading responses. *Monographs of the Society for Research in Child Development,* 1976, *41*(2, Serial No. 165).

Estes, W. K. Intelligence and cognitive psychology. In L. B. Resnick (Ed.), *The nature of intelligence.* Hillsdale, N.J.: Lawrence Erlbaum Associates, 1976.

Fleisher, L. S., Jenkins, J. R., & Pany, D. *Effects on poor readers' comprehension of training in rapid decoding* (Center for the Study of Reading Tech. Rep. No. 103). Champaign, Ill.: University of Illinois at Urbana-Champaign, Center for the Study of Reading, 1978.

Gibson, E. J., & Levin, H. *The psychology of reading.* Cambridge, Mass.: MIT Press, 1975.

Gleitman, L. R., & Rozin, P. Teaching reading by use of a syllabary. *Reading Research Quarterly,* 1973, *8,* 447–483.

Hunt, J. M. *Intelligence and experience.* New York: Ronald Press, 1961.

Resnick, L. B. Task analysis in instructional design: Some cases from mathematics. In D. Klahr (Ed.), *Cognition and instruction.* Hillsdale, N.J.: Lawrence Erlbaum Associates, 1976.

Rosner, J. *Phonic analysis training and beginning reading skills* (LRDC Publication 1971/19). Pittsburgh: University of Pittsburgh, Learning Research and Development Center, 1971.

Venezky, R. L. Research on reading processes: A historical perspective. *American Psychologist,* 1977, *32*(5), 339–345.

Author Index

A

Abelson, R. P., 58, *70*
Abrahams, R., 127, *128*
Acland, H., 153, 176, *177*
Adams, M. J., 11, *24*
Ames, W. S., 93, 98, *108*
Anderson, I. R., 341, *352*
Anderson, J. F., 357, *372*
Anderson, L. M., 305, *305*
Andersson, T., 131, 133, *148*
Anisfeld, M., 327, *353*

B

Ball, S., 155, *177*
Bandura, A., 314, *316*
Bane, M. J., 153, 176, *177*
Baratz, J., 116, 118, 119, *128,* 139, 144, 145, 146, *148,* 338, *352*
Barber, L., 212, *214*
Barik, H. C., 136, *148*
Barker, M. E., 143, *148*
Baron, J., 36, *50,* 329, *352*
Barr, R., 363, *372*
Barron, R. W., 41, *50*
Bateman, B., 182, *194*
Beasley, C. M., 357, *372*

Beck, I. L., 179, 182, *195,* 218, 225, 231, 263, 264, *268*
Berliner, D. C., 176, *178, 184, 194*
Biemiller, A., 96, 98, *106*
Blackman, B., 229, *268*
Blumenthal, S. H., 183, *194*
Bobrow, D. G., 58, *70*
Bogatz, G. A., 155, *177*
Bond, G. L., 156, *177*
Bouma, H., 77, 84, *86*
Boyer, M., 131, 133, *148*
Bransford, J., 291, *293*
Brent, D. E., 346, *352*
Broadbent, D. E., 34, *50*
Brophy, J. E., 305, *305*
Broudy, H. S., 311, *316*
Brown, A. L., 314, *316*
Brown, R., 142, *148*
Bruinicks, R. H., 182, *194*
Buck, C., 94, *107*
Burke, C., 93, *106,* 139, *148*
Buswell, G. T., 6, *24,* 99, *106*

C

Calfee, R. C., 183, 185, *194,* 365, *372*
Campbell, 153, *177*
Campbell, D., 163, 164, *177*

Campbell, R. N., 136, *148*
Carpenter, P. A., 60, *70*
Carroll, J. B., 218, *268*, 313, *316*, 319, *352*
Carter, B., 185, *195*
Cattell, J. M., 6, *24*
Cazden, C. B., 296, 297, 298, *305*
Chapman, R. S., 143, *149*, 365, *372*
Chase, W. G., 60, *70*
Chi, M. T. H., 104, *106*
Ching, D. C., 140, *148*
Chomsky, N., 283, *293*
Clark, H. H., 60, *70*
Clay, M. M., 92, 96, 98, *106, 107*
Clymer, T., 326, *352*
Cohen, A. D., 147, *148*
Cohen, A. S., 97, *107*
Cohen, D., 153, 176, *177*
Cohn, J. A., 99, *107*
Coleman, E. B., 186, *194*
Coleman, J. S., 153, *177*
Collins, A., 11, *24*
Conant, J. B., 318, *352*
Cook-Gumperz, J., 126, *128*
Cooley, W. W., 175, *177*, 313, *316*
Cooper, F. S., 183, *195*
Cronbach, L. J., 181, *194*, 367, *372*

D

d'Anglegan, A., 136, *149*
Danks, J. H., 101, *107*
Davis, F. B., 53, *70*
Dearborn, W. F., 341, *352*
de Hirsch, K., 266, *268*
Deutsch, C. P., 199, *214*
de Voogd, A. H., 77, *86*
Dickinson, D., 303, *305*
Doehring, D. G., 359, *372*
Dooling, D. J., 101, 103, *107*
Douglas, W. O., *132*
Dozier, M. G., 199, *215*
Drake, G. F., 147, *148*
Dreifuss, F. E., 92, *107*
Durkin, D., 153, *177*, 266, *268*
Durrell, D. D., 183, *194*, 202, *214*
Dykstra, R., 156, *177*, 183, *194*

E

Erlebacher, A., 163, 164, *177*
Elias-Olivares, L., 138, *148*

Elkonin, D. B., 183, 185, *194*, 202, *214*
Ellson, D. G., 212, *214*
Emrick, J. A., 175, *177*
Engle, P. L., 135, 142, 145, *148*
Epstein, M., 303, *305*
Ervin-Tripp, S. M., 145, *148*
Estes, W. K., 34, 35, 37, 38, 42, 47, *51*, 357, *372*

F

Fairbanks, G., 99, *107*
Farnham-Diggory, S., 65, 67, *70*
Fosold, R. W., 94, *107*
Fathman, A., 145, *148*
Feigenbaum, E. A., 55, *70*
Feldman, S., 302, *305*
Finn, J. D., 162, *177*
Fischer, F. W., 185, *195*
Fishbein, J. M., 145, *148*
Flavell, J. H., 68, *70*
Fleisher, L. S., 361, *372*
Flesch, R., 7, *25*, 318, *353*
Fletcher, J. D., 230, *268*
Fowles, B. R., 304, *305*
Fox, B., 183, *194*, 339, *353*
Freedle, R., 15, *25*, 286, *293*
Fries, C. C., 7, *25*
Fristoe, M., 199, *214*
Frostig, M., 184, *194*
Frumkin, B., 327, *353*

G

Gage, N. L., 184, *194*
Gagne, R. M., 179, *194*
Galvan, M., 134, *148*
Gardner, G. T., 35, *51*
Gay, G., 127, *128*
Gibbon, S. Y., Jr., 304, *305*
Gibson, E. J., 17, *25*, 34, 41, *51*, 53, 55, *70*, 98, *107*, 202, 203, 214, *214*, 283, *293*, 330, 340, 347, *353*, 355, 359, *372*
Gintis, H., 153, 176, *177*
Glaser, R., 179, *194*, 310, 314, *316*
Glass, G. V., 166, *177*
Gleitman, L. R., 203, *214*, 366, *372*
Goldman, R., 199, *214*
Goldstein, D. M., 183, *194*
Golinkoff, R. M., 95, *107*

Goodman, K. S., 89, 91, 92, 94, 95, 96, 98, 107, 108, 113, 128
Gould, T. S., 202, 215
Greene, D., 347, 353
Greenhalgh, C., 305, 305
Gregg, L. W., 56, 65, 70
Grice, H. P., 121, 128
Griffin, P., 303, 305
Griffiths, N. L., 210, 214
Gumperz, J. J., 122, 123, 126, 128
Gutierrez, A. L., 134, 139, 148

H

Hakstian, A. R., 166, 177
Hallahan, D. P., 181, 194
Halle, M., 283, 293
Hardy, M., 185, 194
Haring, N. G., 346, 347, 353
Harlow, H. F., 45, 51
Harnischfeger, A., 155, 175, 178, 313, 316
Harrington, S. M. J., 183, 194
Harris, A., 155, 175, 177
Harris, P., 212, 214
Hauck, M. A., 346, 347, 353
Herasimchuk, E., 122, 128
Hess, R. D., 296, 305
Heyns, B., 153, 176, 177
Hildreth, G. H., 210, 214
Hively, W., 225, 268
Hobson, C., 153, 177
Hogaboam, T., 95, 108
Horne, D., 184, 194
House, B. J., 47, 51
Huey, E. B., 6, 25
Hunt, B. C., 93, 107
Hunt, J. M., 364, 372
Huus, H., 155, 177

I

Imlach, R. H., 92, 107
Isakson, R. L., 102, 108

J

Jansky, J., 266, 268
Jencks, C., 153, 176, 177
Jenkins, J. R., 361, 372
Johnson, K., 117, 127, 128, 129

Johnson, M., 291, 293
Just, M. A., 60, 70

K

Kaplan, E. L., 99, 100, 107, 141, 149
Kaplan, N. E., 199, 215
Karweit, N., 155, 178
Kauffman, J. M., 181, 194
Kavanagh, J. F., 319, 353
Kennedy, J., 115, 117, 129
Kenny, D. A., 163, 178
Keypart, N., 184, 194
Kline, P. J., 357, 372
Kochman, T., 127, 128, 143, 148
Kolers, P. A., 142, 149
Kozak, N., 303, 305
Kuenne, J. B., 185, 195

L

LaBerge, D., 32, 35, 36, 38, 39, 41, 49, 51, 104, 107
Labov, W. A., 94, 107, 112, 113, 118, 128
Lahaderne, H. M., 176, 178
Lambert, W. E., 136, 147, 149
Lazerson, B. H., 101, 107
Leaverton, L., 145, 149
Lehtinen, L., 181, 195
Leinhardt, G., 313, 316
Lepper, M. R., 347, 353
Levin, H., 17, 25, 34, 51, 53, 70, 98, 99, 100, 107, 141, 149, 202, 203, 214, 214, 229, 268, 283, 293, 330, 340, 347, 353, 355, 359, 372
Lewis, L., 127, 128
Liberman, A. M., 183, 195
Liberman, I. Y., 95, 108, 185, 195
Lindamood, C., 183, 185, 194
Lindamood, P., 183, 185, 194
Lohnes, P. R., 313, 316

M

MacGinitie, W., 183, 195
Mandler, G., 34, 51
Marsh, G., 186, 195
Marston, E., 229, 268
Martin, E., 32, 51
Marwit, W., 117, 128

Mathews, M., 4, *25*
Matthewson, G., 117, 118, *128*
Mattingly, I., 319, *353*
Maugham, W. S., 2, *25*
McConkie, G. W., 78, 79, 83, *86, 87*
McDermott, R. P., 296, 300, 301, *306*
McGauvran, M. E., 210, *214*
McPortland, J., 153, *177*
Mehegan, C. C., 92, *107*
Melmed, P. J., 93, *108, 115, 128, 137, 149*
Melton, A. W., 32, *51*
Menyuk, P., 99, *108*
Meredith, R., 91, *108*
Michelson, S., 153, 176, *177*
Miller, G. A., 34, *51,* 186, *195,* 319, *353*
Miller, J. W., 101, 102, *108*
Mitroff, D. D., 218, 225, 263, 264, *268*
Modiano, N., 135, *149*
Monroe, M., 183, *195*
Mood, A. M., 153, *177*
Moray, M., 34, *51*
Murphy, H. A., 183, *194, 202, 214*

N

Nash, R., 137, *149*
Neisser, U., 283, *293*
Nelson, E., 303, *305*
Nelson, K., 287, *293*
Newman, G., 117, *128*
Nicely, P. E., 186, *195*
Nicholas, D. W., 290, *293*
Nisbett, R. E., 347, *353*
Nolen, P., 117, *128*
Norden, M., 39, *51*
Norman, D. A., 58, *70*

O

Ogden, J., 305, *305*
Olson, D. R., 319, *353*
O'Regan, J. K., 79, *87*
Osterberg, T., 116, 119, *128*

P

Palmer, E. L., 304, *305*
Pany, D., 361, *372*
Pehrsson, R. S. V., 105, *108*

Perfetti, C. A., 95, *108*
Peterson, R. J., 36, 39, *51*
Petty, W. T., 319, *353*
Piaget, J., 66, *70*
Piestrup, A. M., 114, 122, 123, *128, 296,*
    299, *306*
Pittenger, J. B., 41, *50*
Plumer, D., 199, *215*
Politzer, R., 145, *149*
Pollatsek, A., 36, *51*
Popp, H. M., 333, *353*

R

Rayner, K., 78, 79, 80, 82, 83, *86, 87*
Reber, A. S., 319, *353*
Reicher, G. M., 42, *51*
Reinhardt, M., 229, *268*
Rentel, V., 115, 117, *129*
Resnick, D. P., 3, *25*
Resnick, L. B., 3, *25, 99, 108,* 179, 182, *195,*
    231, *268,* 356, *372*
Riegel, K., 15, *25,* 286, *293*
Ringler, L., 182, *195*
Robinson, H. M., 182, *195*
Rode, S. S., 99, 100, *108*
Rosen, C. L., 93, 98, *108*
Rosenberg, S., 325, *353*
Rosenshine, B. V., 176, *178*
Rosinski, R. R., 95, *107*
Rosner, J., 183, *195,* 339, *353, 368, 372*
Ross, A. O., 181, *195, 330, 353*
Ross, M., 347, *353*
Roswell, F. G., 183, *194*
Routh, D. K., 183, *194,* 339, 346, *352, 353*
Rozin, P., 203, *214,* 366, *372*
Ruddell, R. B., 117, *129*
Rumelhart, D. E., 11, *25,* 58, *70,* 96, *108,*
    324, *353*
Rystrom, R., 115, *129*

S

Samuels, S. J., 32, 35, 38, 49, *51,* 104, *107,*
    176, *178,* 181, *195*
Saville, M. R., 133, 134, 139, 140, *149*
Scarborough, D. L., 319, *353*
Schaaf, E., 117, *129*
Schindler, R. M., 36, *51*
Schlesinger, I. M., 99, *108*

Searle, J., 121, *129*
Selig, H., 305, *305*
Selinker, L., 142, *149*
Serwer, B., 155, 175, *177*
Shankweiler, D., 95, *108,* 183, 185, *195*
Shebilske, W., 77, *87*
Sherman, M., 186, *195*
Shiffrin, R. M., 35, *51*
Shuy, R., 139, 143, *149,* 255, 256, *268*
Siler, E. R., 100, *108*
Silverberg, M. C., 92, *108*
Silverberg, N. E., 92, *108*
Simon, D., 339, *353*
Simon, H. A., 55, *70*
Simons, H., 115, 116, 117, 118, *129*
Sims, R., 117, *129*
Smith, E. B., 91, *108*
Smith, E. E., 40, *51*
Smith, F., 198, *215,* 326, *353*
Smith, I., 182, *195*
Smith, M. S., 53, *70*
Smythe, P. C., 185, *194*
Snow, R. E., 181, *194,* 367, *372*
Somervill, M. A., 139, *149*
Spache, G. D., 211, *215*
Spoeher, K. T., 40, *51*
Stennitt, R. G., 185, *194*
Stern, C., 202, *215*
Sternberg, S., 282, *293*
Stevens, A. L., 96, *108*
Stewart, W. A., 116, 117, 119, *129*
Strauss, A., 181, *195*
Strawson, C., 329, *352*
Studdert-Kennedy, M., 183, *195*
Swain, M., 136, 147, *148*

T

Takanishi, R., 296, *305*
Tatham, S. M., 117, *129*
Taylor, W. L., 325, *353*
Templin, M. C., 199, *215*
Thurston, I., 36, *50*

Trabasso, T., 290, *293*
Treisman, A., 34, *51*
Troike, R. C., 133, 134, 139, 140, *149*
Tucker, G. R., 136, 147, *149*
Turner, A., 99, *107*
Turnure, J. E., 176, *178*

V

Vellutino, F. R., 181, *195*
Venezky, R. L., 143, *149,* 192, *195,* 355, 365, *372*
Vernon, M. D., 182, 184, *195*

W

Walker, L., 117, *129*
Wallach, L., 199, 202, 204, 205, *215,* 330, *353*
Wallach, M. A., 199, 202, 204, 205, *215,* 330, *353*
Watson, J., 229, *268*
Weber, R. M., 93, 94, 96, 98, *108,* 141, *149*
Weinfeld, F. D., 153, *177*
Weiss, L., 145, *149*
Well, A. D., 36, *51*
Wepman, J. M., 182, *195*
Whiting, H. T. A., 315, *316*
Wiley, D. E., 155, 175, *178,* 313, *316*
Williams, J. P., 184, 185, *195,* 229, *268*
Winograd, T., 58, *70*
Wittick, M. L., 155, *178*
Wolfram, W. A., 113, *129,* 143, *149*
Woodcock, R. W., 199, *214*

Y Z

York, R. L., 153, *177*
Zeaman, D., 47, *51*
Zhurova, L. E., 203, *215*
Zigmond, N., 184, *195*

Subject Index

A

ABD's of Reading, 179–193
Acquiring reading competence, 7, 19–23, 92, 104, 111, 116, 119, 140–142, 281, 285, 287, 328, 365, 368
Alphabet, 6, 9, 26, 40, 44, 55, 64, 67, 205, 286, 289, 326, 340, 342, 345–346, 365, 367, 369
Alpha-picture, 206–207, 209
Ambiguity, 123
Aptitude-treatment interaction, 366–367
Assessing reading progress, *see also* Student achievement, 153–156, 158, 162–177, 183
Assessing reading progress, 21–23, 73, 115–117, 119–121, 146, 189–192, 210–213, 255–259, 265, 267, 281, 283, 289, 310–312, 314, 328, 362–363, 370
Attention, 14, 34–35, 39–40, 44, 46–47, 62, 64, 105, 181, 198, 235, 284, 297–299, 301–305, 330–331, 337, 368
  and classroom structure, 297–298
  direction of, 297
  focus of, 302–305
Attention, selective, 12, 73, 181, 330, 352
Attitudes, 75
Auditory analysis, 179, 182–186, 307, 366

Auditory discrimination, 115, 181, 183–184, 186, 187, 199, 365
Auditory synthesis, 184–186
Auditory-visual associations, 183, 186, 366

B

Basal approach, 6–7, 155–156, 181–182, 235, 267, 283, 318, 327, 330, 362–363
Base word, 82–83
Basic skills, 307, 313, 332
Behavioral techniques, 18, 23, 346–347
Bigrams, 35–39, 44–47, 49
Bilingual education, history of, 131–133
Bilingual programs, 131–148, 286–287, 336–337
  direct approach, 133, 135–136, 146–147, 336–337
  dual approach, 133–142
  immersion approach, 131, 135–136, 146–147
  native language approach, 133–137, 336
  and research, 133–137, 147–148
  standard native language approach, 143–145
  transfer of reading skills, 134–137, 139–142, 147, 287

Bilingualism, 17, 131–148, 286, 317, 322, 336
Black dialect, 17, 93, 98, 111–127, 137, 139–140, 142–143, 286–287, 299–300, 338–339
Black dialect readers, 145
Black dialect and reading interference, 111–127, 139, 287, 299–300, 338–339
  an alternative explanation, 118–121
  grammatical, 114, 116–118, 338
  phonological, 114–116, 287, 338
Black language, deficit vs. difference viewpoints, 112–113
Blending, 19, 33, 44–45, 179, 181, 183–186, 188, 190, 192, 203, 207–209, 229, 231–234, 244, 255, 266, 289, 369–370

C

Classroom interaction, 111–127, 295–305, 336–339
  linguistic-sociolinguistic approach, 121–122, 338–339
Cloze procedure, 325
Code, 5–7, 9, 32–35, 37–47, 49, 89–91, 327, 363, 367–368
  distinctive features, 41, 43–44
  letter, 37–44, 48
  meaning, 33–35
  perceptual, 32, 34–35, 45–47
  phonological, 9, 32–34, 44–45, 89–91, 327
  verbal, 91
  visual, 32–34, 36, 39, 46–47, 49
  word, 39, 41–44, 46, 49
Code approach, see also Phonics, 8–9, 16, 44, 154, 156, 162, 182, 230, 233, 255, 259, 263, 267, 289–290, 302–303, 307, 309, 318, 327, 329–330, 332–333, 335, 342–345, 359
Code approach, 7, 9, 20, 26, 97, 120, 191, 225, 315, 320, 358–359, 363, 367, 369
Cognitive processes, 72, 76–77, 80–81, 86, 309, 311, 313–315, 320, 351, 356–357, 359
Cognitive psychology, 284–285, 296, 308, 311, 322, 355–358, 371
Cognitive psychology of learning, 359, 371
Cognitive synthesis, 67, 69

Cognitive system, 16, 31, 34–35
Community adults, 204, 210
Compensatory education, 18, 22, 25, 136, 157–160, 162–164, 166–171, 174–176, 369–370
Competence, 201, 204–205, 211–212, 297, 313–314, 320, 325, 328, 336, 356, 362, 364, 366, 371
Complexity, 74–75, 105, 263, 285, 302, 314–315, 322, 336, 345, 349, 358, 368
Comprehension, 4–7, 9, 12–13, 26, 31–32, 34–35, 48, 53–54, 65, 68–69, 80, 85, 89–106, 114–115, 117–119, 122, 154–156, 169, 173, 188, 191, 198, 205, 212, 217–218, 235, 243–244, 259, 262, 281–283, 285, 290, 292, 303, 307–309, 313, 320, 328, 332–337, 339, 341, 348–352, 360–361
  depth of, 348–349
  development of, 348–349
  listening, 92
Constructive reading, 62, 68–69
Content, 218, 259–264
Context, see Cues, context
Contextual nodes, 37–41, 45–50, 283–284, 368
Critical word location, 82–83
Cues, 13, 49–50, 90, 95, 99, 118–119, 122, 124–126, 180, 198, 222, 226–227, 233–235, 244–246, 248, 258–259, 265, 288–291, 304, 307, 325, 331, 334, 343–346, 350–351, 370
  acoustic, 289
  color, 180
  context, 49–50, 90, 95, 122, 124–126, 198, 226–227, 233–235, 244–245, 248, 258–259, 288, 290–291, 307, 325–326, 329, 331, 334, 343–345, 370
    types of, 122, 125
  format, 304
  graphemic, 226–227, 233–234, 265
  letter-sound, 246, 259, 329
  phonic, 326–331, 340, 345, 350–351
  picture, 222, 227, 233, 258–259, 331, 334
  redundant, 118–119, 235, 346
  semantic, 226–227, 233–234, 259
  syntactic, 226–227, 233–234, 259, 265
  teacher prompts, 222, 235
  verbal, 235
  verbal, 13, 289
Cummulative mastery, 204
CVC, 186–187, 190, 208

D

Decision functions, 58–61
Decoding, 4–5, 7–12, 15, 18, 22–23, 26, 31,
    53–54, 65, 75, 89–106, 134, 156, 179,
    182–183, 186–188, 190, 192, 232–233,
    255, 282–283, 288, 301–303, 307–309,
    312, 314–315, 326–333, 341–346, 348,
    350–352, 359, 362
  centrality to early reading, 8–12, 26
Development of reading skill, 13, 20, 119,
    322, 346, 348–349, 356–363
Developmental theory and research, 19–20,
    111, 314, 346, 356–363
Diagnosis, 73, 259, 311, 321, 339, 360
Dialect, 17, 93–94, 98–99, 103, 115, 120,
    299, 338
Dialect features, 115, 120
Dialect speakers, 17, 93–94, 98–99, 103
Difficulty in reading, sources of, 16–19, 22,
    93–94, 98–99, 103, 111–127, 188–189,
    281, 317–352
  cultural and linguistic differences, 17–18,
    93–94, 98–99, 103, 111–127
  individual differences, 18–19, 188–189
Disadvantaged, 25, 155–156, 197–214, 309
Discourse-processing skills, 311
Discovery, 213–214, 343, 358, 367–370
  invention and, 358, 367–370
Discrimination nets, 54
Distar, 16, 18, 304, 348
Dyslexia, 56, 318–319

E

Early reading, focus on, 5–7, 318
  code and meaning, 5–7
Electric Company, 297–298
Encoding, 9, 55
Environmental influences, 193, 296–297,
    299, 302–303, 308, 312, 314, 340, 371
EPAM, 55
Errors in oral reading, 15, 92–103, 105–106,
    117, 124–125, 181, 222, 265, 360,
    362–363
  context-based, 363
  graphic-phonetic, 95–98, 106
  self-correcting, 96–98, 265
  substitution, 96–98, 100–101, 222
  syntactic-semantic, 95–100, 106
ESL, 134

F

Eye movement control, 78–79
Eye movement coordination, 75
Eye-movement research, 15, 71–86
Eye movements, 74, 77–81, 285–286, 295,
    309
  random, 78, 81
  regressive, 74, 80
  rhythmic, 77–79, 81
Eye-voice span, 15, 94, 99–100

Familiarity, 35–37, 39, 47, 49–50, 304, 332,
    346, 348
Feature analysis-by-synthesis, 283
Feature detection, 55–56, 62, 322
Fixation duration, 77–81, 86, 309
  control of, 79–81
Fixations, 73, 77–84, 286
Flexibility, 322, 336
Follow-Through programs, 175
Fovea, 82
French-speaking, 135–136, 142, 146
Functional language approach, 12, 16–17,
    26

G

Game-pictures, 200, 205–209
Generating strategies, 68–69, 104
Good vs. poor readers, 85, 92, 94–97, 102,
    104, 332, 360–362
Grapheme-pnoneme correspondences, *see*
    Spelling to sound correspondences
Graphic information, 268
Graphic processing, 100
Guessing, *see* Hypothesis

H

Hard-to-teach, 18–19, 23, 369–370
Hierarchy, 21, 32–33. 42–43, 49, 58, 106,
    266, 335
Hispanics, 17
Homophones, 114–115
Hyperlexia, 92–93
Hypothesis, 12–13, 61, 68, 71, 78, 89–91, 94,
    99, 101, 103–105, 117, 141, 234, 267,
    282, 296, 308, 331–332, 341, 362

I

Idiolect, 98–99
Inconsistency, 102–103
Independent reading, 245, 341–342, 348
Indirect speech acts, 125–126, 338
Individual differences, 18–19, 188–189, 316,
    364–368, 371
  aptitude matching approach, 364, 366
  readiness approach, 364–366
Individualized instruction, 175, 180,
    217–218, 221, 264–266
  rate or pace, 218, 221, 265–266
Inferences, 13, 21, 74–76, 121, 126, 235, 258,
    291, 309, 325, 349
Instructional approaches, 5–7, 9, 12, 16–17,
    20, 23, 26, 68, 71–74, 97, 120, 134,
    155–156, 162–163, 165, 174, 181–182,
    184, 191, 225, 235, 259, 267, 283,
    315, 318, 320, 327, 330, 358–359,
    361–363, 367, 369
  basal, 6–7, 155–156, 181–182, 235, 267,
    283, 318, 327, 330, 362–363
  code, 7, 9, 20, 26, 97, 120, 191, 225, 315,
    320, 358–359, 363, 367, 369
  functional language, 12, 16–17, 26
  language-experience, 68, 134, 184, 367
  linguistic, 182
  meaning-oriented, 5–7, 12, 23, 97, 120,
    259, 315, 320, 361, 363
  skill-emphasis, 162–163, 165, 174
Instructional goals, 73–75, 159, 162, 193,
    217–218, 222, 225, 262, 267, 335, 357
Instructional implications, 21, 48–49, 61–62,
    71, 73, 75, 81, 84–85, 282, 309, 312,
    361, 363
Instructional materials, 217–219, 221, 329
Instructional sequence, 217, 220, 222, 225,
    228, 230, 331, 334–335, 342, 363
Instructional strategies, 217–218, 226, 230,
    266
Instructional time, 22–23, 153–177, 320, 332
Integrating concrete operations, 69
Interlanguage, 142
Intersentence integration, 101–102
Intonation, 92, 94
Iteration, 64, 66, 69

L

Language-experience approach, 68, 134,
    184, 367

Latency, 36–37, 39, 59–61
Learning disability, 18, 179–193, 218, 266,
    289, 322, 369
Learning psychology, 313–314, 334,
    356–357, 370–371
Letter cards, 208–209
Letter clusters, see Orthographic regularity
Letter discrimination, 307, 311, 320, 336,
    340
Letter drawing, 206–207
Letter recognition, 13–15, 322, 340
Letter-sound correspondences, see Spelling
    to sound correspondences
Letter tracing, 206, 266, 341
Lexical access, 15, 101–102, 105, 307, 362
Lexicon, 15, 95
Literary, 2–5, 16, 19, 111, 210, 286, 319
  rising criteria for, 3–5
  social press for, 2–5
  universal, 2–3
Literary quality, 262–263
Logograph, 67
Look-say approach, see Basal approach

M

Mastery criteria, 205–211
Meaning, 5–7, 12–14, 33–34, 45, 68, 76, 92,
    99, 105, 142, 156, 198, 217–218, 222,
    225–226, 231, 233–235, 244, 258–259,
    268, 289–291, 302, 309, 321, 324, 326,
    328, 333, 341–342, 345, 350, 358–359,
    363
Meaning-oriented approach, 5–7, 23, 97,
    120, 259, 315, 320, 361, 363
Mediation, 324, 326–328, 341–342
Memory, 16, 32–35, 56, 58, 64, 68, 69, 75,
    77, 86, 104, 181, 183–184, 198, 284,
    291, 296, 311, 322, 361
  bottleneck, 361
Minority groups, 143, 146, 201, 286, 319,
    369
Miscommunication, 122, 287
Miscue analysis, 259, 262, 265
Mismatch, 17, 112–113, 116, 287, 299
Modality, 181–182, 185, 283, 366
Models, analytical, of influences on
    achievement, 313
Models of reading, 14–16, 20, 53–70, 89–90,
    282, 284–285, 295, 313–314, 322–336
  audread, 15–16
  decoding-comprehension, 15

Models of reading *(contd.)*
  information-processing, 14, 20, 53–70, 284–285, 295, 313, 322
    operations and programs, 20, 54
    perceptual system, 20, 54–57, 62, 64
    semantic system, 20, 54, 57–62, 64, 66
  informed-guessing, 89–90
  interactive, 282
  learning-theory approach, 313–314, 334
  stage theories, 20, 314, 332–333, 335–336
Models, word processing, 31–34, 39–40, 42–43, 47, 50
  comparison of six models, 42–43
  LaBerge-Samuels, 31–34, 39–40, 47, 50
    intersystem associations, 31–34
    phonological system, 32–34, 39, 47, 50
    semantic-syntactic system, 32–34, 50
    visual perceptual system, 32–34, 39–40
Motivation, 48, 145, 259, 262–264, 308, 325, 332, 335, 340, 346–347, 350–351
  intrinsic vs. reward, 346–347

N

Naming, 32–33, 365
Native language literacy, 133–137, 144–145
Native language, specification of, 137–139
Natural language processes, *see also* Oral languages, 5, 12, 15–16, 117, 144, 146–147, 227, 251, 366
Natural language processes, 5, 12, 15, 67, 262, 322
New Primary Grades Reading System, 217–278, 288–290
Node, 54, 57, 59, 64
Nonoral hypothesis, 341
Nonprofessionals, 212
Nonverbal communication, 123, 127, 296

O

On-line methods of study, 282, 284–285
Open Court, 16
Open Court Reading Program, 348
Oral fluency, 133–134, 146
Oral language, *see also* Natural language processes, 5, 12, 15, 67, 262, 322
Oral language, 5, 12, 15–16, 117, 144, 146–147, 227, 251, 366
Oral production, 90–91, 94, 97, 100–101, 103, 105, 282, 287, 341

Oral reading, 4–6, 15, 89–106, 115, 244–245, 259, 265, 282–283, 287, 299, 341–342, 348, 362
  as comprehension, 89, 91
  as decoding, 89–90
  disfluencies in, 101–106
  and reading level, 103–104
Oral-written language association, 227
Orthographic regularity, 8–9, 12, 15, 32, 34, 40, 43–44, 56, 141, 185, 226, 230–231, 284, 307, 329, 334, 342, 344, 359, 362–363, 368

P

Perceptual learning, stages of, 41–44
Perceptual processes, 72, 78–79, 81, 86, 99, 311
Perceptual span, 15, 71, 73, 79, 81–86, 286
Perceptual units, 6, 14–15, 20, 31–50, 283–284, 308
  difficulties, 49–50
  functions of, 15, 31–35
    filter information, 34
    transform information, 34
  learning new units, 15, 31, 33, 40–49
    familiar levels, 40–44
    instruction and unitizing skills, 46–49
    new levels, 44–46
  selection of levels, 15, 31, 35–40, 283
  sizes of, 31, 34, 284
Peripheral-visual processing, 15, 18, 79, 82, 309
Phoneme analysis, 185–186, 190, 203, 289, 368–369
Phoneme-grapheme correspondences, 8, 18, 95, 140–141, 191, 366
Phoneme identification skills, 197–214, 288–289, 307, 309
Phoneme recognition, *see* Phoneme identification
Phonemic segmentation, 9, 20, 38, 47, 185, 288–289, 329–330, 335, 365, 369
Phonics, *see also* Code approach, 7, 9, 20, 26, 97, 120, 191, 225, 315, 320, 358–359, 363, 367, 369
Phonics, 8–9, 16, 44, 154, 156, 162, 182, 230, 233, 255, 259, 263, 267, 289–290, 302–303, 307, 309, 318, 327, 329–330, 332–333, 335, 342–345, 359
Phonological recoding, 13–14, 358–359
Predictions, 324–325

Prereading, 335–340, 345, 350–352
grapheme discrimination, 336, 340
language development, 336–339
conventions of story telling, 337, 339
language of instruction, 337
motivation, 336, 340
segmentation skills, 336, 339–340, 345, 350–352
metalinguistic skills, 339
Prerequisite skills, 204, 283, 288, 330, 332, 335, 337, 350
Print-to-speech units, 226–235
Processing lag, 80–81
Pronunciation, 32, 98, 102, 104, 114, 124–125, 127, 145, 287, 331, 338, 343
Propaedeutics, 8
Psycholinguistic processing, 75, 78, 82, 86
Psychology of reading instruction, 355–377

R

Readiness, 46, 183–184, 197, 201–205, 210–212, 311, 338, 364–366
curricula, 201–202, 338
low, 203–205, 210–212
Reading disorders, 73, 91, 179–193, 318–319
Reading groups, 297–305
Reading interference, 111–127, 299–300, 337–339
structural vs. functional, 299–300
Reading interference and classroom interaction, 122–127, 287–288, 299–300, 337–339
Reading and language, 15–16, 326–333
Reading-to-learn, 62, 68–69, 332
Reading level, 298–299, 328
The reading problem, *see also* Difficulties in reading, sources of, 17–18, 93–94, 98–99, 103, 111–127
The reading problem, 317–352
Reading problems, 286–288, 308
Reading rate, *see* Reading speed
Reading speed, 14, 32, 104–105, 117, 328, 346
Reading Unlimited Program, 217–278, 288, 290–291, 349
Rebus, 67, 257
Recoding, 231, 233, 255
Recognition, 54, 57, 64, 281
Recognition unit, size of, 64, 66
Rehearsal, 32

Remediation, 18, 73, 92, 346
Research, observational, 295–298, 302, 320, 362
Research and practice in beginning reading, *see also* Theory-practice relations, 23–25, 267–268, 295, 317–352, 355–371
Research and practice in beginning reading, 307–316
curriculum analysis, 309–310
field and classroom research, 312–313
learning and acquistion, 313–314
physiological research and clinical investigations, 309
problem of skill acquisition, 315–316
stages of proficiency, 314–315
teaching practices, 311–312
testing practices, 310–311
Research prescriptive, 308
Research, sociolinguistic, 121–127, 295–296, 300, 338–339
Research, usefulness of, 50, 74–76, 147–148, 192–193, 229–230, 234, 266–267, 282–283, 307–352, 355–371
Retention, 73–74, 86
Rote memorization, 207, 343

S

Saccade, 77–80, 82, 286
Schema, 58–59, 61–62, 67–69
Second-language learning, 17, 113, 116, 133–134, 142–143, 146–147
Segmentation, 19, 183, 192, 284, 329–330, 335–336, 339–340, 345, 350–352, 365–366, 370
Semantic constraints, 95–97, 99, 141, 282, 286
Semantic information, 217, 268, 343
Semantic network, 58–59, 61
Semantic processes, 5, 13, 81, 83–84, 95, 100–101, 105
Semantic representation, 91
Sensory overload, 184
SES, 136, 154, 156–157, 159–165, 167–172, 174–177, 197–214, 286, 296, 319, 340, 369–370
"Sesame Street," 155–156, 304
"Set for diversity," 229
Shared communicative background, 122, 124, 126, 288

Sight-sound correspondences, *see* Spelling to sound correspondences
Sight words, 233, 263, 343
Silent reading, 91, 115, 244–245, 328–329, 341–342, 348
Skill-emphasis, 162–163, 165, 174
Skilled performance and acquisition, development of, 357–363, 371
  contrastive studies, 360–363
  cross-age studies, 360, 362–363
  longitudinal studies, 362–363
Skilled reading, *see also* Skilled reading, nature of, 7–16, 25–26, 35, 44, 72–74, 76–77, 84, 86, 89, 103, 105, 281–283, 285, 288–289, 296, 307, 315–316, 319–335, 341, 345–348, 350–352, 358–362
Skilled reading, 7, 9, 12–15, 19, 35, 72, 314–316, 322, 325, 327, 332, 346
Skilled reading, nature of, *see also* Skilled reading, 7, 9, 12–15, 19, 35, 72, 314–316, 322, 325, 327, 332, 346
Skilled reading, nature of, 7–16, 25–26, 35, 44, 72–74, 76–77, 84, 86, 89, 103, 105, 281–283, 285, 288–289, 296, 307, 315–316, 319–335, 341, 345–358, 350–352, 358–362
  and automaticity, 13–14, 25–26, 35, 44, 285, 328–329, 331–332, 346–348, 350–351, 360–362
  bottom up or top-down, 13–14, 26, 89, 103, 281–283, 288–289, 296, 315–316, 323–326
  converting visual patterns into meaning, 72, 359
  direct or mediated access, 14, 26, 358
  inside out or outside in, 323–326, 329, 334–335, 345, 348, 350, 352
  translation of print to sound, 15, 25–26, 105, 281–282, 307, 321–322, 324, 326–328, 341, 358–359
Spanish dialect readers, 134, 145–146
Spanish-speaking, 134–135, 137–139, 143–146, 286, 336
  dialects of, 137–139, 286
Speech, 89–91, 93, 121–124, 222, 225–226, 281, 284, 292, 324, 326–333
  elocutionary force, 121
  interpretation of, 121–122
  propositional content, 121–122, 124
  situated meaning, 122–124
Spelling patterns, *see* Orthographic regularity

Spelling to sound correspondences, 6, 64–66, 68, 96, 141–142, 179, 182, 185–186, 190, 197–198, 201, 205, 207–209, 213–214, 217, 221, 226–233, 255, 257–258, 263, 265–266, 283, 285–286, 305, 326, 328, 330–331, 334, 338, 342–344, 365, 367–368, 370
Spoken versus written language, 2, 15–16, 20, 26
Stage of practice, 54
Standard English, 93, 112–115, 117–119, 124–125, 139–140, 143–144, 287, 338–339
Stimulus-response viewpoint, 213–214, 267, 313
Strategies for story reading, 235–245
Student achievement, *see also* Assessing reading progress, 21–23, 73, 115–117, 119–121, 146, 189–192, 210–213, 255–259, 265, 267, 281, 289, 310–312, 314, 328, 362–363, 370
Student achievement, 153–156, 158, 162–177, 183
Student expectations, 251, 303–304
Syllable, 32, 34, 47, 95, 179, 183, 185, 190, 284, 288–289, 322, 329, 335, 339, 366
Syntactic constraints, 95–97, 99, 116, 141, 262, 282
Syntactic information, 217, 268, 343
Syntactic processes, 5, 13, 79, 81, 100–101, 105
Syntactic and semantic integration, 101

T

Tachistoscope, 76, 81, 324
Task analysis, 179, 356, 358, 365, 369
Task definition, 124–125
Task demands, 54, 62–69, 73, 86, 99, 104–105, 284–285
  taxonomy of, 20, 54, 62–69, 284
Teachability, 339
Teacher, 6, 22, 48–49, 112–113, 120–127, 132, 143–146, 154–159, 164, 172, 175, 177, 180, 187–191, 211, 218–219, 221–222, 226–228, 231–232, 234–235, 244–246, 251, 259, 262–266, 268, 282, 287–288, 295–305, 310, 312, 314, 316, 318–319, 323, 328, 330, 333, 335, 338–339, 341
  role of, 219, 221–222

Teacher expectations, 144, 301
Teacher training, 126, 144, 297, 319, 321
Text alteration effects, 15, 73, 94, 100–103, 106, 282
Text difficulty, 94, 99, 105
Text structure, 314
Theories of reading process, 281–286
Theory-practice relations, *see also* Research and practice in beginning reading, 307–316
Theory-practice relations, 23–25, 267–268, 295, 317–352, 355–371
Time on task, 296–302, 304–305, 332
Transfer of training, 69, 164, 191–192, 198, 201, 209, 214, 289, 313, 340, 361–363, 366, 370
Transitions in processing, 356–357
Tongue-twister sentence, 203, 205
Tutor, 202–206, 208–212, 265, 288–289, 369
Tutorial program, 204–214, 340

U

Units, 19, 99
  clause, 19, 99
  phrase, 19, 99

V

Verbalization, 297
Verification tasks, 62, 65–69

Visual buffer models, 77–78, 80–81
Visual information, 77, 79–84, 86
Visual-perceptual-motor reading readiness programs, 184, 289
Visual processing, 75, 77, 82, 86, 181, 283, 322, 359, 362, 364
Visual search, 20, 360
Vocabulary, 6, 16, 40, 71, 75, 105, 142, 145, 188, 199, 209, 211, 230, 232, 243, 258, 262–263, 336, 343–345, 349, 351, 370

W

Whole-word approach, *see* Basal approach
Word-attack skills, 334–336, 341, 343
Word callers, 91–93, 97, 103, 302, 341
Word-cards, 209–210
Word length, 79, 82–83
Word-processing skills, 359
Word recognition, 5, 9, 13–15, 20, 31, 35, 53, 95, 114, 124, 155–156, 162, 169, 198, 211–212, 283, 309, 320, 322, 329, 331–332, 334, 343, 346, 351, 359–362, 368
Word shape, 81–82
Word superiority effect, 15, 20, 42, 290
Writing, 21, 155, 226
Writing systems, 140, 326, 329, 342–343, 346